Religious Literacy, Law and History

The book profiles some of the macro and micro factors that have impact on European religious literacy. It seeks to understand religious illiteracy and its effects on the social and political milieu through the framing of the historical, institutional, religious, social, juridical and educational conditions within which it arises. Divided into four parts, in the first one, *One literacy, more literacies?*, the book defines the basic concepts underpinning the question of religious illiteracy in Europe. Part II, *Understanding illiteracies, debating disciplines?*, highlights the theological, philosophical, historical and political roots of the phenomenon, looking at the main nodes that are both the reasons religious illiteracy is widespread and the starting points for literacy strategies. Part III, *Building literacy, shaping alphabets*, examines the mix of knowledge and competences acquired about religion and from religion at school as well as through the media, with a critical perspective on what could be done both in the schools and for the improvement of journalists' religious literacy. Part IV, *Views and experiences*, presents the reader with the opportunity to learn from three different case studies: religious literacy in the media, religious illiteracy and European Islam, and a Jewish approach to religious literacy. Building on existing literature, the volume takes a scientific approach which is enriched by interdisciplinary and transnational perspectives, and deep entrenchment in historical methodology.

Alberto Melloni is a Full Professor of History of Christianity at the University of Modena and Reggio Emilia, director of the Fondazione per le scienze religiose Giovanni XXIII in Bologna and chair holder of the UNESCO Chair on Religious Pluralism and Peace at the University of Bologna. He is principal investigator for the European Infraia RelReS project headed by the Fondazione and coordinator of the Resilience research infrastructure project, and he spearheaded the establishment of the European Academy of Religion.

Francesca Cadeddu is Research Fellow at the University of Modena and Reggio Emilia, and at the Fondazione per le scienze religiose Giovanni XXIII in Bologna. She is affiliated to the Faiths and Civil Society Unit at Goldsmiths University of London and serves as secretary general of the European Academy of Religion. She works on the history of American Catholicism in the twentieth century and on religious literacy in Italy and Europe.

ICLARS Series on Law and Religion

Series Editors:
Silvio Ferrari, University of Milan, Italy, Russell Sandberg, Cardiff University, UK, Pieter Coertzen, University of Stellenbosch, South Africa, W. Cole Durham, Jr., Brigham Young University, USA, and Tahir Mahmood, Amity International University, India

The *ICLARS Series on Law and Religion* is a new series designed to provide a forum for the rapidly expanding field of research in law and religion. The series is published in association with the International Consortium for Law and Religion Studies, an international network of scholars and experts of law and religion founded in 2007 with the aim of providing a place where information, data and opinions can easily be exchanged among members and made available to the broader scientific community. The series aims to become a primary source for students and scholars while presenting authors with a valuable means to reach a wide and growing readership.

Islam, Law and the Modern State
(Re)imagining Liberal Theory in Muslim Contexts
Arif A. Jamal

Atheist Exceptionalism
Atheism, Religion, and the United States Supreme Court
Ethan G. Quillen

Lutheran Theology and Secular Law
The Work of the Modern State
Edited by Marie A. Failinger and Ronald W. Duty

Religious Freedom and the Law
Emerging Contexts for Freedom for and from Religion
Edited by Brett G. Scharffs, Asher Maoz and Ashley Isaacson Woolley

Religion, Pluralism, and Reconciling Difference
Edited by W. Cole Durham, Jr. and Donlu Thayer

Religious Literacy, Law and History
Perspectives on European Pluralist Societies
Edited by Alberto Melloni and Francesca Cadeddu

For more information about this series, please visit:
www.routledge.com/ICLARS-Series-on-Law-and-Religion/book-series/ICLARS

Religious Literacy, Law and History

Perspectives on European Pluralist Societies

Edited by
Alberto Melloni and
Francesca Cadeddu

Routledge
Taylor & Francis Group
LONDON AND NEW YORK

First published 2019 by Routledge

2 Park Square, Milton Park, Abingdon, Oxfordshire OX14 4RN
52 Vanderbilt Avenue, New York, NY 10017

Routledge is an imprint of the Taylor & Francis Group, an informa business

First issued in paperback 2020

British Library Cataloguing-in-Publication Data
A catalogue record for this book is available from the British Library

Library of Congress Cataloging-in-Publication Data
A catalog record for this book has been requested

ISBN: 978-1-138-30364-5 (hbk)
ISBN: 978-0-367-53419-6 (pbk)

Typeset in Galliard
by codeMantra

Contents

Notes on contributors

Francesca Cadeddu is Research Fellow at the University of Modena and Reggio Emilia, and at the Fondazione per le scienze religiose Giovanni XXIII in Bologna. She is affiliated to the Faiths and Civil Society Unit at Goldsmiths University of London and serves as secretary general of the European Academy of Religion. She works on the history of American Catholicism in the twentieth century and on religious literacy in Italy and Europe. Among her recent publications on religious pluralism are *Blasfemia, diritti e libertà. Una discussione dopo le stragi di Parigi*, edited by A. Melloni, F. Cadeddu and F. Meloni (Il Mulino 2015), and 'Sostenere l'islam in Europa attraverso la conoscenza', in *Dall'islam in Europa all'islam europeo. La sfida dell'integrazione*, edited by M. el Ayoubi and C. Paravati (Carocci 2018).

Grace Davie is Professor Emeritus of Sociology at the University of Exeter. She is a specialist in the sociology of religion and has worked extensively on the European case. Her latest publications include *Religion in Britain: A Persistent Paradox* (Wiley-Blackwell 2015) and *Religion in Public Life: Levelling the Ground* (Theos 2017). She was also a co-ordinating lead author for the chapter on religion in *Rethinking Society for the 21st Century*, vol. 3, *Transformations in Values, Norms, Cultures* (Cambridge University Press 2018), which is the report of the International Panel on Social Progress.

Donatella Di Cesare teaches Theoretical Philosophy at Sapienza University in Rome and Philosophical Hermeneutics at Scuola Normale Superiore in Pisa. She is one of the most influential philosophers in the academic and media international debate, and writes on the *Corriere della Sera*. Among her latest publications are *Stranieri residenti. Una filosofia della migrazione* (Bollati Boringhieri 2017), *Heidegger and the Jews: The Black Notebooks* (Polity Press 2018) and *Torture* (Polity Press 2018).

Adam Dinham is an interdisciplinary academic combining theology and religious studies, sociology of religion, social work and social policy, public policy and politics. He is director of the Faiths and Civil Society Unit at Goldsmiths University of London; professor of Religious Literacy at VID Specialized University in Oslo; honorary professor of Religion, Leadership and Society at the University of Sheffield; fellow of the Westminster Abbey Institute for Faith and Public Life; and chair of the BSA Sociology of Religion Study Group (SocRel). He edited *Religious Literacy in Policy and Practice* with M. Francis (Policy Press 2015) and *Re-imagining Religion and Belief: 21st Century Policy and Practice* with C. Baker and B.R. Crisp (Routledge 2018).

Mary Earl has trained teachers of Theology, Religious Studies and Philosophy at the University of Cambridge's Faculty of Education for over twenty-five years. Before that she was a secondary school teacher; then, as now, she maintains a strong interest in inclusive education and disability studies. She has worked, outside education, in the arts and in counselling settings. Her research interests, and those of her higher degree students, include language and learning, museum education, reflexivity and religion, and the pedagogy of Religious Studies teaching. She is a programme manager for initial teacher education courses at the faculty and a subject leader for that course. As a result she is actively involved in mentor training, professional studies training and related activities for the University of Cambridge.

Vincente Fortier is Senior Researcher at the National Centre for Scientific Research and currently runs the joint research unit Law, Religions, Enterprise and Society (University of Strasbourg/CNRS). Her research field is law and religion, and covers family law, labour law, contract law and legal practice linked to religions. Author or co-author of three books, director or co-director of twelve books, she has published over sixty articles in refereed journals or chapters of scientific books. She has given some fifty lectures at national and international conferences. Her latest publications are *L'expression religieuse en entreprise*, edited by S. Marti, V. Fortier, J. Maïla and M. Hunyadi (Le bord de l'eau 2016), and *La circoncision rituelle. Enjeux de droits, enjeux de vérité*, edited by V. Fortier (Presses Universitaires de Strasbourg 2016).

Maria Chiara Giorda is Associate Professor in History of Religions at Roma Tre University in Rome, and since 2012 she has been professor and coordinator of the section Sociology and Media of the master in Religions and Cultural Mediation at Sapienza University in Rome. She is an historian of religions, and she works on religious pluralism in public spaces, religious places in urban spaces and religious diversity at school. Among her latest publications are 'Sacred Places in Urban Spaces: A Interdisciplinary Perspective' (*Historia Religionum* 8, 2016) and *Famiglie monastiche. Il Dominus Tecum di Pra'd Mill* (Aragno 2017).

Robert Jackson is Emeritus Professor of Religions and Education at the University of Warwick. He has contributed to the educational work of the Council of Europe since 2002, including by writing *Signposts* (Council of Europe 2014). His book *Religious Education for Plural Societies: The Selected Works of Robert Jackson* is about to be published by Routledge. In 2017, he was awarded honorary doctorates by NTNU Norwegian University of Science and Technology, Trondheim and the Norwegian School of Theology, Oslo.

Martin M. Lintner is member of the Order of the Servants of Mary as well as professor of Theological Ethics and Theology of Spirituality at the Philosophical-Theological College in Brixen/Bressanone and lecturer of Ethics at the Free University of Bozen/Bolzano. His main research fields are bioethics, sexual moral and family ethics, animal ethics, and fundamental moral theology. His last two publications are *Der Mensch und das liebe Vieh. Ethische Fragen im Umgang mit Tieren* (Tyrolia 2017) and *Von Humanae vitae bis Amoris laetitia. Die Geschichte einer umstrittenen Lehre* (Tyrolia 2018).

Susanna Mancini holds the chair of Comparative Constitutional Law at the University of Bologna School of Law and is a vice president of the International Association of Constitutional Law. She is interested in exploring how race and gender-related social and cultural constructs have shaped the balance of power and privilege in a liberal society, and in the role of the law in perpetuating and/or combating the marginalization of women and racial, religious and sexual minorities. Her work explores issues of law and religion, reproductive rights, the partnership of feminism and multiculturalism, self-determination and secession. Her latest publications include *Comparative Constitutional Law. Cases and Materials,* edited by N. Dorsen, M. Rosenfeld, A. Sajó, S. Baer and S. Mancini (West Academic 2016) and *The Conscience Wars. Rethinking the Balance between Religion, Identity, and Equality*, edited by S. Mancini and M. Rosenfeld (Cambridge University Press 2018).

Alberto Melloni is a Full Professor of History of Christianity at the University of Modena and Reggio Emilia, director of the Fondazione per le scienze religiose Giovanni XXIII in Bologna and chair holder of the UNESCO Chair on Religious Pluralism and Peace at the University of Bologna. He is principal investigator for the European Infraia RelReS project headed by the Fondazione and coordinator of the Resilience research infrastructure project, and he spearheaded the establishment of the European Academy of Religion. He is columnist for the *Corriere della Sera* and *la Repubblica.* Among his latest publications are *I Presidenti della Repubblica. Il Capo dello Stato e il Quirinale nella storia della democrazia italiana*, edited by S. Cassese, G. Galasso and A. Melloni (Il Mulino 2018); *Il Concilio e la grazia. Saggi di storia sul Vaticano II* (Jaca Book 2016); and *Amore senza fine, amore senza fini* (Il Mulino 2015).

Flavio Pajer has been professor of Pedagogy and Didactics of Religions at the Università Pontificia Salesiana in Rome and comparative educationalist of the European educational systems, in particular in the field of public and multifaith Religious Education. He is author of several essays on European policies related to religious freedom in public spaces and editor of a collection of religious syllabuses and textbooks for Italian secondary school curricula. He is also editor of *EREnews*, a quarterly e-journal about current developments of models of teaching about religions and beliefs in the different European countries. Among his latest publications are *Dio in programma. Scuola e religioni nell'Europa unita 1957–2017* (Morcelliana 2017) and *Scuola e religione in Italia. Quarant'anni di ricerche e dibattiti* (Aracne, forthcoming).

Robin Sclafani has over thirty years' experience in developing and delivering anti-bias training programs for various target groups. She was appointed director at CEJI – A Jewish Contribution to an Inclusive Europe in 2006, after serving for five years as its training director. She previously worked for the ADL Anti-Defamation League's A World of Difference® Institute as their New York City project director, where she developed the Peer Training Program, which has reached tens of thousands of high school students across the USA since 1991. As director of CEJI, she is the architect of the suite of training programmes linked to the award-winning project Belieforama: A Panoramic Approach to Issues of Religion and Belief. Since 2009, CEJI is coordinating one of civil society's most promising initiatives in hate crime monitoring and hate speech training, called Facing Facts, which now offers a variety of e-learning modules through the platform Facing Facts Online.

Adam B. Seligman is Professor of Religion and director of the Graduate Program in Religious Studies at Boston University. He is director of CEDAR (Communities Engaging with Difference and Religion), which leads seminars every year on contested aspects of religion and the public square in different parts of the world. His latest publications include *Religious Education and the Challenge of Pluralism*, edited by A.B. Seligman (Oxford University Press 2014), and *Living with Difference: How to Build Community in a Divided World*, edited by A.B. Seligman, R.R. Wasserfall and D.W. Montgomery

(University of California Press 2016). His book – written with R. Weller – *What Counts as the Same: Memory, Mimesis and Metaphor in Social Life* is about to be published by Oxford University Press.

Jennifer M. Taylor is Research Fellow at The Kirby Laing Institute for Christian Ethics in Cambridge and senior contributor at The Media Project in New York. Her main interests are religion and media; in particular her research work focusses on the Christian origins of the press, Evil and the lost language, and Islam and secularisation. Among her latest publications are 'Response to "A Feminine View of Missions and Belonging in the Middle East Context"', in *When Women Speak...*, edited by M. Dale, C. Hine and C. Walker (Regnum Books 2018), and 'The Christian Origins of the Free Press', in *This Book Changed Everything: The Bible's Amazing Impact on Our World*, edited by V. Mangalwadi (forthcoming).

Erdal Toprakyaran is Junior Professor of Islamic History and Contemporary Culture, and executive director of the Center for Islamic Theology at the University of Tübingen. His main research fields are the history and culture of Muslims in the Ottoman Empire and the Turkish Republic, Islamic mysticism and Muslim-Christian relations. His latest publications are 'Krieg und Mystik. Das Narrativ von Atatürk als Gottesstreiter und mystischer Pol', in *Dem Einen entgegen. Christliche und islamische Mystik in historischer Perspektive*, edited by E. Toprakyaran, H. Schmid and C. Ströbele (LIT Verlag 2018), and 'Mercy and Love in Islamic Mysticism', in *Rahma. Muslim and Christian Studies in Mercy*, edited by V. Cottini, F. Körner and D.R. Sarrió Cucarella (PISAI 2018).

Michael Wakelin is an English broadcaster who produced several shows for TV and radio. He currently works as executive producer at TBI Media, and he is head of programmes for Coexist House and chair of the Religion Media Centre in London. His work focusses on the connections between media and religion, and, on a broader level, on interfaith.

John Wolffe is Professor of Religious History and associate dean at the Faculty of Arts and Social Sciences at Open University. His research focuses on religious conflict/antagonism (especially anti-Catholicism and Islamophobia), religious responses to death, religion and national identity, secularization and religious resurgence. His latest publications include 'Towards the post-secular city? London since the 1960' (*Journal of Religious History* 41:4, 2017) and 'Forever England beneath the Cross of Sacrifice: Christianity and National Identity in British First World War Cemeteries', in *Christianity and National Identity in Twentieth-Century Europe*, edited by J. Carter Wood (Vandenhoeck & Ruprecht 2016).

Preface

Alberto Melloni and Francesca Cadeddu

In the last twenty years, the issue of religious illiteracy and its relationship to legal systems, historical events and the construction of memory in western countries has garnered the attention of scholars and policy-makers. The bibliographic references that the reader will find in the following pages lay out the attempt to understand (and a path to counteract) the lack of critical awareness of histories, laws, theologies, doctrines, creeds and cultures that make up the religious and spiritual landscape of Europe and North America. Studies on these issues have produced knowledge as well as works and policies from which two parallel tendencies have emerged: one intent on Religious Education, that is, what gives structure and content to the spaces chosen for the acquisition of awareness concerning religions and creeds, and the other focused on religious alphabetization and the production of knowledge, meaning the acquisition of knowledge about religions and systems of belief as an inter- and transdisciplinary issue.

The most recent project that marked the initial step in the first tendency is REDCo (Religion in Education: A contribution to Dialogue or a factor of Conflict in transforming societies of European Countries). To date, it has produced a 36-volume series that includes the participation of some of the most renowned scholars in Religious Education. It covers a variety of issues and case studies from philosophy, geography, pedagogy and anthropology. In the second case, publications respond to the need to contextualize religious literacy in the time and space of individual nations. On a European and North Atlantic scale, however, we have recently witnessed a growing necessity to offer a complete, global reading on these topics. In this vein, we can include the *Rapporto sull'analfabetismo religioso in Italia*, edited by Alberto Melloni (Il Mulino 2014), which was our first approach to the issue of religious illiteracy and convinced us of the need to broaden our perspective on a European scale; *Religious Literacy in Policy and Practice*, edited by Adam Dinham and Matthew Francis (Policy Press 2015), which came out one year later and mainly focused on the English context; and the renowned works *Religious Literacy: What Every American Needs to Know – And Doesn't* by Stephen Prothero (HarperCollins 2007) and *Overcoming Religious Illiteracy* by Diane Moore (Palgrave Macmillan 2007), both of which concerned the American context.

This volume sets out to move beyond the case studies and pave the way for research that reflects on history, legal structures, systems of thought and the challenges of European religious pluralism as such. The work takes place within a Europe conceived of as a cultural space anchored to the countries of the European Union, but at times, the context also extends into the outlying areas of the Mediterranean, the Balkans, the Middle East, Asia and North America. To this end, the layout of the chapters has been imagined in order that European research, ideas and experiences can be presented in a single framework that is deliberately interdisciplinary and diverse, according to the 'alphabets' used by individual authors. As it were, these contributions are not necessarily exhaustive.

This volume is not a handbook for politicians, teachers or interested parties nor is it a set of solutions to the pressing consequences of religious illiteracy or the outcome of a single line of research. It is, however, an attempt to stimulate politicians, teachers and other interested parties to grasp the true value of knowledge as the only tool for facing the complexity of what we define as 'religion in the public space' and to answer the questions that naturally arise when discussing such issues, like 'Are religions violent?' or 'Why do we have to teach them at school?' For this, each author was invited to analyze critically the causes of religious illiteracy from the specific point of view of their own discipline or profession and to set aside momentarily the search for its solutions in order to give space to the reasons that have generated and nourished it.

The various contributions have given rise to four distinct sections. The first, *One literacy, more literacies?*, identifies the four main questions from which our reflection develops. We asked ourselves what the historical origins of religious literacy might be and if they may be connected to the institutional systems of modern Europe. And wherever possible – and indeed, it was – to identify common causes, we then investigated when and why different definitions of this phenomenon emerged and whether we should, in fact, consider more than one religious alphabet. In the last ten years, a wide variety of codes have emerged (e.g. schools, social work, business, privileged majorities and creative minorities) from the literature and the debate set in motion by study groups (including informal ones) on religious literacy. This has led us to believe in the need for greater contextualization for individual state scenarios and specific social and educational systems. Consequently, the question arises as to whether the religious and institutional diversity that marks Europe today is a bearer of different forms of religious literacy and is therefore in need of different educational, instructional and institutional approaches.

For this, we sought contributions that could frame the role of Religious Education on a historical-juridical level in the context of the guaranteed rights and freedoms in Europe. The goal was to understand to what degree the recognition of religious rights is passed on through the understanding – acknowledged, taught or produced – for religious people and for the religiously literate. The issue has been, and remains, controversial. This is not only due to the problems it raises in countries where secularism has become a standard-bearer or in countries characterized by a religious culture that predominates. The question of Religious Education also poses an epistemological problem inasmuch as there is competition among forms of knowledge that are termed 'neutral' (and are they?), forms presented as 'validated' (and they are) and forms that derive their solidity from disciplinary statutes (every history is history, every law is law, etc.). The use of one approach or another in the fight against religious illiteracy has brought scholars and policy-makers to underestimate the responsibilities that other fields of knowledge have in the absence of constructing religious literacy in Europe, pay little attention to the biases that each of these fields has produced in public discourse and neglect an inter-sectorial or inter-hermeneutic approach: religious literacy cannot be passed on solely through the school, social workers, the media or any other sector, if only done exclusively.

The second and third sections of the volume emerge out of these circumstances, with *Understanding illiteracies, debating disciplines?* and *Building literacy, shaping alphabets.* In the former, on the one hand, we sought to investigate the disciplines that are often marginalized from the reflections on the early symptoms of the problem – philosophy, theology and law – and, on the other hand, we examined a number of interdisciplinary and, in a manner of speaking, classical nodes: secularism, violence and symbols.

Philosophy, theology and law have been called to action specifically to understand how the construction of meanings, the reading of the Scriptures, the formulations of doctrines and subsequent rights have contributed to (and, in a vicious circle, in turn, registered) the disconnect between a reality that is increasingly religiously diversified and 'another reality', and the tools, notions and methods that could have supported their understanding. Current events regularly remind us of this disconnect: every Christmas, every act of fundamentalism and every woman with a veil generates hours of discussion concerning the role that religion should have in public spaces, and this is without counting the regular media stereotypes and counter-stereotypes, clichés and counter-clichés. The great limit of these debates is that they fail to create any honest reflection on the significances and real consequences of the choices that policy-makers, educators and scholars (formal and informal) make whenever they dwell in that same area of disconnect.

To this end, in the section entitled *Building literacy, shaping alphabets*, we focused the debate on the presence of religions in school and on the formation of language passed on through mass media. The aim of these three contributions is to describe and to start discussion on the role of formal educators (teachers) and non-formal ones (in this case, media actors) in the process of conveying knowledge about religions (in their theological 'autonomy', in their diversity and in the relationships that emerge from historical experiences or from their newfound proximity to public spaces). In addition, these contributions examine the awareness that the education of new generations and of public opinion passes through these large channels of communication. Starting from the education of the figures mentioned earlier, from the method and content selected to convey information, from the spaces that educational systems and means of information offer to religion, we consider whether we can begin to turn around the illiterate tendencies in which we find ourselves today.

Lastly, the section *Views and experiences* was conceived to represent – without pretending to be exhaustive – a wide range of initiatives, subjective proposals and exemplifying experiences from different situations and contexts. We wished to propose projects, actions, initiatives and reflections that have emerged from a number of diverse, real experiences. These include the work of Jennifer Taylor, an English journalist involved in religious literacy in the areas of communication; Robin Sclafani, the director of the Jewish European Network working to fight discrimination and prejudice; and Erdal Toprakyaran, the director for the Center for Islamic Theology in Tübingen, Germany. Each of these experiences and analyses opens a window onto the most successful and critical aspects of every attempt at literacy, inevitably involving ideologies, theologies and internal dynamics in communities of faith.

All of these works have been imagined and carried out with the ambition of creating a framework for debate among not only scholars but also (and above all) policy-makers, teachers of Religious Education and other disciplines not apparently connected with religions, and journalists and organizations working in social contexts. We have deliberately chosen a liberal scientific method with the conviction that only through an inclusive and interdisciplinary research method can we produce inclusive policies and choices that respect diversity.

Acknowledgements

This volume has been made possible by funds allocated to the Department of Education and Humanities of the University of Modena and Reggio Emilia by the Italian Ministry for Education, University and Research (MIUR), together with the scientific, operational and organizational assistance of the Fondazione per le scienze religiose Giovanni XXIII in Bologna. The initiative is part of a broader research project on religious illiteracy that began at the Fondazione in 2012 and continues today with the research team involved in the Resilience project. Warm thanks and gratitude to the publisher and Alison Kirk, in particular, who with patience and care worked for this volume's publication.

Part I

One literacy, more literacies?

1 European religious illiteracy

The historical framework of a removed agenda

Alberto Melloni

Introduction

The definitions of religion accumulated over the years have often been studied in terms of their reach and development.[1] Such a variety allows me to resort to my own formulation and to regard religion as the 'free assumption of a superior moral obligation by men and women immersed in a culture'. I use this formulation not due to any illusion that it should convince someone or to the presumption that it is immune from critical remark but solely because it is one that I believe allows me to say that everything that is attributed to this sphere – freedom, processes of engagement, translations of moral obligation, conceptions of superiority and, of course, culture – is expressed *historically*. Moreover, it all unravels in a time of languages[2] shaped by texts, hermeneutics, practices, gestures, inhibitions, missions, symbols and doctrines that, in turn, produce other doctrines, symbols, missions, inhibitions, gestures, practices, hermeneutics and texts. This series of edifications and deconstructions would appear to some uncontrolled and to others free: a megalopolis of signs and meanings that develop according to

> procedures that, far from being regulated or eliminated by panoptic administration, have reinforced themselves in a proliferating illegitimacy, developed and insinuated themselves into the networks of surveillance, and combined in accord with unreadable but stable tactics to the point of constituting everyday regulations and surreptitious creativities that are merely concealed by the frantic mechanisms and discourses of the observational organization.
>
> (de Certeau 1984: 95–6)

Such 'languages' can, and sometimes do, convey – both verbally and nonverbally – cultural expressions, ethical attitudes, philosophical convictions and imaginations of the cosmos and the self as well as epistemological postulates or political products. They may take on

1 For a framework, cf. Platvoet and Molendijk (1999), including eighteenth-century positions (Christian Wolff) on the right of God to impose obligations whose violation infringes upon obligations of justice, and which in my view – besides the not insignificant point of personal adherence to the obligations themselves – strikes an essential point; on the Bonhoeffer perspective of the age of autonomy and the reading of Dilthey, we can see the initial observations of Ernst Feil (1999: 125–7). In this sense, the use of the category of Nonbelief as Belief is pleonastic because even individual and collective abstention or refusal, neutral distance or active hostility in the face of religion are 'religious acts'.

2 The problem of cultures, symbols and semantics exploded during the 1960s and a debate commenced alongside the ceaseless discussion on the 'definition' of religion: from religion as a 'cultural system' in Clifford Geertz (1966) to that of Peter L. Berger (1969: 3–4) as a cultural given, open 'to all', cf. the popular work by Jeppe S. Jensen (2014) and for a more scientific approach, see Filoramo (2004).

relationships of synergy, conflict or identity with other languages, whether silent or voiced. They lay boundaries or traverse worlds that are often defined as 'denominational', and they can be understood or ignored without the act – understanding, ignoring – determining either historical development or social and political incisiveness.

This lengthy preamble serves to help us comprehend the point of view assumed here in the face of religious illiteracy[3] in Europe: that it is not only a sociologically documented fact but also the historical outcome of an abandonment of the understanding of these 'languages'. Such an outcome is so incredibly vast and profound that it not only involves those who believe themselves to be, or to have become, foreign to these systems of signs and meanings (the expunction of religious dimensions from the House of European History in Brussels does not need to be amended in order to bear testimony to the lowest point in the inculturation of the Union) but also affects those who consider or declare themselves to be believers.

Secularizations

'It's secularization, stupid!'. It is Bill Clinton's famous phrase, but also the motto of the sorrowful monotonies of a religious integralism that looks back nostalgically to the mythical times of a 'Christian' Europe – the 'medieval' one of Novalis's[4] pietism (Menozzi 2005), the wholly Latin one of Gregory VII, if not the imperial one of Constantine (Zamagni 2012, Melloni 2013). It has also been the adage of those who in the last two centuries defined by the term *secularization* the undefeated enemy to whom we attribute the sociological regression of the religious and the resounding echo of the 'ego and its desires'.[5] But the same phrase will be uttered by methodological agnosticism, which, animated by a 'missionary' fervor, will see in secularization – secularism, for shorthand – the measure of a civilization that has extended beyond an enchantment of the divine and sees in religious violence the confirmation that without secularism, it would be impossible to encounter *Fortschritt*.[6]

In some respects, these exact interpretations, with their symmetric simplicity, can be taken as the signs of such profound religious illiteracy that it speaks of 'secularization' as if it were a single thing and as if the viability of nonbelief (Taylor 2007, Schoenberg and Majeran 2016) were our destiny, laid out in the monochrome Eden of modernity.[7]

Unitarian secularism?

In point of fact, the research – endowed with the term secularization by jurists working on the 1648 Treaty of Westphalia and then redetermined semantically by Émile Durkheim[8] – has

3 In English, this concept is usually translated as 'illiteracy' and not the outdated 'analphabetism'. There is, however, a difference between these two expressions that I believe should not be underestimated: the opposite of 'illiteracy' is the verified possession of 'literacy', while the opposite of 'analphabetism' is 'alphabetization', supposing instead a structured act. On its definition cf. the chapter 'Alphabétisation et alphabétisme, quelques définitions' in *Rapport mondial de suivi sur l'éducation pour tous 2006*, Paris, UNESCO, 2006, 155–69, www.unesco.org/education/GMR2006/full/chap6_fr.pdf, last accessed 20 June 2018.

4 On the pitfalls of modernity and its unforeseen effects, see Kracht (2004).

5 Joseph Ratzinger, homily *pro eligendo pontifice*, given in St Peter's Cathedral on 18 April 2005, www.vatican.va/gpII/documents/homily-pro-eligendo-pontifice_20050418_it.html, last accessed 20 June 2018.

6 The work of Reinhart Koselleck (2006) remains essential to this issue.

7 For a discussion starting from the position of Niklas Luhmanns that extends far beyond the German context, cf. Pollack (2012).

8 Cf. Durkheim (1968: 305) on the 'aptitude de la société à s'ériger en dieu ou à créer des dieux'.

advanced so far as to distinguish phases, traits and aspects that, while not always persuasive, at least disrupt the trivialization of a 'unitarian' secularism. Charles Taylor's tripartition, which is well accepted in the field,[9] established the following in a long, cinematic sequence: (1) *political* secularization, (2) secularization involving *individual* behaviors and (3) the *cultural* secularization of the postmodern age.

1 'Political' secularization is a thing apart (this does not necessarily imply that it is historically set above other forms). This secularization is referred to as 'political' because it moderates, expunges or prohibits discussions, elements and 'religious' convictions from institutions and the 'public' sphere through a process that others subsequently interpret as an incubator of a 'liberal' state (cf. Habermas 2005). It is a process of disestablishment that, in all honesty, does not historically respond to the various positions of science and reason. Rather, it rises as a (believing) attempt to put an end to the carnage of religious wars (Tierney 2014: 215–90). There is little doubt that after the Enlightenment – when conceptions of science and reason held powerful sway – the Revolution and the Napoleonic age 'secularized' (are we still using the Westphalia meaning?) decisive features of public life: sovereignty as the origin of *nomos*, the school as the root of *ethos*, the registry office as a standardization of the *oikos*, the hospital as a form of control of science over *thanatos* and the large-scale army as the place of the civil sacrifice of *demos* (cf. Baubérot 2013). Following the close coupling between the popular masses and the nationalisms of World War I, political secularization found a variant – interpreted as a degeneration – in European fascism.[10] It reappears, however, without any significant changes in the affluent society of the war's aftermath, valorizing the possibility of extending the principle of equality to unthinkable contexts within the rigid framework of bourgeois modernity: sexuality, ethnicity, gender, bioethics, family models, etc.
2 The other secularization involving the self-understanding of the self and the world is the one that, in Charles Taylor's language, upsets, on the one hand, the cosmic imaginary and, on the other, the penetrability of the ego. Taylor sees both as products of the Lutheran Reformation.[11] Emmanuel Lévinas (who for obvious reasons could not be content with such a classical explanation so profoundly steeped in 'Catholic' suspicions toward *Glaubenspaltung*) believed that he could trace the re-understanding of the modern world back to the origins of technique,[12] when technique was still too slow and incapable of involving individual bodies. Choices by individuals and religious affiliations conveyed in class segmentations are assumed, therefore, to have resulted in a system of thrust and counterthrust that was to produce cultural secularization, which would then proceed uninterrupted for the decades from Schleiermacher to 1968.[13]

9 In a perspective that mixes John Rawls and Ratzinger, see the stance of Areshidze (2016) on the need to separate state secularization from that of society in order to save liberal principles.
10 Incapable of resisting the seduction of 'totalitarian religions', the two secularizations did not experience any guilt at the subordination to fascisms or cultural complicity in the Shoah – epic crimes to which theological cultures were just as vulnerable as regimes of confessionalization. If anything, it is the position of churches that do question themselves on the 'silence' in the face of genocide, at most to deny accusations through a fanciful rereading of the critical historical evidence, but the ability of the 'leading' ideology to cut through cultural secularizations like butter is easily exempted by *Schuldfrage*.
11 Taylor had already been reproached for this subordination to the Catholic stereotype; see Benson (2008).
12 Emmanuel Lévinas, *Sécularisation et faim* is an essay from 1976, now in Lévinas 1991.
13 Cf. the stance of Baubérot (2004: 53), which reads secularization as 'perte de pertinence sociale [...] des univers religieux'.

3 According to Taylor, a third secularization joins the fray, which he fully deems *a Secular Age*. This secularization renders acceptable and dominant both nonbelief (the focus of Taylor's research) and the multiple recompositions of the religious (which appear to reemerge from an underground calling for blood and deadly identities). Cultural secularization allowed for the transition from a world where each segment of reality was solidly embedded within a superior framework – 'human agents are embedded in society, society in the *cosmos*, and the *cosmos* incorporates the divine' (Taylor 2007: 152) – into a world of disembedding the real segments into a framework of an exclusivist 'humanism' (sic!). It is the selfsame 'clockmaker' god[14] – constructing mechanisms of such mathematic perfection as to conceal his hand in their making – who allows for 'science and reason' to outclass the function carried out by 'religion and superstition' (273).[15] Only after this step developed and was then fragmented by the culture of Romanticism in the nineteenth century would the nationalist culture of the twentieth century generate an 'immanent frame'. In this new setting, religious belonging would disunite (and, if anything, reunite) on the basis of a need for 'authenticity' to which 'established' communities of faith cannot always respond. Subsequently, this produces aggregations, 'fervours' and inspirations in search of new equilibriums.

Illiteracy as a historic fact

I have turned to this excessively schematic synthesis of Taylor's positions only to say that those who are dissatisfied with simply brandishing the category of secularization as an indeterminate amulet during the crisis of liberal democracies (Böckenförde 2007) would be well served if European religious illiteracy were considered neither the premise nor the product of a secularization of the public space, of behaviors or of what generates Taylor's 'immanent frame' in this day and age. Instead, it is to be understood as a historic fact.

In short, European religious illiteracy is not the result of a shift in the religious landscape. It is, rather, the *theologische Unklarheit* that encompasses that landscape. Illiteracy is not the pessimistic and blame-casting definition of an indifference to the religious that has lost its serenity and must, in spite of itself, take on the knowledge rendered necessary by the cohabitation of faiths and fundamentalist infiltrations. Rather, it is the darkness that envelops indifference and cohabitations. It is not a dilemma created by the migrations of far-off religious universes, filtered over centuries through the eyes of colonialism. It is what the end of colonialism and the uncontrollability of migratory processes shed light upon.

It is a condition that can, and must, be defined thus: 'illiteracy', not for the convenience of a metaphor but rather to deny any assimilation of the 'fact' in question with a limit with which to come realistically to terms or a statistically unavoidable error in a society that is far too complex. Like any form of illiteracy, religious illiteracy is a social evil where the victims are the bearers of the damage, and it must be tackled with the same perspective as that by which basic illiteracy was approached. Basic illiteracy excluded the subordinate from reading and writing, and was used as a tool of public policy not to extend political participation and civil development. Can the same be said of European religious illiteracy? I believe so.

14 See again the exemplary research of the late Randi (1987).

15 For doubt on the actual overcoming of the spell of monarchy, cf. Manow (2008: 8–12).

1 On a global scale, religious illiteracy cannot be explained by the end of religious influence (whether understood as part of devotion or of superstition) in the public sphere or with its reduced capacity to control personal customs, thus relegating it to the sphere of preference. Religious illiteracy proceeds, on the contrary, from the rupture of an existential metric system that is typical of modernity *à l'ancienne*: this involved a sequence that saw the individual move toward what we would call 'self-secularization' as a haven in one's journey through life. The link between religious knowledge gained in an educational phase and its use in actual observance ceases at a precise point or stage in life. The rupture of a condition of subjective constraint becomes the emancipation from a universe of the religious and 'practice'. The multiplication of this journey led to an era (which, in Taylor's categories, is assumed to be pre-immanent) when people abandoned or rejected adherence to precepts, figures, symbols and practices that were well known to them on both an existential and a doctrinal level. These people were still willing to educate their children *for a certain time*, often in their original community of faith, beginning from the concepts and teachings that had been rejected, and then to shape them with the same kind of transition toward agnosticism. This agnosticism, however, was in fact filled with meanings and values of religious foundation.

The end of true socialism has led to a lesser need to assess the 'religious' as generally in conflict with state atheism and as an act of opposition toward the totalitarian imposition of ideological atheism. This has resulted in the increasingly rapid accumulation of generations that did not depart from lands of belief in order to come ashore on distant, non-religious lands but are rather natives of the irreligious. What Taylor calls the immanent 'era' in the eyes of the historian seems to be more like a generation than an age: it is the melding together of the first truly agnostic 'next generation', endowed from infancy with a religious *tabula rasa*. Members of this generation are capable of either the most exaggerated eradication of any spiritual instance or of subjecting themselves to the unbridled fascination of unknown religious cocktails, fervent 're-bornisms' and religious obsessions on the edge of salvation/well-being (cf., for example, Spector 2009, Smith 2013).

2 The religious illiteracy that is revealed in the rupture between the self-secularized and 'native' agnostics has been reinforced by an equally important rupture within the knowledge and learning pertinent to the religious sphere. Within this field of study, there is an ongoing diatribe concerning the preconditions of such learning that have so weakened its fruitfulness. On one side, we find the range of theories that, with a multitude of internal nuances, believe that a 'neutral' knowledge of religion is the most qualitatively distinct and superior form. This form could *only* be practiced by those who do not partake in any religious substances or at least have cut down their dosage to acceptable forms (academic instruction in secular institutions) at appropriate times: to give an example, such conceptions do not believe that theology can be seated among the admissible learnings at the assembly of 'secular' research on religions since theology is not the rational exploration of conceptual links and languages over the course of time but will always and forever remain apologetic or at best mild sectarianism. There is the opposite conviction, also crisscrossed by internal variations, with which a multitude of religious authorities willingly identify: namely that the religious can be known through 'further' knowledge, positioned beyond 'mere' historical fact. Greater understanding on a quantitative and qualitative level can be provided *solely* to and from whoever adheres to the internal truth of the subject under study. Hence, to demonstrate this by means of another example, there are two histories of sanctity: one that is superficial and limited to the surface of things, and one that by contrast may adhere to dimensions

unattainable to those outside the community of faith. Ultimately, there is the attempt – and this is the lesson for historians of figures such as Roger Aubert and Giuseppe Alberigo, a group in which I myself identify – to explain that just as there are not two mathematics, one believing and one atheist, there are not two histories, two philosophies, or two theologies. Rather, there is a single rational effort to answer the questions about the *res* in question, about how and what they are, how they have emerged or changed. This acknowledges that, like any history, even religious history must endeavor to go beyond its limits, despite the understanding that there is a limit that exists. This limit involves the sphere of intentions of both those who investigate and those who are investigated, and we may only go beyond this limit with great care and modesty.

The historical-religious scientific field (whose boundaries differ in the various cultures of the West and have already been fragmented by the fundamental epistemological questions driving it) has progressed over the course of the last two centuries. This has led to a growth in specialization in critical knowledge. The history of science teaches us that specialization is common and customary in all learning. This being the case, all pertinent disciplines have been added into the historical-religious field (theology, religious history, exegesis, religious philosophy and cultural anthropology), leading to an increasingly acute segmentation, the result of which is now that a form of knowledge once central in western culture, which had been the critical restraint to non-*moderate devotion*, the antagonist of the *sacra potestas* itself, has now been split into a series of incommunicable splinters where no dialogue can exist and with which no other form of knowledge must necessarily interact. This splintering has had at least two effects: a reduction in the demand for intellectual education in the field of religious practices – since in this area the various needs of the communities of faith seem to be satisfied by the abilities of those working within them; and the instructional offerings which have provided knowledge that is highly concentrated on its own 'neutrality', regardless of the actual capacity to explore the intrinsic profundities of the issue in question.

A European gauge

Religious superpluralism – which is not simply a religious variant of superdiversity but rather the area where history-rich diversities encounter one another – has thus moved into a context of religious illiteracy where it has certainly paid its dues. Turning to outdated solutions bound to national cultures has proven useless: *laïcité*, which perfectly regulated the relationship between Christians and ex-Christians, and whose aim was the immunity of public space;[16] the *separation* that governed the relationship among believers on the basis of the immunity of the individual's conscience, which found itself facing the issue of the corporate rights of the minorities; the systems pertaining to concordats, which have had to come to terms with the idea that not every interlocutor on the religious scene wishes to adapt himself or herself to a system that protects the relation among powers; and the 'structured dialogue' implemented by the European Union, which addressed religious authorities as if they were general stakeholders of interests that were otherwise impossible to weigh – they all leave the European Union constantly a step behind court law.[17] In numerous contexts, the fear of the complexity of it all has driven some to use religious symbols as amulets of identity in the dream of an impossible simplification of the religious landscape.

16 For the effect on Roman Catholicism after Vatican II, see Gabriel, Spieß and Winkler (2010).
17 Cf. Petty (2016), Orofino (2014) and for the Italian context, see Ventura (2013).

In fact, illiteracy has hindered recognition of one of the most relevant outcomes in the judicial-political history of religious Europe: that in the absence of agreement, without directives, and in the prudence of the Union's bodies, Europe has developed a 'non-model' of religious pluralism and liberty (Kracht 2003),[18] which finds its strength in that it is a non-model. The Union has a history of diverse religious violence, confessional or non-confessional impediments placed at the head of political systems and divergent regulations on the formation of leaders in communities of faith and on their governance and practices that are irreconcilable with the management of religious symbols. What has emerged from all this is a system of freedom with its own homogeneity, which, even recently, has shown itself capable of evolving with political lacerations that are compatible with democratic systems. Instead of establishing rigid systematics that would prove difficult to use in disparate systems, it is as if a pragmatic patchwork of systems has been established that, in their divergence, is capable of producing equivalent liberties (Basdevant-Gaudemet and Messner 1999, Ferrari 2012).

This non-model appears to suit European religious illiteracy very well, but in the medium term, it cannot help being put at risk by the indefinite growth of the very same illiteracy.[19] In other words, European religious illiteracy does not intend to diminish the value or need for analysis on a national or regional scale but rather posits the necessity to place it within public policies on a European scale in order to avoid relegating religious issues to a normative taboo or a research-oriented fragment of 'fear management'.[20]

Models of public policy

Like all illiteracies, the religious one can be measured either in accordance with the abstract fixation of a standard – the historical-theological equivalent of Read-Write-Count or the Dublin Descriptors – or starting from the hypothesis that educational systems are those that should provide this knowledge, along with the other learning they impart, and that it is in their insufficient performance that problems in need of solution begin to lurk. There are countless reports and essays that could be cited and studied, but I shall limit myself to three. These are set within the framework of the twenty-first century, and they address profoundly different education systems;[21] I believe them to be the most significant.

The first is the report drafted by the commission established by Jack Lang, French Minister of National Education. Its aim was to reflect on the educational transfer of knowledge concerning the religious experience in nondenominational schools in France. Presided over by Régis Debray, the commission wrote *L'enseignement du fait religieux dans l'école laïque*, published in April 2002.[22] It is divided into five brief but dense parts, examining expectations, resistance and the constraints of teachings that clash with the loss of historical depth

18 In an attempt to make a distinction, which today is less convincing than it was twenty years ago, Kallscheuer (1996: 181–210).

19 Well-placed preoccupations had already emerged in Shadid and van Koningsveld (2002).

20 The website of the DG Research and innovation of the European Commission provides an adequate presentation of religious studies as an instrument to contrast radicalization, and of religious diversity as a mere analogy with present diversity rather than a peaceful composition of bloody conflicts.

21 See the overview of the place of religion in the history of European schools in Smyth, Lyons and Darmody (2013).

22 For example, it moves in a different direction from the *Toledo Guiding Principles* drafted in 2006 under the direction of Cole Durham and Silvio Ferrari. The Toledo Principles started from the curricular need for teaching that is inspired by the idea that curriculum can facilitate teacher fairness with respect to decisive questions for the European Union (respect for minorities, human rights, legal issues).

as a fundamental educational syntax. The report proposed a reinforcement of the humanistic disciplines that, without 'confusion des magistères' (Debray 2002: 42), do not bring God or the relativism of the family *paideia* to school but rather lead from 'd'une laïcité d'incompétence (le religieux, par construction, ne nous regarde pas) à une laïcité d'intelligence (il est de notre devoir de le comprendre)' (43). Twelve recommendations suggest a critical and comparative approach to programs for primary and secondary schools, coupled with strengthened teacher training and a heightening of the École Pratique des Hautes Études. In reality, the simple Institut européen en sciences des religions, directed by Claude Langlois and Debray himself, would undertake certain initiatives. The perspectives in Debray's report were crystal clear: secularism is not one spiritual choice among or in competition with others; rather, it is what makes religious *coexistence* possible. This comes from the principle that what unites us has greater value than what divides us; furthermore, what is now needed is not an extra hour of classroom time but a reassessment of the curriculum and of teaching itself.[23]

This issue was to witness a significant development in Diane Moore's research addressed to the US context.[24] Moore's work is worth mentioning not only for its intrinsic value but also for its capacity to highlight (albeit indirectly) the immaturity of European reflection at the same chronological height. Take, for example, a type of text of an entirely political nature, such as the resolution of the parliamentary assembly of the Council of Europe in October 2005,[25] where unresolved aporias were abundant, which can be easily deduced from the appearance in the text of adversative propositions (the 'however arguments'). In its opening, the assembly

> forcefully reaffirms that each person's religion, including the option of having no religion, is a strictly personal matter. However, this is not inconsistent with the view that a good general knowledge of religions and the resulting sense of tolerance are essential to the exercise of democratic citizenship.

23 Debray (2002: 60ff.). Released shortly after Debray (2005). This pedagogic perspective would swiftly be set aside by significantly different political choices. The President of the French Republic, Jacques Chirac, instituted a new commission, presided over by Bernard Stasi – Commission de réflexion sur l'application du principe de la laïcité dans la République – wherein Debray would also take part. This commission published a document (called *Rapport Stasi*), delivered to the Élysée on 11 December 2003. It intervened in schools by stating that, like other public buildings, ostensible symbols that express religious or political belonging (crucifixes, kippahs, headscarves) should be prohibited. The Stasi Commission is actually the only one to pose the problem of cultural modification within Islamic thought, probably following the suggestion of Mohammed Arkoun, and to evoke the more rational movements within it that rejected the confusion between political power and spiritual power. The Stasi Commission gave rise to the foundation of the Loi Peillon, which banned symbols of religious belonging within public and scholastic buildings, thus limiting the *visible ostension* of one's belonging.

24 Despite referring to the American context, Diane L. Moore's book provided another perspective in the twenty-first century to the debate without having any public mandate: Moore (2007) examines the struggle against religious illiteracy in the secondary education system in America. It does so by starting not from the issue of secularism but rather from a philosophy of education involving the construction of an openness to diversity, and in this framework, it indicates 'why religion should be included in public school education' (27–52). What to teach and who can teach 'about Religion' are only steps toward the formation of a learning community where diversity itself becomes a factor in growth (on this issue, for example, see the chapter 'A Case Study: Teaching about Islam', 111–38). In Moore's idea, this community can be achieved by modifying the curricula of certain disciplines, such as history and literature but also economics and biology, contentious subjects for biblical fundamentalists in the southern USA.

25 Assembly debate on 4 October 2005 (27th Sitting, Doc. 10673, report of the Committee on Culture, Science and Education, rapporteur: Mr Schneider), adopted on the same day and in the same session.

That the knowledge of a thing is not inconsistent with its knowledge is highly banal: it demonstrates how immature the issue truly was.[26] The formula used in the third point of the resolution is also of interest:

> The family has a paramount role in the upbringing of children, including in the choice of a religious upbringing. However, knowledge of religions is dying out in many families. More and more young people lack the necessary bearings fully to apprehend the societies in which they live and others with which they are confronted.

This attributes the necessity of knowledge to the atheism of families who are incapable of providing the necessary information and instructional set needed to understand one's self and others. In a series of recommendations filled with truisms and wishful thinking, the text asks states to provide 'objective' knowledge, despite recognizing the complexity of an understanding of religious conflict and of teachers' inadequate qualifications.[27]

Entirely weak and passive in the face of the French choice to prohibit the 'visible ostentation' of symbols of religious belonging at school set forth by the Stasi Commission,[28] Resolution 1720, with similar frivolity, assumed still more truisms. This included the one stating that the knowledge of religious diversity would be the only one among all others present in the educational system to be carried out not for knowledge of the subject but for the sake of comparison.

The guiding principles of Toledo

This is one of the many points that emerged from the work promoted by the OSCE (Organizzazione per la Sicurezza e la Cooperazione in Europa) office and completed in 2007: about forty jurists and pedagogues called by the OSCE Office for Democratic Institutions and Human Rights (ODIHR) spent one year developing the *Toledo Guiding Principles on Teaching about Religions and Beliefs in Public Schools.*[29] It is a concise document[30] based on a clear human rights framework and on the postulate that respectful teaching means affirming the dignity of religious and nonreligious convictions, and teaching them on an equal level. The 'better understanding of religions and beliefs', therefore, is a tool for deconstructing stereotypes. For this reason, the document is

26 The same form of balance returns in Point 5: 'Politics and religion should be kept apart. However, democracy and religion should not be incompatible. In fact, they should be valid partners in efforts for the common good. By tackling societal problems, the public authorities can eliminate many of the situations which can lead to religious extremism'.

27 Cf. the paragraphs on education and the struggle against stereotypes (see Appendix II, § 6), on school as the educator of tolerance and on how 'understanding the history of political conflicts in the name of religion is essential' (§ 7). On the principle that 'knowledge of religions is an integral part of knowledge of the history of mankind and civilizations. It is altogether distinct from belief in a specific religion and its observance', on the idea that teaching 'the origins of all religions' is possible (§ 8) and on the varieties in European systems (§ 9).

28 On Loi Peillon, see the report on its application one year after implementation, Cherifi (2005).

29 *Toledo Guiding Principles on Teaching about Religions and Beliefs in Public Schools*, OSCE/ODHIR 2007, www.osce.org/odihr/29154?download=true, last accessed 20 June 2018.

30 See the summary by Catherine Syms, head of religious teaching at the diocesan School for Girls in Auckland, New Zealand, cf. *Enhancing the effectiveness of Religion and Values Education within ISNZ Schools*, www.osce.org/odihr/29154?download=true, last accessed 20 June 2018.

expressed using the term 'teaching *about* religion' (159 times), which runs through the four parts of the text that tackle 'legal issues' related to this teaching 'about Religions and Beliefs', questions of curricula, and suggestions for teacher training that, having to suit fifty-seven different countries, could not but remain generalized. Very frequently (precisely twenty-eight times), it has to settle for limiting affirmations through concessions ('A is true, however B is necessary'), which we had already seen in the Council of Europe – for instance, the affirmation that uses (*apax*) theology as a form of competence represented in the editorial board:

> The Guiding Principles combine the legal, educational and theological expertise of both academics and practitioners to ensure the right balance between substance and practicability. With the different approaches to teaching about religions and beliefs being taken into account, the Toledo Guiding Principles are intended to serve as a tool that teachers and educators can relate to from the point of view of their respective national systems. Having individuals from different religious and belief viewpoints involved in developing these Guiding Principles has helped to ensure that the perspective of religious and belief communities is reflected and that the final product is as balanced and inclusive as possible in its scope and approach and the resulting sense of tolerance are essential to the exercise of democratic citizenship.
>
> (27)

Yet what is truly interesting is the approach to comparative studies, referred to seven times, as one of the tools (nothing short of the form of a real research institute) to be adopted in order to promote certain principles destined to enjoy scant reception, at least in Europe. In fact, the Toledo Principles picked up a tendency – which was already seen in Europe until 1995 – that viewed the issue of knowledge of religious fact as part of the struggle against racism and xenophobia.[31] The Toledo Principles led to the European Monitoring Centre on Racism and Xenophobia (EUMC), which then became the European Union Agency for Fundamental Rights (FRA), which had published teaching tools aimed at fighting Islamophobia.[32] In this form, the issue of religious pluralism entered the European research program under the category 'Citizens and governance in a knowledge based society'. With very modest sums, it financed the first research projects, where – still in a solely contemporary dimension and only with socio-juridical tools – it engaged the topic of 'dialogue' with and among religions (Jackson, Miedema, Weisse *et al.* 2007). The distance of these programs from the fields of historical, exegetic and theological research rendered the principles useful to those who least needed it incomprehensible to those who most needed it, and ended up interpreting a moment of knowledge within a framework of actionable rights.

God's revenge, in which the Eternal takes scornful revenge on the theoreticians of his death, exhausted his own ability to explain Jihadi terrorism (Kepel 2000).

31 Resolution of the Council and the representatives of Member States' Governments meeting within the Council of 23 October 1995 on the response of educational systems to the problems of racism and xenophobia, *Official Journal* C 312, 23 November 1995, https://eur-lex.europa.eu/legal-content/EN/TXT/?uri=CELEX:41995X1123, last accessed 20 June 2018.

32 Cf. EUMC, *Muslims in the European Union: Discrimination and Islamophobia*, December 2006, https://fra.europa.eu/sites/default/files/fra_uploads/156-Manifestations_EN.pdf, last accessed 20 June 2018.

The counterevidence of vocabularies

If we want counterevidence, all we need is to consider how the religious violence of the self-proclaimed jihad has been described.[33] This concept has seen all languages converge on a single French term that itself is worthy of a biography: *radicalization*.

The history of French and European political radicalism is lengthy and consecrates the word as an almost technical term, indicating a political stance that shuns mediation. A telling episode from 1988 with the first dual for power between François Mitterrand and Jacques Chirac, a long-time deputy of the Union for French Democracy who had moved to the National Front eight years before deciding to resign from the party in protest of its *radicalization*.[34] It was an entirely political move that, even in the 2017 campaign, Macron made use of as an effective controversial argument against his adversary Fillon.[35] In Anglo-Saxon gray literature, the adjective 'radical' still has a technical value but with some differences. It indicates those groups who aim to achieve political goals that are already present on the stage by using extreme or violent measures if necessary. Radical left terrorism is one example used to designate armed groups in western Europe from the 1960s to the 1980s (Malkki 2012). It is in early twenty-first-century France that the term comes into use as associated with Islam,[36] first in a nonspecific manner and then basically as a synonym of Islamic terrorism, quickly assuming a global scale.[37]

Without entering the dispute between Olivier Roy and Gilles Kepel on whether Islamic terrorism is an Islamized nihilism or a politicized Islam, it seems clear to me that the increasingly massive and uncritical appeal of the category of radicalization expresses a singular conception of religious experience. Indeed, when factual evidence has established that 'self-radicalization' is possible, whether carried out via web in isolation or in the proximity of the family, we realize that we are dealing with something where the religious component in its strictest sense must be marked either by fanaticism or by an illiteracy such that it leads the second generation unsurprisingly to consider Islam or the Islamic as a behavior that is typical of ideological groups.

The acritical adoption of the category of 'radicalized' as a description of individuals who engage in an entirely standardized form of terrorist strategy (Schmid 2012) has also led to the

33 Analysts identify different strategies and, in part, seasons of jihad ideology in the Sunni field: (1) the first, exemplified by the military stance of al-Qaeda, which aims at mass Islamic insurrection and views its mortal enemy as the USA, with the attack of 11 September 2001; (2) a second position aims at mass Muslim insurrection in Arab countries, such as the attempt in Algeria in the 1990s, and aims to create state bases in the likes of al-Baghdadi's Daesh; (3) the third aims and strikes everywhere but especially in Europe: it seeks to produce the greatest amount of fear to move towards repressive national policies that strengthen recruitment to assist in the overturning of the internal sectarian balance between Sunni and Shiite on a global scale. Besides the historical-political nature of these analyses over the long term, it has already been documented how these lines have leveraged European religious illiteracy, leading to a number of highly significant distortions of language.

34 'L'OPA du RPR sur les députés du Front national', *Le Monde*, 12 March 1988.

35 For example, 'Mort du front républicain: Macron parle de "radicalisation" de Fillon et Mélenchon', *Valeurs actuelles*, 5 May 2017, www.valeursactuelles.com/politique/mort-du-front-republicain-macron-parle-de-radicalisation-de-fillon-et-melenchon-82719, last accessed 20 June 2018.

36 Cf. Aziz 1996 includes the report from the French Internal Ministry concerning the dangerousness of Islamic youth movements. It would prove interesting to conduct a study on the possible relationship between the politics of the Algerian civil war, which advocated the eradication of violent Islam, and its identification as radical.

37 A journal such as *Terrorism and Political Violence* used the term 'radicalism' until 2007 to refer to the Israeli right in 2007 and for new religious movements in 2009; the general use still appeared in the important essay by the social psychologist McCauley and Moskalenko (2008), and later in the reviews of Coolsaet (2008), where the term was employed specifically.

equally slippery antonym of 'moderate' Islam. Here again, the French language is a harbinger (Laird 1996), and this usage does not spread through its remote and perhaps unconscious evocation of the *gouvernement modéré* of Montesquieu – which is moderate solely because it is constrained by laws. This jargon asserts itself by creating an antonymic correlation between moderatism and radicalism – similar to the wording that defines consumerism – correlations that are innocent enough as long as they stay within their controlled and measurable environs and harmful, becoming vices, when they lose contact with a socially accepted measure.[38]

If the vocabulary used to define Islamic terrorism lies on a politically sensitive terrain, it is not the sole environment where the gravity and seriousness of religious illiteracy is manifested. Consider, for example, the apparently diametrically opposed preaching against terrorism, which strives to delegitimize religious terrorism and rightfully denounce its abuse of the name of God by those who are believed to use his name to excite their own homicidal delusions. Within, however, the historical area of Europe that has been consumed over a long period, particularly in the last century, by a sequence of horrors – the *unicum* of the Shoah, the Balkan Wars, the civil war in Ulster, ethnic cleansings, Sunni terrorism, war among Christians in the Ukraine, etc. – to say that these were committed through an abuse of the name of God is akin to organizing a heartfelt ceremony in front of the lion's cage where everyone holds a sign reading 'a true king of the jungle is a vegetarian'. These horrors involved perpetrators who were convinced that they honored his Name, victims that invoked that Name in vain and expressed the passivity of the great mass of people who did not feel the contradiction that today seems so strikingly self-evident.

Conclusion

Reflecting, therefore, on European religious illiteracy in its historical dimension means looking at a decisive problem for the future of European societies in the medium term. To think that curing it – pumping knowledge into educational and research systems with the same energy and confidence as if it were a limb that had lost its flow of blood – can solve the problems in the next five years would be illusory. However, to think that the dilemma of a religious climate change, in which we are presently immersed, with its effects on the European landscape in the next fifty years, can do without a significant quantity and quality of adequate knowledge would be an even more dangerous wager and an even greater illusion.

Bibliography

Areshidze, Giorgi 2016. *Democratic Religion from Locke to Obama. Faith and the Civic Life of Democracy*, Lawrence, University Press of Kansas.

Aziz, Philippe 1996. *Le paradoxe de Roubaix*, Paris, Plon.

Basdevant-Gaudemet, Brigitte and Messner, Francis (ed.) 1999. *Les origines historiques du statut des confessions religieuses dans les pays de l'Union Européenne*, Paris, PUF.

Baubérot, Jean 2004. *Laïcité 1905–2005, entre passion et raison*, Paris, Seuil.

Baubérot, Jean 2013. 'Sécularisation, laïcité et laïcisation', *Empan* 90:2, 31–8.

Benson, John 2008. 'Some Thoughts on Charles Taylor's A Secular Age', *Dialog: A Journal of Theology* 47:2, 88–90.

38 See the essay cited as the founder of the study of the subject by Dodge and Benedict (1915).

Berger, Peter L. 1969. *The Sacred Canopy. Elements of a Sociological Theory of Religion*, New York, Doubleday.

Böckenförde, Ernst-Wolfgang 2007. *Der säkularisierte Staat. Sein Charakter, seine Rechtfertigung und seine Probleme im 21. Jahrhundert*, München, Carl Friedrich von Siemens Stiftung.

Chalier, Catherine and Abensour, Miguel 1991. *Lévinas* (Cahiers de l'Herne), Paris, Éditions de l'Herne.

Cherifi, Hafifa 2005. *Application de la loi du 15 mars 2004 sur le port des signes religieux ostensibles dans les établissements d'enseignement publics*, Paris, La Documentation française.

de Certeau, Michel 1984. *The Practice of Everyday Life*, Berkeley, University of California Press.

Debray, Régis 2002. *L'enseignement du fait religieux dans l'école publique*, Paris, Odile Jacob.

Debray, Régis 2005. *Les communions humaines. Pour en finir avec «la religion»*, Paris, Fayard.

Dodge, Raymond and Benedict, Francis G. 1915. *Psychological Effects of Alcohol. An Experimental Investigation of the Effects of Moderate Doses of Ethyl Alcohol on Related Group of Neuro-Muscular Processes in Man*, Washington, DC, The Carnegie Institution.

Durkheim, Émile 1968. *Les formes élémentaires de la vie religieuse*, 5th edn, Paris, PUF.

Feil, Ernst 1999. '"Religio" and "Religion" in the 18th Century. The Contrasting Views of Wolff and Edelmann', in Jan G. Platvoet and Arie L. Molendijk (ed.), *The Pragmatics of Defining Religion. Contexts, Concepts and Contests*, Leiden, Brill, 125–48.

Ferrari, Silvio 2012. 'Models of State-Religion Relations in Western Europe', in Allen D. Hertzke (ed.), *The Future of Religious Freedom. Global Challenges*, Oxford/New York, Oxford University Press, 201–14.

Filoramo, Giovanni 2004. *Che cos'è la religione. Temi metodi problemi*, Torino, Einaudi.

Gabriel, Karl, Spieß, Christian and Winkler, Katja (ed.) 2010. *Religionsfreiheit und Pluralismus. Entwicklungslinien eines katholischen Lernprozesses*, Paderborn, Schöningh.

Habermas, Jürgen 2005. 'Religion in der Öffentlichkeit. Kognitive Voraussetzungen für den "öffentlichen Vernunftgebrauch" religiöser und säkularer Bürger', in Jürgen Habermas (ed.), *Zwischen Naturalismus und Religion. Philosophische Aufsätze*, Frankfurt am Main, Suhrkamp, 119–54.

Jackson, Robert, Miedema, Siebren, Weisse, Wolfram *et al.* (ed.) 2007. *Religion and Education in Europe: Developments, Contexts and Debates*, Münster, Waxmann.

Jensen, Jeppe S. 2014. *What Is a Religion?*, Abingdon/New York, Routledge.

Kallscheuer, Otto (ed.) 1996. *Das Europa der Religionen. Ein Kontinent zwischen Säkularisierung und Fundamentalismus*, Frankfurt am Main, Fischer.

Kepel, Gilles 2000. *Jihad. Expansion et déclin de l'islamisme*, Paris, Gallimard.

Koselleck, Reinhart 2006. '"Fortschritt" und "Niedergang" – Nachtrag zur Geschichte zweier Begriffe', in Reinhart Koselleck (ed.), *Begriffsgeschichten. Studien zur Semantik und Pragmatik der politischen und sozialen Sprache*, Frankfurt am Main, Suhrkamp, 159–82.

Kracht, Hermann-Josef Große 2003. 'Selbstbewusste öffentliche Koexistenz. Überlegungen zum Verhältnis von Religionen und Republik im Kontext moderner Gesellschaften', in Karl Gabriel (ed.), *Religionen im öffentlichen Raum. Perspektiven in Europa*, Münster, Regensberg, 225–72.

Kracht, Hermann-Josef Große 2004. 'Religiöse Fremdlinge in der modernen Welt? Ultramontane Katholiken im 19. Jahrhundert und die Frage nach den Entstehungskontexten einer zivilgesellschaftlichen Demokratie', in Ralph Jessen, Sven Reichhard and Ansgar Klein (ed.), *Zivilgesellschaft als Geschichte. Studien zum 19. und 20. Jahrhundert*, Wiesbaden, Springer, 89–113.

Laird, Robbin 1996. 'France, Islam and the Chirac Presidency. Strategic Choices and the Decision-Making Framework', *European Security* 5:2, 219–39.

Malkki, Leena 2012. 'Radicalisation and Terrorism in History: Lessons from the Radical Left Terrorist Campaigns in Europe and the United States', in Rik Coolsaet (ed.), *Jihadi Terrorism and the Radicalisation Challenge: European and American Experiences*, 2nd edn, Farnham, Ashgate, 69–81.

Manow, Philip 2008. *Im Schatten des Königs. Die politische Anatomie demokratischer Repräsentation*, Frankfurt am Main, Suhrkamp.

McCauley, Clark and Moskalenko, Sophia 2008. 'Mechanisms of Political Radicalization: Pathways toward Terrorism', *Terrorism and Political Violence* 20:3, 415–33.

Melloni, Alberto (ed.) 2013. *Costantino I. Enciclopedia Costantiniana sulla figura e l'immagine dell'imperatore del cosiddetto editto di Milano*, 3 vols., Roma, Istituto della Enciclopedia Italiana.

Menozzi, Daniele 2005. 'La "cristianità" come categoria storiografica', in Giuseppe Battelli and Daniele Menozzi (ed.), *Una storiografia inattuale? Giovanni Miccoli e la funzione civile della ricerca storica*, Roma, Viella, 191–228.

Moore, Diane L. 2007. *Overcoming Religious Illiteracy. A Cultural Studies Approach to the Study of Religion in Secondary Education*, New York, Palgrave Macmillan.

Orofino, Marco 2014. *La libertà di espressione tra Costituzione e Carte europee dei diritti. Il dinamismo dei diritti in una società in continua trasformazione*, Torino, Giappichelli.

Petty, Aaron R. 2016. 'Religion, Conscience and Belief in the European Court of Human Rights', *George Washington International Law Review* 802, www.gwilr.org/wordpress/wp-content/uploads/2017/02/ILR-Vol-48.4_Aaron-Petty.pdf, last accessed 20 June 2018.

Platvoet, Jan G. and Molendijk, Arie L. (ed.) 1999. *The Pragmatics of Defining Religion. Contexts, Concepts and Contests*, Leiden, Brill.

Pollack, Detlef 2012. *Säkularisierung – ein moderner Mythos? Studien zum religiösen Wandel in Deutschland*, 2nd edn, Tübingen, Mohr Siebeck.

Randi, Eugenio 1987. *Il sovrano e l'orologiaio: due immagini di Dio nel dibattito sulla 'potentia absoluta' fra XIII e XIV secolo*, Firenze, La Nuova Italia.

Schmid, Alex P. 2012. 'The Revised Academic Consensus Definition of Terrorism', *Perspectives on Terrorism* 6:2, 158–9, www.terrorismanalysts.com/pt/index.php/pot/article/view/schmid-terrorism-definition/385, last accessed 20 June 2018.

Schoenberg, Phillip W. and Majeran, Roman 2016. 'Varieties of Humanism for a Secular Age: Charles Taylor's Pluralism and the Promise of Inclusive Humanism', *Roczniki Filozoficzne/Annales de Philosophie/Annals of Philosophy* 64:4, 167–97.

Shadid, Wasif A.R. and van Koningsveld, P. Sjoerd (ed.) 2002. *Religious Freedom and the Neutrality of the State: The Position of Islam in the European Union*, Leuven, Peeters.

Smith, Robert O. 2013. *More Desired than Our Own Salvation. The Roots of Christian Zionism*, Oxford/New York, Oxford University Press.

Smyth, Emer, Lyons, Maureen and Darmody, Merike (ed.) 2013. *Religious Education in a Multicultural Europe: Children, Parents and Schools*, New York, Palgrave Macmillan.

Spector, Stephen 2009. *Evangelicals and Israel. The Story of American Christian Zionism*, Oxford/New York, Oxford University Press.

Taylor, Charles 2007. *The Secular Age*, Cambridge, MA, Harvard University Press.

Tierney, Brian 2014. *Liberty and Law: The Idea of Permissive Natural Law, 1100–1800*, Washington, DC, The Catholic University of America Press.

Ventura, Marco 2013. *Law and Religion in Italy*, New York, Kluwer Law International.

Zamagni, Gianmaria 2012. *Fine dell'era costantiniana. Retrospettiva genealogica di un concetto critico*, Bologna, Il Mulino.

2 Religious literacy in modern Europe

Grace Davie and Adam Dinham

Introduction

This chapter has two substantive sections. The first section summarises the religious context in modern Europe, and the factors that must be taken into account if this is to be properly understood. It exposes the reasons for religious illiteracy in this part of the world and the negative consequences that follow from this. The second section introduces two specific responses to this situation, recognising that the response to religious illiteracy – religious literacy – is not a unitary concept. Far from it: it varies considerably between sectors, settings and problems, a point made clear in our conclusion.

Understanding religion in modern Europe: the factors to take into account

This section draws primarily on a growing corpus of work by Grace Davie – in particular on two articles that introduce a series of factors that are currently shaping the religious life of Europe, and a more recent exposition focussed on the British case (Davie 2006a, 2006b, 2015). The crucial point to grasp is that these factors not only change and adapt over time but also push and pull in *different* directions. They can be listed as follows:

1. The role of the historic churches in shaping European culture
2. An awareness that these churches still have a place at particular moments in the lives of European people, though they are no longer able to influence – let alone discipline – the beliefs and behaviour of the great majority of the population
3. An observable change in the actively religious constituencies of Europe, which operate increasingly on a model of choice, rather than a model of obligation or duty
4. The arrival into Europe of groups of people from many different parts of the world, and with very different religious aspirations from those seen in the host society
5. The reactions of Europe's secular constituencies to the increasing salience of religion in public as well as private life
6. A growing realisation that the patterns of religious life in modern Europe should be considered an 'exceptional case' in global terms – they are not a global prototype.

Each of these factors is developed later in order to construct a rounded picture of religion in early twenty-first-century Europe, and to discern the reasons behind the growing concern about religious illiteracy.

Cultural heritage

The first factor concerns the role of the Judaeo-Christian tradition as one influence among others in the formation of European culture.[1] This is easily illustrated in the imprint that the Christian tradition has had on time and space in all European societies – in other words on some of the most fundamental categories of human existence. Regarding the former, it is clear that calendars, seasons, festivals, holidays, weeks and weekends are all premised on the Christian narrative. It follows that the rhythm of the workplace, to take one example, favours those of the Christian tradition, whether active or not. Members of other faiths may well be accommodated – sometimes generously, sometimes less so – but their 'fit' cannot simply be assumed. They are, for instance, very likely to need time off work to celebrate their major festivals. In terms of space, the most obvious exemplars are a comprehensive network of geographical parishes and the dominance of Christian buildings. The skyline itself is an important indicator both of past history and present developments. It is equally clear that some modifications to this profile are more acceptable than others. A good example can be found in the close scrutiny given to the planning applications for buildings belonging to other faith communities. The protracted controversy regarding the building of a mosque in Athens is a case in point, an unease that could be replicated many times over.[2]

Europe's historic churches: the inherited model

Central to Europe's history is the presence of a dominant church (or in one or two cases churches) in each European nation with close links to the state and therefore to territory. The model works at national (state), regional (diocese) and local (parish) level and is pervasive from one end of Europe to the other. The fact that this model is currently under strain in many parts of the continent does not detract from its underlying influence in shaping the ways that Europeans think about religion. Such sentiments can be captured in an understanding of the state church (or its successor) as a public utility: an institution that is there at the point of need for those who so desire and who live in a designated territory. Davie has developed a series of concepts in order to capture the essence of this relationship. The first of these is the notion of 'believing without belonging' (Davie 1994); the second – and more apposite – is 'vicarious religion' (Davie 2000, 2007). Both concepts focus on the middle ground seeing this as the most interesting, but also the most contested, area of European religion – a point developed at length in the more recent *Religion in Britain* (Davie 2015).

It is, moreover, this dimension of Europe's religious life which is most subject to the process of secularisation, with the effect that institutions that once had a hands-on role in the daily lives of most European citizens are now quite other. The situation varies across the continent, but the erosion – best understood as a series of generational shifts – is evident across a wide range of indicators: practice, membership, affiliation and belief.[3] This does not mean, however, that Europe's historic churches have entirely lost their *raison*

1 The influence of Roman organisation and Greek secularism should also be taken into account.

2 For a full discussion of the controversies surrounding the building of this mosque, see Danopoulos (2004) and Triandafyllidou and Gropas (2009).

3 See, for example, the data brought together by the European Values Study, www.europeanvaluesstudy.eu/, last accessed 25 October 2017, and the International Social Survey Programme, www.issp.org/, last accessed 25 October 2017.

d'être. Despite their relative secularity, Europeans are likely to return to these institutions at moments of celebration or grief (whether individual or collective). The frequency with which they do this differs from place to place, but in some sectors of the continent (Nordic Europe, selected Catholic countries and most of the Orthodox world), baptism rates remain remarkably high. Elsewhere they have dropped noticeably. The proportion of burials is more stable, but that too is falling in some places (Britain offers a good example). Particular buildings very often symbolise these connections and remain significant, both for those who use them and those who do not – unsurprisingly in that they house the many-layered minutiae of individual as well as collective memories.

A shift from obligation to consumption

That, however, is not the whole story. An observable change is taking place in the church-going constituencies of Europe, which are increasingly operating on a model of choice, rather than a model of obligation or duty. The latter was very much associated with the state church, though less so as the centuries passed. Churches that were excluding and exclusive in the early modern period have had, bit by bit, to learn to live with difference as religious minorities established themselves all over the continent. There were in addition marked differences *within* the historic churches themselves. The present situation should be seen as the continuation of this trend. In recent decades, however, the process has accelerated to the point that in some parts of Europe the notion not only of choosing one's religion but of changing it is increasingly common. One set of choices, moreover, involves stepping out of religion altogether: the 'secular' is an increasingly popular option.

Without doubt the number of alternatives is growing, bearing in mind two things: that the range of possibilities in Europe remains limited if seen in global terms, and that the 'market' in question overlays an earlier model. In other words, it runs alongside rather than replaces the parish system. In short this is a both/and rather than either/or situation: the incipient market caters for those whose aspirations exceed the older model; the public utility – though fading – continues as one choice among many for the actively religious and as a safety net for those who do not want to choose at all. The co-existence and gradual re-balancing of two religious economies, which are in partial tension but also overlap, captures a great deal about the religious situation in Europe since 1945.

An additional point is worth noting. Until relatively recently, it was broadly the case that the traditional pattern of religion in Europe was more durable in rural areas than it was in cities. Indeed much of the work on secularisation in the late nineteenth and early twentieth centuries focussed on the progressive detachment from the church of the urban working class. Opinions differed regarding the extent and timing of this drift, but there was no doubt about the subject matter. The twenty-first century has seen a different picture emerge. More often than not, it is the rural churches that are struggling. This is unsurprising given that they are deprived of people on the one hand and burdened by the maintenance of inappropriate – if architecturally significant – buildings on the other. Europe's larger cities, however, are seeing new forms of religion emerge, a pattern driven as much by immigration as by the indigenous population. The case of London will be considered later.

New arrivals

Immigration stimulates choice – predictably in the sense that the newly arrived bring with them new ways of being religious, both Christian and other faith. Europe's post-war decades have seen a marked growth in this respect in a movement which is economically rather than religiously motivated. There are four phases to consider. The first took place in the late 1950s and 1960s as the major economies (Britain, France, West Germany and the Netherlands) expanded fast, requiring new sources of labour. A second wave in the 1990s led to a much more widespread phenomenon, which stretched from the north to the south of Europe. It included the Nordic countries, the Mediterranean rim and Ireland, many of which had been countries of emigration for most of the twentieth century. The third wave was rather different. Post-2004 a reconfigured European Union permitted the movement of labour from east to west, leading to a partial rebalancing of religions within the continent as a whole. Significant numbers of Polish Catholics, for example, moved west.

Equally important in the whole story, however, are the economic downturns – in, for instance, the 1970s, in the early 1990s and, very abruptly, in 2008. Not only do these periods of decline depress immigration (and at times reverse it), they lead in addition to growing tensions – notably in terms of entitlement to jobs, housing, healthcare and education. Such tensions dominated the headlines as a fourth phase took shape in 2015–16, the point when large numbers of refugees fled to Europe from the escalating violence in the Middle East. It is abundantly clear that this movement of people has seriously destabilised not only the European societies more immediately affected by the influx, but the European institutions as a whole. The political consequences are still unfolding.

Right from the start, moreover, the implications for religious life have been immense. As indicated, both the growing presence of Christians from the global South and the arrival of significant other faith communities have altered the religious make-up of very many if not all European cities. Regarding the former – and to give but one example – a comprehensive survey carried out in London in 2012 revealed not only that church attendance among Christians had grown from just over 620,000 in 2005 to just over 720,000 in 2012 (a 16% increase in seven years) but that the growth was particularly – if not exclusively – evident in black majority churches and a wide variety of immigrant groups.[4]

Regarding the latter, the consequences are far-reaching. Simply by their presence, other faith communities are challenging some deeply held European assumptions, notably the notion that religion should be considered a private matter. The existence of sizeable Muslim minorities is crucial in this respect. The Muslim population in Europe is noticeably varied, but these diverse communities share certain attributes: a need to express their faith in public (in, for example, the wearing of the veil) and a desire to protect Islam from satire or vilification (in publication, in the media or in film). A whole series of episodes have erupted for these reasons: the *affaire du foulard* in France, the Rushdie controversy in Britain, the murder of Theo van Gogh in the Netherlands (together with the subsequent defection of Hirsi Ali to the USA) and the furore over the Danish cartoons of Muhammad and debate which subsequently spread to Sweden. More recent debates concerning dress have centred on the wearing of the burqa and raise rather different issues, notably those of security. Violent attacks in France, Belgium, Germany and the UK (2015, 2016 and 2017) have exacerbated the tensions. Finding resolutions to these intractable issues has demanded sustained attention from both scholars and policy-makers, both in the European institutions and in the member states. It has, moreover, brought religion to the fore of public debate in a way that was not expected in the immediate post-war period.

4 See 'London's Churches are growing', www.brierleyconsultancy.com/capitalgrowth, last accessed 25 October 2017. For a fuller discussion of recent changes in London, see Davie (2015: 107–9) and Chartres (2015).

Secular reactions

Europeans react variously to this evolving situation. Some welcome the greater attention to religion in public life brought about by immigration, whilst others are not so sure. Conspicuous in this respect are the sometimes vehement reactions of Europe's increasingly vocal secularists, many of whom have difficulty coming to terms with this change in priorities. In many respects this is paradoxical. Secular voices were often at the forefront when welcoming newcomers of different ethnicities. This is much less the case when exactly the same populations begin to assert a religious affiliation as their primary allegiance, a switch which is likely to happen where the provenance and ethnicities of the Muslim community in question are diverse (in the United Kingdom, for example).[5]

A further point should, however, be noted: the secular constituencies of Europe are as varied as their religious counterparts. French secularism, for example, is as much French as secular and markedly different from its British, rather more pragmatic, counterpart. And quite apart from national differences, secular viewpoints range along a continuum from indifference or mild agnosticism at one end to moderately aggressive atheism at the other. The secular, moreover, is gradually emerging as a category in its own right. The epithet 'nones' is still found in the literature to denote those that place themselves outside the purview of religious institutions. They are on the rise in most parts of Europe. More constructive, however, are the attempts to understand the secular, or rather the non-religious, as a positive rather than negative category, seeing this – like religion itself – as a lived reality as much as a cognitive choice. Lois Lee develops this theme in some detail (Lee 2015).

Europe as an exceptional case

The final factor is a little different. It can be found in a gradual, if uneven, realisation that the patterns of religious life in modern Europe should be considered an 'exceptional case' – they are not a global prototype (Davie 2002). In short, Europeans are slowly beginning to grasp that Europe is relatively secular not because it is modern, but because it is European. It is equally true that some Europeans welcome this insight; others are disconcerted by it. Those who welcome it are likely to be more favourably disposed to the growing religious diversity of the continent than those who cling to earlier ways of thinking. Among the latter are two rather different groups of people. There are those that assume that Europe is Christian and will (or should) remain so. A second cluster perceives secularisation as an inevitable part of modernisation – a situation in which religion declines rather than grows in social significance and can therefore be safely set on one side. Both are discomfited by growing religious diversity, and the debates that emerge from this, but for very different reasons.

One point, however, is clear: the situation in Europe is complex, and to understand it fully, it is necessary to see the factors listed earlier in the round. The result is a paradox. On the one hand, religion has re-entered the public square and demands a response. On the other, an increasingly secular population (brought about by a persistent drift from the historic, and other, churches) has difficulty dealing with these issues, in the sense that most, if not all, Europeans are rapidly losing the concepts, knowledge and vocabulary that

5 The reason, however, is clear enough: acceptance of ethnic identities fitted well with the agenda of primarily left-wing people; religious allegiances do not. Similar reservations towards specifically religious nomenclature can be seen in the social scientific community which, by and large, has been more at ease dealing with the secular categories of race and ethnicity.

are necessary to address the difficult questions that arise in the management of difference. What follows is a public conversation about faith, which is of poor quality – at best ill-informed, often ill-mannered and at times dangerously provocative. It is this situation that accounts for widespread concern about religious literacy in this part of the world.

Religious literacy in action

These conundrums have provoked a growing number of responses across Europe, in higher education, schools, law, media and health and social care, among others. The following section draws primarily on a body of work by Adam Dinham which strives to connect theoretical analyses to practical action. Two examples are highlighted and used to illustrate the issues in question. They are the Religious Literacy in Higher Education Programme in the UK and religious literacy training for health and social care professionals in Norway.

The Religious Literacy in Higher Education Programme

The Religious Literacy in Higher Education Programme was established in England and Wales in 2010 (Dinham 2016b). It began with a theoretical analysis of the problem of its inverse – religious illiteracy. Quickly revealed was the paucity of attention to religion in higher education. That said a small body of literature has emerged which examines the history of religion in higher education (Reuben 1996, Hart 1999, Roberts and Turner 2000), alongside another on the recent 're-emergence' of religion on university campuses (Edwards 2008, Wuthnow 2008) and the implications of increasing religious diversity for teaching and research (Edwards 2006, Tisdell 2008). Together this reveals considerable anxiety: where has all this religion come from, why is it back and what should we do about it? The literature also renews an old debate about the responsibilities of universities in a world marked by the 'complex co-presence' (Ford 2004) of often competing religious and secular philosophical traditions. Universities turn out to be particularly revealing of how religion and belief questions often confuse or elude people's ability to address them. Knowledge is regarded as post-religious. Science and religion are often counter-posed. Religion is frequently regarded as threatening to liberal values and freedoms and as having no place in the universities which espouse them. Assumptions of secularity are continuously mistaken for neutrality. And all too often this lands us in muddled thinking about whether and how to talk about religion at all. We – and a number of others – argue that the education system, and particularly universities, should play a vital role in addressing this loss of religious literacy (Gilliat-Ray 2000, Ford 2004, Prothero 2007, Woodhead 2012). This has made universities a useful place to start.

The Religious Literacy in Higher Education Programme undertook empirical research to flesh out how these analyses play out in practice. One focus was on what preoccupies university leaderships. Another was on operational staff in practical higher education roles. Both were approached to find out what sorts of issues were being encountered.

In research undertaken with vice chancellors in 2009–10, the programme identified four university leadership stances, perhaps indicative of stances in wider society (Dinham and Jones 2012). In the first type, 'soft neutral', society is conceived of as a secular space where public institutions remain as far as possible neutral and education avoids mentioning religions or belief. A firmer line actively seeks the protection of public space from religious faith, asserting a duty to preserve public bodies, such as universities, as secular. We called this group 'hard neutral'. A third group – the largest – saw religious faith as a potential learning and formation resource upon which to draw. We called this group 'Repositories and Resources'. The fourth type aims to offer education 'for the whole person', incorporating a specifically religious or belief dimension. This perspective was more common in universities which were founded as religious institutions. We called this group 'formative-collegial'.

We also asked what issues about religion preoccupy vice chancellors. We found that practical and policy concerns were prominent. Vice chancellors were concerned about issues in four key areas. First, they were focussed on legal action arising out of possible discrimination on the grounds of religion and belief; second, on campus extremism and violence; third, on marketing their universities to students of all religion and belief backgrounds, and none; and fourth, on appealing to international students, from all parts of the world and from all religions and beliefs. This analysis appears to balance perceived risks (about violence and litigation) with perceived opportunities (about 'widening participation' and attracting international students).

Finally we conducted case study research in three universities to understand something of the experience of students and staff. We found religious students who had not felt able to attend for interviews, for exams or for Saturday lectures. There were anxieties about public speakers, especially on the topic of Israel and Zionism. Timetabling staff were concerned about the coincidence of exams and Ramadan. Canteens and bars were taking positions for or against halal food, alcohol-free events and single-sex socials. There were sports societies whose members were teasing a Sikh for wearing the 5 K's (worn by orthodox Sikhs: ***kesh*** – uncut hair; ***kara*** – armband; ***kangha*** – comb; ***kacchera*** – knee-length shorts; and ***kirpan*** – sword). Residences were confused about kosher kitchens and women-only halls. Campus banks either could or could not handle the requests of Muslim students for halal borrowing for student fees, and some counselling services felt they could not discuss religion with religious students. Above all, these staff and students were strongly aware of an absence of policies and guidance to frame the conversation. On religion as such, there is almost always institutional silence.

In short we found great diversity of both need and response underneath the religious literacy umbrella, just within this one sector, in this country alone, as the previous examples reveal. We concluded that religious literacy is both a stretchy and a context-specific idea. The challenges in a medical school in a highly diverse area of London are not the same as those in a social work department in more homogenous, especially rural, parts of England. We suspected that this applies across different sectors too, and further religious literacy work in schools, law and media reinforce this (Dinham and Francis 2016). Reading across to cultural and spatial specificities, we also anticipated that religious literacy will look different from one country to another. An example of both is in religious literacy training in health and social care in Norway.

Religious literacy in health and social care in Norway

Colleagues in Norwegian higher education connected with the Religious Literacy Leadership Programme in the UK in 2012 because it resonated with the challenges of increasing religious plurality in their countries as a result of new and very rapid migration. While the interest was good-willed, it was also anxious, reflecting the tension found in the UK experience between accommodating and 'othering' difference, especially in the context of extremism. In Norway this took a particular urgency after Anders Breivik's crimes in Oslo in 2011. Though this was quickly characterised as motivated by the politics of the far-right, rather than religious extremism, Breivik himself quite clearly saw his actions as resistance to religious plurality caused by immigration.

The motivating issue in Norway, like Britain, has been the perceived prominence of Islam in a context of sharply increased migration. An important difference, however, is that ethnic and religious diversity is much newer to Norway. Indeed it was perceptions of the UK's relative experience with multiculturalism that led Norwegian colleagues to connect with the Religious Literacy Leadership Programme. As with the UK, there was a sense that education could be an essential component in recalibrating the debate away from defensive 'othering' and towards hospitality. But in this assumption, too, another important difference is apparent. This is located in the nature of the higher education institution involved – VID Specialised University in Oslo. This is a Diaconia institution, a framing which itself confuses or evades many Europeans in ways which shed light on the problem of religious literacy in Europe. Diaconia, New Testament Greek for service, is interpreted as a Christian call to respond to a need in keeping with the social gospel. This describes an agenda which Christian democrats regard as translating the Christian theologies of 'love of neighbour', forgiveness, hospitality, peace and reconciliation into the politics of social justice, welfare and redistribution. Diaconal work is therefore Christian-rooted, faith-motivated work for social justice and provision of social care, dating in Norway from the 1860s and emanating from their then established (Lutheran) Church, though bureaucratically independent of it.

In Norway, the Diaconia institutions are by far the largest educators in the field of social services. This is in some ways unsettling because in most of Europe health and social care are regarded as secular professions, de-coupled from their faith-based roots by the growth of state welfare in the first half of the twentieth century (Dinham 2016a). Structurally Diaconia institutions behave as state universities, producing secular professionals. Yet they talk of religious values guiding their work, including love for one's neighbour and social justice. They stand, therefore, on an apparent front line between the secular and the sacred, which both poses and reflects the religious literacy challenge: how are we to think about religion in a Europe which had come to think of itself as post-religious, and yet finds itself highly religiously plural after all? The 'diaconal' factor in particular raises the question set out in the first half of this chapter: how is a culturally Christian Europe to think of itself in a context of increasing religious plurality? What does this say about the actual or proper role of religion in the European public sphere? Questions which have long exercised those who imagine Europe to be secular – about the boundaries between the sacred and secular, private and public – are reasserted.

Diaconia institutions are also interesting to religious literacy because of their position as providers of health and social care in particular. This challenges the assumptions of a secular/sacred binary, within which the large majority of professionals have been seen as on the supposedly secular side. Instead, such institutions draw attention to the fact that Europe is in fact complexly post-religious, secular, Christian and plural all at once. The boundaries between religion, non-religion and secularity are blurred, if they exist at all. This matters because health and social care present among the largest frequency of encounters between religious and non-religious providers and service users in the public sphere. This is a pervasive, ordinary, everyday space, and the playing out of religious and non-religious identities within it is of enormous theoretical interest in terms of Europe's ability to understand and talk well about its religion and belief.

It is also of great practical importance, making religious literacy both innovative and pressing for a number of other reasons. Health and social care professions embody a systemic understanding of the person as physical, mental, social and spiritual. Across Europe, many health and social care providers and educators employ chaplaincies as a resource for all, and in some cases these are legally mandated (e.g. in UK hospitals). Yet curricula for professional education appear to neglect religion and belief, and the resources – including chaplaincies – associated with them are widely regarded as separate, private spaces within the otherwise public service. Training has largely reflected a wider secularised sensibility in higher education which emphasises natural scientific paradigms and epistemologies. Within this, health and social care education tends towards a medical model and social scientific accounts of the person which can obscure the religious and the spiritual (Furness and Gilligan 2012). At the same time, many health and social care systems are at least part-public. This puts them on another front line, with public policy-making, which is itself heavily inflected with secular assumptions which also militate against more open-minded religiously literate practices of health and social care (Dinham and Francis 2016).

VID's role in this is as Norway's second-largest private university with 3,300 students on four campuses in Bergen, Oslo, Sandnes and Stavanger. It offers fifty study programmes in health sciences, social sciences, theology and religious studies, and leadership studies. Programmes comprise bachelor degrees in Nursing, Social Work, Social Pedagogics, Theology and Occupational Therapy, and master's degrees in Health and Social Services for Elderly People, Social Work, Diaconia and Christian Social Practice, Value-based Leadership, Family Therapy, Citizenship and Rehabilitation, Intercultural Communication, Theology and Religion, and Globalisation. The connections between Diaconia and training for the health and care professions consolidated around the religious literacy idea in 2014 when VID initiated a new PhD programme which self-consciously takes up religious literacy as a core perspective. The focus is on the interplay of faith-based religious practice (Diaconia), values and professional practice. It also introduced a new MA programme on religion and belief for health- and social care professionals, focussed on the impact of religion and values on care and welfare needs, and on care and welfare practices. Several of the research groups at VID Specialised University have since committed to a similar focus: see, for instance, the group 'Competence in questions of religions and world views in the framework of health care and social services' and the group 'Cracks and in-betweens: Religion, migration and transnational relations'.

Conclusion

Religious literacies

These two initiatives are closely related – indeed, one gave rise to the other – yet have clear context-dependant differences. Religious literacy in both starts as a response to anxiety about newly prominent Islam, and both emphasise the rebalancing of perceptions of religion in terms of risk and opportunity. Yet, in the UK, the most pressing challenge is to establish religion as a legitimate issue for public discussion in the first place, requiring the shedding of assumptions of secularity which are all too often interpreted to mean neutrality. Whereas in Norway the diaconal framework establishes a very different set of popular boundaries between the public, professional and private in relation to religion and belief in which church-based social work seems perfectly normal.

Related work in the fields of media, law and schools also illuminates the context-specific nature of religious literacy, prompting our conclusion that what is needed is not religious literacy but religious literacies, plural. Thus, in law, a key challenge is for employers, service providers, lawyers and judges to be able to access deep theological meanings on the one hand, as well as to understand how they relate to the diverse ways in which individuals live them out (Dinham and Shaw 2013). Since law differs from place to place the religious literacy required in different jurisdictions is itself context-specific. In media, there is agreement that the presenting task in the UK is to equip media professionals to report religion with an understanding of internal diversity rather than as monolithic blocks of fossilised doctrine, and to do so in real time (Wakelin and Spencer 2016). In France, conversely, it may be regarded more as a matter of freedom of speech in the face of attacks on liberal values, and the power of *laïcité* will likely prevent any sort of initiative in the UK mould. In education, about a third of schools in England are church schools, and the 1944 Education Act mandates Religious Education and a daily act of collective worship for all. Hence the key question: what should Religious Education be for, and what should we teach within it (Dinham and Shaw 2015)? In France, the starting point is quite different: should we teach religion in schools at all?

The religious literacy umbrella

That said – and whilst religious literacy is most certainly context-specific – we argue that there are a number of shared positions which make it a meaningful umbrella term.

First, religious literacy is a particular problem of the developed West in that it is ill-conceived secular-mindedness – what has sometimes been called subconscious secularity – that assumes a post-religious world and seeks to act as though it is one. Thus the secular paradigm, in all its varying and contested forms, is itself a product of western intellectual life and tradition, rooted in Enlightenment philosophy, scientific method and, it must be said, in the discipline of sociology. This combination lies at the root of the challenge as to whether religion is a legitimate topic for public conversation in the first place. It follows that clarity on this point is essential if religious literacy is to flourish.

Second, religious literacy is not a Muslim issue, though it often starts as one. Most certainly it needs to respond in part to the perceived and actual challenges of Islamism – not to be confused with Islam – and of increasing religious diversity more broadly. But this is not the only issue or even the biggest one. The discourse, however, has focussed far too much on religion as risk, and not nearly enough on its opportunities and enrichments, in education, welfare, informal care and community-building. Religious literacy draws attention to this and in doing so is likely to produce a less ill-tempered quality of conversation.

Third, it is a liberal endeavour. It stands within the liberal tradition of human rights, social justice and freedoms of speech and thought, and invites people of all religions, beliefs and none to engage with religion and belief diversity in this spirit. It does not extend as far as respecting and tolerating any and all expressions of religion or belief, where those expressions cut across liberal ones. It is unlikely to attract the most illiberal, though they are perhaps most in need of the conversation, but that should not stop the rest of us from engaging our differences. It is thereby normative, in that it has purposes and goals: peaceful, informed encounter across religion and belief differences. It emphasises a respectful conversation, rather than a tolerant one, regardless of one's own religion, belief or none.

So one size does not fit all. Understanding and responding to the real religious landscape and challenges of any particular sector or setting is the key task of religious literacy. Under the umbrella of the critiques and values commonly accepted, it must be approached anew each time in every setting and sector. Thus religious literacy is a framework which needs always to be populated with specific facts and circumstances. Networks of actors, such as those in this volume, will recognise this. Sharing the challenges and responses will strengthen the burgeoning of religious literacy initiatives both across Europe and beyond.

Bibliography

Chartres, Richard 2015. 'New Fire in London', *Lambeth lecture*, 30 September 2015, www.archbishopofcanterbury.org/articles.php/5621/bishop-of-london-delivers-lambeth-lecture-on-church-growth-in-the-capital, last accessed 25 October 2017.

Danopoulos, Constantine 2004. 'Religion, Civil Society, and Democracy in Orthodox Greece', *Journal of Southern Europe and the Balkans* 6:1, 41–55.

Davie, Grace 1994. *Religion in Britain since 1945: Believing without Belonging*, Oxford, Blackwell.

Davie, Grace 2000. *Religion in Modern Europe: A Memory Mutates*, Oxford, Oxford University Press.

Davie, Grace 2002. *Europe: The Exceptional Case. The Parameters of Faith in the Modern World*, London, Darton, Longman & Todd.

Davie, Grace 2006a. 'Is Europe an Exceptional Case?', *The Hedgehog Review* 8:1–2, special issue *After Secularization?*, 23–34.

Davie, Grace 2006b. 'Religion in Europe in the 21st Century: The Factors to Take into Account', *Archives européennes de sociologie/European Journal of Sociology/Europäisches Archiv für Soziologie* 47:2, 271–96.

Davie, Grace 2007. 'Vicarious Religion: A Methodological Challenge', in Nancy T. Ammerman (ed.), *Everyday Religion: Observing Modern Religious Lives*, Oxford/New York, Oxford University Press, 21–36.

Davie, Grace 2015. *Religion in Britain: A Persistent Paradox*, 2nd edn, Oxford, Wiley-Blackwell.

Dinham, Adam 2016a. 'Religious Literacy and Welfare', in Adam Dinham and Matthew Francis (ed.), *Religious Literacy in Policy and Practice*, Bristol, Policy Press, 101–12.

Dinham, Adam 2016b. 'Developing Religious Literacy in Higher Education', in Kirstin Aune and Jacqueline Stevenson (ed.), *Religion and Higher Education in Europe and North America*, Coventry, Routledge.

Dinham, Adam and Francis, Matthew (ed.) 2016. *Religious Literacy in Policy and Practice*, Bristol, Policy Press.

Dinham, Adam and Jones, Stephen 2012. 'Religion, Public Policy and the Academy: Brokering Public Faith in a Context of Ambivalence?', *Journal of Contemporary Religion* 27:2, 185–201.

Dinham, Adam and Shaw, Martha 2013. *Religious Literacy for Equality in Religion or Belief: Overall Programme Summary*, www.gold.ac.uk/faithsunit/current-projects/religious-literacy-in-equality-and-human-rights/, last accessed 25 October 2017.

Dinham, Adam and Shaw, Martha 2015. *REforREal: The Future of Teaching and Learning about Religion and Belief*, www.gold.ac.uk/media/documents-by-section/departments/research-centres-and-units/research-units/faiths-and-civil-society/REforREal-web-b.pdf, last accessed 25 October 2017.

Edwards Jr., Mark U. 2006. *Religion on Our Campuses: A Professor's Guide to Communities, Conflicts, and Promising Conversations*, New York, Palgrave Macmillan.

Edwards Jr., Mark U. 2008. 'Why Faculty Find it Difficult to Talk about Religion', in Douglas Jacobsen and Rhonda H. Jacobsen (ed.), *The American University in a Postsecular Age*, Oxford/New York, Oxford University Press, 81–98.

Ford, David F. 2004. 'The Responsibilities of Universities in a Religious and Secular World', *Studies in Christian Ethics* 17:1, 22–37.

Furness, Sheila and Gilligan, Philip 2012. 'Faith-Based Organisations and UK Welfare Services: Exploring some Ongoing Dilemmas', *Social Policy and Society* 11:4, 601–12.

Gilliat-Ray, Sophie 2000. *Religion in Higher Education: The Politics of the Multi-Faith Campus*, Burlington, VT, Ashgate.

Hart, Darryl G. 1999. *The University Gets Religion. Religious Studies in American Higher Education*, Baltimore, MD, The Johns Hopkins University Press.

Lee, Lois 2015. *Recognizing the Nonreligious: Reimagining the Secular*, Oxford, Oxford University Press.

Prothero, Stephen 2007. *Religious Literacy: What Every American Needs to Know – and Doesn't*, San Francisco, CA, HarperSanFrancisco.

Reuben, Julie A. 1996. *The Making of the Modern University: Intellectual Transformation and the Marginalisation of Morality*, Chicago, IL, University of Chicago Press.

Roberts, Jon and Turner, James 2000. *The Sacred and the Secular University*, Princeton, NJ, Princeton University Press.

Tisdell, Elizabeth J. 2008. 'Spirituality, Diversity, and Learner-Centered Teaching: A Generative Paradox', in Douglas Jacobsen and Rhonda H. Jacobsen (ed.), *The American University in a Postsecular Age*, Oxford/New York, Oxford University Press, 151–66.

Triandafyllidou, Anna and Gropas, Ruby 2009. 'Constructing Difference: The Mosque Debates in Greece', *Journal of Ethnic and Migration Studies* 35:6, 957–75.

Wakelin, Michael and Spencer, Nick 2016. 'Religious Literacy and the Media', in Adam Dinham and Matthew Francis (ed.), *Religious Literacy in Policy and Practice*, Bristol, Policy Press, 117–36.

Woodhead, Linda 2012. 'Religion in Britain Has Changed, our Categories Haven't', http://faithdebates.org.uk, last accessed 25 October 2017.

Wuthnow, Robert 2008. 'Can Faith Be more than a Sideshow in the Contemporary Academy?', in Douglas Jacobsen and Rhonda H. Jacobsen (ed.), *The American University in a Postsecular Age*, Oxford/New York, Oxford University Press, 31–44.

3 Different illiteracies for different countries

Are there no data for religious illiteracy?

Maria Chiara Giorda

Illiteracy, a dark horse

Religious illiteracy is difficult to define. On the one hand, we are accustomed to reading in more or less scientific journals that religion-related incidents and arguments are caused by widespread public ignorance about religion. It is also true that so far this 'religious illiteracy' people have started talking about has no certain, thorough explanation. It is not clear, however, whether this illiteracy is a European illiteracy or whether it has as many forms as European countries have. Its impact on Europe and its countries has not been investigated enough, but they should be able to overcome it legally and culturally. In this chapter, I present a study on religious illiteracy connected to young people of school-age. The school environment has been uniformly studied by a few, albeit not many, scholars in different European countries. I chose the school age related to the issue of illiteracy since the world of education reveals numerous cases and, at the same time, owns the means to defeat illiteracy and teach religious culture. However, despite limiting the study of religious illiteracy to young students, there are still not enough data to effect a complete research.

The answer to the initial question as to whether there are different forms of religious illiteracies or not calls into question the question itself. Before answering it, it is necessary to explain what religious illiteracy (or illiteracies) is, along with its causes, signs, processes and consequences, which I do in the first section. In the second, I show the result of a few studies on religious literacy by scholars in different European countries. In the third, I provide a list of the major European research projects along with the relevant publications on the topic of 'literacy'. In the fourth, I talk about a few researches in which the causes and consequences of illiteracy have been analysed. In my conclusion, I stress the fact that religious illiteracy has still not been investigated in depth, that there is no specific language pertaining to it and that there are not enough relative concepts. However, even if we (in Europe and in other countries) do not possess enough data on religious illiteracy, we are struggling to investigate and set up a religious literacy effective enough to overcome this so scarcely-known illiteracy.

To give an example of ignorance/illiteracy, we can take what happened in an average-sized city in Italy. There, children who do not eat pork or non-halal meat are called Islamic 'fundamentalists': the word is used to describe this group of people's rules and way of living, but, unfortunately, it ends up by discriminating them (Giorda 2014). Another example can be the fact that German students take Buddha for Ganesha, Abraham for Mosé, Alì for Ali Baba. French students take bar mitzvah to mean circumcision and the Torah for the Quran (Michon 2011). Moreover, many French students have never heard of monotheism, Easter, Pentecost, Annunciation, Ascension (Tincq 1988, Defois and Tincq 1997).

Moreover, what can one say about the following sentences?

'Islam promotes violence and discrimination against women'; 'Hinduism is a cult'; 'America is a Christian nation'; 'Homosexuality is a sin'; 'In their heart of hearts, all Muslims are terrorists'; 'Buddhists aren't violent'; 'Mormons aren't Christian'; 'Religion and reason are incompatible'; 'Christianity is a peaceful religion'; 'Jews killed Christ'.

The foregoing quotes represent what US students, friends, professionals, professors and researchers (other than religious scholars) think and say (Moore 2007). Misunderstanding comes easy: people who run public debates about religion do not possess enough knowledge to criticise their guests and find it difficult to conduct intelligent debates (Giorgi 2017). The result is that debates are superficial. For example, sectarian claims are not criticised and people who believe that all religions are the product of blind naïveté or fanaticism cannot be asked intelligent and deeper questions about the topic. We do not know how (or why) this has happened. It may have been due to superficiality, carelessness, prejudice or misjudgement. It is not clear how such a lack of education, communication and information has brought about this misuse of vocabulary. Above all, it is not clear what all the consequences of this phenomenon are.

However, as I have said, there is no common definition of illiteracy, but its existence is taken for granted among scholars interested in these issues. Although there are studies on how to defeat it, what is lacking is a shared view of it. Its causes and the complexity of its processes are not investigated enough and, indeed, with this term we refer to many different phenomena.

Despite Grace Davie's oft-repeated dictum that 'at precisely the moment that we need them most, we are losing the vocabulary, concepts and narratives that are necessary to talk intelligently about religion', there is still a great deal to be investigated in order to develop the concept of religious (il)literacy and its uses and applications (Day and Lövheim 2015).

For this reason, we need to think up suggestions that are neither obvious nor biased ideas. We cannot stand against rules with which we do not agree, nor do we need to criticise, yet we must propose tools and methods that will increase literacy.

The other side of the coin: religious literacy

Some studies from various European countries offer us elements and different points of view concerning the opposite side of illiteracy, which is religious literacy: how we can form it, who the main characters are and which instruments we possess.

The notion of religious literacy has been significantly investigated in Religious Education in recent years, especially in Andrew Wright's works (1993, 2007, 2011, see also Conroy and Davis 2008). This does not reveal an attachment to any particular religion or doctrine *per se* but a general knowledge, the relevant vocabulary, the concepts and the practices as well as some grasp of the complexities, the contradictions and the challenges that are the components of the numerous religious traditions and histories.

The need to answer the question 'Why is religious literacy needed?' is the starting point from which many studies have been carried out. What kind of teaching do we need to guarantee a better one? The latter question is too difficult to answer without giving a biased answer, and this is harmful for the good functioning of scientific research. In the 1970s–80s, scholars from many European countries started noticing that at school there was a lack of the correct instruments to promote good religious literacy. Some school programmes were then changed and various attempts to improve the situation were made.

Over the last ten years, in Europe, many proposals have been discussed, thus in many European countries (Pajer 2013, 2016). There is no doubt that this renewed interest in education/religion is directly connected to the multiple secularities which characterise our society and to its great religious differences (Burchardt, Wohlrab-Sahr and Middell 2015, Giorda 2015).

Among the most recent works we can find the Toledo Guiding Principles and the *Signposts* that investigate what the goals that the teaching of religions must pursue are.[1] Nevertheless, they do not investigate whether 'religion(s)' should be an autonomous subject to be taught, but they analyse rather *how* to teach them. Many studies and conferences have been held to find an effective way to improve this type of literacy in order to find the correct Religious Education that is suitable for Europe. I mention, for instance, Robert Jackson's large bibliography (Jackson 2016). In Jackson's recent work *The Future of Religious Education in Europe* edited by Kristina Stoeckl and Olivier Roy, he investigates the Religious Education models and didactic methods in the context of religious and non-religious (cultural) differences. In the introduction to the same book, he says that religious knowledge is very important in secular societies (Stoeckl and Roy 2015).

The British author tried to classify religious literacy:

> Religious literacy can be a useful expression. However, like various terms in this field – including the term 'religious education' itself – it is used by different writers to mean some different things. I will outline 3 uses of the term (there are more in the literature). I would argue that a combination of 1 and 2 is appropriate for learners in schools – such as community schools – which have students and teachers from a variety of religious and nonreligious backgrounds:[2]

1 'Religious literacy' means having the capacity to understand as much as possible the key concepts of the various religions. It also includes the capacity to understand the use that individuals or groups make of such concepts in relation to their religious beliefs, values and practices.
2 Students should have the capacity to analyse and discuss such concepts, beliefs and practices with the teacher and their peers. They should also be able to relate both reflection and critical thinking that they have been engaged in to their personal and social experience.
3 Both of these models are different from initiation or nurture into a religion or 'learning religiously'. Learning religiously is a legitimate approach in state schools where there is a strong religious component, provided that young people learn not only their own religion, but also elements about religious diversity in nowadays society.

1 *Toledo Guiding Principles on Teaching about Religions and Beliefs in Public Schools*, OSCE/ODHIR 2007, www.osce.org/odihr/29154?download=true, last accessed 5 January 2018; for the Italian edition, with other articles of comment, see Bernardo and Saggioro (2015). For a critical approach, see Jensen (2008). See Council of Europe, *White Paper on Intercultural Dialogue*, www.coe.int/t/dg4/intercultural/Publication_WhitePaper_ID_en.asp, last accessed 5 January 2018; the NEF reports on Religion and Democracy in Europe, dossiers 2010: Luce Pépin, *Report on Teaching about Religions in European School Systems*; Beate Küpper and Andreas Zick, *Report on Religion and Prejudice in Europe, New Empirical Findings*; more recent Council of Europe's publication *Signposts* (Jackson 2014).

2 Robert Jackson, 'Religious Literacy', unpublished paper submitted to the All-Party Parliamentary Group on Religious Education (call for evidence on the importance and development of Religious Literacy), April 2016.

In the same country, Adam Dinham and Matthew Francis published a miscellaneous monograph on *Religious Literacy in Policy and Practices* (2016). The literacy concept is explained as follows:

> Religious literacy begins with an understanding of this – that religion or belief pervade as majority, normal and mainstream, whatever one's own position or stance. Clarity about the category of religion and belief is the beginning of religious literacy – it requires a willingness to recognise it as relevant. This precedes knowledge about specific religions and beliefs themselves, which can only effectively follow on from intelligent, thoughtful, informed understanding of ideas about religion and the secular – an understanding of how the conversation is framed.
>
> (Dinham and Francis 2016: 11)

The same volume contains a text by James Conroy (Conroy, Lundie, Davis *et al.* 2013, Conroy 2016) that is an analysis of *Religious Illiteracy in School Religious Education*; this investigation was carried out in the UK and may be useful to our discussion. In this article, Conroy attempts to explore two central concerns in and for Religious Education in a liberal democratic society. The first is a marked decline[3] in functional religious literacy, and the second is that such functional illiteracy both feeds off and nurtures a kind of pathology in the practices of Religious Education that militate against the seriousness of claims to the theological. The sources of his analysis can be found in a major three-year ethnographic study of Religious Education practices in twenty-four schools across the UK. This is an attempt to investigate some of the manifestations of religious illiteracy. The attempt is based on conceptual and factual 'errors' (Conroy 2016: 169) that the authors witnessed in the classroom and offers a catalogue of them. In the final section Conroy suggests some interrelated causes for the failure of compulsory Religious Education used to defeat religious illiteracy. The conclusions are interesting as they show some causal connections that it would be interesting to prove:

> Whereas in the US the absence of RE in the public school has fostered unthinkingness and the consequent growth of fundamentalism, in Britain RE that has failed to pay attention to the relationship between the self and 'religious objects' has also produced an unthinkingness, manifest not as fundamentalism, but as profound disassociation, scepticism and lack of interest.
>
> (184)

I argue this reveals a lack of objectiveness in the analysis: religion literacy is based on the knowledge of religious vocabulary and on the capacity to contextualise the concepts within their historical, ethical, epistemological and social context. Religion illiteracy, instead, does not include the aforementioned elements which religious literacy is based on. Religion illiteracy is basically confusing the information, is giving partial explanations that become partial understandings: in the UK school quality and quality teaching are to be blamed for this (Conroy 2016: 170).

This perspective fits fairly well within the contest of this book, which is considered to face a huge lack of religious literacy. The authors think that nowadays many people are ill-equipped to engage with religion and belief when they encounter them in their daily lives (in relationships, law, media, professions, business and politics, among other venues). This

3 We shall see in the following sections that considering former days better than today's is another particular feature of the studies on literacy.

book brings together theory and policy and contains more investigations carried out by expert scholars who analyse what religious literacy is, why it is needed and what can be done to improve it. The writers' intent is to provide the people with an instrument that may be useful in order to learn to live with the plurality and pervasiveness of many religions and beliefs, whatever their personal beliefs may be.

In the introduction to the book, Dinham states:

> We are not going to suggest that the answer lies in a return to the past – more confessional RE in schools, a re-valorised Church of England, and a return to predominantly church-based welfare services. The clocks are not going back, even if we wanted them to (which, for the record, we don't). But we do want to challenge a number of assumptions which have taken hold about religion and belief in the public sphere during the second half of the 20th century, push at them firmly, and the assumptions soon fall away. What is left, we have found, is frequently a positive, healthy space for a far better quality of conversation about religion and belief than we thought had become the case.
> (Dinham and Francis 2016: 4)

Drawing on Dinham's earlier work with Stephen Jones (2012), religious literacy is a civic endeavour, beyond any religion. It aims to teach people of all faiths (or none) to know and live together with the increasing plurality of religions and beliefs that everyone encounters in their paths as a result of migration and globalisation. 'It is made all the more difficult by decades of non-confessional Religious Education in schools, the marginalisation of Theology and Religious Studies in universities, and the traction of assumptions of secularity' (Dinham and Jones 2012, Dinham and Francis 2016: 16). There is not only a lack of knowledge about religion but also about traditions in general. In Chapter 4 of this book, Stephen Prothero and Lauren Kerby carry out a different type of investigation: they tried to trace this loss in the history of Christianity in the US. They started analysing the relevant legal cases from the 1960s back to the nineteenth century, when Christian denominational differences were minimised in order to Christianise the nation. The way religion is taught in schools is limiting, teachers are often unwilling to expand beyond the limits the textbook sets. The combined effect of these deficiencies is that Religious Education in school reduces religious practice to a private form and religious feelings to private sentiments. 'The corollary of this argument is that [...] religious literacy is only possible where a meaningful engagement with religion takes place, not a light-touch, postmodern relativisation of religious thought' (Dinham and Francis 2016: 21; see also Moulin 2011, 2015a, 2015b, 2016, Conroy, Lundie, Davis *et al.* 2013). A catalogue of compelling cases is the basis for a better quality education concerning religion and belief (Dinham and Francis 2016: 17).

Across the Atlantic, in the US, scholar Diane Moore is also coordinating a research group driven by the same need to offer the right instruments to create a strong religious literacy (Moore 2007: 1–14). She is the author of the most famous book on illiteracy. The official website of the Religious Literacy Project at Harvard Divinity School says that this school is dedicated to enhancing and promoting the public understanding of religion.[4] It provides resources and special training opportunities for educators, journalists, public health workers, foreign service officers, interfaith/multifaith groups, students and others wishing to understand better the complex roles that religions play in contemporary global, national and local contexts. In her book, Moore aims to understand the complex religious influences because there is a critical dimension of understanding modern human affairs across the full spectrum of

4 See http://rlp.hds.harvard.edu, last accessed 5 January 2018.

endeavours in local, national and global arenas. The aim of her investigation is to find out the better methods to diminish religious illiteracy. Providing resources useful to recognise, understand and analyse religious influences in contemporary life (Moore 2007: 20) is an important goal she aims to reach. The definition of religious literacy was articulated in 2006 by Moore. Such a definition was later adopted by the American Academy of Religion (AAR) in order to help educators understand what is required for a basic understanding of religion and its role in the human experience.[5] The author thinks that much misrepresentation and misunderstanding stems from Enlightenment definitions of secularism that spread widely through colonialism and deeply influenced all the cultures worldwide. The aforementioned study is helpful to identify the misinterpretations and to understand better the multivalent dimensions of how religions function in contemporary life. These foundations provide the best instruments to understand the complex roles that religions play in life, and understanding them will help diminish the negative consequences of the widespread religious illiteracy (Moore 2007: 37).

Bruno Michon's point of view is far different. He discussed his PhD dissertation in Strasbourg (Michon 2011) on religion culture among French and German teenagers. He affirms that illiteracy is a loss and a reduction but he never assesses it by acting as a *laudator temporis acti*. Michon's investigation is located in France, but its scheme could be used throughout Europe. He chose to carry out his study in schools as he is interested in young students. Michon argues that this emptying of religious cultures can be analysed both from a personal and cultural perspective and from an alterity standpoint (to learn about religions different from one's own). Michon tries to analyse the studies that have been carried out concerning religious culture in France over recent decades. He analysed more than sixty works and scientific articles dealing with this topic. Sixty-six per cent of them were implemented in France. He discovered that 'religious culture' (*culture religieuse*) does not have a definite meaning but is actually used by many authors who implicitly accept its different uses. Here are some examples: Charles Taylor (1989), who makes use of this term to refer to believers that are part of the religious culture, then an article written by two US criminologists that investigate the connection between religious culture and an attitude towards violence (Ellison, Burr and McCall 2003): in both cases 'religious culture' involves economic, social and political issues. We witness religious culture influencing symbols and meanings that are part of our lives. In 1969, the Jesuit Raymond Deniel wrote on *Social Compass*, reporting the fact that Christian believers knew little of their own religious culture (Deniel 1969). This is a cognitive/scientific approach to culture: the assessment of the knowledge about one's own religion and of other religions. This kind of approach is part of an *a priori* framework that must be read critically according to the 'ideal education' of the humanistic perspective. Of these *a priori* arguments, the first that is worth mentioning is the positive role of the education perspective: culture means knowledge, and knowledge means behaving well towards others and towards the world in which we live (Flahault and Schaeffer 2002).

In the fields of sociology and pedagogy (Michon 2014), many French scholars (far more than English and German ones) used Michon's two approaches as *définition culturelle et définition savante*. What is noteworthy is that this approach was used to explain some social phenomenon without ever being defined, analysed or measured.

Until now, illiteracy has not been investigated and this proves that the studies on it are still too weak. In the majority of investigations, in point of fact, illiteracy is something that is missing

5 See *Guidelines for Teaching about Religion in K-12 Public Schools in the United States*, American Academy of Religion, April 2010, www.aarweb.org/sites/default/files/pdfs/Publications/epublications/AARK-12CurriculumGuidelines.pdf, last accessed 5 January 2018.

or something that has been lost. Europe refers to illiteracy as if it were a lack of knowledge and a loss of memory (Ognier 2003). In 1901, the Ligue Française de l'enseignement proposed to teach the history of religions to prevent the loss of religious culture, and since then France has been trying to use the teaching of history of religions to combat 'inculture' and 'exculturation' (Hervieu-Léger and Willaime 2001, Hervieu-Léger 2003). On the other hand, the loss of a personal religious culture has been worrying theologians, priests and scholars since the end of the nineteenth century and never ceased to concern them throughout the entire twentieth century. To emphasise the significance of this point, it is worth mentioning the Catholic militant Joseph Santo's work *Effarante ignorance religieuse d'incroyants et croyants* (1934) (Michon 2011: 33).

In Germany, although scholars are open to a public debate and are interested in gaining knowledge about religions (Jödicke 2009), they consider illiteracy as a loss of memory (Käbisch 2014a, 2014b). They think that ignorance (illiteracy) comes as a second instance. First, there is the loss of religious culture from both a cultural perspective and from a cognitive outlook, and horizontally from both a religious and a non-religious point of view.

In her work *Schulischer Religionsunterricht* (Frank 2009: 33–47) on the Swiss situation, Katharina Frank explains how the fear of losing the catechism- and confession-based uses of Christianity are the true reasons why traditional Christian Churches are concerned. They are worried that education may become secular. In Switzerland, the fear of losing one's own religious uses is one of the main arguments in discussions on today's religious diversity, and this fear involves the loss of one's own identity, values and a basic knowledge about religion (Rota 2017). There are as many arguments as there are Swiss cantons. In actual fact, however, one of the conclusions of the project conducted by Jödicke and Rota is that, despite the historical differences among the cantons, the arguments are very similar across the whole country. For example, the arguments put forward in the canton of Geneva are very similar to those in France (Hutmacher 1999). In addition, 'illiteracy' is seldom mentioned (*analphabétisme religieux*), but the discourse revolves rather around a number of potential losses, e.g., culture, social cohesion and identity, which are sometimes bundled together under the label of 'ignorance' (Jödicke and Rota 2010, Rota 2015).

In Italy, some sections of the Catholic Church think that religious ignorance is a loss of knowledge and memory about religious culture: there is an ongoing research on CEI (Italian Episcopal Conference) documents and the vocabulary used in textbooks whose results are not still available, but researchers are pondering the existence of an insider reading of religious culture.[6] We must also recall that in the UK various discussions concerning religious illiteracy as the loss of traditional religious heritage have been held: some Christian organisations have carried out research revealing a loss of knowledge about Christianity.[7]

6 A survey about Documenti dell'Istituto has been carried out and researched on the website www.lasalliana.it (last accessed 5 January 2018), Cahiers Lasalliens, Cahiers MEL and Études Lasalliens.

7 See Bible Society, *Pass It On*, 2014, www.biblesociety.org.uk/uploads/content/projects/Bible-Society-Report_030214_final_.pdf, last accessed 5 January 2018; Christian Institute, *Christmas Knowledge Survey*, 2013, www.comres.co.uk/wp-content/themes/comres/poll/Christian_Institute_Christmas_Knowledge_Survey_December_2013.pdf, last accessed 5 January 2018. Some warn that a loss of knowledge about traditional Christianity in British society means more assertive/less tolerant forms of Christianity are coming to the fore: 'BBC head of religion warns of "chronic lack of religious literacy" in the UK', *The Independent*, 18 March 2016, www.independent.co.uk/news/uk/home-news/bbc-head-of-religion-warns-of-chronic-lack-of-religious-literacy-in-the-uk-a6940041.html, last accessed 5 January 2018; Sylvia Collins-Mayo and colleagues pick up the theme of a loss of religious memory (using Hervieu-Léger) in Collins-Mayo, Mayo, Nash *et al.* (2010). The findings of their research in church youth clubs suggest that young people make do with a watered-down version of the faith rather than search for religious or spiritual meaning elsewhere. See also Collins-Mayo's chapter, 'Young People and Residual Christian Culture', in Day and Lövheim 2015: 179–94.

Ambiguity of the concept and lack of a definition of it (is it culture? is it literacy? or is illiteracy intended as an isolated concept, not as a lack of literacy?) should be always kept in mind and must be a leading thread in investigations in this field. From this perspective, Michon's work concerning France and Germany should be used to compare his results with those of other European countries. However, there is no sign of this study/comparison being effected.

European projects: an oriented perspective?

Judging from the aforementioned researches, it may seem that the common (national and European) perspective is willing to try to build a religious culture based on a positive and constructive policy rather than one of indifference/negligence. It is worth noting that many projects that have been published have attempted to propose and regulate models, instruments and teaching methods in the religious field. However, the results they have attained in the assessment of the state of knowledge can easily be challenged. Of these major projects I shall briefly analyse the goals of European Network for Religious Education in Europe through Contextual Approaches (ENRECA), Religare, Religion and Democracy in Europe and REDCo (Religion in Education: A contribution to Dialogue or a factor of Conflict in transforming societies of European Countries) with the subsequent publications.

The ENRECA was set up in 1999 as a forum for mutual cooperation and reflection on the changing role of Religious Education in Europe. It brought together scholars from England, Germany, the Netherlands, Norway, Sweden and Wales. Scholars are engaged in empirical and theoretical research into aspects of religion and education in relation to intercultural issues. The fundamental concern is the danger that Religious Education, while firmly rooted in many European traditions, might become more marginalised and weakened in our education systems.

Two perspectives were important for ENRECA's vision: religious contextuality, with a focus on religious life in particular cultural situations and at local levels, and religious competence as the ability of a student to negotiate religious meanings.

In January 2007 the Network of European Foundations (NEF) launched a special initiative on Religion and Democracy in Europe. The second phase of the Religion and Democracy in Europe initiative (2008–9) aims to develop a series of reports addressing specific aspects of the interaction both between the state and religion and between religion and society. The reports are an exercise mapping existing practices and different approaches to specific issues, set within the broader context of the religion and democracy debate. They target practitioners, policy-makers and agents in civil society. The reports have been developed by renowned experts and address the following topics: Religion and Healthcare in the European Union; Teaching about Religions in European School Systems; Conflicts over Mosques in Europe; Religion and Prejudice in Europe.

In Religion and Prejudice in Europe by Beate Küpper and Andreas Zick, eight countries were selected for this research: Britain, France, Germany, the Netherlands, Italy, Portugal, Poland and Hungary. The results of the research could be used to organise a similar research on illiteracy. The more religious people are, the more prejudiced they usually are. This holds true for the largest Catholic and Protestant countries no matter their level of religiosity. Religious people show more anti-Semitism, negative attitudes towards Muslims and immigration and racism based on skin colour than non-religious ones.

If belonging to a religious group makes people being more prejudiced and creates stereotypes, then we should investigate whether illiteracy may be the result of such prejudice and stereotypes. Religious people also use their religion to legitimise their attitudes and as a means of self-protection.

From a different perspective we could say that the knowledge of religions may be an instrument to defeat prejudices. This is what it is said in *Religious Diversity and Intercultural Education* edited by John Keast (2007): it is a reference book for schools published by the Council of Europe in 2007. It is based on some investigations carried out in Austria, Cyprus, France, Germany, Greece, the Holy See, Norway, Slovenia, Spain and the UK.

The Religare (2010–13) project concerned religions, belonging, beliefs and secularism in Europe.[8] It examines the legal rules protecting or limiting (constraining) the experiences of religious or other belief-based communities. Where the practices of communities or individuals do not conform to state law requirements, or where communities turn to their own legal regimes or tribunals, the reasons behind these developments need to be understood. It comprised thirteen universities and research centres throughout the European Union and Turkey. Religare wanted to contribute to enhancing interdisciplinary cooperation in the area of religious pluralism in Europe and examining new legal frameworks in the field of religion and secularism with a view to making policy recommendations for improvement.

The international research project REDCo addressed the question of how religions and values contribute to dialogue or tension in Europe. Empirical studies, targeting pupils in the fourteen- to sixteen-year age group, looked into their own perceptions of dialogue or conflict within the different national contexts. Eight European countries were involved: Estonia, Russia, Norway, Germany, the Netherlands, France, England and Spain.[9] The main aim of REDCo project was to define and compare the potentials and limitations of religion in the schools in different European countries. This comparison can help us to find different approaches in the field of Religious Education and to promote dialogue in the European context. The project aimed at analysing conceptual and practical approaches to mutual understanding in the field of Religious Education. This project analysed the theoretical and practical approaches in schools and universities that encourage dialogue with others and mutual respect. These approaches can be strengthened without underestimating the conflicts between people of a different religion, culture and political opinion. I merely want to mention the conclusions of this project in order to demonstrate that illiteracy still needs to be investigated in far greater depth.

> Mais on peut évaluer ce qui retirent les élèves d'un tel enseignement? Les enquêtes RedCo ne permettent pas de le dire et c'est une question qu'il faudra un jour aborder [...]. Pourquoi ne pas tenter d'évaluer les performances respectives de l'enseignement des faits religieux en France, de la *religious education* en Angleterre, du *Religionsunterricht für alle* du Land de Hambourg... du point de vue des acquis des élèves? Les résultats d'une telle analyse internationale pourraient révéler des surprises et l'on peut même conjecturer qu'en matière de connaissance des faits religieux, la France ne serait pas mal classée. Que le pays de la laïcité s'en tire mieux que les autre dans ce domaine serait évidemment une heureuse surprise!
>
> (Béraud and Willaime 2009: 243–5)

8 See www.religareproject.eu/content/what-religare, last accessed 5 January 2018.
9 REDCo, *Final Report Summary*, http://cordis.europa.eu/result/rcn/47525_en.html, last accessed 5 January 2018.

This text mentions arguments that are still topical, and not much progress has been made since then. Just as Michon compared France and Germany (Alsace, Baden, Württemberg, Berlin, Brandenburg), so should Europe and the US do likewise (Berger, Davie and Fokas 2008). Speaking from a methodological perspective, anyone wishing to study the (il)literacy issue in the two continents should start from an accurate analysis of the actual school systems: however, the origins of the subject are not clear.

Very first steps in the analysis of causes and symptoms

Religious culture seen from a cognitive perspective has been studied in depth by Michon, to whom we owe many reflections. These reflections may be very useful in investigating the roots of illiteracy in the different Europe scenarios. First of all, if the subject of this study is teenagers, we cannot limit our research to the school systems, but we need to include: catechism; the time dedicated to Religious Education outside school (for instance Quran schools, Hebrew schools, Bible classes); internet or other media talking about religion – whether directly or indirectly (for instance in Italy teenagers watching *The Simpsons* learn a great deal about religion); then family and friends. These sources that are different from school play a great influence on teenagers and should be carefully studied, as some countries such as Italy, France and Germany (Melloni 2014) have already done. The media play an important role and often have more educating power than school itself. This is why scholars should focus not only on Religious Education but on the different forms of teaching in/outside/from/about religion(s). All these approaches have positive aspects, but also limitations. They are limited because the transmission of knowledge about religions is not effective enough. Much still has to be done concerning school programmes content and their goals. Furthermore, a comparative perspective has not been adopted yet. It is also worth noting the importance of the relationship between formal and informal sources, conflicting and non-conflicting sources on the same entity, in a complex system connected to the decline of institutions, to secularisation processes and to the many sources of information.

At school, there are two important factors that help the spread of religious knowledge: the teacher's ability to hold students' attention and, above all, textbooks. The results of a research carried out in Italy, France, Germany, Norway, Sweden, Portugal and the UK[10] show that textbooks often encourage the growth of illiteracy (rather than literacy). Over the last ten years, an increasing number of researchers have shown how far textbooks have helped the authoritative perspective towards religions to develop and become established. One example is the journal *Religion*, which in 2013 launched a feature series exploring the use of textbooks in the study of religions at University. The journal now regularly prints review essays on textbooks (Giorda and Caramagno 2017) that have been influential or have

10 See *School Textbooks and Religion*, www.gei.de/en/departments/textbooks-and-society/school-textbooks-and-religion.html, last accessed 5 January 2018, and *Research on Textbooks in the Study of Religion*, www.gei.de/fileadmin/gei.de/pdf/publikationen/Bulletin/Bulletin_15/GEI_Bulletin2015_Andreassen.pdf, last accessed 5 January 2018. See also Pingel (2000), Andreassen and Lewis (2014), Giorda (2012), Willaime (2014). For Portugal, see Comissão da Liberdade Religiosa (Commission for Religious Freedom) who conducted a research in 2007 to textbooks (see Esther Mucznik, *A religião nos manuais escolares*), where negative stereotypes towards minority groups, such as the Jewish and the Muslim, were identified. Other religions were virtually absent from the textbooks: www.clr.mj.pt/sections/agenda/estudo-a-religiao-nos/2007-estudo-a-religiao/downloadFile/attachedFile_f0/Religiao_nos_manuais_escolares_estudo.pdf?nocache=1268737957.04, last accessed 5 January 2018.

drawn special attention within the study of religion. As far as Italy is concerned, for example, the methodological assessment of textbooks offers a unifying frame of analysis across a wide range of texts with reference to different religious traditions and different subjects (Literature, Philosophy, History and obviously Religious Education). Since the results of the research are slow to find their way into textbooks, the gap between academia literacy and school literacy will remain wide and stereotypes will increase.

France and Germany have different formal and informal sources, teaching methods, textbooks and assessing methods, which it is important to know if we aim to analyse the various European scenarios in depth. In France, Religious Education is not an important school subject, therefore the relevant information is acquired thanks to the media and during time outside school in general. In Germany, Religious Education is fundamental to the school system because religion plays a great cultural role in the country.

Furthermore, differences among the local politics and culture of every city in a given country that, willingly or not, influence the Religious Education should also be analysed.

The different types of 'exculturation' and 'popularisation' processes are playing an important role in the creation of new religious knowledge in more or less secularised contexts. In this case, the concept of religious literacy is more complex and can be described with difficulty: it can be approached from different perspectives, including cultural, cognitive, existential, identity and popular aspects (Michon 2011: 515).

There are many options that still need to be investigated. Even though a secular Religious Education in which many religions are taught might work from a cultural and political point of view, and from a religious diversity and secular perspective, provided that this takes place in a non-confessional school environment where studies on Religious Education[11] have been carried out for years, it cannot be excluded that differences in theory, taught contents, methods, instruments and side effects will be so important and extensive that they may invalidate the objectives and results. Would it be unexpected if those who own a better literacy are those who received a confessional Religious Education? It is worth remembering that there is a truly wide gap between theory and practice.

Religious prejudices and stereotypes, clichés and poor education (which have never been investigated enough) are often assumed to be the cause of such a negative situation. Jenny Berglund (Berglund 2015) carried out an investigation into the signs of ignorance in Sweden and another eight European countries and into the goals that should be achieved in the teaching on Islam at school. Strategic differences in perceptions of social cohesion in different countries shape Islamic education. Her goal was the knowledge and control of this aspect of culture, and the map is useful in order to analyse which and how the different countries reach this goal. Anders Sjöborg, on the contrary, thinks that religious illiteracy is the stigmatisation of Islam. In Sweden, public discussions on human rights are divided into three parts: consensus on human rights discourse in general; awareness of the need for constant refinement regarding the application of human rights; a rising awareness of the stigmatisation of Islam which can be seen as a sign of a lack of religious literacy (Sjöborg 2015).

Scholars or politicians are accustomed to pondering and judging negative events that frequently occur. The work of Jenny Berglund, Yafa Shanneik and Brian Bocking, *Religious Education in a Global-Local World* (2016), reveals a critical analysis of the situation

11 Cf. Wanda Alberts and Tim Jensen's panel in Annual Conference of EASR 2016 'Relocating Religion' (Finland, University of Helsinki, 28 June–1 July 2016), about 'Discrepancies Between Teacher Training Programmes in the Study of Religions and the Aims, Contents, and Didactics of Related School Subjects'.

today. In this work they tried to investigate how religious literacy can be brought about in different countries. The book, indeed, examines Religious Education in over ten countries, including Australia, Indonesia, Mali, Russia, the UK, Ireland, the USA and Canada. Investigating Religious Education from a global and multi-interdisciplinary perspective, it presents research on its diverse past, present and possible future forms. In doing so, it enhances the public and professional understanding of the complex issues and debates surrounding Religious Education around the world. The volume emphasises a student-centred approach, viewing any kind of Religious Education, or its absence, as a formative, living experience for pupils. It stresses a bottom-up, sociological and ethnographic/anthropological research-based approach to the study of Religious Education, rather than the 'top-down' approaches which often start from prescriptive legal, ideological or religious standpoints. The twelve chapters in this volume regard Religious Education as an entity that has multiple and contested meanings and interpretations that are constantly negotiated. For some, Religious Education means religious nurturing, either tailored to parental views or meant to inculcate a uniform religiosity. For others, it means learning about the many religious and non-religious views and secular ethics, not promoting one religion or another. Some seek to avoid the ambiguous term 'religious education', replacing it with terms such as 'education about religions and beliefs' or 'the religious dimension of intercultural education'. The approaches are many but they are all at risk (Conroy, Lundie and Baumfield 2012).

The academic world is very interested in the fact that illiteracy is kept alive by prejudices, stereotypes and clichés. The process is similar for all of them: stereotypes empty things of meaning. They make people think that difference implies something inferior, something hostile. Stereotypes generate prejudices and justify acts of discrimination. According to classical studies, prejudice is what makes people exhibit discriminatory behaviour towards groups or individuals that are considered inferior.

The religious diversity we are experiencing nowadays has changed our needs and educational goals. It is also true that the different levels of literacy (or illiteracy) in every country change our interpretation of diversity. Illiteracy plays an important role, as shown by the Food&Religion investigation carried out in some European cities (Giorda and Bossi 2016), whose results relating to Italy reveal as follows (Figure 3.1).

There is a great difference between people's perception and reality. In a primary school in Milan (cf. Giorda and Bossi 2016), the pupils' parents were asked how many pupils from a different religion were enrolled at the school. The parents' perception was that they were many more than they actually were in reality. As I have already said, there are many studies that try to defeat illiteracy by increasing the literacy level. They look for a solution, taking for granted that there is a problem.

Conclusions (or rather, a new beginning)

Andrea Rota's book on Religious Education in Switzerland shows a really good description and classification of different types of religious ignorance. Rota actually notes that the phrase 'religious illiteracy' is rather more prominent than the polemic about education in France (Rota 2015, see also Urbanski 2013, 2016). Davie thinks that 'religious illiteracy' became famous after the publication of Henri Tincq's article 'Analphabétisme religieux' in *Le Monde* (1988) in which he talked about some examples of religious ignorance (Davie 2000).

This should be a reason to start analysing the causes and the consequences of religious illiteracy. Dealing with ignorance is not simple if the causes and the processes have not

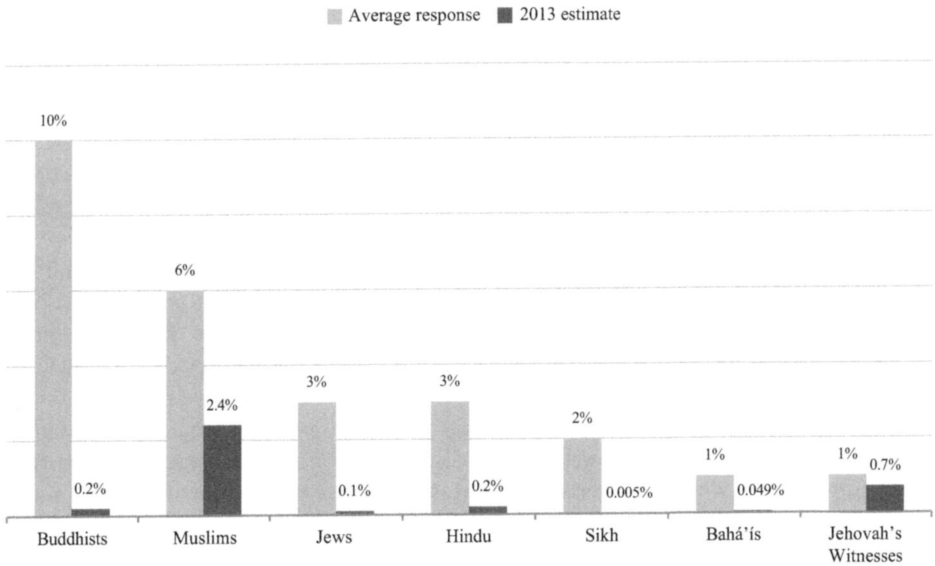

Figure 3.1 Italian families' perception of religious diversity in Italy.

been previously thoroughly analysed. I think that some actions can be taken to improve the situation:

1 Providing all the European countries with a better description of what religious illiteracy/ignorance is, from all the useful perspectives. Religious illiteracy is not a memory loss but a lack of religious knowledge. We could use Michon's questions: What is religious illiteracy? What do the different countries call it (if they give it a name)? What are the causes? Are there any sources that can help us identify the factors behind it?

   In this context, it is difficult to decide what we need to know to avoid being ignorant. Religious ignorance among teenagers can be seen from different perspectives (Estivalèzes 2005, Michon 2011: 475, Rota 2015: 274–7): (a) the cognitive perspective: it is related to the study and the knowledge about religion and religions but it is too frequently controlled by politics; (b) the memory and identity perspective: the acquisition of enough knowledge about our identity. From a Christian-centred point of view, a Christian knowledge should be learnt before any other religious knowledge (above all of Islam); (c) social and regulations perspective: religious culture can be a social glue for different cultures. We often talk about loss of values: but which values?; (d) the existential dimension as a loss of spirituality and meaning of life which represents an unmet anthropological need.
2 What can the social, cultural, religious and political reasons for its growth in our educational systems, causing more prejudices, clichés, psychological and emotional closeness blocks, be? If a teenager has a great religious culture (both of its own religion and of others), it does not mean he is less ignorant or illiterate. To put it with Becker – as cited by Rota –, in public arenas social groups establish forms of knowledge and attitudes whose lack or infringement is considered ignorance (Becker 1963).

Relating to the way in which education should be changed, I think that there is no longer any time for abstract reasoning. It is time to analyse and criticise present practices in order to identify the differences between theory and practice: student's curriculums, the type of education teachers have received (Rota and Bleisch 2016), textbook contents and what happens in classrooms.[12]

3 What must be analysed is the consequences for individuals and stakeholder groups (school classes, religious teenager groups).

The consequences should be further divided into two more groups: (a) the consequences within the religious community may increase sectarian points of view, internal discriminations, violent radicalisations (Roy 2008); (b) the consequences outside the religious community can be minority discrimination, non-recognition, clichés, stereotyping what is 'different'.

The following questions should be asked: are teenagers who have studied and have knowledge consequently more open and tolerant? What is the relation that links belief and knowledge? What is the impact that religious diversity has on knowledge nowadays? Furthermore, on the other hand, what are the consequences that illiteracy and literacy have on religious diversity?

A multilevel approach entails rethinking the evaluative approach, starting from the systemic perspective on the evaluation object of religion, such as regulatory reporting, to curricula and who has materialised from the inductive perspective, in terms of subject assessment and the entire complexity of the student. The Assessment Tool that has been suggested for the evaluator is an integrative one, an opportunity to see the process, be aware of the process by which it is evaluated, develop the ability to track what is happening in this process and intervene. It concerns a formative assessment, as long as the proposed instrument 'crosses the boundaries of various learning activities'. As a school subject, 'Religions' is an integrative one (contributing to, and complementing, the student's general education) and an integrator (harmonising the pupil's various skills) (Lazār 2016).

4 In the end, the connection between ignorance and evil and literacy and goodness is worth criticising. We often say that knowledge defeats fanaticism but I think that this connection is merely wishful thinking of which we have no evidence. This would imply that the various recommendations on a vaguely defined and tricky literacy, with its incentivisation of instruments, occasions and methods, are considered as an antidote to a poison that has hitherto never been identified and analysed.

From a more in-depth perspective, I may affirm that the concerns about religion should be compounded by a lack of expertise and knowledge regarding religious diversity, what some have called 'religious illiteracy' (Bramadat and Koenig 2009, Bramadat and Seljak 2009). Such 'illiteracy' has placed local authorities in a situation of discomfort, vulnerability and insecurity when dealing with religious matters and requires the development of new, innovative policy approaches.

In the end, I conclude by saying that there are different types of illiteracy for different countries but there are no data for investigating it.

Bibliography

Andreassen, Bengt-Ove and Lewis, James R. 2014. *Textbook Gods. Genre, Text and Teaching Religious Studies*, Sheffield/Bristol, Equinox.

Aslan, Ednan and Rausch, Margaret (ed.) 2018. *Religious Education. Between Radicalism and Tolerance*, Wiesbaden, Springer.

12 See the project 'Religions, discriminations et racisme en milieu scolaire': www.redisco.hypotheses.org, last accessed 5 January 2018.

Becker, Howard S. 1963. *Outsiders. Studies in the Sociology of Deviance*, New York, The Free Press.

Béraud, Céline and Willaime, Jean-Paul (ed.) 2009. *Les jeunes, l'école et la religion*, Paris, Bayard.

Berger, Peter L., Davie, Grace and Fokas, Effie 2008. *Religious America, Secular Europe? A Theme and Variations*, Aldershot, Ashgate.

Berglund, Jenny 2015. *Publicly Funded Islamic Education in Europe and United States*, The Brookings Project on U.S. Relations with the Islamic World, Analysis Paper 21, April, www.brookings.edu/wp-content/uploads/2016/06/Final-Web-PDF.pdf, last accessed 5 January 2018.

Berglund, Jenny (ed.) 2018. *European Perspectives on Islamic Education and Public Schooling*, Sheffield/Bristol, Equinox.

Berglund, Jenny, Shanneik, Yafa and Bocking, Brian (ed.) 2016. *Religious Education in a Global-Local World*, Berlin, Springer.

Bernardo, Angela and Saggioro, Alessandro (ed.) 2015. *I Princìpi di Toledo e le religioni a scuola. Traduzione, presentazione e discussione dei 'Toledo Guiding Principles on Teaching about Religions and Beliefs in Public Schools' (OSCE/ODIHR)*, Roma, Aracne.

Bramadat, Paul and Koenig, Matthias (ed.) 2009. *International Migration and the Governance of Religious Diversity*, Montréal/Kingston, McGill-Queen's University Press.

Bramadat, Paul and Seljak, David (ed.) 2009. *Religion and Ethnicity in Canada*, Toronto, University of Toronto Press.

Burchardt, Marian, Wohlrab-Sahr, Monika and Middell, Matthias 2015. *Multiple Secularities Beyond the West: Religion and Modernity in the Global Age*, Boston, MA/Berlin/München, Walter de Gruyter.

Collins-Mayo, Sylvia, Mayo, Bob, Nash, Sally *et al.* 2010. *The Faith of Generation Y*, London, Church House Publishing.

Conroy, James C. 2016. 'Religious Illiteracy in School Religious Education in UK', in Adam Dinham and Matthew Francis (ed.), *Religious Literacy in Policy and Practice*, Bristol, Policy Press, 167–86.

Conroy, James C. and Davis, Robert A. 2008. 'Citizenship, Education and the Claims of Religious Literacy', in Michael A. Peters, Alan Britton and Harry Blee (ed.), *Global Citizenship Education: Philosophy, Theory and Pedagogy*, Rotterdam, Sense, 187–203.

Conroy, James C., Lundie, David and Baumfield, Vivienne 2012. 'Failures of Meaning in Religious Education', *Journal of Beliefs and Values: Studies in Religion and Education* 33:3, December, 309–23.

Conroy, James C., Lundie, David and Davis, Robert A. *et al.* 2013. *Does Religious Education Work? A Multi-dimensional Investigation*, London, Bloomsbury.

Davie, Grace 2000. *Religion in Modern Europe. A Memory Mutates*, Oxford, Oxford University Press.

Day, Abby and Lövheim, Mia (ed.) 2015. *Modernities, Memory and Mutations: Grace Davie and The Study of Religion*, Farnham, Ashgate.

Defois, Gérard and Tincq, Henri 1997. *Les médias et l'Église. Evangelisation et information: le conflit de deux paroles*, Paris, CFPJ.

Deniel, Raymond 1969. 'Croyances religieuses en milieu urbain: Ouagadougou', *Social Compass* 16:1, 101–8.

Dinham, Adam and Francis, Matthew (ed.) 2016. *Religious Literacy in Policy and Practice*, Bristol, Policy Press.

Dinham, Adam and Jones, Stephen 2012. 'Religion, Public Policy and the Academy: Brokering Public Faith in a Context of Ambivalence', *Journal of Contemporary Religion* 27:2, 185–201.

Ellison, Christopher G., Burr, Jeffrey A. and McCall, Patricia L. 2003. 'The Enduring Puzzle of Southern Homicide. Is Regional Religious Culture the Missing Piece?', *Homicide Studies* 7:4, 326–52.

Estivalèzes, Mireille 2005. *Les religions dans l'enseignement laïque*, Paris, PUF.

Flahault, François and Schaeffer, Jean-Marie 2002. 'Présentation', *Communications* 72, 5–16.

Frank, Katharina 2009. *Schulischer Religionsunterricht. Eine religionswissenschaftlich-soziologische Untersuchung*, Stuttgart, Kohlhammer.

Giorda, Maria C. 2012. 'Religione cattolica e insegnamento nell'Italia unita. Il Risorgimento nei manuali di storia della scuola superiore', *Rivista di storia del Cristianesimo* 1, 89–116.

Giorda, Maria C. 2014. 'A tavola con le religioni. Il cibo plurale delle mense scolastiche', *Politeia* 30:114, 70–93.

Giorda, Maria C. 2015. 'Religious Diversity in Italy and the Impact on Education: The History of a Failure', *New Diversities* 17:1, 77–93.

Giorda, Maria C. and Bossi, Luca 2016. 'Mense scolastiche e diversità religiosa. Il caso di Milano', *Stato, Chiese e pluralismo confessionale* 24, www.statoechiese.it, last accessed 5 January 2018.

Giorda, Maria C. and Caramagno, Giovanna 2017. 'Italian Religious Textbooks: An Historical Analysis', in Zrinka Štimac (ed.), *Schulbuch und religiöse Vielfalt. Interdisziplinäre Perspektiven*, Göttingen, Vandenhoeck & Ruprecht, 177–98.

Giorgi, Alberta 2017. 'Il soggetto religioso femminile nello spazio pubblico e la questione dell'agency', *Religioni e Società* 88, 63–73.

Hervieu-Léger, Danièle 2003. *Catholicisme, la fin d'un monde*, Paris, Bayard.

Hervieu-Léger, Danièle and Willaime, Jean-Paul 2001. *Sociologies et religion. Approches classiques*, Paris, PUF.

Hutmacher, Walo (ed.) 1999. *Culture religieuse et école laïque – Rapport du groupe de travail exploratoire sur la culture judéo-chrétienne à l'école*, Genève, SRED.

Jackson, Robert 2014. *Signposts: Policy and Practice for Teaching about Religions and Non-Religious Worldviews in Intercultural Education*, Strasbourg, Council of Europe.

Jackson, Robert 2016. 'Inclusive Study of Religions and World Views in Schools: Signposts from the Council of Europe', *Social Inclusion* 4:2, 14–25.

Jensen, Tim 2008. 'RS based RE in Public Schools: A Must for a Secular State', *Numen* 55:2/3, 123–50.

Jödicke, Ansgar 2009. 'Das Verhältnis der römisch-katholischen und der evangelischen Kirche in Deutschland zum Ethik-Unterricht am Beispiel Berlins. Religionswissenschaftliche Perspektiven', in Mariano Delgado, Ansgar Jödicke and Guido Vergauwen (ed.), *Religion und Öffentlichkeit: Probleme und Perspektiven*, Stuttgart, Kohlhammer, 221–41.

Jödicke, Ansgar and Rota, Andrea 2010. *Unterricht zum Thema Religion an der öffentlichen Schule: Untersuchung im Rahmen des NFP 'Religionsgemeinschaften, Staat und Gesellschaft'*, Freiburg, Universität.

Jödicke, Ansgar and Rota, Andrea 2014. 'Patterns of Religious Education Policy in Switzerland. The Long Arm of Distanced Christians?', *Journal for the Scientific Study of Religion* 53:4, 722–38.

Käbisch, David 2014a. 'Konfessionslosigkeit Konfessionslosigkeit als Thema von Lern und Anwedungsaufgaben. Fachdidaktische Perspektiven', *Zeitschrift für Pädagogik und Theologie* 66:3, 252–61.

Käbisch, David 2014b. *Religionsunterricht und Konfessionslosigkeit. Eine fachdidaktische Grundlegung*, Tübingen, Mohr Siebeck.

Keast, John 2007. *Religious Diversity and Intercultural Education: A Reference Book for Schools*, Strasbourg, Council of Europe.

Lazăr, Emil 2016. 'Learning Results and Evaluation through Levels Given by the Results in Religious Education', *Social Sciences and Education Research Review* 3:1, 141–6.

Melloni, Alberto (ed.) 2014. *Rapporto sull'analfabetismo religioso in Italia*, Bologna, Il Mulino.

Michon, Bruno 2011. *La culture religieuse des adolescents en France et en Allemagne. Des connaissances aux défis de l'exculturation, de la popularisation et de l'altérité*, PhD. Thesis, Université de Strasbourg/Technische Universität Berlin.

Michon, Bruno 2014. 'L'école, la culture religieuse et le vivre-ensemble: une perspective comparative', *Revue française de pédagogie* 1:186, 85–97.

Moore, Diane L. 2007. *Overcoming Religious Illiteracy: A Cultural Studies Approach to the Study of Religion in Secondary Education*, London, Palgrave Macmillan.

Moulin, Daniel 2011. 'Giving Voice to "the Silent Minority": The Experience of Religious Students in Secondary School Religious Education Lessons', *British Journal of Religious Education* 33:3, 313–26.

Moulin, Daniel 2015a. 'Doubts about Religious Education in Public Schooling', *International Journal of Christianity & Education* 19:2, 135–48.

Moulin, Daniel 2015b. 'Religious Identity Choices in English Secondary Schools', *British Educational Research Journal* 41:3, 489–504.

Moulin, Daniel 2016. 'Reported Schooling Experiences of Adolescent Jews Attending Non-Jewish Secondary Schools in England', *Race Ethnicity and Education* 19:4, 683–705.

Ognier, Pierre 2003. *La méconnaissance de l'histoire obère toujours le débat actuel sur la laïcité*, http://ens-religions.formiris.org/userfiles/files/er_3742_1.pdf, last accessed 5 January 2018.

Pajer, Flavio 2013. 'Jeu des problématiques européennes', in Luc Collès and René Nouailhat (ed.), *Croire, savoir: quelles pédagogies européennes? Données empiriques, analyses et questions pour l'avenir*, Brussels, Lumen Vitae, 95–118.

Pajer, Flavio 2016. 'L'educazione al fatto religioso in Europa e in Italia', in Associazione Treelle (ed.), *Educare a vivere con gli altri nel XXI secolo: cosa può fare la scuola? I casi di Francia, Germania, Italia, Polonia, e la 'global citizenship'*, Genova, TreEllle, 117–36.

Pingel, Falk 2000. *The European Home: Representations of 20th Century Europe in History Textbooks*, Strasbourg, Council of Europe.

Rota, Andrea 2015. *Etat des lieux des politiques de l'enseignement religieux en Suisse latine*, Gollion, Infolio.

Rota, Andrea 2017. *La religion à l'école. Négociations autour de la présence publique de communautés religieuses*, Zürich, Seismo.

Rota, Andrea and Bleisch, Petra B. 2016. 'Representations and Concepts of Professional Ethos among Swiss Religious Education Teacher Trainers', *British Journal of Religious Education* 39:1, 75–92.

Roy, Olivier 2008. *Sainte ignorance. Le temps de la religion sans culture*, Paris, Seuil.

Sjöborg, Anders 2015. 'Negative and Positive Freedom of Religion: The Ambiguous Relation of Religion and Human Rights in Sweden', in Hans-Georg Ziebertz and Gordan Črpić (ed.), *Religion and Human Rights: An International Perspective*, Berlin, Springer, 173–205.

Stoeckl, Kristina and Roy, Olivier (ed.) 2015. *The Future of Religious Education in Europe*, Firenze, EUI.

Taylor, Charles 1989. *Sources of the Self: The Making of Modern Identity*, Cambridge, Cambridge University Press.

Tincq, Henri 1988. 'L'analphabétisme religieux', *Le Monde*, 10 November.

Urbanski, Sébastien 2013. 'L'enseignement du fait religieux à l'école publique. Influence des paradigmes de la sécularisation et de la recomposition du religieux', *Revue des sciences sociales* 49, 114–21.

Urbanski, Sébastien 2016. *L'enseignement du fait religieux. École, république, laïcité*, Paris, PUF.

Willaime, Jean-Paul (ed.) 2014. *Le défi de l'enseignement des faits religieux à l'école. Réponses européennes et québécoises*, Paris, Riveneuve.

Wright, Andrew 1993. *Religious Education in the Secondary School: Prospects for Religious Literacy*, London, David Fulton.

Wright, Andrew 2007. *Critical Religious Education, Multiculturalism and the Pursuit of Truth*, Cardiff, University of Wales Press.

Wright, Andrew 2011. 'Beyond Fundamentalism: Spiritual Realism, Spiritual Literacy and Education', in Mervyn Hartwig and Jamie Morgan (ed.), *Critical Realism and Spirituality*, London, Routledge, 75–89.

4 Religious rights, educational duties?

Flavio Pajer

Introduction

The title suggests a bipolar strain between two epistemologically independent and highly significant issues throughout the world that, in fact, interface and are interdependent. The conscious exercise of a right presupposes education. Education – in constructing awareness, consciousness and competencies – allows for the full enjoyment of a right along with the execution of its respective duties. If this is true in general, then it is also valid in the specific case of religious rights and the corresponding Religious Education.

No one can ignore that if it was ever peaceful and painless, this bipolar tension has become fraught with problems in our day and age. The question in the title allows for suspicion and asks for thorough analysis. On the one hand, we find the universe of religious rights that has been upset by well-known opposing and contradictory phenomena, such as interethnic mobility *versus* collective closure, the relentless escape from churches *versus* the explosion of new religions and the regressive revenge of fundamentalism *versus* the rushing ahead of post-religious or humanist groups. On the other hand, we have the universe of educational duties, whose actors – individuals along with institutions – in a context of late western modernity, tinker with the age-old alliances such as family and community, state and churches, among personal and interpersonal rights and duties that are manageable in private or collective spaces, and institutional rights and duties that can be managed in the public space.

The data of the problem

Today, religious diversity seems to be the phenomenon that most disrupts traditional educational arrangements. It does so at a historical moment when open, secularized and pluralist societies have adopted the acknowledgment of religious freedom as a founding principle. On the one hand, religious freedom is seen as an inalienable individual right based on human dignity.

> Beliefs or doctrines do not have rights, but people do. They have the right and the duty to follow their own conscience without coercion. The truth cannot be imposed coercively; it must be received freely. To this end – and this is the radical novelty of the new secular condition – neither truth nor error have rights *per se*. People have the right and the duty to seek the truth, to pursue their own happiness without coercion and to follow their own conscience.
>
> (Casanova 2017: 15)

On the other hand, although at times they may spontaneously aggregate, religious communities are generally also formative and regulatory. All those who belong to a community – by birth or choice – subject themselves to an initiating and educational process in order to assimilate a cultural heritage (consisting in beliefs, notions, stories, customs, rules and values) that identifies and distinguishes one religious community from another. The right of a person to believe goes alongside the right of a community to form itself. This formation may, in turn, take the specific form of a personal initiation, strictly linked to the community, or in parallel it may also take the shape of a formal cultural or fact-finding education about the religion in question. In this case, the educational responsibility can be delegated to other extra-confessional organizations, such as the public school system. This comes with a degree of ambiguity and dissent concerning the legitimacy of the educational competencies that the collective-confessional space and the civil-public space may claim, given that, within the person being educated, questions on the rights of the believer and the rights of the citizen are put at stake (or in potential conflict).

In order to smooth out pragmatically these contrasts over the years, a number of relevant distinctions have been introduced on both a theoretical and a practical level. One of the first conceptual distinctions, which is only apparently academic, lies in the difference between faith and religion. Here, for faith (*fides qua*, or religiosity) we generally mean the subjective right to adhere to the belief of a religious tradition or, similarly, to harbor convictions based on an immanent vision of life (humanist beliefs, nonreligious worldviews). For religion – particularly in the prevalent jargon of schools, universities and social media – one often tries to outline the symbolic capital that is historically generated by faiths (*fides quae*). As such, an individual may be susceptible to cultural information, to systematic and critical teaching/learning, without necessarily becoming involved in the conscious acceptance of either the teacher or the student.

On a personal level, here we find the source of a dual order of rights in terms of religion: the right to believe freely (in a theist and atheist sense) and the right to the rational understanding (e.g. historical-critical or philological-exegetical) of religious phenomena. These phenomena are understood as the entirety of facts inherent to universal human culture, beginning from the history and the ethos of populations and their religious traditions to the biographical experience of an individual person. Along with this, what follows is a dual order of educational responsibilities: that of the religious community to initiate their followers into 'cultual' practice (teaching/learning into faith) and that of civic organizations (foremost the school) to guarantee that their citizens receive adequate cultural literacy on religious issues (teaching/learning about religion).[1]

A second significant distinction is asserted in the thought and praxis of modern constitutional law and is part and parcel of the secular statute of the state and its institutions.

1 The distinction came of age at the end of the twentieth century in the context of the English educational system. The educationalist Michael Grimmitt formalized it in particular, distinguishing three types of approach to religious phenomena: a participatory or confessional approach (learning into religion), a learning or notional approach (learning about religion/s) and an interpretive-hermeneutic approach (learning from religion/s) (Grimmitt 1987: 213–55). To refine the approaches, we could include a fourth type: the extra-religious approach (learning out of religion). This was adopted in the French educational system following the Régis Debray report (2002), where 'religious phenomenon', which does not qualify as an independent discipline, is recognized only as an episodic element within other scholastic learning and is therefore elaborated following the epistemology of the individual 'profane' disciplines and with a professionally neutral behavior – *laïcité oblige!* – both on the part of the teachers as well as the students.

The modern, post-confessional state is characterized by a form of secularity that is no longer the anti-religious laicism of the nineteenth century or the Bolsheviks. This secularity does not deny the rights of religious groups within society, does not relegate them to the private sphere and does not privilege the religion of the majority at the cost of the religions of minorities. Quite the contrary, the democratic state not only respects the freedom of religion of every citizen, but it also uses legal tools suited to the historical context (concordats, agreements, bilateral conventions) (cf. Colaianni 2012) to recognize the plural legitimacy of the institutional expressions of religious communities. Furthermore, it recognizes its citizens' right to profess nonreligious viewpoints and allows their communities the same dignity and freedom it grants to religious organizations and viewpoints (Parisi 2011, Jackson 2014).[2] The secular state affirms that, if not entirely agnostic in religious material, it is at least theologically unequipped to arbitrate religious disputes; it gives up its role as protector of orthodoxy and the one 'true religion'; it does not abusively establish itself as an 'ethical state'; if anything, it takes it upon itself to protect religious minorities from the discriminatory invasiveness of one or another majority church, and as impartial arbiter, paves the way for free and democratic discussion among different value systems.

A look at international and European documents

The charters of international law do not oblige states to engage directly in Religious Education for their citizens; on the contrary, they distrust educational politics that might open up a path toward state proselytism. Measures of this kind are plausible, or even necessary, in our contemporary context. Nonetheless, there are plenty of clear official declarations directed towards the principle of regulating public education. For example, Art. 26.2 of the *Universal Declaration of Human Rights* (1948) assures that

> education shall be directed to the full development of the human personality and to the strengthening of respect for human rights and fundamental freedoms. It shall promote understanding, tolerance and friendship among all nations, racial or religious groups, and shall further the activities of the United Nations for the maintenance of peace.

A kindred declaration is found in Art. 29.1.d of the *Convention on the Rights of the Child* (1989), which commits states to guarantee 'the preparation of the child for responsible life in a free society, in the spirit of understanding, peace, tolerance, equality of sexes, and friendship among all peoples, ethnic, national and religious groups and persons of indigenous origin' (cf. Smith Foster 1996, Long 2007: 101–22).

2 In October 2013, the publication of the official curriculum of Religious Education for England and Wales used the expression 'religions and worldviews' in setting forth the core of its content, specifying that this expression 'is used in this document to refer to Christianity, other principal religions represented in Britain, smaller religious communities and non-religious worldviews such as Humanism' (Religious Education Council of England and Wales 2013: 11 n. 7). In October 2016, a document on the 'promotion of freedom of religion and conviction', developed by sixty experts from an initiative of the Faculty of Law at the University of Oslo, was drafted for 'persons with theistic, non-theistic and atheistic beliefs, as well as those who do not profess any religion or belief'. See *Oslo Principles on promotion of Freedom of Religion or Belief*, www.jus.uio.no/smr/english/about/programmes/news/docs/oslo-principles-on-promotion-of-freedom-of-religion-or-belief_2016.pdf, last accessed 26 October 2017.

Art. 30 of the same convention more explicitly assures that

> in those States in which ethnic, religious or linguistic minorities or persons of indigenous origin exist, a child belonging to such a minority or who is indigenous shall not be denied the right, in community with other members of his or her group, to enjoy his or her own culture, to profess and practise his or her own religion, or to use his or her own language.

The United Nations *Declaration on the Rights of Persons belonging to National or Ethnic, Religious and Linguistic Minorities* (1992) directly intervenes on the part of minority rights, reaffirming the rights of said people 'to enjoy their own culture, to profess and practise their own religion, and to use their own language, in private and in public, freely and without interference or any form of discrimination', and '[...] to participate effectively in cultural, religious, social, economic and public life' (Art. 2.1–2).

What remains a fundamental priority in international law is the educational responsibility of parents. 'Parents have a prior right to choose the kind of education that shall be given to their children' (*Universal Declaration of Human Rights*, Art. 26.3); children shall have 'the right [...] to freedom of thought, conscience and religion'; and 'States Parties shall respect the rights and duties of the parents and, when applicable, legal guardians, to provide direction to the child in the exercise of his or her right in a manner consistent with the evolving capacities of the child' (*Convention on the Rights of the Child*, Art. 14.1–2).

In similar terms, the *African Charter on Human and People's Rights* (1981) affirms 'the State shall have the duty to assist the family which is the custodian of morals and traditional values recognized by the community' (Art. 18.2).

Previously, an important document released by UNESCO in 1960 was the standard – the *Convention against Discrimination in Education* – which considered nondiscriminatory

> the establishment or maintenance, for religious or linguistic reasons, of separate educational systems or institutions offering an education which is in keeping with the wishes of the pupil's parents or legal guardians, if participation in such systems or attendance at such institutions is optional and if the education provided conforms to such standards as may be laid down or approved by the competent authorities, in particular for education of the same level.
>
> (Art. 2.b)

The document later emphasizes the need to respect parental rights, along with the principle that

> it is essential to respect the liberty of parents and, where applicable, of legal guardians, firstly to choose for their children institutions other than those maintained by the public authorities but conforming to such minimum educational standards as may be laid down or approved by the competent authorities and, secondly, to ensure in a manner consistent with the procedures followed in the State for the application of its legislation, the religious and moral education of the children in conformity with their own convictions; and no person or group of persons should be compelled to receive religious instruction inconsistent with his or their convictions.
>
> (Art. 5.1.b)

Considering the 'theocratic' vision that Islam holds in regards to family education and the management of public education, a western reader will not be especially surprised to see that the *Cairo Declaration on Human Rights in Islam* (1990) assures that

> every human being has a right to receive both religious and worldly education from the various institutions of teaching, education and guidance, including the family, the school, the university, the media, etc., and in such an integrated and balanced manner that would develop human personality, strengthen man's faith in Allah and promote man's respect to and defence of both rights and obligations.
>
> (Art. 9.b)

In presenting a brief review of a number of regulatory issues in and for a European context, it is necessary to mention a foundational text. The *European Convention for the Protection of Human Rights and Fundamental Freedoms* (*ECHR*) led to further legal and administrative documents. It was released by the Council of Europe and signed in Rome on 4 November 1950, shortly after the *Universal Declaration* in 1948. Above all, the definition of religious freedom is emblematic:

> Everyone has the right to freedom of thought, conscience and religion; this right includes freedom to change his religion or belief and freedom, either alone or in community with others and in public or private, to manifest his religion or belief, in worship, teaching, practice and observance.
>
> (Art. 9.1)

Alongside this article, Art. 14 states:

> The enjoyment of the rights and freedoms set forth in this Convention shall be secured without discrimination on any ground such as sex, race, language, religion, political or other opinion, national or social origin, association with a national minority, property, birth or other status.

This definition of the freedom of religion was then adopted almost word for word by the *Charter of Fundamental Rights of the European Union* (2000), Art. 10.

Beginning with the *ECHR*, the aforementioned *Charter of Fundamental Rights* and the subsequent wealth of interpretative literature that has followed in recent decades, the European doctrine on religious freedom has reconciled a vast range of rights, which have been summarized by contemporary scholars (Cardia 1999: 172, Ventura 2001: 55–89, Ferrari 2012): (1) the right to express freely one's religious faith through adherence to a religion, following an individual religious belief system, or by creating new religious or nonreligious belief systems; (2) the right not to belong to any religious faith or to adhere to any other ideological or philosophical orientation, whether it be religious, agnostic, rationalist or atheist; (3) the right to change one's religious orientation and opinion at any time; (4) the right to promote and proselytize one's own beliefs and convictions through the writing, printing and circulation of religious materials; (5) the right to teach a religion or conviction in suitable locations; (6) the right to worship in private and in public; (7) the right to found associations of religious and cultural character, and to participate in associations and existing aggregations.

In spite of the substantial transnational consensus on these principles, certain interpretations of religious and educational rights have not been resolved in the public space in certain member states. One example is the ardent and unmoving secularity adopted by the French in contrast to the more conciliatory and cooperative models of other countries. It is difficult to find a compromise, and this brought about the adoption of the *EU Guidelines on the Promotion and Protection of Freedom of Religion or Belief* by the Foreign Affairs Council of the EU in 2013. The Guidelines not only are a practical and nonbinding manual intended for the delegates of the twenty-seven member states but are also offered up to the entire international community. It affirms that religious freedom is an individual right and not a privilege of a single religion or ideology, and it insists on the duty of public authorities 'to promote, through the educational system and other means, respect for diversity and mutual understanding by encouraging a wider knowledge of the diversity of religions and beliefs within their jurisdiction' (Art. 34.b); it also recalls the need to defend

> the right of children to learn about the faith/belief of their parents, and the right of parents to teach their children in the tenets of their religion or belief. It also includes the right to peacefully share one's religion or belief with others, without being subject to the approval of the state or another religious community. Any limitation on freedom of religion or belief, including regarding places of worship and state registration of religious or belief groups, must be exceptional and in compliance with international standards. (Art. 40)

The European Court of Human Rights has intervened a number of times to avoid any form of indoctrination: (1) on the part of a state, whose relevant authorities are responsible for guarding against offenses to parents' religious or philosophical convictions through imprudence, negligence or lapses in judgment or untimely proselytism. This also applies to teachers of public schools, who must demonstrate discretion and objectivity in their judgment and behavior; and (2) on the part of parents who might become 'excessive', violent or arbitrary in their educational conduct, along with other groups or other sectarian movements (cf. Boucaud 2016: 209ff.).[3]

The contribution of the Council of Europe

In terms of the legal framework (of which we have mentioned a number of exemplary documents), let us now examine the executive framework and specific educational policies that stem from European bodies. It is essential to examine the central role played by the Council of Europe, which as mentioned before, has a primary mandate to survey and promote cultural affairs. Since its origin (1949) until the 1980s, it abstained from intervening in religious affairs, with the widely shared assumption that Europe should work from a societal project where religious convictions were, if not completely concealed, at least held at the margins of public debate. There was a clear change in perspective in the mid-1980s[4]

3 In terms of scholastic Religious Education, see especially Belgiorno de Stefano (2008). On the distinction between education and indoctrination, see Hull (2004: 9–10).

4 In 1985, the Council of Europe, in dealing with the teaching of human rights in schools, identified that within 'moral and religious education there was a particular area for the initiation of young people to more abstract notions of human rights'; in 1987, a scientific seminar, before a series of study conferences on the promotion of ethical culture in Europe, shed light on 'the irreplaceable contribution of Judaism on European culture', while a similar seminar in 1991 explored the contribution of the Islamic civilization to European Culture (Pajer 2006, Ventura 2014).

that was solidified in 1989 and then during the 1990s with the fall of Communism and the laws on religious freedom introduced in post-communist and central-eastern European countries. Two European seminars in 1993, respectively on the 'fight against racism, xenophobia and intolerance', and on 'religious tolerance in a democratic society' elaborated the stance that the study of religion was a necessary tool for creating a more realistic and more true vision of contemporary society. An official Recommendation by the Council (no. 1178, 1992), prepared and destined for the educational ministers of the member states, proposed that 'the programmes of the compulsory educational system should involve concrete and objective information concerning the major religions and their main variants on principles of comparative religion, ethics, and individual and social rights'. A later Recommendation (no. 1202, 1993) foresaw the need to 'provide for courses of religious and moral education in school curriculum for all pupils' and invited to promote 'a diverse and accurate presentation of religions in textbooks, especially in historical texts, in order to improve and deepen the understanding of different religious traditions'. Another study seminar (held in Donaueschingen in Germany in 1994) stated:

> if religion is an integral part of cultural identity, it is the responsibility of educational authorities to promote a cultural, social and historical approach to religions in their curriculum. This approach must be marked by tolerance, be multilateral and be absent of any and all clericalism or ideological indoctrination.

Specifically, the seminar formalized a number of proposals, including: (1) that every member state of the Council of Europe would insert a non-confessional course on Religious Education within its common curriculum. This course would be held by a qualified teacher capable of acting as a reference for the study of religious affairs within a variety of school subjects; (2) that such teaching would be carried out in a complementary manner, such as for anthropological, historical, philosophical or ethical analysis, or for experiential analysis within literary or artistic works; (3) that university departments for religious studies would offer their competencies to the training of instructors called upon to teach religion.

The Commissioner for Human Rights – one of the most active bodies of the Council of Europe – has promoted a considerable number of European meetings with heads of religious organizations (both Christian and non-Christian), in order to identify the contribution that these organizations may have in maintaining democratic rights and the respect of fundamental liberties within states.[5] Such initiatives have sought to demonstrate how the 'religious factor', far from being marginalized in schools or being reserved solely for believers, is instead becoming a significant stepping stone in the education of all European citizens; it reaches across boundaries of scholarly knowledge and becomes an important feature in political and legal mediation, besides being essential for ecumenical and theological dialogues.

Furthermore, it is important to recall that the well-known Report to UNESCO of the International Commission on Education for the Twenty-First Century also addressed the

5 The seminars took place: in 2000 in Syracuse, on the role of monotheistic religions in the face of armed conflict; in 2001 in Strasbourg, on the competencies of the church and states concerning the exercising of religious freedom; in 2002 in Leuven, on the confluence and divergence between human rights and religion; in 2004 in Malta, on religion's contribution to the education of tolerance; in 2006 in Kazan, Russia, on the dialogue between European religious communities and the school. See official documentation in www.coe.int/, last accessed 26 October 2017.

issue of religious rights and education.[6] What inspired the report was clear: far more than simply reducing the issue to the functional economism of educational training, it calls for a return to the social and personalist priorities of education. An understanding of religious heritage and the values and meaning inherent within that heritage is necessary to achieve the cultural and civic education of generations of Europeans.

Religions and Christian churches between rights and duties

Human beings have the capacity to fashion themselves with convictions according to their conscience, to elaborate them, convey them and even change them. They also have the right to conform their lives according to their convictions, whether religious or not. Religious functions, rituals, celebrations and holidays, dietary rules and the education of future generations are just some of the expressions of these convictions. To this end, adequate infrastructures exist, such as synagogues, churches, mosques, temples, schools and associates, etc. From this perspective, religions are substantially the historical and contextual embodiment of a universal need. Over time, every religion develops a doctrinal and institutional body that serves to identify and demarcate itself from other groups, and sometimes even to overpower others. On the strength of this social dynamic, religious traditions have worked out their own system of rights that, over the course of history, may enter into conflict with others or even into conflict with civil or human rights in general. This occurs especially in traditionally religious societies that become secularized or democratized (Berman 1995: 88–9).

It is useful, however, to recall how religions share an ethical foundation and how that foundation has given rise to human rights in general. The theologian Hans Küng, historical advocate for the worldwide ethics project (*Weltethos*), reminded us of this at the Worldwide Conference on Religion and Peace held in Kyoto in 1970:

> As we sat down together facing the overriding issues of peace we discovered that the things which unite us are more important than the things which divide us. We found that we share: a conviction of the fundamental unity of the human family, of the equality and dignity of all human beings; a sense of the sacredness of the individual person and his conscience; a sense of the value of the human community; a realization that might is not right; that human power is not selfsufficient and absolute. A belief that love, compassion, selflessness and the force of inner truthfulness and of the spirit have ultimately greater power than hate, enmity, and self-interest; a sense of obligation to stand on the side of the poor and oppressed against the rich and the oppressors; and a profound hope that good will finally prevail.[7]

6 A passage on the right to an education that teaches the values of 'living together' is of particular interest: 'The Commission has put greater emphasis on one of the four pillars that it proposes and describes as the foundations of education: learning to live together, by developing an understanding of others and their history, traditions and spiritual values and, on this basis, creating a new spirit which, guided by recognition of our growing interdependence and a common analysis of the risks and challenges of the future, would induce people to implement common projects or to manage the inevitable conflicts in an intelligent and peaceful way. Utopia, some might think, but it is a necessary Utopia, indeed a vital one if we are to escape from a dangerous cycle sustained by cynicism or by resignation' (Delors, al-Mufti, Amagi *et al.* 1996: 20).

7 Disarmament/Development/Human Rights the Findings of the World Conference on Religion and Peace, Kyoto, Japan, 16–21 October 1970. Tristram Engelhart has sought to clarify the point concerning the potential for a universal ethics (Engelhardt 2014).

To return to our argument, what we wish to take stock of here is merely an outline of the positions that religions and churches have assumed on the issue of education, which is one of the crucial junctures where the right to religious freedom and Religious Education can come into conflict with that of human rights.

Above all, it is worth emphasizing that the religious world is often the source of substantial criticism towards the world of education. An example of such criticism is the extent to which educational systems uncritically submit themselves to the imperatives of the market and economic efficiency, privileging the promotion of skill sets and marginalizing access to humanistic knowledge. It is clear that believers feel their religious sensibility to be expropriated of symbolic capital – that of meaning, values, of 'useless knowledge' – which they instead consider fundamental. Perhaps more than ever, we no longer count the critical positions that religions take on public education policies. These positions are taken and conveyed not only in the name of religious rights but also in the name of human rights themselves. On this latter point, religions are not the only ones to raise their voices, as they often find themselves in agreement with nondenominational militant organizations or exponents of an enlightened humanism that is shared by nonbelievers and believers of different faiths.

A documented review of the positions of individual religions and denominations concerning the educational rights-duties would go beyond the modest ambitions of this paper. Nonetheless, we have a notable and up-to-date collection of literature to draw from in order to present an essential bibliographic exploration.

On the problematic relationship between religions and human rights, a monographic issue of the international journal *Concilium* (2, 1990) set out to respond to two significant questions: how do human rights come to be motivated in every great world religion, and what are the key points at their foundation? What are their weaknesses or debatable aspects that can be perceived in the theories and practice of those religions? Judaism teaches that no one may deprive an individual of the fundamental value that God has granted to everyone and that God, too, will never take away. Here there is the possibility, or rather the duty,

> to develop one's own human endowments through personal confidence, to respect one's own private life and reputation through further education and free time, through work, to be recompensed, to acquire property, to marry and build a family [...]. All of this is so fundamental for Judaism that it is only rarely explicitly conveyed in the Bible or in the Talmud.
> (Borowitz 1990: 46)

Human rights have enjoyed highs and lows in the Christian tradition:

> The Christian Church began splendidly during the pre-Constantine era, only to be mired in the corruption of power [...]. Even the great Augustine wrote against those who followed their own conscience [...]. Fortunately [...] Thomas Aquinas, following in the footsteps of Albertus Magnus, came out in favour of whomsoever followed their own conscience, even if the pope himself declared it erroneous!
> (Swidler 1990: 33)

Despite Luther's undeniable contributions, 'even Protestant theology until the 20th century manifested a distant relationship with human rights. In terms of the values and victories of western Enlightenment and the modern European revolutions, its behaviour was defensive, akin to even that of the Catholics [...] Christian Churches on the whole had difficulty recognizing the rights of man up until the middle of the twentieth century' (Walf

1990: 57–8), until they appeared in Pope John XXIII's *Pacem in terris* (1963) and in the Vatican Council II declaration *Dignitatis humanae* (1965).

The relationship between Islam and human rights is certainly more problematic, given the original asymmetry between western Judeo-Christian culture and the world of the Middle-Eastern and Arab culture. This dissimilarity was illustrated by Roger Garaudy, who as a Marxist convert to Islam, arrived with a sorrowful three-fold admonition to 'put an end to the triumphalism of a tradition that sees itself as the best as it ignores all others'; to 'put an end to the static literalism of the Koranic exegesis that ignores how God speaks through history and how he should be listened to through history'; and to 'put an end to the legalism that deprives Islam of its interior dimension and love' (Garaudy 1990: 81–2). In fact, within the Islamic community in recent years there are promising signs of reflection on certain principles that until now had been considered impossible to reform. The 'Letter of 138 Muslim Scholars to the Pope and the Leaders of the Christian Churches' (Samir 2007) and the *Marrakesh Declaration* (2016) are examples of this. This Declaration lists the measures that are considered urgent within the educational field; it states:

> Urge Muslim educational institutions and authorities to conduct a courageous review of educational curricula that addresses honestly and actively any material that instigates aggression and extremism, leads to war and chaos, and results in the destruction of our shared societies.

A number of contemporary scholars have attempted comparative approaches to the problem of 'religion – education', identifying them according to historical, phenomenological and theological criteria, and sometimes all of these criteria together (Sforza 1994, Scheuer 2003, Margotti 2012: 70–84).[8] The risks of comparison are well known, especially in the area of religion: first of all, there is the illusion of taking one religion *a priori* as the standard for the others; attributing the analyzed religions with categories of improper or even deviant judgments; putting myths and doctrines, rituals and initiations, truth and heresy, iconic language and verbal language on the same level; finally, there is the inherent risk of accusing another of illiteracy because of an ignorance of textual scriptures, of mnemonic notions or of rational argumentation, while the religious experience – we all know – generally goes beyond the dimensions of the here and now, and beyond these parameters of assessment.

The American scholar Gabriel Moran understood this aporia when he noted,

> the modern world tends to consider scholastic teaching as the prototypical didactic form. The teacher seeks to convince by providing explanations and reasons; at school the teacher represents the community, but his or her persuasive authority rests mainly on clarity and rationality. In these conditions, no single religion could survive scholastic teaching; all religions in a school environment would be subjected to the threat of subversion.
>
> (Moran 1995: 130)

8 Also the *Dictionnaire des faits religieux*, edited by Régine Azria and Danièle Hervieu-Léger, Paris 2010, reserves substantial entries to the individual great religions (e.g. 'Bouddhisme', 'Catholicisme', 'Dar Al-Islam', 'Judaïsme'), emphasizing the typical structures of cultural transmission and their educational potential. For more detailed information on the educational policies of Christian denominations and of other religions concerning the specific issue of public schools and Religious Education in Europe, see the monographic issue edited by Flavio Pajer (2012), with contributions on the educational policies of Judaism (Amos Luzzatto), Roman Catholicism (Flavio Pajer), Protestantism (Peter Schreiner) and Islam (Peter Antes).

Rather than accusing the educational system of eventual or actual deficits in religious literacy, it should be recalled that there is an irreversible cultural gap – or amnesia, as the theologian Christian Duquoc dubbed it – that has interrupted the communicative flow between generations and historical periods.

> The current amnesia is not forgetfulness, it is the result of judgment: for many of our peers, Christianity is none other than an archaic monument not unlike that of Gregorian music, Romanesque art or Greek tragedy. It may be beautiful, but it no longer provides us with truth. We find ourselves locked in a paradox: wishing to wrench these Christian monuments away from cultural oblivion does not necessarily mean we render service to the spreading of faith, it means insisting that faith be identified for what it is. However, our manner of grasping truth and meaning nowadays runs the risk of being no less devoid of relevance than the writing of a new Gregorian piece or the construction of another Romanesque building.
>
> (Duquoc 1999: 158–9)

This pertinent observation moves the responsibility for the so-called lack of religious culture from the didactics of notional education to the much more arduous hermeneutic function of enculturation.

Nonetheless, religions today are not generally willing to abandon the battleground of the school, including public schools, to close themselves up within the private sphere of esoteric communication. Rather, they demand rights from public authorities to enter into the international flow of democratic diffusion, not only to guarantee an obvious social visibility but also for the opportunity to engage with different positions of scientific production (universities), for a foundational disciplinary literacy (schools) and for popular divulgation (media). Although there are many examples one can mention, the Catholic Church, for example, in the name of religious freedom solicits the authorities of civic society to provide for places and instruments for the promotion of religious culture (religious literacy) that are worthy of an open and pluralist society. The main document that attests to this openness is the *Dignitatis humanae* council declaration,[9] specifically Paragraph 6 where it affirms that 'Cura iuris ad libertatem religiosam tum ad cives tum ad coetus sociales tum ad potestates civiles tum ad Ecclesiam aliasque communitates religiosas spectat'.

Dignitatis humanae for the right to public Religious Education

This conciliar text[10] lists five specific subjects on which to work in order to promote – according to the different contexts and respective levels of competency – conditions for the effective exercise of religious freedom. From these five subjects I shall limit my analysis to one, the *potestates*

9 In reference to the *Dignitatis humanae* and its 'subversive' importance, it is worth recalling Giuseppe Alberigo, when he wrote, 'the Vatican II marked an unquestionable and macroscopic inversion of tendencies in regards to prevalent Catholic orientation in the last four centuries. The emblematic resolution – more than anything else – of the conciliar wish to recover the original and foundational values of the Christian faith is found in the declaration on religious freedom *Dignitatis humanae*. Perhaps no other decision has demanded such effort from the council fathers, as it was necessary to recognize the intangibility of the conscience of every person in order to overcome a series of daunting historical encrustments: that is, the convictions that the authenticity of Christian revelation can (and must) be imposed through the forcing of consciences' (Alberigo 2002: 187–8).

10 To contextualize the innovative reach of this document through a precise recognition of its elaboration, see Scatena (2003). An up-to-date reading, including a theological perspective, can be found in Siebenrock (2016).

civiles: the public or state authorities.[11] More specifically, among the various duties attributed to the said authorities and civic institutions for fostering religious freedom, I intend to focus my attention on the formative duty endowed to the public education system, especially to the plausibility of the specific disciplinary figure that is (or should be) education *about* and *from* religion, understood here as an informational and critical curricular approach toward the universal religious phenomenon, its history and its different forms and interpretations.

On the issue of the promotion and safeguarding of the religious freedom of pupils as individuals and future citizens, I shall start from the hypothesis that the authorities of public schools – without prejudice for primary family rights – cannot limit themselves to delegating to churches or religious communities the duty of selectively and respectively instructing pupils in the understanding of their own faith's traditions (as is still common practice in numerous countries with concordat regimes), but they can and must indiscriminately guarantee to the entire school population the acquisition of the minimum cognitive tools necessary to be able to read and interpret the religious phenomenon as it is objectively understood. These tools must be suitable – especially in the emerging contexts of secularized, multicultural and religiously mixed cultures in the western world – for a wider and more understanding exercise of the freedom of religion. This will be without prejudice to any such parallel or complementary course of confessional Religious Education that is instituted or may be instituted in scholastic or extracurricular contexts, of which ecclesiastic communities or other religious communities are the legitimate holders, in consistency and compatibility with the framework of the various national or local legal and educational systems.

It is therefore necessary to discern whether and under which conditions civil authorities – who are institutionally responsible for the common good and the peaceful, orderly coexistence of citizens of different religious beliefs – can institute common, objective courses on religious subjects in public schools to guarantee a comprehensive, unbiased understanding of different religious identities, with obvious priority accorded to the religions present in the territory. This would help establish the prerequisites for the mutual recognition of different religious identities. Such recognition would certainly make use of other formal legal tools, but it goes without saying that a significant propaedeutic cultural role would have to be carried by school education. This role would include fostering processes of intercultural didactics where the religious factor normally acts as one of the more constant and conspicuous keys to reading human cultural heritage, as well as involve creating paths aimed at recognizing and understanding religious language and symbolism as found in the variety of their anthropological roots and their historical morphology.

Actually, the *Dignitatis humanae* declaration does not go so far as to attribute explicitly public schools with such an educational responsibility.[12] Instead, at first glance,

11 I have updated a previous article in this second part (Pajer 2007).

12 Mainly because it did not have the competence or the right since the public education system is a civic institutional environment that is normally regulated and managed by independent state, regional or city authorities. In democratic societies, these authorities operate as representatives and are at the service of a civic society, which by law and in fact is not extended to a religious society. Second, because the prevalent cultural climate during the years of the Council was inadequate for soliciting specific attention on public authorities in this sense. Recall that forty years ago these recent cultural phenomena of globalization had yet to become so conspicuous. These phenomena are now spreading rapidly throughout the West and are called by many names (some evocative, others semantically fluctuating), such as religious comeback, God's revenge, migrations of the sacred, postmodern devoutness, post-secular laity, de-privatization of religion, de-secularization, identity communitarianism, theologies of religious pluralism, interreligious dialogues, etc.

it appears quite restrictive in this issue. In point 5, it emphasizes parents' fundamental rights to educate their children and affirms that those rights are considered violated in two cases: (1) when children are forced to attend school lessons that do not correspond to their parents' religious persuasion; (2) when a single form of education is imposed that excludes any and all Religious Education.[13] In fact, our present hypothesis does not fall under the first case, because an *objective* course on religious phenomena does not interfere *per se* in the sphere of people's *subjective* persuasions any more than a history, philosophy or any other humanistic lesson would. It does not fall into the second case, either. In fact, it would actually be a corrective because it strives to overcome the archaic secularism that has ignored or fought against any religious presence in schools whatsoever. Instead, it would promote a *positive and comparative intelligence* of religious phenomena. Or better: these contents, precisely because they come from and epistemologically make use of religious sciences (value-free knowledge) and are not conjectured solely from theological sciences (value knowledge), are such that – if proposed by schools with the appropriate intellectual honesty and didactic impartiality – do not require any absence of faith or any shift in personal convictions. Rather, they would allow for an informed, comparative and reasoned understanding of religious phenomena, founded on common processes of historical and empirical observation, of linguistic and symbolic analysis of documents, of comparison and contrast of interpretations, etc. It is clear that a militant believer interested in school solely as a means to educate other believers – and hence with a relationship of exclusive and all-absorbing identification with the languages and behaviors of his or her faith and nothing else – would find an unbiased and non-confessional approach to religious issues insufficient, if not impertinent and deviant. It is equally as clear, however, that if the specific competence of public schools is to elaborate culture and to elaborate it in terms and with methods suitable for different disciplines, scholastic authorities are then legitimized in taking charge of the knowledge of religious phenomena as something that belongs to universal experience and to human history. It is, therefore, educationally pertinent and even unavoidable in today's climate that public schools elaborate religion as a cultural object, following their own methodologies and competencies in the teaching of what for believers is primarily an object of faith.

To further justify the urgency of this hypothesis, it is helpful to recall the well-known historical circumstances of recent decades following the Vatican Council. The cultural revolution of 1968, new religious and spiritual movements, Assisi 1986, the fall of the Berlin Wall and the end of the bipolar system, the insurgence of bloody ethnic-religious conflicts in various regions of the globe, the migrant movements that have blended cultures and religious faiths, 11 September and its political and military aftermath, the unresolved issue of Israel and Palestine, etc.: there have been hundreds of other events that reveal a profound and dramatic transformation in the new social visibility and geo-political role of religions, beginning with the important roles played by the great monotheistic traditions of Abraham. These events spill over from their own natural cultural and religious contexts into political and civic spaces and could not then, nor can they now, fail to affect civic authorities and institutions, especially those in charge of safeguarding human rights (of which religious rights are a non-negotiable component) and educational policies for schools and universities.

13 On these provisions, I have previously cited specific prescriptions in international and European documents, see notes 11, 14, 16.

Public school and the right-duty of religious literacy

The drafting of the *Dignitatis humanae* took place in a worldwide post-war climate effected, among others, by the then recent *Pacem in terris* (1963). The period was still strongly compromised by ideological tensions between the two blocs, and the Church felt the need to affirm the rights of religious freedom, claiming them not only for their own believers but also for all people on the basis of their common dignity. Today, the shift in socio-religious conditions, the macroscopic socio-political relevance of religious issues and the legal and cultural evolution of basic concepts (such as the concept of religious freedom, secularism, religious instruction/education or of non-confessional religious knowledge) require the public school system to assume independent, suitable initiatives in the area of religious literacy. This clearly must take shape through the necessary and opportune dialogue with the religious authorities involved and with the democratic representatives of the citizens who participate (especially with parents of the pupils), to avoid simple ideological misunderstandings and, above all, conflicts in competencies on an institutional level.

In the fifty years since the drafting of the *Dignitatis humanae*, there have been notable transformations in the production of legal and political doctrine concerning the secular nature of the state and its schools, democratic citizenship and its respective rights, and religious culture and its public transmission. This is not the forum to investigate deeply into these broad topics, but it is important to take note of recent developments and tendencies. These developments help us intuit how one might plausibly imagine, at least in Europe, a specific intervention in public schools aimed at fostering religious freedom:

1 A move from a modern conception of human rights (the rights of individual and social liberty sanctioned by the state-nation as guarantor of equal opportunities for all citizens) towards a conception of those same rights in a globalized, postmodern world (the rights to individual and group diversity within both the public and private sphere, the assertion of cultural and religious identity at a local/regional and supranational level, the coexistence of multiple cultures in the same social space). Today's multicultural society is aware of the urgency to prevent the impending specter of a 'clash of civilizations' and understands the need to begin in schools to foster the capacity to engage in debate and dialogue that is non-emotive, not solely self-referential and no longer Eurocentric with the great cultures and religions of our globalized planet (Bein Ricco 2005a: 5–45, 2005b, Tamayo 2005).
2 The right to religious freedom as one of the fundamental rights of a person and citizen is amply codified – as we have seen – in the statutes of international bodies and national constitutions. Instead of the restrictive concept of religious liberty understood until recently as the mere subjective possibility to believe or not, it would be significantly more opportune to achieve a more social and concrete concept of advancement than that of the prior conditions. This would foster the personal exercise of religious freedom. It is clear that within our current situation of growing religious pluralism an objective and critical understanding of religious phenomena and their meanings is a necessary condition to guarantee younger generations (and not only these generations) the tools they need. These tools act as prevention against the aggressive intrusiveness of the proselytizing of identity groups, an antidote to the emotional seduction of fundamentalisms, and finally and most importantly, as a supplementary cognitive resource to act on or perfect one's own religious choice with greater freedom and awareness (Berlingò 1987, Gervasio 2004, Dieni, Ferrari and Pacillo 2005).

3 From a 'neutral secularist' model that relegates religious conviction and ethical choices to the private sphere of the individual, and which has given rise to the often conflictual and debatable parallelisms between the public or 'neutral' school and a denominational school, between profane culture (for everyone) and religious instruction (for believers), towards 'comparative secularities', an 'asymmetrical laity' (Ferrari 2006). This form of secularism no longer denies the differences in life perspectives in prejudicial ways but rather recognizes and integrates them into the democratic and public space, which is the school for everyone. In a society with significant cultural heterogeneity, this prevents the school from becoming an easy ground for constructing communities based on ethnic, religious or ideological bases.

4 In a move 'from agnostic ignorance towards secular intelligence of religion' (Debray 2002: 43), the public school can remain open not only to specific educational collaboration on the part of teachers certified in religious, mono-confessional instruction but can also seek out and activate further independent and common courses on trans-denominational 'religious culture'. This can be carried out seamlessly with the educational content and the objectives of related subjects to promote the necessary understanding of the plurality of religious forms present in history and in the social surroundings. These forms, which are often ignored in school curricula or misrepresented by current prejudice, often end up becoming perceived as threats to the safety and cohesion of a multicultural society (Genre and Pajer 2002).

5 As a consequence of important academic developments in religious sciences – in parallel if not in direct contact with theologians throughout the twentieth century[14] – religious didactics in school has been testing a significant distinction between the confessional teaching *of* religion or faith (think of the classic figure of the scholastic catechesis from the post-Trent era), to a cultural education *about* religion:[15] the former is destined mainly to educate faithful pupils who belong to a specific mono-cultural community in their own faith, while the latter seeks instead to instruct on the multiple religious realities that a culturally and religiously heterogeneous school population possesses (in the presence of students of various faiths, nonbelievers and those who may be searching for faith). A system of this kind must garner the primary values and cultural features of religious phenomena in order to understand their historical and human significance. It then must combine the ideal values coming from respective religious identities with the common values of citizenship (Campiche 2003, Council of Europe 2005).

6 Move from the principal reasons or opportune arguments toward facts. There are many national education systems in western secular societies (Anglo-Saxon Europe, Canada, Brazil and Australia) (Pajer 2014) that have introduced, experimented with and verified – using unilateral state legislation, but often also with the positive consensus of churches and families – forms of objective, multi-denominational or comparative studies of religions. These studies reconcile diverse paths and approaches (symbolic, historical, ethical, phenomenological, etc.) that are adaptable according to the school grade; such courses, which are managed by the state or by local authorities according

14 Two different European dictionaries that came out at the same time are evidence of this: *Dizionario del sapere storico-religioso del Novecento*, edited by Alberto Melloni (2010) and *Dictionnaire des faits religieux*, edited by Régine Azria and Danièle Hervieu-Léger (2010).

15 A distinction that in many respects is the normal didactic corollary on a scholastic level for that which, at university level, has two channels: the confessional and non-confessional production and spreading of religious knowledge (see note 2). Cf. also Mazzola (2001), Mazzola (2014), Pajer (2000).

to the situation, can sometimes coexist with optional, confessional courses held by churches, and sometimes be substitutes for such courses.[16]

The educational system at the service of knowledge and values

In relation to the promotion of religious freedom in a multi-religious society, the principal duties of states and international organizations express themselves on two levels: that of issuing laws and provisions aimed at preventing and censuring acts of violence and discrimination, whether they be physical or symbolic, especially in religious matters; and to foster the development of a civic society capable of respecting the plurality of coexisting religious systems and to promote tolerance among individuals and groups of believers and nonbelievers. These may create the conditions for democratic coexistence established on the acknowledgment of differences and their interactions. In terms of activities of prevention and promotion, public authorities must clearly turn to the educational system as the primary engine to convey knowledge and values democratically, to impart the necessary critical thinking skills and abilities to assess issues ethically, and to shape behavior that is consistent with the commonly held values shared in all democratic societies represented within their constitutions. Therefore, in their educational policies, public authorities must avoid privileging one religion over another, emphasizing significant religious systems while silencing others, or even taking the place of choice within civic and religious society and thus assuming the domineering role as an ethical and educating state (thus negating the primacy of the individual as citizen, and potentially, as believer).

The areas where educational policy can intervene in the promotion of religious freedom can be spread out over a wide range of sensitive issues that precede and accompany the management of religious instruction. Following is a short list:

1 The orientation of educational policy linked to the growing fundamental needs for multi-religious contexts, such as intercultural pedagogy, the education of democratic citizenship against racism and intolerance, education intended to handle cultural differences and axiological conflicts, or more generally, to foster social and cultural integration in a manner that does not aim to assimilate minority cultures and religions into the hegemonic system of the majority, but rather operates with a view toward the evolution of all of society toward a greater balance in recognized and legitimated diversity.
2 Verifying cultural contents of various school subjects on issues concerning the history of religious traditions, their texts and doctrines, and their effects on culture and customs. It is the responsibility of the drafters of ministerial programs concerning humanistic subjects, such as history, law, philosophy and art, to approach these subjects with impartial reasoning, objective data and interpretations related to religions, and thus

16 The latter case occurs when churches or other religious organizations prefer not to avail themselves of public structures and instead opt for Religious Education that they seek to provide themselves within their own educational structures (families, communities, youth groups), leaving the public school system with the sole responsibility of providing non-confessional courses; or when the legal and economic conditions of free education are such in a nation that the request for religious instruction by families of faith can generally be satisfied by a network of free, denominational schools. This exonerates the public system from the responsibility of instituting confessional courses that would be manifestly disregarded by a public that, free to choose, has presumably chosen the public school for its impartial tendencies in religious matters.

avoid omissions or 'silences' on the religious phenomena of culture, biased assessments inspired by anti-religious ideologies and the inverse apologetic, inopportune overemphasis of that phenomena; similar intellectual responsibilities rest with authors and editors of scholarly textbooks and didactic subsidization in general.

3 Education and training of teachers of different humanistic subjects (but not only of humanistic subjects) to be able to analyze correctly and secularly – consistently with the epistemological rules of the subject in question and without introducing undue 'theological' or spiritualistic arbitrary interpretations – the religious or symbolic dimension that is often inherent or mixed into the subjects they teach. Regardless of their personal religious convictions, it is the professional duty of instructors alone to shed light on the multitude of cultural features and potential ethical-religious meanings of the knowledge with which they deal, and this responsibility ought to be supported by the same public structures that trained them and with which they collaborate.[17]

4 Education and training of teachers to be experts in religious sciences, nominated to hold public school courses on religious or ethical culture that are managed by scholastic authorities and potentially proposed as an option or replacement for confessional courses managed by churches or other religious communities.

Protection of religious freedom in the school environment does not fall only to the institutions and individuals involved in managing public instruction. Besides the content and manner of instruction, there are delicate problems concerning the management of religious symbols, as seen with recent cases regarding the Islamic veil or the crucifix in classrooms. Besides the reasons behind allowing or not allowing these symbols to be publicly displayed, it is still necessary to develop critical, meta-confessional discourse that can provide students with the cognitive tools needed to dissuade intolerant behavior (Dieni, Ferrari and Pacillo 2005).

Religious freedom at the service of human dignity

Religious freedom is a fundamental human right, whose foundation lies in the dignity of the person him- or herself. The building blocks of that dignity are what define the nature of people: reason, free will and moral responsibility (*Dignitatis humanae* § 2). It follows that freedom of religion should be regulated alongside freedom of thought and freedom of conscience. These three indivisible liberties do not consist solely in the right not to be individually subjected to state coercion, but rather in the right to have a positive acknowledgment of the said liberty on the part of public authorities. This acknowledgment – much more than a simple and foregone tolerance – involves the recognition of opinion, religious creed and ethical choice. In this view, the *Dignitatis humanae* represented a sea change: the top-down, external tradition of tolerance became bottom-up, projecting from the center of the person and with clear reference to the common good (Scatena 2003).

17 The legislation concerning the French educational context is emblematic of this. In recent years, all candidates for primary and secondary education, especially those receiving training in humanistic subjects, have specific courses in their initial training on historical-religious sciences; similar courses are offered in programs for those who are currently teaching as well. Certain centers of higher education are specialized in training teachers to recognize and elaborate systematically 'the religious dimension of school subjects'. Furthermore, we must remember that these initiatives are activated in a legislative context of historical separation between church and state, which not only does not authorize any confessional religious teachings in public schools but does not even allow alternative courses on the history of religion or anything similar.

In order to guarantee the conditions to allow individuals and social groups to enjoy their civil liberties, public authorities can and must contribute to guaranteeing the conditions for the private and public exercise of religious freedom. This necessitates a clear relationship of distinction-subsidiarity between public authorities and religious authorities in the various areas in question, especially in education. For example, where the church has the right/responsibility to shape the religious conscience of its followers, the state has the right to shape the historical-religious conscience of its citizens; where the church carries out its ministry of teaching the Truth in virtue of its divine mandate founded on revelation, the state has the authority to produce other readings of religious heritage, which are non-theological but no less plausible from the perspective of truth in terms of reasoning and scientific veracity; readings that may be a suitable stimulus for the faithful to verify their own religious conceptions and for the non-faithful may offer a possible meaning and, above all, raise awareness and prosperity for humanity. It is especially clear in the area of religion that the possibility of free choice expands according to the degree to which an individual has been prepared to understand and compare: the broadest exercise of liberty stems from the awareness, not the ignorance, of values, from multi-faceted debate and dialogue, not from indoctrination.

Scholars of religious law follow a similar path: in order to develop a critical understanding of the relationship between rights and religion and to compare correctly the religious rights of different traditions, it is always necessary to start from the cultural and historical premises of the laws of religions themselves, not only from canon law. Canon law is a relevant legal assessment for the 'Christian' western world, but appears hopelessly provincial if applied on a global scale (Ferrari 2002: 284).

In the conclusion to these brief notes, we have sought to point out the guiding thread that links the two fundamental rights to believe and to understand with the duty to educate and to train:

1 *The freedom to believe* is one of humanities' fundamental rights and as such is safeguarded as a civil right by national and international judicial systems; it is largely a virtual freedom, especially in infancy and adolescence, inasmuch as the individual is not in full possession of the conditions and tools needed to exercise definitive, personal, responsible choices; the development of this freedom – which on principle also includes the freedom not to believe or to change belief – is entrusted to the individual, but also to a variety of educational institutions, the school in particular; the school, in turn, does not conceal the 'religious problem' or see it as a problem solely for the religious community but instead faces it as a cultural issue, offering all students without distinction the specific informational, analytical and comparative skills necessary to engage in a search for meaning; in the absence of these tools, a real exercise of free and mature religious choice is wanting.
2 *The right to know* is also a fundamental right of an individual and citizen, even more so in our day and age as our societies desire to view themselves as 'exploratory': whether a person is a believer, a nonbeliever or has different beliefs, he or she has the right to learn about religious phenomena because they represent a historical dimension of humanity. Religion represents the roots of past and present cultures and civilizations, it is a horizon of meaning with which to interact; the public school, when it is not ideologically precluded against religious knowledge, has the authority and the tools to satisfy this need to know, which is the right of every student.
3 *The duty to train* is the obvious practical corollary that enters into the political agenda of every state that wishes to be active in the face of the real demands of a

new, multi-religious society; this duty falls under the purview of public educational structures (schools and universities): these structures possess the specific and defined competencies that do not diminish, much less eliminate, the corresponding and complementary competencies of religious communities. These communities can operate within and outside schools, depending on the independent national regulations. These competencies are needed in order to make the commonplace idea that the state remains 'incompetent in religious matters' less and less sustainable.

Bibliography

African Charter on Human and People's Rights, www.achpr.org/instruments/achpr?prn=1, last accessed 26 October 2017.

Alberigo, Giuseppe 2002. 'Forme e problemi dell'autunno della cristianità', in Gianfranco Bottoni (ed.), *Fine della cristianità? Il cristianesimo tra religione civile e testimonianza evangelica*, Bologna, Il Mulino, 175–200.

Azria, Régine and Hervieu-Léger, Danièle (ed.) 2010. *Dictionnaire des faits religieux*, Paris, PUF.

Bein Ricco, Elena (ed.) 2005a. *Libera Chiesa in libero Stato?*, Torino, Claudiana.

Bein Ricco, Elena 2005b. 'I diritti tra modernità e postmodernità', *Protestantesimo* 60:4, 267–81.

Belgiorno de Stefano, Maria G. 2008. 'L'insegnamento della religione sotto il controllo della Corte Europea dei Diritti umani', *Stato, Chiese e pluralismo confessionale* June, www.statoechiese.it, last accessed 26 October 2017.

Berlingò, Salvatore 1987. *Libertà d'istruzione e fattore religioso*, Milano, Giuffrè.

Berman, Harold J. 1995. 'Diritto e religione', in Mircea Eliade (ed.), *Enciclopedia delle religioni*, vol. 5, Dario M. Cosi, Luigi Saibene and Roberto Scagno (ed.), *Lo studio delle religioni. Discipline e autori*, Milano, Jaca Book, 88–9.

Borowitz, Eugene 1990. 'La Torah scritta e orale e i diritti umani. Fondazione e carenze', *Concilium* 2, 43–54.

Boucaud, Pascale 2016. 'Le droit à l'éducation au regard de la discrimination et de l'endoctrinement', *Pedagogia e vita* 74, 193–216.

Cairo Declaration on Human Rights in Islam, www.fmreview.org/sites/fmr/files/FMRdownloads/en/FMRpdfs/Human-Rights/cairo.pdf, last accessed 26 October 2017.

Campiche, Roland J. 2003. 'La régulation de la religion par l'État et la production du lien social', *Archives de sciences sociales des religions* 121, 5–18.

Cardia, Carlo 1999. *Manuale di diritto ecclesiastico*, 2nd edn, Bologna, Il Mulino.

Casanova, José 2017. 'Lo Stato post-secolare e il pluralismo religioso', *Vita e Pensiero* 100:1, 15–21.

Charter of Fundamental Rights of the European Union, www.europarl.europa.eu/charter/pdf/text_fr.pdf, last accessed 26 October 2017.

Colaianni, Nicola 2012. *Diritto pubblico delle religioni. Eguaglianza e differenze nello Stato costituzionale*, Bologna, Il Mulino.

Convention against Discrimination in Education, http://portal.unesco.org/en/ev.php-URL_ID=12949&URL_DO=DO_TOPIC&URL_SECTION=201.html, last accessed 26 October 2017.

Convention on the Rights of the Child, www.ohchr.org/EN/ProfessionalInterest/Pages/CRC.aspx, last accessed 26 October 2017.

Council of Europe 2005. *The Religious Dimension of Intercultural Education*, Strasbourg, Council of Europe.

Council of Europe 2013. *EU Guidelines on the Promotion and Protection of Freedom of Religion or Belief*, Foreign Affairs Council meeting, Luxembourg, 24 June, https://eeas.europa.eu/sites/eeas/files/137585.pdf, last accessed 26 October 2017.

Debray, Régis 2002. *L'enseignement du fait religieux dans l'école publique*, Paris, Odile Jacob.

Declaration on the Rights of Persons belonging to National or Ethnic, Religious and Linguistic Minorities, www.un.org/documents/ga/res/47/a47r135.htm, last accessed 26 October 2017.

Delors, Jacques, al-Mufti, In'am, Amagi, Isao *et al.* 1996. *Learning. The Treasure Within. Report to UNESCO of the International Commission on Education for the Twenty-First Century*, Paris, UNESCO.

Dieni, Edoardo, Ferrari, Alessandro and Pacillo, Vincenzo (ed.) 2005. *Symbolon/Diabolon. Simboli, religioni, diritti nell'Europa multiculturale*, Bologna, Il Mulino.

Duquoc, Christian 1999. 'Fede cristiana e amnesia culturale', *Concilium* 1, 155–62.

Engelhardt, Tristram H. 2014. *Dopo Dio. Morale e bioetica in un mondo laico*, Torino, Claudiana.

European Convention for the Protection of Human Rights and Fundamental Freedoms, www.echr.coe.int/Documents/Convention_ENG.pdf, last accessed 26 October 2017.

Ferrari, Silvio 2002. *Lo spirito dei diritti religiosi. Ebraismo, cristianesimo e islam a confronto*, Bologna, Il Mulino.

Ferrari, Silvio 2006. 'Religione civile in Europa. Laicità asimmetrica', *Il Regno. Attualità* 6, 200–12.

Ferrari, Silvio 2012. 'La Corte di Strasburgo e l'articolo 9 della Convenzione europea. Una analisi quantitativa della giurisprudenza', in Roberto Mazzola (ed.), *Diritto e religione in Europa. Rapporto sulla giurisprudenza della Corte europea dei diritti dell'uomo in materia di libertà religiosa*, Bologna, Il Mulino, 27–53.

Garaudy, Roger 1990. 'I diritti dell'uomo e l'Islam. Fondazione, tradizione, violazione', *Concilium* 2, 68–83.

Genre, Ermanno and Pajer, Flavio 2005. *L'Unione Europea e la sfida delle religioni. Verso una nuova presenza della religione nella scuola*, Torino, Claudiana.

Gervasio, Giuseppe 2004. 'Ordinamenti giuridici, fattore religioso, fenomeno religioso', *Rivista di teologia dell'evangelizzazione* 8:16, 479–99.

Grimmitt, Michael 1987. *Religious Education and Human Development: The Relationship between Studying Religions and Personal, Social and Moral Education*, Great Wakering, McCrimmons.

Hull, John M. 2004. 'Practical Theology and Religious Education in a Pluralist Europe', *British Journal of Religious Education* 26:1, 7–19.

Jackson, Robert 2014. *Signposts: Policy and Practice for Teaching about Religious and Non-Religious World Views in Intercultural Education*, Strasbourg, Council of Europe.

Küng, Hans and Moltmann, Jürgen 1990. 'Etica delle religioni universali e diritti umani', *Concilium* 2, 15–16.

Long, Gianni (ed.) 2007. *Libertà religiosa e minoranze*, Torino, Claudiana.

Margotti, Marta 2012. *Religioni e secolarizzazioni: ebraismo, cristianesimo e islam nel mondo globale*, Torino, Rosenberg & Sellier.

Marrakesh Declaration, www.marrakeshdeclaration.org/files/Bismilah-2-ENG.pdf, last accessed 26 October 2017.

Mazzola, Roberto 2001. 'L'organizzazione non confessionale del "sapere" religioso in Italia', *Quaderni di diritto e politica ecclesiastica* 9:1, 141–52.

Mazzola, Roberto 2014. 'Confessioni, organizzazioni filosofiche e associazioni religiose nell'Unione Europea tra speranze disilluse e problemi emergenti', *Stato, Chiese e pluralismo confessionale* 3, www.statoechiese.it, last accessed 26 October 2017.

Melloni, Alberto (ed.) 2010. *Dizionario del sapere storico-religioso del Novecento*, 2 vols., Bologna, Il Mulino.

Moran, Gabriel 1995. 'Educazione religiosa', in Mircea Eliade (ed.), *Enciclopedia delle religioni*, vol. 5, Dario M. Cosi, Luigi Saibene and Roberto Scagno (ed.), *Lo studio delle religioni. Discipline e autori*, Milano, Jaca Book, 126–31.

Pajer, Flavio (ed.) 2000. 'L'insegnamento delle scienze religiose in Europa', *Religioni e società* 15:2, 3–126.

Pajer, Flavio 2006. 'L'istruzione religiosa nelle politiche scolastiche europee', in Nella Borri (ed.), *Pluralità delle culture e pluralismo religioso*, Perugia, L'altrapagina, 187–204.

Pajer, Flavio 2007. 'Libertà di credere, diritto di conoscere, dovere di formare. Il diritto alla libertà religiosa e la competenza educativa della scuola pubblica', in Manlio Sodi (ed.), *'Ubi Petrus ibi Ecclesia'. Sui 'sentieri' del Concilio Vaticano II*, Roma, Las, 758–71.

Pajer, Flavio 2012. 'L'istruzione religiosa pubblica in un'Europa multireligiosa. Le politiche educative del cattolicesimo romano', *Historia Religionum. An International Journal* 4, 23–38.

Pajer, Flavio 2014. 'Les systèmes éducatifs européens vont-ils généraliser des approches post-confessionnelles dans les cours en matière de religions?', in Brigitte Caulier and Joël Molinario (ed.), *Enseigner les religions. Regards et apports de l'Histoire*, Québec, Presse de l'Université Laval, 311–26.

Parisi, Marco 2011. 'Ateismo, neutralità dell'istruzione pubblica e pluralismo delle opzioni formative', *Quaderni di diritto e politica ecclesiastica* 19:1, 127–46.

Religious Education Council of England and Wales 2013. *A Curriculum Framework for RE in England*, October 2013, www.resubjectreview.recouncil.org.uk/media/file/RE_Review_Summary.pfd, last accessed 26 October 2017.

Samir, Khalil 2007. 'The Letter of 138 Muslim Scholars to the Pope and Christian Leaders', *Asia News*, 17 October, www.asianews.it/news-en/The-Letter-of-138-Muslim-scholars-to-the-Pope-and-Christian-Leaders-10577.html, last accessed 26 October 2017.

Scatena, Silvia 2003. *La fatica della libertà. L'elaborazione della dichiarazione 'Dignitatis humanae' sulla libertà religiosa del Vaticano II*, Bologna, Il Mulino.

Scheuer, Jacques (ed.) 2003. *L'Éducation. Ce qu'en disent les religions*, Paris, Éditions de l'Atelier.

Sforza, Giulio (ed.) 1994. *Religioni ed educazione. Dialogo delle civiltà*, Roma, Anicia.

Siebenrock, Roman A. 2016, 'Il vangelo della dignità dell'uomo. *Dignitatis humanae*, una provocazione continua', *Concilium* 4, 41–52.

Smith Foster, Michael 1996. 'I diritti dei minori', *Concilium* 32:2, 163–73.

Swidler, Leonard 1990. 'Diritti umani: una panoramica storica', *Concilium* 2, 30–42.

Tamayo, Juan José 2005. 'Religiones y derechos humanos: una relación conflictiva', in Juan José Tamayo (ed.), *10 palabras clave sobre derechos humanos*, Estella, Editorial Verbo Divino, 349–59.

Universal Declaration of Human Rights, www.un.org/en/universal-declaration-human-rights/, last accessed 26 October 2017.

Ventura, Marco 2001. *La laicità dell'Unione Europea. Diritti, mercato, religione*, Torino, Giappichelli.

Ventura, Marco 2014. 'Religione e scuola. Sviluppi nazionali e indirizzi europei', in Antonio Mantineo, Domenico Bilotti and Stefano Montesano (ed.), *Insegnamenti e insegnanti di religione nella scuola pubblica italiana*, Milano, Giuffrè, 219–37.

Walf, Knut 1990. 'Vangelo, diritto canonico e diritti umani', *Concilium* 2, 55–67.

Part II

Understanding illiteracies, debating disciplines?

5 The ethics of the Torah compared to neo-paganism

Donatella Di Cesare

Religions in the age of the McWorld

In recent years we have been speaking of a 'religious comeback' within the public sphere. This term fails to do justice to what is a truly complex phenomenon. Religion was never actually driven out. It was relegated to the private sphere in an affected and ahistorical manner, only to be reproached whenever it dared overstep its boundaries. However, those who had pointed to irreversible development through secularization have been proven wrong. Nothing could, or should, have hindered the progress of reason, which – in gradually allowing autonomy and emancipation from any and all religious tutelage – would guarantee a better future. As this wondrous and progressive destiny has not come to pass, secularization has run aground in an arid, sterile riverbed and is unable to provide answers to the difficult and troubling questions of our new century. As Habermas often said, today we live in a 'post-secular society' (cf. Ratzinger and Habermas 2005).[1] We see secularization as a process that, if it has not yet completely run its course, appears to be moving toward decline.

An unusual and unexplored context has thus been laid out. It would be a mistake to desire to bring this context back to previous conventions. One example of this kind of schematization is the widespread attempt to read the contemporary landscape as a new clash of civilizations, not in the way that Huntington considered it, but rather as a 'war of the holy' against secular reason (Huntington 1996). It goes without saying that, in this convention, the 'holy' is the vehicle for all evils and the root of every conflict. In short, it represents the last, great obstacle that reason must overcome to pave the way for a new Enlightenment and open the doors to the final chapter in human progress. Just such an accusation against religion was raised, in all its one-sidedness, by Christopher Hitchens in his 2007 book *God Is Not Great: How Religion Poisons Everything*, though many other titles could be mentioned as well.

Such positions betray a fundamental difficulty in reading the present, reveal the uncertainty of those who had wished the course of history had taken another turn and lay bare a sense of disorientation. The belief that religion is simply violence and represents useless, even harmful, obscurantism is a reckless way to seek a remedy in the tormented scenarios of our modern times. Furthermore, those who believe in the 'original sin' of religion can hardly tolerate its return. Despite interpreting religion as a sort of last-ditch attempt or parting shot, it manifests all the irritation and exacerbated disenchantment in the face of a complex event moving forward alongside globalization.

1 As well as the volume that collects the largest amount of material on this subject is Habermas (2005). On the relationship between religion and the public sphere, cf. Cunico (2009).

In this respect, we must not forget that secularization has always been linked to the nation-state. It was able to establish itself in modern times as politics began to conceal its own religious foundations, and as politics sought to justify itself, it ended up making the state sacred and thus became a sort of civil religion (Graziano 2014: 17ff.). The decline of the nation-state, however, leads to a crisis in secularism arising from a fictitious separation between religion and politics that eventually leads to the failure of secularization. Laical voices appear unable to speak beyond the confines of the nation-state, while religions – which came before – reacquire space and allow those boundaries to be crossed. Paradoxically, in the current 'McWorld', religions play the main role not only in private life but also in public. It is impossible to imagine interpreting the international landscape if we disregard religions.

In short, we can say that the crisis of modernity is characterized by a return of religion, or better, of religions, which escape from the private sphere to reemerge within public spaces to regain the political dimension that they had never actually renounced. The question then arises as to whether in this role, which secularism would like to impede, religions constitute the place of intrinsic violence and fundamental extremism, whether they represent the weapon of a new totalitarianism bent on dominating the world even at the cost of global war, or whether, instead, they may be able to steer the great ethical choices of politics to call for justice and inspire peace.

Religion beyond the limits of simple reason

The great religious awakening of recent years has long been underestimated in the West. It has been considered an antiquated oddity, the remnants of obscurantism and a phenomenon admissible at best in the so-called 'third world'. Particularly in places such as France, where secularism appeared to be a timeless virtue and where the legally sanctioned hundred-plus years of separation between church and state should be undisputed, the effects have been disastrous. As we well know, this clash is the result of the entrance of Islam into the nation.

While Judaism and Christianity, in renouncing numerous privileges, accepted from the outset of modernity an *agreement* with the state in recognition of its sovereignty, Islam has only just begun to enter the nation and that 'lay agreement'. The entrance of Islam into the realm of European citizenship has shed light on a number of difficulties linked to other religions as well. Judaism and Christianity, in fact, have had to give up their political dimensions, without this renunciation ever being definitive. Perhaps this is because the separation between religion and politics is a demand of secularism that is as fictitious as it is unattainable.

Throughout the western world, the clash with Islam has reignited friction with religions, especially with the traditional and monotheistic ones. This front, which cuts across the one opened by the 'clash of civilizations', separates secularism in all of its forms and nuances from the interreligious coalition that some would call the 'holy alliance'. This is yet more evidence of the multiplicity and complexity of the fronts in our globalized world.

But how is the disagreement between secularism and religions interpreted and experienced? The versions range widely, and this is a further reason why this issue touches a raw nerve in current debate.

Religions look upon the court of Gentiles with a certain mistrust and unhidden preoccupation; above all, they refuse to recognize in secularism a neutral ground where exchange and debate among different ethical standpoints may occur, or as a shared morality that, as a universal language, should guarantee a kind of collective identity. They call into question – some more than others – that secular agreement which seemed dysfunctional before and has now been laid bare in all its impotency.

For its part, secularism looks down with its enlightened reasoning upon religions from on high, passing judgment on them as expressing superfluous dogmas and harmful superstitions. In separating religions from culture and stigmatizing them as non-culture, they have expunged them from common cultural heritage. The repercussions of this act of so-called post-Enlightenment are devastating. Secularism projects age-old, deeply rooted prejudices and preconceptions onto religions. Instead of being deconstructed, these prejudices and notions are then reasserted and reintroduced in new and equally violent forms.

Contemporary criticism of monotheism

Monotheism is often accused of being both new and altogether ancient. If 'God is violence', the cause must be found in its singularity. A recent formulation of this can be found in the pages of Michel Onfray's book, *Atheist Manifesto: The Case against Christianity* (2011), which has been highly successful in France and has become a bestseller.

Onfray takes aim at monotheism without mincing words: 'Monotheism is fatally fixated on death. It loves death, cherishes death; it exults in death, is fascinated by death' (176). Killings, massacres, heinous crimes: 'Behind all these abominations stand verses from the Torah, passages from the Gospels, and suras from the Koran, legitimizing, justifying, blessing' (177).

Similar texts circulate throughout Europe. But Onfray's position, which owes much to the books of Jean Soler (2002–4, 2009), is emblematic for other reasons as well. Above all, in order to strike at the source of monotheism, it lashes out at the Jews. 'Let us give credit where it is due. The Jews invented monotheism and everything that went with it'. In fact, they invented 'holy war' (Onfray 2011: 178). Onfray claims that the concept of jihad is found in the Torah. 'An only God, bellicose, mail-clad, merciless, fighting and giving no quarter, capable of exterminating the enemy without a twinge of conscience, galvanizing his troops'. This was the God of the Jews, from whom they would never distance themselves. 'For two thousand five hundred years, no leading figure descended from the chosen people has declared that these pages are rooted in fable' (180). Although Onfray's work went unnoticed in the Jewish Italian world, it sparked sharp criticism in France. Shmuel Trigano, one of the most authoritative voices in French Judaism, accused him of 'enormous violence' and of a 'profound lack of culture' that opens the door to anti-Semitism (Trigano 2015: 512–13).

Within the pages of Onfray's book, a theologically and politically significant theory takes shape. 'Every theocracy is a denial of democracy' (Onfray 2011: 177). This continues to refer to the Jewish people, who carry with them both the responsibility of an only God as well as the idea of theocracy.

In a different way, Jan Assmann advances a theory that equates an only God, a single-minded thought and the specter of a totalitarian regime. As a successor of the German tradition where this theme had been discussed at great lengths, Assmann points his finger at the inherent intolerance of monotheism. In his most successful, albeit controversial, book, he speaks of 'the mosaic distinction' to indicate the shift from polytheism to monotheism. For the first time, this distinction would establish the limit between the true God and the false gods (Assmann 2002, 2010). Assmann sees this shift, in which Israel plays the main role, as decay. The God who presumes himself to be chosen wishes to undermine the other gods – jealous and intolerant, he cannot bear to have them alongside. So, in claiming to be the only true God, he passes the others off as false gods and idols.

At first, the ancient religions tolerated one another; the various peoples had no real difficulty relating their gods to the others. Only when Israel entered the scene did 'holy war' begin. Violence was thus inaugurated, and other monotheisms such as Christianity and Islam would take it up in milder forms. As a scholar of theological politics, Assmann (2013: 64ff.) would go a step further: monotheism would be seen as a theological paradigm of dictatorship. In contrast, polytheism could allow for democratic overtures and pluralistic debate. Where there are gods, there is tolerance; where a single God dominates, there is violence.

Assmann's work continues to spark heated debate. Although it was well received in Europe, especially Germany, the Jewish community criticized it with valid reasoning. Ultimately, Assmann ended up correcting his thesis, recognizing that within the book of Exodus there is no role for the distinction between right and wrong, while instead the question of slavery and liberty is decisive. Although Assmann has proclaimed Judaism as the 'religion of difference', that is indifferent to the gods of others, his accusatory framework against monotheism remains intact.

Many, in fact, have taken up his thesis – most recently Peter Sloterdijk in his book entitled *God's Zeal* (2009; see also 2013). In general, the idea that monotheism is a source of violence and potential worldwide dictatorship has spread not only throughout philosophy, but within culture in general, to the point that it appears as an almost foregone conclusion.

Notes on the name of God

The new critique of monotheism reveals a trivial conception of God, which was taken up by paganism and mainly projected onto Judaism. It is an unjust projection and, for this very reason, exemplary. It reveals the way in which those who know neither the tradition nor the content set about dismissing 'religion' from the outside.

What does 'God' mean? Is it perhaps an overused word, deprived of reflection upon its significance and its etymology? In Romance languages, for example, 'Dio' in Italian, 'Dieu' in French, it derives from the Indo-European *Dieus, linked to *deiwa, and indicates the brightness of the heavens, from which *Zeûs*, *deus*, *divus*, *Dio* is the common name of a class of superior beings. It is the remnant of a series of gods.

This is not the God of the Torah, the 'God' that recapitulates Himself in others, the only one remaining from a series of gods. For this 'God' would keep a solid bond with the other gods. In the Torah, rather, the Tetragrammaton, four letters that cannot be uttered, indicates the proper (not common) Name of the absolute Other. A Name that cannot be uttered, as if one could expect to define it without respecting its ineffability, as if one could dominate it without raising one's gaze toward transcendence (cf. Di Cesare 2011: 65ff.).

The shift from polytheism to monotheism was revolutionary. Jacob Taubes emphasizes this point using words that Assmann appears to have forgotten. The pagan seeks out the numinous and sacred: a star is a goddess, a river is a god (Taubes 1997: 37ff.). He moves from one idol to the next, incapable of moving outside the world. Israel de-sacralizes the world, it removes magic and breaks from idolatry. No ground can be given – not even toward the sacred that spatializes itself. The Jews remain faithful through the centuries to the unmentionable Name that is separated from the numerous local divinities, guiding the history of the universe. Imagine the irritation of Roman soldiers upon entering the Temple only to find it empty. How could that sovereign people adore Absence with such fervor? An absence that was strikingly present and infinitely Other.

If we cannot project the pagan conception of God onto Judaism, as Assmann does, must we perhaps allow that Jewish monotheism is a totalitarian paradigm and that no democracy can exist where there is theocracy?

To address this question, it suffices to turn to Spinoza. According to an ancient etymology, *Israel* means 'he that striveth with God' and can be translated in Greek as theocracy, power of God. In this political form, 'no one was subject to his equal' (Spinoza 2007: 224; cf. Di Cesare 2012). In Spinoza's view, theocracy, which remains a regulative ideal, is a condition for democracy. In the covenant with the subversive God of Exodus, in the experience of liberation from slavery, in the equality for all that excludes all dominion except that of the absolute Other, democracy emerges for the first time.

If religion is not culture. 'Holy Ignorance'

Many other instances of critique or unjustified attacks on monotheistic religions could be brought forth. What is really important, however, is to grasp the phenomenon in all its gravity. In its most recent and extreme versions, secularism reacts to the return of religions to the public sphere – a return it is unable to explain – by backing and even promoting the gap between culture and religion.

This multi-faceted gap has spread throughout the globalized world. The religious revival has undoubtedly provoked it. Whether this revival is a return or a conversion, religions often present themselves in the secularized public space with unsoiled vestments and a militant character. In this sense, the revival both responds to and is a product of secularization. This is why it is ambiguous to speak simply of a 'return' of religion. This implies that religion is returning in its traditional forms. In this sense, only the most fundamentalist and charismatic of religious forms assert themselves (Salafism, neo-Sufism, Evangelism, etc.). This is where the gap between culture and religion plays out.

These new forms reduce the polyphony of tradition from which they come into the unison of a single truth. In militancy, there is no time for the hermeneutics of texts. 'Religion' in its etymological sense deals with the bonds of tradition and with readings. But reading is an interpretative exercise that sets the text in motion again; it does not petrify it. To read does not mean to idolize a text, but rather to open it up to an infinity of meanings. For example, this is why in Islam the front line cuts through the text and divides the exegetes from the doctrinarians. It is a battle between those who read and interpret the texts and those who would appropriate them in order to dominate.

This occurs under less convulsive aspects in other religions. Olivier Roy spoke of a 'holy ignorance' to indicate the widespread phenomenon in globalization of religions without culture. He states,

> It is the relationship between religion and public life that is changing, for religious revival in the public sphere no longer takes on the form of cultural visibility but becomes a display of religious 'purity', or of reconstructed traditions. [...] in all cases it is the so-called 'fundamentalist' or 'charismatic' forms of religion that have seen the most spectacular growth, be it Protestant evangelicalism or Muslim Salafism. There has been a similar increase in hardline orthodoxy in the Catholic Church and Judaism, and even in Hinduism. Fundamentalism is the religious form that is most suited to globalization, because it accepts its own deculturation and makes it the instrument of its claim to universality.
>
> (Roy 2013: 5)

In the militant and fundamentalist version of religion, there is no request for knowledge and awareness, only faith. Here we find the indifference to traditional culture whence that indifference itself derives. God speaks without context. In contrast to what is often claimed, violence is not found within the text, but rather in the way that text is used, or better, abused. In this context, the text is ignored or reduced to a list of dogmas or even a manual for terror. The departure from hermeneutics is dictated by the presumption of being able to take a text to the letter – for example, the Torah as ***verbum misticum***. It is no coincidence that, in the Jewish tradition, the Talmud is decisive. The Talmud is the reading of the Torah that encompasses it in open dialogue.

Another way to say 'departure' from hermeneutics is 'deculturation' (Roy 2013: 5ff.). Roy sees this as the source of neo-fundamentalism. It is, in fact, right to state that the path toward peace and dialogue passes through the hermeneutics of the texts, especially those of one's own tradition. No dialogue can be had with the religion of another if you know little or nothing of your own. Only those who read the texts can open themselves to others and begin to see the affinities. When we are unaccustomed to the hermeneutics of texts or to reflection on religious concepts, we stand silent in the face of the ostentation of an alleged 'truth', which instead should be deconstructed immediately. Religious fundamentalisms seek to separate from the culture of origin. The Quran, the Gospels, the Torah require interpretation.

'Holy ignorance' wreaks disaster. It erects barriers between believers of different faiths as well as between believers and nonbelievers. All intermediary space is abolished and mediation becomes impossible. The common ideas and values that might tie the believer to the nonbeliever are disregarded or even removed. The believer stands as the sole exponent of what is holy against a profane environment that spreads to include anyone who might otherwise appear to be a doubtful believer or non-practicing believer. This is how polarization between neo-fundamentalists and secular partisans of modernity is created.

The traps of secularism

When we speak of 'holy ignorance', it is necessary to underline that deculturation is favored by the 'secular culture'. Furthermore, upon closer examination, a fanatic is none other than the mirror image that secularism projects onto religion.

If religion is blind faith, superstition, an accumulation of dogmas, slavery and alienation, it is the 'opium of the people' (according to a misunderstood passage by Marx), then there is no sense in studying or understanding it. In fact, Marx also considered religion exciting and a form of 'protest' against misery (Marx 1975: 394). If the former were the case, what would there be to learn or to know? If anything, religion would be an obstacle to culture that ought to be removed with a single, peremptory stroke. In this vein, secularism often appears no less factious than the fanatic.

What is the use of reading the Bible if you presume to know those pages contain only dogma and acts of violence? Not only do you ignore and brandish ignorance, but the old stereotypes burst forth with a vengeance. What can be more violent to others you do not know than to attribute them with an image they do not possess? Here, the doors of anti-Semitism swing open alongside those of Islamophobia.

The claim set forth by the 'culture of secularism' that mutual ground for debate may be created thanks to multiculturalism proves incomprehensible. In a world fraught with intermittent global war, the outcomes of such a debate are clear to all. In its proclaimed universality, multiculturalism is a kind of artificial language without depth that ignores and abolishes language. In this historical void where there is neither the sharing and exchange of memory nor the promise of a future, multiculturalism imposes bonds that remain abstract and ideas that are destined for uncertainty. Multiculturalism teaches neither the grammar of reciprocity nor the syntax of otherness.

Multicultural secularism does not mediate among different religions. Rather, it promotes deculturation and contributes to the widening gap between the religious and the lay. Here we find a significant difference with respect to the past. In the paradigmatic clash between Marxism and Christianity, there was ample and profound exchange starting from the questions raised and from the criticisms of the common experience of an unjust society. There is a wealth of examples that could be brought forth in this context, but it is enough to recall the theology of liberation. Starting from the 1960s in Latin America, the atheist left found a formidable ally in the anti-imperialist prophetism of the priests from the *favelas* who, in appealing to a sense of justice and equality, combined the gospel with class struggle. Here we find the link between modern socialism and ancient Judeo-Christian Messianism, which had previously been evoked by Rosa Luxemburg.

Today, the clash between the religious and the secular could not be more different, and this conflict is often anything but monolithic. Even the terms for the dispute are up for discussion. One must not fall into the trap of accepting the single version offered by secularism; on the one hand, there is the individual who with his or her unbridled freedom refuses all norms, and on the other, the believer who is subjugated by a transcendent and irrational order. Instead, they are two interpretations that are distant from modernity and two conceptions of human beings and their relationships with others that are almost irreconcilable.

Ethics drawn from the scriptures and neo-paganism

This clash is apparent in contemporary philosophy where it has been outlined in great detail over recent decades. The area where two opposing visions face off is in ethics. After Auschwitz, philosophical reflection has returned primacy to ethics, thanks mainly to Emmanuel Lévinas.

To prevent western civilization from drifting backward to a totalitarian or all-absorbing universalism, we must return to the texts, above all to the Torah. Only the study of texts can treat a sick western world as well as bear witness to the possibility of a new way of acting even before the act of thinking. The ethical primacy of action, as shown in the Scriptures, brings every secular illusion of autonomy into play and unmasks the western person who demands independence and the ability to dictate laws as he or she sees fit. It exposes the obsolete presumption of ethical autonomy and teaches ethical heteronomy. The unconditional assumption of the Law of the Other means that ethics exist wherever the other is welcomed. What would the 'I' be without the other who always precedes it? It is the recognition not of an abstract freedom, but of a liberation that, as in Exodus, is achieved each time with the other and within the other (Lévinas 1986: 72ff., cf. also 2016).

For Lévinas, the exodus from the being to the other is required to escape from this autistic syntax, this expectation of being the lawmaker of the universe and of settling everything by enveloping oneself in it and annihilating the other. Without this *ethic*, meaning a movement away from oneself and towards the other, the 'I' would not exist either. The world did not begin with me. Before me there was past immemorial, there is always the other that summons me, that questions me and to whom I am called upon to respond – simply pointing me towards the one who calls me. There is no choice, because in this turning towards whoever calls me is where the 'I' is constituted. Responsibility precedes liberty.

No command is needed to inform me of my obligation that ties me to the other: *hinneni*, 'here I am!' It is impossible to derive or explain this obligation, where my 'being there' always coalesces. The unconditional response becomes the shape of a new and ancient universal ethic (Lévinas 1983: 21ff.).

A close reading of texts accompanies a critical vision of modernity. In this sense, modern individuals, basking in the marvels of their western freedoms, are accused of being sovereigns solely preoccupied with their sovereignty, rendered helpless only in the face of death. In the manifestation of one's own emphatic identity and superb priority, this detestable 'I' is freed from any and all responsibilities and sets off in search of meaning for its life.

The condemnation could not be any clearer. While secularism clambers for and lays claim to freedom, this ethic opposes responsibility. But the difference becomes even more drastic. Beyond being secular or perhaps profane, the 'culture of secularism' appears instead to be pagan or neo-pagan. It is difficult, therefore, to find a common ground. This is the unprecedented phenomenon that has been emerging in recent years.

Criticism of paganism has been described by a number of scholars, including Hans Jonas. To this end, a tradition that was already consolidated in philosophy and theology is taken up again. But what does paganism mean?

Pagans are the stone walls of Mesopotamia, the hieroglyphs sculpted in the rocks of Egypt, and pagans are the oriental astral myths that designed the cosmic year, describing the eternal cycles of nature and even the Greek gods where those myths converge. A star is a goddess, a river is a god (cf. Taubes 1997: 37ff.). The search for the numinous and the sacred is pagan because it is the inability to move outside of the world. In the pagan world, folded in on itself, no one expects more than the eternal return of sameness. Not because the pagan world is uneventful, tragic or devastating. But here, life is carried out in that eternal return of sameness, which by no coincidence was celebrated by Friedrich Nietzsche at the dawn of the new European paganism. Tragedy is its representation.

In tragedy, where blame and punishment are muddled, pagans are tormented because they realize they are better than their gods, and so they rebel within that tormented world where ethical order has not been reestablished. But their brief revolt is no more than a symptom of their immaturity, or – as Walter Benjamin put it – of their 'moral infantility'. It is the simple impossibility of finding the path toward freedom. In tragedy, redemption – if there is one – is only occasional and limited. Franz Rosenzweig wrote that pagans are the self 'shut in itself', incapable of escaping from the elementary immanence of the world they see as concrete and eternal (Rosenzweig 1992: 222, Benjamin 1999: 111–12, 2014: 34–5). They end up setting the rhythm of their life to the cycle of nature in order to root themselves in that immanence and to devote themselves to worldliness.

In today's world, one can view liberty as simply a never-ending race from one idol to the next, with that same impossibility of moving outside the world. And neo-paganism may be hailed, proclaimed, even motivated under a theological and philosophical profile, or it may instead be a phenomenon that is unaware that it is often no different from the uncritical adherence to the religion of capitalism.

Bibliography

Assmann, Jan 2002. *Potere e salvezza. Teologia politica nell'antico Egitto, in Israele e in Europa*, Torino, Einaudi.

Assmann, Jan 2010. *The Price of Monotheism*, Stanford, CA, Stanford University Press.

Assmann, Jan 2016. *Il disagio dei monoteismi. Sentieri teorici e autobiografici*, Brescia, Morcelliana.

Benjamin, Walter [1919] 2014. 'Destino e carattere', in Walter Benjamin, *Angelus Novus. Saggi e frammenti*, Torino, Einaudi, 31–8.
Benjamin, Walter [1962] 1999. *Il dramma barocco tedesco*, Torino, Einaudi.
Cunico, Gerardo 2009. *Lettura di Habermas. Filosofia e religione nella società post-secolare*, Brescia, Queriniana.
Di Cesare, Donatella 2011. *Grammatica dei tempi messianici*, Firenze, Giuntina.
Di Cesare, Donatella 2012. 'De Republica Hebraeorum. Spinoza e la teocrazia', *Teoria* 2, 213–28.
Graziano, Manlio 2014. *Guerra santa e santa alleanza. Religioni e disordine internazionale nel XXI secolo*, Bologna, Il Mulino.
Habermas, Jürgen 2005. *Zwischen Naturalismus und Religion: Philosophische Aufsätze*, Berlin, Suhrkamp.
Hitchens, Christopher 2007. *God Is Not Great: How Religion Poisons Everything*, New York, Warner Twelve.
Huntington, Samuel P. 1996. *The Clash of Civilization and the Remaking of World Order*, New York, Simon & Schuster.
Lévinas, Emmanuel [1961] 2016. *Totalità e infinito. Saggio sull'esteriorità*, Milano, Jaca Book.
Lévinas, Emmanuel 1983. *Altrimenti che essere o al di là dell'essenza*, Milano, Jaca Book.
Lévinas, Emmanuel 1986. 'Esigente ebraismo', in Emmanuel Lévinas, *L'Aldilà del versetto. Letture e discorsi talmudici*, Napoli, Guida, 71–9.
Marx, Karl 1975. 'Critica della filosofia del diritto di Hegel. Introduzione', in Karl Marx, *Scritti politici giovanili*, Torino, Einaudi, 394–412.
Onfray, Michel 2011. *Atheist Manifesto: The Case against Christianity, Judaism, and Islam*, 2nd edn, New York, Arcade Publishing.
Ratzinger, Joseph and Habermas, Jürgen 2005. *Etica, religione e Stato liberale*, Brescia, Morcelliana.
Rosenzweig, Franz [1921] 1992. *La stella della redenzione*, ed. by Gianfranco Bonola, 2nd edn, Genova, Marietti.
Roy, Olivier 2013. *Holy Ignorance: When Religion and Culture Part Ways*, 2nd edn, New York, Oxford University Press.
Sloterdijk, Peter 2009. *God's Zeal: The Battle of the Three Monotheisms*, Cambridge, Polity Press.
Sloterdijk, Peter 2013. *Im Schatten des Sinai: Fußnote über Ursprünge und Wandlungen totaler Mitgliedschaft*, Berlin, Suhrkamp.
Soler, Jean 2002–4. *Aux origines du Dieu unique*, 3 vols., Paris, Éditions de Fallois.
Soler, Jean 2009. *La violence monothéiste*, Paris, Éditions de Fallois.
Spinoza, Benedict de 2007. *Theological-Political Treatise*, Cambridge, Cambridge University Press.
Taubes, Jacob 1997. *Escatologia occidentale*, Milano, Garzanti.
Trigano, Shmuel 2015. *Quinze ans de solitude. Juifs de France: 2000–2015*, Paris, Berg.

6 Theological roots of religious illiteracy

Martin M. Lintner

The ambiguity of 'religious illiteracy'

In his homily during Holy Mass on the solemnity of Pentecost 2016, Pope Francis spoke of an 'all-too-common spiritual illiteracy' that leads to an inability to pray and to recognize in every human being a brother or a sister. Spiritual illiteracy, he explained, is an expression of a paradox characterized by an 'attempt to be free of God, even if accompanied by a desire for his presence'.[1] Pope Francis did not use the term 'illiteracy' in the sense of a lack of *religious knowledge* but rather in the sense of an *existential experience* of a 'spiritual homelessness' as an effect of the loss of faith and trust in God as father of all human beings.

Even though spiritual and religious illiteracy are not the same, they are linked to each another. Spirituality is the very personal way of interpreting one's life in the light of faith. It is an expression of the quality of being concerned with religious matters and questions and as such it interferes with knowledge about religion and religious issues as a public or social phenomenon, besides with the personal ability to understand and use religious terms and symbols. Stephen Prothero, the chair of the Department of Religion at Boston University, defines religious literacy as 'the ability to understand and use the religious terms, symbols, images, beliefs, practices, scriptures, heroes, themes, and stories that are employed in [...] public life' (2007: 13). He diagnoses that Americans are deeply religious and at the same time more and more ignorant about religious traditions. He argues that an increasing importance of religion in modern society does not necessarily correspond to a better understanding of what people profess to believe. Believing often goes hand in hand with an increasing ignorance not only about other religious traditions but also about what a person believes in, and therefore is somehow related to a widespread religious illiteracy.[2]

In a similar vein, the Italian Church historian Alberto Melloni (2014: 5) understands religious illiteracy as an accepted lack of meaningful knowledge of experiences of faith, of Holy Scriptures as their basis, of ritual practices, of internal and external norms and of historical dynamisms in which they are integrated and by which they are formed. According to Melloni, religious illiteracy (in Italy) is both a 'religious phenomenon' of the present times as well as an integral part of an ongoing cultural development of school education and school politics. This, he maintains, reduces Religious Education to a superficial sharing of information concerning (the Catholic) religion (even though the term 'Catholic' does

1 See https://w2.vatican.va/content/francesco/en/homilies/2016/documents/papa-francesco_20160515_omelia-pentecoste.html (15 May 2016), last accessed 10 January 2018.

2 He says this in regard to the US-American society, but it undoubtedly also applies to the European context.

not describe religion *per se* but rather one confession within the Christian churches). In this light, religious illiteracy in Italy is the fruit of a radical laicism as well as of a short-sighted clericalism. On the one hand, laicism regarded theology to be a nonacademic, narrow discipline with the consequence of having it excluded from state-run universities. On the other hand, clericalism upheld improving the quality of Religious Education of the clergy by promoting the pious devotion of students rather than their intellectual capacity for theological reflection and critical comparison (Melloni 2014: 1–12).

Religious illiteracy becomes then a kind of precise indicator of a lack of cultural formation and of a critical intellectual capacity that reflects on various cultural, political and anthropological questions. Moreover, it provokes a lack of ability to face cultural and political developments, along with other religions and expressions of faith, critically. These three examples of spiritual and religious illiteracy, of Pope Francis, Prothero and Melloni, reveal the profound ambiguity of this phenomenon.

The present article will examine some theological roots of religious illiteracy. First, a differentiated understanding of the phenomenon of secularization will be elaborated as an inevitable framework within which to perceive religious illiteracy. Then, fundamental theological core issues that question faith in God, such as theodicy, Nietzsche's dictum of God's death or the real exigencies of atheism, will be explored in greater detail. Finally, the article will deal with the complex problem of the knowledge of God and of the understanding of theology as a science.

The context of secularization

The sociological as well as the theological roots of religious illiteracy cannot be understood without a deeper and a differentiated understanding of the process of secularization and the ideology of secularism. Both have characterized the history of religions in the different areas of Europe.

The ambiguity of the 'return of religion' in modern society

The thesis that religion would lose its public significance in the modern, enlightened world while being confined to the private life of believers has been proven to be unfounded (Kruip 2014: 85–6). There is no automatic relationship between the process of secularization or modernization on the one hand and the end of religion on the other. Religion is going through a stage nowadays during which it is regaining a new role in public life. Modern societies not only claim to be secular, but they are indeed pluralistic realities. Single members of a social community no longer share the same faith, traditions or world-view. Europe has also changed to such a degree that it can no longer claim to be Christian or to be characterized by a Christian view of the world.

The European religious landscape has become pluralistic to such an extent that one can find all kinds of religions and faiths here, and people from those who are explicitly agnostics or atheists, to those who do not confess or profess any religious belonging.[3] Having said this, it is imperative for citizens to find *common* values as a basis for their day-to-day life in a community. While these values might not necessarily be rooted in, or founded on, a common faith, they certainly have to be justified and presented through a reasonable and a

3 A brief, concise overview of socio-religious changes is offered by Regina Polak (2012: 81–5).

meaningful discourse. At the same time, each member of a society lives and acts according to a personal view of the world, which becomes evident in one's private life and in the public sphere, whether it is an explicitly religious view or not.

Different social studies on values, particularly that of the German futurologist Matthias Horx, have demonstrated a development characterized by what he calls a 'mega-trend religion' or a 'mega-trend spirituality'. Horx argues that while our times are witnessing a 'return of religion', its form is not an institutional one but rather characterized by new individual spiritualities (cf. Zulehner and Denz 1993, Denz 2002, Polak 2011), whose main traits are their lack of reference to institutional churches.

Similar literature asserts that 'spiritual life is no longer governed by bishops and clergy, but rather by the conscience of the individual and the insight from self-reflection, literature, meditation, discussions with friends and spiritual guides' (Mariański and Wargacki 2012: 26). These new forms of alternative religiosity are characterized by individualization, subjectification and the privatization of what people believe, and often do not face the challenge of an academic, theological verification. This also radically changes the way religions appear and leads churches to carry out a thorough assessment of why they are not able to respond appropriately and satisfactorily to the religious questions and needs of modern people (cf. Knapp 2006: 10, Amor 2014: 270–1). If one considers that 'the *Theologein* in preaching, catechism, liturgy, magisterial proclamation is a confessing, witnessing speech [...], a God-speech, which in its credibility and identification directly involves the speaker with his/her faith, just as it engages the "we" of the faithful in Christ and speaks to listeners and addressees in their individuality' (Hünermann 2014: 13), the churches have to ask themselves why their testimony and their God-speech in the ears of so many does not sound very credible.

However, since the horrific event of 11 September 2001, a new and a dramatic return of religion into the public life and political sphere can be noticed. The fundamentalist and violent face of a perverse manifestation of religion disseminates fear of, and resistance to, any form of religion. This may give rise to prejudices against religions in general, seeing them as dangerous and as an ongoing source of conflicts and violence. In this sense, religions would be seen part and origin of various problems, rather than contributing to practical and reassuring solutions.

This dramatic return of religion urges the western world and its secularized society to deal with issues of religion again. It proves that religion is not a mere private question of single believers but has a deep social and political impact. Religious institutions do not simply have a social function serving as a charitable enterprise in which their social role is often looked upon and tolerated in a secular contact. The return of religion is arousing not only a fresh, frequently ambiguous, interest in religion and in religious topics but is revealing anew a kind of helplessness to which religious illiteracy leads in a critical confrontation, especially with Islam.

Ignorance about religion itself and about the basic tenets of religious traditions produces a lack of tolerance and leads to deep cultural and social conflicts (cf. Moore 2007). The knowledge of one's own religion, or religious tradition, as well as the willingness to appreciate religious belief as such (instead of discriminating it as irrational obscurantism), together with the ability to understand and use religious terms and symbols, are indispensable conditions for a constructive dialogue among religions. These conditions are only occasionally met at present, for example in regard to the dialogue with Islam. However, from a sociological-empirical perspective, it is quite clear that pluralism is not a cause of religious illiteracy but rather reveals its serious and problematic nature.

Secularization and secularism

The development demonstrated creates challenges, one of which entails recognizing religion as a part of modernity. The process of modernization cannot be understood as a process of overcoming religion since tensions between religion and modernity are characteristic of the modern era. Conflicts between different spheres of values are home to modernity (cf. Gabriel 2008 who refers to Pollack 2003: 77–131). The willingness and the ability to engage in a critical and a fundamentally constructive dialogue with the modern world are required, which will occur by acknowledging the values and positive developments of the modern era and by overcoming the anti-modernistic notions of a 'bad', 'decadent' and 'antireligious' modern world. Religions, in their turn, have to accept that each one of them has lost its monopoly status and that the modern context is an open field of competing worldviews and different nuances of meaning.

For too long, the process of secularization has been understood by the magisterium of the Catholic Church in a purely negative sense. It is true that the historical process of secularization, which began in the late eighteenth century with the French revolution and was initially intended as the seizure of ecclesiastical property, was linked to a fierce struggle against ecclesiastical authorities and privileges. In this process, religious authorities and institutional religions lost their influence, including their social, cultural and political roles and governance itself. It was, of course, also a painful process of emancipation on the part of the Catholic Church. Nonetheless, the inappropriate, largely self-centered defense of its own privileges and power, as well as its sovereignty in the interpretation of religious truths, gave way to other values propagated by the process of secularization. Alternatively, emphasis now fell on the role of autonomous reason, the respect for individuals, the distinction between the reality of God and the secular world and, finally, the recognition of the autonomy and differentiation among secular spheres such as the state, the economy and science.

This self-defensive attitude did not permit the church to recognize the deeper Judeo-Christian roots of this process and to engage in a critical but constructive dialogue with secularization. Historically speaking, secularization is an exclusive phenomenon of the western or the Latin Christian world. It is not only one of the major consequences of the loss of religious unity in the Christian West but is more deeply rooted in the separation between immanence and transcendence, the profane/secular and divine spheres, norms and conscience (cf. Böckenförde 1977). These dualistic distinctions led to further divisions, such as those between law and morality, institutions and personal conviction, exteriority and interiority, objectivity and subjectivity, to mention just a few. These distinctions undoubtedly influenced the relationship between the churches and the upcoming nation-states by separating the church and the state, as well as religious and secular authorities (cf. Isensee 2008: 19–20).

However, this process was lamented as a loss of the church's social influence rather than an opportunity to regain authenticity and religious credibility, which were lost as a result not only of the political involvements of religious institutions but also of the dramatic religious wars in Europe. The real problem, that is to say, the decline of religious beliefs and practices in modern societies, was not recognized for a long time.[4] Religious institutions were far too busy fighting for their own social status and privileges, instead of responding to the existential needs and religious demands of the people.

4 According to José Casanova (2006), a leading scholar in the sociology of religion, European secularization has to be understood precisely in this sense.

However, the process of secularization offers religions new possibilities. Secularization requires the religious and ideological neutrality of the state, which has to protect the rights of both individuals and religious communities. The separation of church and state is based on an understanding that the respective religious and state authorities set the other's limits. Secularization, moreover, has to be distinguished from an ideology of secularism. Secularism, alternatively, can be understood as an extreme form of secularization which emphasizes not only the distinction between the divine and the profane spheres but goes further by denying any transcendent dimension. In this sense, secularism seeks to eliminate a person's transcendental aspirations and motivations. It requires the autonomy of secular spheres by denying the existence of God, hence not permitting any realities other than the secular and profanes ones. This standpoint does not acknowledge that religions and religious institutions indeed have something meaningful to say about the world and human life (Szaniszló 2014: 340). Therefore, whereas secularization is not necessarily hostile to religion, secularism is explicitly irreligious.

It is interesting to notice that in Europe there is a remarkable difference between the western and central-eastern countries. While new forms of spirituality are not strongly linked to traditional religious institutions, they are rooted close to traditional churches. In this sense, they are truly a western European phenomenon. In the eastern European countries, after the political upheaval of 1989 with the overcoming of state-sanctioned secularism, the Catholic Church did not go through a period of reinforcing its position, as it would have wished, nor were there developments of new forms of alternative religiosity (Gabriel 2008).

The percentage of people without any religious confession or practice is as high as before the political turning-point in 1989. However, these religiously unreachable persons are continually increasing both in the West and in central-eastern European regions, and the spread of religious illiteracy expresses a complete lack of any basic religious knowledge and of any interest in religions or religious issues. It can thus be characterized as religious indifference.[5]

The broad scenario reflects a complexity of religious illiteracy across the board. Having said this, a distinction needs to be made between those who are estranged or alienated from their religious roots, traditions and communities, those who are merely unaffected and untouched by religions and religious issues and those who see themselves as noncommittal nonbelievers (Tiefensee 2011: 161).

God's death and the theodicy

Theology after Auschwitz?

Johann Baptist Metz, a renowned German theologian, evaluates critically the aforementioned 'mega-tendency spirituality' or 'return of religion'. Instead of a renaissance of faith, he identifies an attitude that is friendly to religion but hostile to God (*religionsfreundliche Gottlosigkeit*). This leads him to speak of a return to 'religion without God' (Metz and Peters 1991: 14–67). Religion, he explains, is mistaken for a source of individual happiness, where there is a boundless tendency to seek a self-fulfillment that offers 'spiritual wellness'.

5 Cf. for a Polish and a Czech perspective Glombik (2014) and Kaplánek (2014).

According to Metz, religion loses its strength as a revolt against injustice and suffering by betraying the very nature of the biblical monotheism. In other words, religion is no longer a cry for justice and reconciliation. He continues that the most disturbing theological question concerns God and the suffering of human beings. His major theological concern is to reflect on 'God-speech after Auschwitz': which understanding of God can be found after Auschwitz, and how can one speak about it?[6] Without entering into an in-depth discussion of this very thorny issue of theodicy after Auschwitz, Metz's deep concern must be seen as a criticism of traditional theology, which often appears to be too idealistic and dogmatic.

In this light, theology must not be a closed system of unhistorical reflections on the articles of faith or doctrines. Otherwise, this would lead to a sterile discourse about God that is unable to face the realities of human suffering. Moreover, people do not need such a discourse that is foreign to the historic and personal dimensions of all human realities (cf. Metz 1984). Alternatively, theology has to be grounded in human abysses. It has to be a truly meaningful discourse, 'a speech of faith, hope and love, and as such it is not a speech about God and his salvation but a *Theo-logein*, in which God and his salvation refer to the One who empowers, creates memories and sends out people' (Hünermann 2014: 13) to those who suffer, who are victims, who are thirsting for meaning or feel the desire for love, justice and reconciliation.

Friedrich Nietzsche's proclamation of God's death

The following reflections recall the infamous Nietzschean *dictum* 'God is dead'.[7] There are undoubtedly different meanings of the proclamation of 'God's death' by the German philosopher and poet. It can be understood as a passionate rebellion against an oppressive weight of Christianity that was reduced to its caricature as a rigid, self-righteous moralization. It is also the rejection of the political abuse of God and religion. The very core of the axiom 'God's death' touches on the deeper dimensions of western philosophy and theology. It is neither the atheistic proclamation of God's nonexistence nor the personal profession not to believe (any longer) in a personal God.

The utterance of the expression 'God is dead' is nothing less than a clear realization that Christianity is no longer the prevalent force in people's lives. Christian faith, in this sense, no longer provides credible answers to the very existential questions of human beings. 'God's death' is the end of systematic answers to questions regarding man, nature and the meaning of life, the loss of a comprehensive mental horizon which guarantees the close relationship between divinity and reason, between the distinct but associated divine and secular spheres. The 'old world' with its flawed order has been totally forgotten. Religion has lost its 'innocence' because of its unnecessary political involvements and ulterior interests. Its understanding as a kind of existential insurance and orientation has become obsolete.

For some people, the Christian faith is no longer considered worthy of profession since it has lost its credibility. 'God is dead' is the definitive end of a 'sound trust' in God. It is revealing that Nietzsche understands religion as belief, i.e., as assenting to propositions and

6 Metz, together with Jürgen Moltmann and Dorothee Sölle, belongs to the first generation of German theologians who dealt with this issue, seen in the light of their own biographical experiences. Their prime concern was to develop a theology that is sensitive to the suffering of men, especially of the victims of violence and injustice. On this subject of 'Theology after Auschwitz', its different settings of priorities and its historical and theological development, see e.g. Ginzel (1980) and Kellenbach, Krondorfer and Reck (2001).

7 For the following understanding of Nietzsche's 'God is dead', see Lintner (2011).

assertions on the world and human life assuming them to be true. For him, religion becomes some kind of game of make-believe in which there could be a transcendental order, direction and sense, even though there is no sufficient reason for it. At any rate, Nietzsche does not understand the very nature of religion as faith in God. He misses the fact that religion is essentially a way of life and that it could be seen as an intense relationship with a personal God in whom the faithful can trust.

To Nietzsche, one could add other critics of religion, including Auguste Comte, Ludwig Feuerbach, Karl Marx, Albert Camus and Jean-Paul Sartre, among others. Their criticisms are expressions of the many faces of atheism starting from a methodological scientific one to a more practical and existential one. One also notices an atheism that is anthropological in nature 'in the name of men's dignity and human independence' and another one that is purely theological as a 'protest against God in the face of suffer and injustice'.[8]

It was too late when the church acknowledged not only that 'atheism has been accounted among the most serious problems of this age' but that it 'deserves a closer examination'.[9] Besides the admission that 'believers can have more than a little to do with the birth of atheism',[10] the church recognized her duty to 'strive to detect in the atheistic mind the hidden causes for the denial of God; conscious of how weighty are the questions which atheism raises, and motivated by love for all men, she believes these questions ought to be examined seriously and more profoundly'.[11]

Facing the true exigencies of atheism

Another German thinker, Klaus Müller, argues that theology from the outset of the modern era did not really do its 'homework' in carrying out a serious and critical confrontation with the real exigencies and the reasonable questions of atheism (Müller 2008: 48–50). This German philosopher and theologian identifies a double obligation on the part of both the church and theology.

The first concerns the hermeneutical question of the exegesis of the Holy Scripture. The historical-critical method is necessary but not sufficient. Müller explains that there is still the challenge of revealing how the interaction between history and fictionality originates speech acts which are truthful and, therefore, are capable of withstanding ontological requirements. Otherwise, there is the danger of reducing exegesis into social history (Müller 2007: 556, 2008: 49).

The second obligation is that systematic theology has to come to face the true needs of atheism. In other words, theology has to find answers to legitimate and reasonable inquiries. If this is not done, then one's faith remains immature. Moreover, one's perception of God remains anchored in a time when catechism had been taught in primary schools. Müller asks whether the lack of religious maturity is not a clear indication of profound deficiencies in the common theological education (Müller 2007: 556–7, 2008: 49–50).

8 Recent years have seen the comeback of a militant scientistic atheism, represented e.g. by Michel Onfray, Richard Dawkins, Daniel Dennett, Christopher Hitchens, Michael Schmidt-Salomon. See: Amor (2014: 270–1) and Striet (2008).

9 Cf. Vatican Council II, *Gaudium et spes*, § 19.

10 The Council text continues: 'To the extent that they [the believers] neglect their own training in the faith, or teach erroneous doctrine, or are deficient in their religious, moral or social life, they must be said to conceal rather than reveal the authentic face of God and religion' (*Gaudium et spes*, § 21).

11 *Ibid.*

It is in this same direction that the Jewish philosopher Emmanuel Lévinas tried to lead this conversation. He raised the question of God-talk radically in the face of the suffering of the innocent.[12] He stressed that the question has to be put in the right way, i.e., in the way that God must not be thought of as being part of the world. The question of theodicy has to be posed 'as if God did not exist', because God is not just an answer to the fact of senseless suffering and injustice. He is not just a consolation for the crying and lamenting victims. He is not just an assurance that 'in the end everything will be ok'. If that were the case, he would be 'part of the picture', but he is not.

The just person's suffering for the sake of justice urges theology rather to think radically about the absence of God from the world. Therefore, theology must overcome and move beyond false and infantile notions of God. Lévinas speaks about the need 'to void the child's heaven' in order to become an adult in faith. Lévinas claims that 'true monotheism must frame answers to the legitimate demands of atheism. An adult's God reveals himself precisely in the emptiness of child's heaven. That is [...] the moment when God withdraws Himself from the world and veils his countenance' (Lévinas 1995: 29).

Lévinas's reflection is not just an answer to the paradox that the absence of God, revealed by the suffering of the innocent, does not mean his nonexistence but rather puts radically into question any metaphysical notion of God as well as any – be it positive or negative – declaratory God-speech. True monotheism must not only meet the real requirements of atheism but must also come close to a practical atheism. It avoids God's thematization, even if it is a knowledge by analogy of the attributes of God (Lévinas 1991: 78). It is not possible to go into greater depth here of the question whether, according to Lévinas, the absent God becomes present in the responsibility of the subject towards the other. The metaphysical question of God turns into an ethical one: 'This reveals a God who, while refusing to manifest Himself in any way as a help, directs His appeal to full maturity of the integrally responsible person' (Lévinas 1995: 29). This raises, of course, new questions. Would not the only way to ensure any kind of God-speech be a kind of Biblicism, of positivism of Revelation? Or how can the faith in such a God be distinguished from agnosticism, in other words, how can a God about whom I cannot say anything be distinguished from a God who does not exist at all?

At this point, it may suffice to say that God should never be used as an existential insurance, as a consolation for the suffering, as a satisfaction of human desires or as an excuse not to raise an objection to sufferance and injustice. As Nietzsche said, faith in such a God has lost all credibility.

Theology as a scientific discipline and theological tendencies

The question of the theological roots of religious illiteracy touches on the concept and self-understanding of theology. It poses not only the question of what men can know about God but also that of who has the power to decide who can know what about God. It might be interesting to note at this point that one of the fruits of the Enlightenment was the distinction between authority and competence. Unquestioning acceptance of, or subservience to, authority was replaced by autonomy and personal responsibility (cf. Immanuel Kant's *sapere aude*). This criticism of authority provoked without a doubt a widespread aversion to authority and doctrines.

12 Cf. Lévinas's essay 'Aimer la Thora plus que Dieu' (1955), in *Difficile liberté: essais sur le judaïsme* (Paris, Albin Michel, 1963, 201–6); translation in Lévinas (1995: 27–32).

The tense relationship between Roman Magisterium and theology

In the Roman Catholic Church there are often tensions between the Magisterium and academic theology.[13] It is well known that besides the fundamental question of the correct understanding of the churchliness of Catholic theology, there exists a conflict between the Roman Magisterium and many theologians. The procedure of obtaining the *nihil obstat* on behalf of the Congregation for Catholic Education for faculty appointments in countries with concordats with the Holy See, as well as investigations of the Congregation for the Doctrine of the Faith into theologians, have caused, and still continue to cause, tensions (cf. Gaillardetz 2012).[14] At this point, the issue that has to be seen in the light of the understanding of the scientific character and of the scientific freedom of theology, especially in the secular context, will not be discussed any further.

If theology and theologians are suspected of not being intellectually free, they are not considered serious interlocutors. Whether justified or not, in the secular world there are reservations regarding the academic discipline of theology. The church historian Hubert Wolf reveals its historical roots in what he calls the 'invention of the ordinary Magisterium' in the nineteenth century as a consequence of the church's self-defensive attitude toward the Enlightenment and secularization. He characterizes this development provocatively as turning from 'It is taught what is true' to 'True is what is taught' (Congar 1976, Wolf 2010, Leven 2016). While referring to reason and history, many refused to obey ecclesiastical authorities. The reaction was that the Magisterium claimed ultimate doctrinal authority not only in the matter of the tradition of the *depositum fidei* but also of its authentic interpretation and evolution. The question is undoubtedly very complex, but the present religious illiteracy may be one of the consequences of these developments with their profound impact both on theological education and on the public perception of theology and its role in the academia.

Until the present time, the understanding of theology as a science that claims the scientific freedom of those who as theologians are engaged in academic theological research has presented a great challenge (Leven 2016). If this academic freedom is restricted by emphasizing an unquestioning obedience to the Magisterium, this represents a danger not only for the scientific character of theology but also for the academic credibility of theologians and the legitimacy of theology as a scientific discipline within the framework of universities. The academic context of universities urges theology to develop and profile its scientific methods, and the interdisciplinary dialogue and critical confrontation with other scientific disciplines help theology to understand better the world and human beings, facilitating the encounter between theology and present times. There is no doubt that Catholic theologians should be committed to the practice of the faith and to a sense of loyalty to the Magisterium, otherwise theological research would tend to be reduced to religious studies. However, this commitment must not be at the cost of academic quality and credibility. Theology has the role of both competent preparatory work for the Magisterium and a critical evaluation in regard to the Magisterium's pronouncements. Academic theology should not

13 Among the countless publications, see e.g.: International Theological Commission 1975. *Theses on the Relationship between the Ecclesiastical Magisterium and Theology*, www.vatican.va/roman_curia/congregations/cfaith/cti_documents/rc_cti_1975_magistero-teologia_en.html, last accessed 10 January 2018; International Theological Commission 2011. *Theology Today: Perspectives, Principles and Criteria*, www.vatican.va/roman_curia/congregations/cfaith/cti_documents/rc_cti_doc_20111129_teologia-oggi_en.html, last accessed 10 January 2018; Brinkman, Schreurs and Vroom (2003), Pottier (2016).

14 Cf. also the letter to the Congregation for the Doctrine of the Faith, in which theologians and bishops call for reform of Vatican doctrinal investigations (February 2016).

be understood as an interpretation and explanation of what the Magisterium says but has a true function as a sentinel against constrictions or even erroneous shifts. In order to fulfill this role, theology must be free from the exertion of ecclesiastic influence. Such a theology is of great significance for the Magisterium itself.

However, in the past as well as in the present times, the relationship between academic theology and the Magisterium has not been free of tensions. The concern of the Roman curia that academic freedom of theology would endanger orthodoxy has led too often to emphasizing the binding character of loyalty towards the Magisterium in terms of obedience, to the disadvantage of the academic character of theology. Such a theology risks being limited to the internal ecclesiastic sphere and no longer being able to face an open encounter and critical confrontation with the world, its challenges and questions. It is not able to face the challenge of a religious illiteracy that in part may be caused or reinforced by an academically weak theology or the absence of an intellectually strong theology in public education.

Theological tendencies

An even more thought-provoking question concerns what a person can know about God. It must always be taken into account that any speech about God remains anthropomorphically and historically mediated. Furthermore, according to Klaus Müller, theology did not sufficiently consider that any dogmatic God-speech remains conditioned by Genesis 3, i.e., the Fall of man (2007: 556–7, 2008: 49–50). In the perspective of a Protestant anthropology, there is the danger of falling into an 'epistemic pessimism' which is unable to recognize the true ability of human reason to apprehend the contents of the faith (Stubenrauch and Seewald 2015).

Luther's statements on the human ability to know God are ambiguous. On the one hand, he acknowledged that God has given every human being the ability to know Him, but, on the other hand, he claims the need for revelation to know God because of men's sinfulness. Without revelation, men would turn God into an idol, created by human desires (Kasper 2012: 75). On the contrary, the Catholic neo-Scholastic tradition developed two different theologies, commonly referred to as 'the natural' and 'the supernatural' (the so-called 'two-story-model' of theology). This ended up in a precise distinction between reasonable knowledge and faith and between the secular sphere and religion. Furthermore, in the framework of the doctrine of grace, the separation of the two spheres was reinforced by the construction of the idea of the ***natura pura***, i.e., of a 'pure human nature', which is understood independently of God's grace. This concept severed grace from nature, because grace was seen strictly as extrinsic to nature. Besides a natural knowledge of God, a supernatural one could be perceived thanks to grace and revelation. The problem was the unavoidable failure to find a relationship between the natural and the supernatural dimensions (Pröpper 2011: vol. 1, 271–319). Consequently, God's action of grace was marginalized to the private sphere, while social life and public issues, i.e., the secular sphere, were related to the 'natural order' (Long 2010: 141–3).

The Austrian philosopher Augustinus Wucherer-Huldenfeld elaborates the idea that faith is threatened by atheism as much as by fideism (Wucherer-Huldenfeld 2014).[15] If atheism is a lack of faith, fideism is a kind of 'too much' faith, confusing God's revelation

15 Thanks for this literature reference to Regina Polak, University of Vienna.

with one's own image of God. Fideism is not a belief in God but rather a declaration that one's own concept of God is true, which is based on a positivism of Revelation. As one's own idea of God remains between the religious experience of the inscrutable God and the world, this idea becomes an obstacle to recognizing the world as a source of spirituality and as knowledge of God. In such a fideistic theology, in the end, there remains no space for experience, feelings and self-understanding. It becomes a theoretical and doctrinal God-speech, a self-referential monologue, unable to engage in dialogue or afford (self)criticism.

Final considerations

There can be no doubt about a widespread religious illiteracy. The lack of a meaningful knowledge of experiences of faith, of ritual practices, of the ability to understand and use religious terms, symbols, images, etc. has a strong impact on both the individual level and on the public sphere. It affects believers, insofar as due to a lack of religious knowledge they may not understand what they profess they believe. It also concerns those who do not believe but may feel a deep desire for God's presence even though they reject God or any religious confession. Finally, it also regards those who consider themselves nonbelievers, for being unaffiliated with any religion may have roots in deep theological questions and concerns. Religious illiteracy, however, affects not only a person on the individual level but also the public sphere because religious traditions, practices and issues are part of public life. The process of secularization did not silence religions or drive them back into the private sphere of believers but also produced a pluralistic society in which religions gain a new importance and role. Dealing with religious traditions, issues, terms, etc. assumes all the more significance in a pluralistic context.

As theologians, we should not complain about religious illiteracy but rather seek reasons for it and find ways of overcoming it. The present article has examined some of its theological roots, such as the difficult questions about how to face human suffering, to cope with the experiences of human abysses or respond to fundamental theological core questions, including the human ability to know God and the Judeo-Christian roots of secularization. It has also dealt with historical failures to engage in a serious dialogue with fundamental questions that critics direct at religion. Furthermore, the open confrontation with atheism, in accepting its rightful needs, has also been explored. Finally, the article has tried to clarify whether religious illiteracy is the result of a false understanding of obedience, tolerance and openness to pluralism and of a mistrust of dialogue, as well as of reasonable reflection.

Even though the following words of Pope Francis were expressed in a different context (in that of the current reality of families), they may equally serve as an appropriate conclusion to the present reflection: 'We [...] need to be humble and realistic, acknowledging that at times the way we present our Christian beliefs and treat other people has helped contribute to today's problematic situation. We need a healthy dose of self-criticism'.[16]

16 Pope Francis 2016. *Amoris laetitia. Post-Synodal Apostolic Exhortation on Love in the Family*, March 2016, § 36, http://m.vatican.va/content/dam/francesco/pdf/apost_exhortations/documents/papa-francesco_esortazione-ap_20160319_amoris-laetitia_en.pdf, last accessed 10 January 2018. At the end of this contribution, I'd like to thank my colleagues, the Dogmatists Christoph Amor in Brixen and John A. Berry in Malta for their useful suggestions and critical feedback, and (the latter) for proofreading this paper.

Bibliography

Amor, Christoph 2014. '(Vor-)Überlegungen zu einer Theologie, die an der Zeit ist', in Martin M. Lintner (ed.), *God in Question. Religious Language and Secular Languages*, Brixen, Weger, 263–81.

Böckenförde, Ernst-Wolfgang 1977. 'Zum Verhältnis von Kirche und Moderner Welt. Aufriss eines Problems', in Reinhart Koselleck (ed.), *Studien zum Beginn der modernen Welt*, Stuttgart, Klett-Cotta, 154–77.

Brinkman, Martien E., Schreurs, Nico F.M., Vroom, Hendrik M. *et al.* (ed.) 2003. *Theology between Church, University, and Society*, Assen, Royal Van Gorcum.

Casanova, José 2006. 'Rethinking Secularization: A Global Comparative Perspective', *The Hedgehog Review* 8:1–2, special issue *After Secularization?*, 7–22.

Congar, Yves 1976. 'Bref historique des formes du "magistère" et de ses relations avec les docteurs', *Revue des sciences philosophiques et théologiques* 60, 99–112.

Denz, Hermann (ed.) 2002. *Die Europäische Seele. Leben und Glauben in Europa*, Wien, Czernin.

Gabriel, Karl 2008. 'Jenseits von Säkularisierung und Wiederkehr der Götter', *Aus Politik und Zeitgeschichte* 52, 9–15.

Gaillardetz, Richard R. (ed.) 2012. *When the Magisterium Intervenes. The Magisterium and Theologians in Today's Church*, Collegeville, MN, Liturgical Press.

Ginzel, Günter B. (ed.) 1980. *Auschwitz als Herausforderung für Juden und Christen*, Heidelberg, Schneider.

Glombik, Konrad 2014. 'Narrative Theologie im Dialog mit dem Indifferentismus', in Martin M. Lintner (ed.), *God in Question. Religious Language and Secular Languages*, Brixen, Weger, 177–87.

Hünermann, Peter 2014. 'Introduction', in Martin M. Lintner (ed.), *God in Question. Religious Language and Secular Languages*, Brixen, Weger, 13–14.

Isensee, Josef 2008. 'Europas christliche Wurzeln. Prägekräfte der europäischen Identität', *Die Politische Meinung* 461, April, 19–24.

Kaplánek, Michal 2014. 'Zum Dialog mit den "religiös Unerreichbaren"', in Martin M. Lintner (ed.), *God in Question. Religious Language and Secular Languages*, Brixen, Weger, 203–10.

Kasper, Walter 2012. *The God of Jesus Christ. New Edition*, London, A&C Black.

Kellenbach, Katharina von, Krondorfer, Björn and Reck, Norbert (ed.) 2001. *Von Gott reden im Land der Täter. Theologische Stimmen der dritten Generation seit der Shoah*, Darmstadt, Wissenschaftlicher Buchverlag.

Knapp, Markus 2006. *Verantwortetes Christsein heute. Theologie zwischen Metaphysik und Postmoderne*, Freiburg i.Br., Herder.

Kruip, Gerhard 2014. '"Die Hilfe, welche die Kirche von der heutigen Welt erfährt" (GS 44). Chancen und Herausforderungen der Säkularisierung für die katholische Kirche am Beginn des 21. Jahrhunderts', *Studia Nauk Teologicznych* 9, 85–101.

Leven, Benjamin 2016. *Unabhängige Theologie: Gefahr für Glaube und Kirche?*, Freiburg i.Br., Herder.

Lévinas, Emmanuel 1991. *Totality and Infinity. An Essay on Exteriority*, 3rd edn, Dordrecht/Boston, MA/London, Kluwer.

Lévinas, Emmanuel 1995. 'Loving the Torah more than God', in Zvi Kolitz (ed.), *Yossel Rakover Speaks to God. Holocaust Challenges to Religious Faith*, Hoboken, NJ, KTAV, 27–32.

Lintner, Martin M. 2011. 'Weh dem Entwurzelten, oder: Moral gibt Halt. Ein kritischer Dialog mit Friedrich Nietzsche', in Jörg Ernesti, Ulrich Fistill and Martin M. Lintner (ed.), *Orte des Glaubens. Christsein zwischen Beheimatung und Heimatlosigkeit*, Brixen-Bressanone/Innsbruck, Weger/Tyrolia, 69–81.

Long, Steven A. 2010. *Natura Pura: On the Recovery of Nature in the Doctrine of Grace*, New York, Fordham University Press.

Mariański, Janusz and Wargacki, Stanisław 2012. 'New Spirituality as a New Social and Cultural Mega-Tendency', *Anglojęzyczny Suplement Przeglądu Religioznawczego* 1, 19–39.

Melloni, Alberto 2014. 'L'analfabetismo religioso in Italia. *Actio finium regundorum*', in Alberto Melloni (ed.), *Rapporto sull'analfabetismo religioso in Italia*, Bologna, Il Mulino 1–12.

Metz, Johann B. 1984. *Glaube in Geschichte und Gesellschaft. Studien zu einer praktischen Fundamentaltheologie*, 4th edn, Mainz, Grünewald.

Metz, Johann B. and Peters, Tiemo R. 1991. *Gottespassion. Zur Ordensexistenz heute*, Freiburg i.Br., Herder.

Moore, Diane L. 2007. *Overcoming Religious Illiteracy. A Cultural Studies Approach to the Study of Religion in Secondary Education*, New York, Palgrave Macmillan.

Müller, Klaus 2007. 'Neuer Atheismus. Alte Klischees, aggressive Töne, heilsame Provokationen', *Herder-Korrespondenz* 61:11, 552–7.

Müller, Klaus 2008. 'Atheismus als Gegenreligion. Die Gottesfrage als öffentlich-politisches Thema – und was Theologie daraus zu lernen hat', in Magnus Striet (ed.), *Wiederkehr des Atheismus. Fluch oder Segen für die Theologie?*, Freiburg i.Br., Herder, 29–56.

Polak, Regina (ed.) 2011. *Zukunft, Werte, Europa. Die europäische Wertestudie 1990–2010; Österreich im Vergleich*, Wien, Böhlau.

Polak, Regina 2012. *Mission in Europa. Auftrag – Herausforderung – Risiko*, Innsbruck, Tyrolia.

Pollack, Detlef 2003. *Säkularisierung – ein moderner Mythos? Studien zum religiösen Wandel in Deutschland*, Tübingen, Mohr Siebeck.

Pottier, Bernard 2016. 'Théologie scientifique et théologie ecclésiale. Prendre soin du corps vivant de l'Église', *ET-Studies* 7, 107–27.

Pröpper, Thomas 2011. *Theologische Anthropologie*, 2 vols., Freiburg i.Br., Herder.

Prothero, Stephen 2007. *Religious Literacy: What Every American Needs to Know – and Doesn't*, New York/San Francisco, CA, HarperCollins.

Striet, Magnus (ed.) 2008. *Wiederkehr des Atheismus. Fluch oder Segen für die Theologie?*, Freiburg i.Br., Herder.

Stubenrauch, Bertram and Seewald, Michael (ed.) 2015. *Das Menschenbild der Konfessionen – Achillesferse der Konfessionen?*, Freiburg i.Br., Herder.

Szaniszló, Inocent-Mária V. 2014. 'Unumgänglichkeit der Säkularisierung und Ablehnung des Säkularismus in der heutigen postmodernen Gesellschaft', in Martin M. Lintner (ed.), *God in Question. Religious Language and Secular Languages*, Brixen, Weger, 339–50.

Tiefensee, Eberhard 2011. 'Die Gottesfrage in einem religiös indifferenten Umfeld', in Konrad Glombik and Benedikt Kranemann (ed.), *Die Rezeption des Zweiten Vatikanischen Konzils. Erfahrungen der polnischen Volkskirche und der ost- und mitteldeutschen Diasporakirche*, Oppeln/Erfurt, Redakcja Wydawnistw Wydziału Teologicznego Uniwersytetu Opolskiego, 157–70.

Wolf, Hubert 2010. '"Wahr ist, was gelehrt wird" statt "Gelehrt wird, was wahr ist"? Zur Erfindung des "ordentlichen" Lehramts', in Thomas Schmeller, Martin Ebner, Rudolf Hoppe *et al.* (ed.), *Neutestamentliche Ämtermodelle im Kontext*, Freiburg i.Br., Herder, 236–59.

Wucherer-Huldenfeld, Augustinus K. 2014. *Philosophische Theologie im Umbruch. Zweiter Band: Wider den ungöttlichen Gott*, 2 vols., Wien/Köln/Weimar, Böhlau.

Zulehner, Paul M. and Denz, Hermann 1993. *Wie Europa lebt und glaubt. Europäische Wertestudie*, Düsseldorf, Patmos.

7 Philosophical implications of religious illiteracy

Adam B. Seligman

Introduction

The 'collapse of the great secular ideologies' of the nineteenth and early twentieth centuries has left religion as a primary venue for the inculcation of meaning within diverse populations worldwide (Seligman 2014: 2). In traditional societies, but increasingly in secular European societies as well, the problems of meaning, of understanding our place in creation, the definitions of good and evil, as well as of the good life, of virtue and of moral action, are addressed primarily in religious terms. Despite the promise of the Enlightenment and of the nineteenth-century ideology of progress, it seems impossible to come to grips with these issues today without having recourse to religious languages, traditions and frames of reference.

The problem with this scenario is that it then becomes impossible to provide a framework of shared meaning without, at the same time, invoking a language of community; of belonging (and hence also one of borders, of definitions, of who is like me and who is not like me or who is like 'us' and unlike 'us'); of whom we can trust and whom we cannot; of the terms of moral credit, where granted (and to whom) and when withheld; and of where and in what circumstances the values of peace, empathy and community will trump those of abstract justice, security and individual rights.

If religious belonging is tied to ethnic and national belonging, as indeed it always is (and thus to their terms of trust and collective membership as well), and if religion is also seen as the realm par excellence of meaning and the inculcation of virtue and if societies are made up of different communities of meaning and belonging, as is increasingly the case in today's world, then the problem of shared social life takes on a significant new dimension (Eisenstadt 1995). In such circumstances, it can be argued that our attitudes toward our own margins, to the 'other within' becomes the defining matrix of our civilizational endeavor. Difference, whether communal, ethnic or religious, becomes the overwhelming challenge for which our received categories of rational thought are not always adequate (see recent controversies in Germany over infant male circumcision, in Sweden over kosher and halal slaughter or, in a somewhat more positive light, the emergence of multi-cultural jurisprudence and what is called in legal parlance, 'the cultural defence').[1]

The languages of belonging, of meaning, of definitions of good and of the *summum bonum*, are also always the languages of different religious traditions, beliefs and practices. The increasing religious illiteracy in contemporary Europe is thus of grave political

1 On circumcision, see the German court ruling, Landgericht Köln, 7 May 2012, 151 Ns 169/11. On halal and kosher ban, see Withnall (2014). On multicultural jurisprudence, see Renteln and Foblets (2009).

consequence as we seek to measure up to the rapidly changing societies we inhabit. The following chapter attempts to chart out some of what is at stake in our current circumstances and what we lose when we fail to come to terms with our own religious traditions.

Axial religions and the importance of transcendence

Max Müller, the nineteenth-century doyen of religious studies, famously remarked about the study of religion that 'He who knows one, knows none'. The comparative project was, in his mind, inherent to any real understanding of the religious impulse whose role in the lives of humanity could only be ascertained through rigorous, comparative study. Without understanding religions, there could be no understanding of Religion and hence a huge breach in our ability to apprehend the very project of human life on earth. Today, of course, it is the very study of any religion that is under siege as university enrollments continue to drop and scholarship is often caught behind the latest fads and popular publications in an ever-renewed debate between self-defined secularists and adherents of one faith or another.

Given the very strong connection of the religious impulse to what we term human freedom, or free-will, or perhaps, if we are social scientists, 'human agency', the current ignorance about the religious impetus in humankind is especially troubling. If we are to see in the human actor something more than a utility maximizer, or a function of predetermined biological settings or social controls and role compliancy, we shall need, at the end of the day, to encounter, or re-encounter the transcendent dimension of existence and the stand that we, as individuals and societies, do or do not take towards that dimension (Seligman 2000, 2009).

By religion, I refer here to those religions of the Axial Age, that period as defined by Shmuel Eisenstadt in which they emerged and became constitutionalized, that is to say, in the period between 500 BC and 600 CE.

> A conception of a basic tension between the transcendental and the mundane orders, a conception which differed greatly from that of a close parallelism between these two orders or their mutual embedment which was prevalent in so-called pagan religions, in those very societies from which these post-Axial Age civilizations emerged.
>
> (Eisenstadt 1982: 294)

The emergence of these Axial civilizations followed a period of institutional breakdown characterized by a similar breakdown of cosmological symbolism. This period, in Eric Voegelin's terms, of 'cosmological disintegration' resulted in a new appreciation of the relations between the individual and society to the cosmic order.[2] The change was accomplished through the fundamental restructuring of the relations between mundane and transcendent orders. As Eisenstadt and others have noted, the emergence of this conception in the civilizations of ancient Israel, Christianity, ancient Greece, China, Hinduism, Buddhism and Islam constituted a major force in the restructuring of the terms of collective life and of the principles of political legitimation (Eisenstadt 1982: 300, 301). For with the conception of a higher, transcendent order to which the political realm had to orient and legitimize itself, the 'King-God' disappeared and was replaced by the notion of the accountability of rulers and collectivities to a higher order.

2 On the symbolization of cosmic order and on times of troubles, see Voegelin (1954: 1–13, 52–110).

The Axial break (and the emergence of what has in other contexts been termed the great civilizations or historical religions) presumed a fundamental reordering of the nature of relations between society and 'the powers governing the cosmos'.[3] Breaking down their mutual interpenetration, the Axial Age posited a new conception of the social order, autonomous of, but in tension with, the cosmic (henceforth conceived of as transcendent) sphere. With the institutionalization of such a conception of a chasm between mundane and transcendent orders (between society and the cosmos) and the concomitant search to overcome this chasm, the idea of salvation entered the human consciousness.

With the invention (or discovery) of transcendence in this period, the magical, rather unitary and undifferentiated vision of cosmic existence became bifurcated by the ethical, by the call of a transcendent Being. Otherness was no longer represented as the otherness of demons, diverse deities or wandering souls. That *Hinterwelt*, the 'world behind the world' formerly attributed to magical coercion, was thenceforth projected outwards beyond the world of daily affairs and events (Schluchter 1979: 23). In this move, the otherness of enchanted nature took on transcendent properties. Within the western religious tradition, otherness was apotheosized in the logos of a personal Creator God. This was achieved primarily in the radical transcendence of the Jewish Yahweh (Berger 1969: 113–18). Against this transcendent being and its authority, totally beyond and outside the cosmos as it was, the very historicity of human existence was defined.

It is the authority of this transcendence that Søren Kierkegaard plumbed in the image of the binding of Isaac and which provided a new moral locus of self-identity (Kierkegaard 2009).

To quote Karl Jaspers:

> For the first time philosophers appeared. Human beings dared to rely on themselves as individuals. Hermits and wandering thinkers in China, ascetics in India, philosophers in Greece and prophets in Israel all belong together, however much they may differ from each other in their beliefs, the contents of their thought and their inner dispositions. Man proved capable of contrasting himself inwardly with the entire universe. He discovered within himself the origin from which to raise himself above his own self and the world.
>
> (Jaspers 1953: 3)

What was countenanced from a religious position was thus a grounding of the individual, not in a socially determinant yet accidental community of his or her birth but in a set of 'ultimate concerns', to use Paul Tillich's phrase (1957). This has provided an argument for human dignity and worth in all the monotheistic traditions. It is rooted in the very breakthrough to transcendence that characterized the Axial Age. Within the western tradition, with the institutionalization of the Axial chasm, the individual came to exist primarily as an individual-in-relation-to God, which, as Jaspers noted, is precisely what provided the 'resoluteness' of 'personal selfhood [...] experiencing the highest freedom in the limits of freedom in nothingness' (1953: 65, 63).

Each individual became a unique entity 'immediately responsible to God for the welfare of his soul and the well-being of his brother' (Nelson 1981: 43). The valorization of the individual is through his 'consecration to God'. It is, in Troeltsch's words, 'only fellowship with God which gives value to the individual' (1960: 55). As pointed out by Marcel

3 For this terminology and additional perspectives on religious evolution, see Bellah (1964).

Mauss (1985: 19–20), the notion of the person – as a rational substance, individual and indivisible – owed its metaphysical foundation to Christianity. And while one could argue with Mauss about Christianity as perhaps too highly contested a category, the connection to the Axial Age and the emergence of transcendence is not to be doubted.

Thus, the transcendent, the first fully generalizable other, becomes the basis for an unnegotiable sacred, one seen to exist beyond all possible social constructions, beyond all negotiations. It provides the definitive description to reality, especially to normative reality or rather to the normative aspects of our material reality. Transcendence, or rather the authority inherent to it, reorganizes the relations within the mundane realm. In this, it is quite distinct from magic, which relates to the supernatural precisely as another form of the natural that requires its own set of tools to mediate the impact of the supernatural on the world of man. Magic does something similar in the realm of the supernatural. Thus one may, in particular circumstances, need to sacrifice one's daughter in order to rouse the wind in order to continue the course of the fleet to Ilium (Seligman 2000). Indeed, a comparison between the sacrifice of Iphigenia and that of Isaac highlights precisely this difference between a magical manipulation of the cosmos and the bending of the will to the dictates of a transcendent deity. For transcendence is not concerned with building houses or keeping the wind in one's sails but rather with reorganizing the mundane world in accordance with principles now deemed transcendent in nature.

In this reorganization, the individual emerges as a moral evaluator (as, for example, in the prophet Nathan's admonishment of King David). The idea of transcendence provides a locus of moral authority and selfhood, albeit one foreign to modern sensibilities. It does so, moreover, without falling back on ascriptively defined and primordial categories of selfhood. However paradoxical it may seem to us, its very authority calls the self into being a moral evaluator, an agent in a sense other than power. Problematizing existence, transcendence drives the self to encounter Being. In this encounter, agency can become an existential and moral endeavor rather than simply the exercise of power.

A heteronomously constituted self is constructed in tension with transcendent dictates. This tension was expressed rather movingly by Voegelin as follows:

> These experiences [of transcendence] become the source of a new authority. Through the opening of the soul the philosopher finds himself in a new relation with God; he not only discovers his own psyche as the instrument for experiencing transcendence but at the same time discovers the divinity in its radically non-human transcendence. Hence, the differentiation of the psyche is inseparable from a new truth about God. The true order of the soul can become the standard for measuring both human types and types of social order because it represents the truth about human existence on the border of transcendence. The meaning of the anthropological principle must, therefore, be qualified by the understanding that not an arbitrary idea of man as a world-immanent being becomes the instrument of social critique but the idea of a man who has found his true nature through finding his true relation to God. The new measure that is found for the critique of society is, indeed, not man himself but man in so far as through the differentiation of this psyche he has become the representative of divine truth. [...] The truth of man and the truth of God are inseparably one.
>
> (1952: 67–9)

It is this that provides what Charles Taylor (1989: 93) termed that 'constitutive good' upon which individual selves as moral evaluators can rest. It is moreover, this truth that for philosophers like Hermann Cohen provided the basis for ethics in general, of which tolerance, is an instance. Thus, he notes:

> The correlation of man and God is in the first place that of man, as fellowman to God. And religion proves its own significance first of all in this correlation of the fellowman to God, in which, indeed, man as fellowman becomes a problem and is engendered through this problem. The share of religion in reason is the share of religion in morality, and no problem of morality takes precedence over this problem of the fellowman. The possibility of ethics is tied to this problem.
>
> (1995: 114)

The problem of the 'fellowman' is the problem of tolerance. And here we find a basis for human validation, mutuality, respect and tolerance predicated, not on any set of rights that the human subject carries, but rather on the very constitutive conditions of human existence in the world.

This is an idea shared among all the monotheistic, Axial religions in whose image of a Creator God the human was formed. Whether we look to Quranic injunctions against coercion in matters of religion, or to biblical decrees on justice for the stranger or yet again to the Sermon on the Mount: all give expression to a shared and fundamental truth of human existence as being somehow correlative to God and Being.

Religion and rights

As argued by some scholars, the very contemporary concern with individual rights, choice, the freedom of conscience and so much of what we consider morally, even ethically, irrevocable in the modern world, rests on these foundations.[4] An important example of this, which illustrates just how indebted modern ideas of individual rights are to religious principles, can be found in the interweaving of religious and secular dimensions that came to characterize the reconstruction of natural law doctrines in eighteenth-century America and the related idea of the individual as constitutive of the political community. This development was analyzed by George Jellinek, whose work served as an inspiration for Max Weber's own. As early as in 1895, Jellinek compared the American Bill(s) of Rights (from different states), the French Déclaration des droits de l'homme et du citoyen and, more significantly, the English Bill of Rights of 1689, the Habeas Corpus Act of 1679 and the 1628 Petition of Right. His conclusions are worth quoting as the USA has become in so many ways the 'ideal' type of western modernity:

> The American bills of rights do not attempt merely to set forth certain principles for the state's organization, but they seek above all to draw the boundary line between state and individual. According to them the individual is not the possessor of rights through the state, but by his own nature he has inalienable and indefeasible rights. The English laws know nothing of this. They do not wish to recognize an eternal, natural right, but one inherited from their fathers, 'the old, undoubted rights of the English people'.
>
> (Jellinek 1901: 48)

4 A recent example of such in the case of human rights can be found in Perry (1998). See also my critique of these very assumptions in *Human Rights Review* 1:3, 2000, 140–9.

As Jellinek sees it, English law offers no autonomous grounding of individual rights in a set of natural principles but grounds them solely in tradition, in 'the laws and statutes of this realm' (53). He looked to the defining traits of Congregational Puritanism to explain how the 'inherited rights and liberties, as well as the privileges of organization, which had been granted the colonists by the English kings' became transformed in the New World to 'rights which spring not from man but from God and Nature' (80).

The very success of natural law doctrine – based on self-sufficient individuals endowed with reason – as the foundation of the American political community rested on the synthesis of these ideas with the tradition of the Holy Commonwealth of visible saints, the transcendent subject of Protestant belief. Not only (transcendental) reason but also (transcendent) grace, redefined in the inner-worldly terms of individual conscience, continued throughout the eighteenth century to define the terms of individual and social existence in the civil polity. It was the very continuity of this religious heritage that made the positing of a political community of individuals – united by compacts – possible in eighteenth-century America and beyond. And thus Jellinek further concluded:

> In the closest connection with the great religious political movement out of which the American democracy was born, there arose the conviction that there exists a right not conferred upon the citizen but inherent in man, that acts of conscience and expressions of religious conviction stand inviolable over against the state as the exercise of a higher right. This right so long suppressed is not 'inheritance', is nothing handed down from their fathers, as the rights and liberties of Magna Charta and of the other English enactments – not the State but the Gospel proclaimed it.
>
> (74–5)

As Jellinek realized, individual rights in America were not derived solely from positive law but had acquired a transcendent justification unique in the modern world. Indeed, this situation constituted the foundation of modernity itself. It is, then, the religious or transcendent grounding of rights in that polity most defined by their existence – the USA – that has provided rights with their charismatic force in organizing the institutional aspects of social life. The challenge we face today, however, is precisely that of maintaining an ideology, and even more important a practice, of rights, without the transcendent locus that lent them their meanings in the first place.

In fact, the maintenance of pluralistic forms of society and a tolerance of constitutive difference may paradoxically turn on our ability to re-engage with other (often older) traditions and eschew the 'trump' of individual rights that has come to define our secular and liberal political order. One of the major questions we face is, in fact, whether religious belonging can be a forum for such re-engagement, one which can lead to new understandings of pluralism and recognition of ethnic and religious minorities – for which, of course, an engagement with religious traditions, rather than their current public dismissal, is called for.

Belonging

This is a major issue, precisely because that public reason upon which our liberal-constitutional and rights-based social order is predicated, has also left us bereft of a sense of collective belonging. By a sense of belonging, I refer to claims that can be made on us, or which we can make on others, that appeal to no sense of abstract justice or right, but solely on a shared sense of solidarity, trust and mutuality. To give a sense of what I mean,

I would like to quote the words of the local Boston ward-leader Martin Lomasney, which he related to Lincoln Steffens (1931: 618) at the beginning of the twentieth century: 'I think – said Lomasney – that there's got to be in every ward somebody that any bloke can come to – no matter what he's done – and get help. *Help, you understand, none of your law and justice, but help*'. This was famously quoted by Robert Merton (1967) to explain the perseverance of the political machine in American political culture. Legalized assistance, doled out by cold, bureaucratic organizations (welfare agencies, settlement houses, legal aid clinics, public relief departments, etc.) were all seen as involving a loss of self-respect. In an impersonal society, the political machine provided, in Merton's terms, for humanized and personalized manners of assistance that did not degrade the recipient. What the quote refers to is the chasm between enacting a regime of abstract rights and life in a human community of mutual care and shared belonging. As can be well imagined, each provides very different social spaces, experiences and models of civil life and civic enculturation. These are, if you will, precisely the differences between the rights-based provisions for communal membership, on the one hand, and a type of dense community based on principles of membership of the other.

The human needs for empathy, trust and solidarity are, of course, recognized today, as they were in the past, yet they are – to great extent – accepted aspects of the private realm, while the public arena is ruled by the dictates of an increasingly abstract reason. In more sociological terms, we may claim that the division of public and private realms (upon which so much in our conceptualization of citizenship rests) is, in many western societies, a parallel to a division between truth and trust, reason and empathy, justice and mercy. But, of course, the extremely complicating variable in today's world is how religious communities have come to represent that side of the equation associated with trust, empathy and mercy. And whatever else they are, religious communities are decidedly not universal, which is precisely where they come up against the rules of an abstract and universal reason and hence questions raised as to their relevance as models of civic identity; which is very much the situation in which so many find themselves today.

Liberal-individualist and rights-oriented societies have an idea of the public order which is secular, predicated on the idea of the morally autonomous individual and oriented toward the preservation of different sets of individual rights rather than the realization of an idea of *Good*. At the same time, however, we have more and more communities within the nation-state made up of individuals who do not understand themselves to be morally autonomous (but see themselves as enacting different sets of God-given commandments), who are not at all secular and who have very clear ideas of a public Good – indeed of a divine Good – that trumps the legal recognition and assurance of individual or citizen rights. The result is the establishment of two competing arenas of social interaction, expectations, mutuality, identity and indeed of civil commitment. The one defined by what I call *trust*, the other by what we could term *confidence* (Table 7.1).

To a great extent, today as in the past, the communities of trust, belonging, moral credit and shared moral dispositions are religious communities: replete with their own boundaries, terms of inclusion and thus exclusion, as well. They engage with the 'fellowman' (in Cohen's terms) precisely because they engage with particular individuals in particular languages of home, meaning and shared understanding. They defy abstraction and generalization and so challenge the very basis of abstract reason upon which contemporary societies are predicated.

For better or worse, they cannot, it seems, be denied and our refusal to engage with their claims does, it would seem, leave room for very different particularistic and exclusive

Table 7.1 Two competing arenas of social interaction, expectations, mutuality, identity and civil commitment

Trust	*Confidence*
Shared dispositions	Multicultural values
Moral community	Communities of rights bearers
Value of peace	Value of justice
Familiarity	Strangeness
Sameness	Difference
Shared moral dispositions	Disparate moral values
Shared experience	Dissimilar experience
Moral credit granted to communal members	No credit granted/Knowledge demanded
Others experienced as risk	Others experienced as dangerous
Risk leaves room for doubt	Danger requires security
Our group	Other group

terms of belonging and definitions of home (Eisenstadt and Giesen 1995). I am referring, of course, to the rise of right-wing, anti-immigrant and anti-Muslim parties and sentiments in Europe and the USA. For the particularism of primordially defined civic identities is of a very different nature than the particular languages of transcendent religions whose very engagement with the universal dimension of existence imposes obligations not otherwise apprehended or accepted.

Conclusion

To a great extent, it can be said that the twentieth century in Europe both began and ended in Sarajevo. The murder of Archduke Franz Ferdinand on 28 June 1914 and the outbreak of World War I brought an end to the complacent belief in material progress and amelioratory politics that had characterized nineteenth-century European civilization. Heir to Cartesian method and positivist science, the nineteenth century – more than any other period – believed that rational thought, empirical investigations and a presuppositionless universality would provide sufficient bases for the correct organization of the social world. World War I put an end to these assumptions.

What followed – communism, fascism, Nazism, the anti-colonial and national struggles of the twentieth century – were all, whatever else they were, forms of what Voegelin termed 'modern gnosticism': that is, movements focused around a divinized people, or elite (or class), who would usher in the *Endzeit*. Through correct knowledge of the true telos of history, modern gnostic movements sought to realize salvation through their own actions in history. However, as Voegelin warned, 'Self salvation through knowledge has its own magic and this magic is not harmless' (2000: 256). Though the destruction unleashed by these secular messianisms was incalculable, many continued to believe in their emancipatory potential throughout the twentieth century. The genocidal wars in the former Yugoslavia carried out in the midst of a largely silent Europe were the final act in the horrific dramas of the twentieth century.

An end, it was also a beginning. The mass murder and ethnic cleansing of Europe's major indigenous Muslim population, carried out in full view of the world, was to herald our contemporary reality of intransigent religious identities, the so-called 'clash of civilizations' and an increasing inarticulateness of all attempts at dialogue between different people, religions and worldviews.

For, rather than opening ourselves up to dialogue, we are, increasingly, closing ourselves off from the other. Civilization, in the sense of an organizing center of values, goals and structuring premises can only exist when it is open to its margins, to its limits and boundaries. When it turns in on itself and abandons its margins, it abandons itself. 'Civility' for Samuel Johnson meant 'politeness, the rule of decency and freedom from barbarity'. 'To civilize' was 'to reclaim from savageness and brutality' (1815). In many respects, our own conditions would seem to be of an increase in savageness and in brutality. The barbarians may indeed be at the gates – but only in so far as the gates are closed.

To remain open to the other and so to our own margins is a tremendously difficult enterprise. It involves recognizing our own extremely limited apprehension of truth. It involves our admission that transcendent Truth is, in its very transcendence, inaccessible to us. What must ensue from this realization is nothing less than a constitutive modesty in our epistemological assumptions. Truth can only develop in conversation, in dialogue – that is, through engagement with what is beyond ourselves, beyond our boundaries. What we reclaim from savageness and barbarism is, in the final analysis, nothing less than ourselves.

Not surprisingly, this theme – of the transcendent nature of the One truth and the consequent plurality of truths accessible to mankind, and the tolerance of difference that must ensue – was the subject of a crucial set of lectures given by Karl Jaspers in the University of Groningen in 1935 and later published as *Reason and Existenz* (1955).

There he noted that since it was impossible for man to have Transcendence as a knowable object, the highest demand of truthfulness was for each to act, according to his own truth – bearing in mind that this was his own truth only, and only apparently incompatible with the truths of others.

Jaspers is making a claim for the plurality of truths accessible to humankind, for difference, indeed for the ontological necessity of difference arising from the contingent, mutable and immanent nature of our own understandings. He is demanding a stoicism in the face of uncertainty and calls on us to recognize the particular nature of our own truth claims while, at the same time, refusing to retreat into an easy relativism. He is, in fact, articulating a call to tolerance, predicated on a belief not in relativist truths but in transcendent ones.

> There is the sophistry of easy tolerance which wishes to be valid, but not to be really touched. On the other hand, there is the truth of tolerance which listens and gives and enters into the unpredictable process of communication by which force is restrained; in such a process, man reaches from his roots to the heights possible for him.
>
> (103)

Tolerance of difference, of the other who is different, is for Jaspers not based on either indifference or relativism – but rather on principled engagement with the other, on a process of dialogue and communication that is, itself, structured by the very recognition of the transcendent nature of truth. Tolerance is thus not the solution to all contradictions. It does not make a fractured universe whole – as those modern gnostics noted earlier – but it does preserve the integrity of self, of the other and of their interaction. For without it, we are left with the eradication of difference which inheres to all attempts at overcoming multiplicity and plurality and which is in the final analysis but a succumbing to a form of narcissism, whether collective or individual. A mature discipline in face of the human condition is the best we can do if we are to avoid doing ill.

This is a voice we have heard often – though, indeed, we have continually failed to hearken to. It is the voice of Reinhold Niebuhr. It is the voice of Martin Buber and of

Emmanuel Lévinas. It is the voice that calls on us to see God in our responsibilities before the other. It is the voice which admits of the infinite plentitude of the I-Thou, and of the obligations it entails. It is, however, also a voice that is lost when we lose the language of transcendence and their 'carriers' in the great religious traditions of human history.

Bibliography

Bellah, Robert N. 1964. 'Religious Evolution', *American Sociological Review* 29:3, 358–74.

Berger, Peter L. 1969. *The Sacred Canopy. Elements of a Sociological Theory of Religion*, Garden City, NY, Anchor Books.

Cohen, Hermann 1995. *The Religion of Reason Out of the Sources of Judaism*, 2nd edn, Atlanta, GA, Scholars Press.

Eisenstadt, Shmuel N. 1982. 'The Axial Age: The Emergence of Transcendental Visions and the Rise of Clerics', *European Journal of Sociology* 23:2, 294–314.

Eisenstadt, Shmuel N. 1995. *Power, Trust and Meaning. Essays in Sociological Theory and Analysis*, Chicago, University of Chicago Press.

Eisenstadt, Shmuel N. and Giesen, Bernhard 1995. 'The Construction of Collective Identity', *European Journal of Sociology* 36:1, 72–102.

Jaspers, Karl 1953. *The Origin and Goal of History*, New Haven, CT, Yale University Press.

Jaspers, Karl [1935] 1955. *Reason and Existenz. Five Lectures*, New York, Noonday Press.

Jellinek, Georg 1901. *The Declaration of the Rights of Man and of Citizens: A Contribution to Modern Constitutional History*, New York, Henry Holt and Company.

Johnson, Samuel 1815. *A Dictionary of the English Language*, 14th edn, London, F.C. and J. Rivington *et al.*

Kierkegaard, Søren 2009. *Fear and Trembling*, New York, Feather Trail Press.

Mauss, Marcel 1985. 'A Category of the Human Mind: The Notion of the Person, the Notion of the Self', in Michael Carrithers, Steven Collins and Steven Lukes (ed.), *The Category of the Person. Anthropology, Philosophy, History*, Cambridge, Cambridge University Press, 1–25.

Merton, Robert K. 1967. *On Theoretical Sociology: Five Essays, Old and New*, New York, The Free Press.

Nelson, Benjamin 1981. 'Self Images and Spiritual Directions', in Toby E. Huff (ed.), *On the Roads to Modernity: Conscience, Science and Civilizations*, Totowa, NJ, Rowman and Littlefield, 34–66.

Perry, Michael J. 1998. *The Idea of Human Rights. Four Inquiries*, Oxford/New York, Oxford University Press.

Renteln, Alison D. and Foblets, Marie-Claire (ed.) 2009. *Multicultural Jurisprudence: Comparative Perspectives on Cultural Difference*, Oxford, Hart Publishing.

Schluchter, Wolfgang 1979. 'The Paradox of Reationalization: On the Relations of Ethics and the World', in Günther Roth and Wolfgang Schluchter (ed.), *Max Weber's Vision of History, Ethics and Method*, Berkeley, University of California Press, 11–64.

Seligman, Adam B. 2000. *Modernity's Wager: Authority, the Self and Transcendence*, Princeton, NJ, Princeton University Press.

Seligman, Adam B. 2009. 'Il secolarismo: condizione necessaria della scienza sociale?', in Sergio Belardinelli, Leonardo Allodi and Lorenza Gattamorta (ed.), *Verso una società post-secolare?*, Soveria Mannelli, Rubbettino, 57–82.

Seligman, Adam B. 2014. 'Introduction: Living Together Differently, Education and the Challenge of Deep Pluralism', in Adam B. Seligman (ed.), *Religious Education and the Challenge of Pluralism*, Oxford/New York, Oxford University Press, 1–24.

Steffens, Lincoln 1931. *The Autobiography of Lincoln Steffens*, New York, Harcourt, Brace & Co.

Taylor, Charles 1989. *Sources of Self. The Making of the Modern Identity*, Cambridge, Cambridge University Press.

Tillich, Paul 1957. *The Dynamics of Faith*, New York, Harper and Row.

Troeltsch, Ernst 1960. *The Social Teachings of the Christian Churches*, 2 vols., New York, Harper and Row.

Voegelin, Eric 1952. *New Science of Politics. An Introduction*, Chicago, University of Chicago Press.

Voegelin, Eric 1954. *Order and History*, vol. 1, *Israel and Revelation*, Baton Rouge, Louisiana State University Press.

Voegelin, Eric 2000. *Modernity without Restraint*, Columbia, University of Missouri Press.

Withnall, Adam 2014. 'Denmark Bans Kosher and Halal Slaughter as Minister says "Animal Rights Come before Religion"', *The Independent*, 18 February, www.independent.co.uk/news/world/europe/denmark-bans-halal-and-kosher-slaughter-as-minister-says-animal-rights-come-before-religion-9135580.html, last accessed 12 January 2018.

8 Is religious illiteracy a private or a public issue?

Vincente Fortier

Introduction

'*Laïcité*,[1] the word produces a smell of gunpowder', wrote Jean Rivero in 1949, in an article devoted to the legal concept of *laïcité*, adding that

> it awakens conflicting passionate echoes [...]. When the threshold of law is crossed, quarrels remain; for the legal expert, the definition of *laïcité* does not raise any major difficulty; very different designs have been developed by politicians in the heat of public meetings; but only one has found a place in official documents: legislative texts, parliamentary reports which accompanied their implementation have always understood *laïcité* in a single direction, that of the religious neutrality of the state.
>
> (Rivero 1949: 137)

Rivero's sentences have lost none of their relevance. On the contrary, today it is around this notion (which is a value for some and a principle for the others) that conflicts crystallise. Widely discussed, deconstructed, revisited, the concept of *laïcité* is the focus of all discussions. For some, it has become a magic word, as if mentioning it is sufficient to solve the related tensions of religious pluralism but especially, we dare to say, to fight Islam (radical Islam). For others, it is repulsive, as if it invoked an anathema on all religions. The fuss around the concept, the mass of conflicting information that accompanies it and the passionate tone of the debate give rise to confusion and misunderstandings in French civil society.

Becoming once again a controversy, *laïcité* generates deep rifts among the French population even if, and this is the paradox, it involves equality in the treatment of different religions, state neutrality towards the religious and freedom (of religion) guaranteed to all. While it soothed the tensions in 1905 by separating politics and religion (even if it does not use the term *laïcité*, this law is the keystone of *laïcité*), *laïcité* seems to be have become an anti-religious weapon and even more, 'according to the law built in 1905, an anti-theocratic weapon' (Valentin 2015).

In contemporary French society, several meanings of *laïcité* are combined – philosophical, sociological and legal ones[2] – which diverge, or at least overlap. This has always been the

1 We consider that it is impossible to translate the word *laïcité* because its equivalent in English does not exist. So in this paper we use the French word. However, we use 'secularism' for the French Observatoire de la laïcité (Secularism Monitoring Centre) because this Centre has itself translated the term *laïcité*.

2 As a short, French and relatively recent bibliography (because it is impossible to quote all the books on *laïcité*): La Morena (2016), Philip-Gay (2016), Hermon-Belot (2016), Leschi and Debray (2015), Baubérot (2012, 2015), Portier (2016), Willaime (2008), Roy (2005), Pena-Ruiz (1999).

case due to its polysemy. For some, *laïcité* is synonymous with religious eviction and wider, spiritual exclusion and leads to their denial. Others conclude that a set of humanistic convictions exists between believers and non-believers, to which everyone has agreed or should adhere. Others make of *laïcité* a kind of singular philosophical corpus, competing, should the occasion arise, with any religious body or other philosophical corpus. From a philosophical point of view, the concept is an intellectual construction which aims to prevent the influence of any denomination on civil society. Consequently, it does not allow the imposition of a civil religion in politics while referring spiritual affairs to the private sphere. While all these ways of considering *laïcité* are respectable and interesting, nonetheless some of them lead to an instrumentalisation of the notion, using it to control believers and aiming for a total eradication of religion from the public space, taken in its widest sense. Moreover, they can generate confusion and errors of justice when they are presented as legal consequences.

As recent examples of this evolution in France, we can mention that in the name of *laïcité*, the assessor of a poll insisted that a rabbi could not wear his kippah on his head when voting;[3] an advertisement announcing a fundraising concert in benefit of an association for Christians in the Orient was forbidden by the advertising office of the public bus company (RATP);[4] and, of course, there is a debate regarding faith-based meals served in public canteens.[5] Here the principle of *laïcité* is used in order to justify the prohibition of faith-based meals, which is a legal mistake and a perversion of the meaning of *laïcité*.

Such an evolution, whose typical example is the extension of the scope of *laïcité*, demonstrates how far it has been perverted and reveals a corrupt vision of the concept due to an illiteracy of the legal meaning – whether wilful or not – intended in 1905. At a time when France, in particular, is being struck by mortal attacks committed in the name of God, we can understand such a hardening of standpoints. For some politicians or intellectuals, it is the answer to religious radicalisation and violent extremism, according to the following reasoning: the attacks are committed in the name of God, so we need to be protected against this religion; *laïcité* is a protection; therefore, we have to fight religion in its name (Valentin 2015). But this is a 'falsification (misrepresentation) of *laïcité*', to quote the title of Jean Baubérot's book.

In this chapter, we wish to show that the illiteracy concerning the judicial and legal content of the concept not only leads to aberrations from a legal point of view but is also dangerous as far as fundamental rights and freedoms are concerned. Moreover it causes deep divisions in French society, which is pluralistic. In other words, what is at stake today in France is the illiteracy relating to the judicial content, the legal meaning of *laïcité*, whose consequence is an ideological and philosophical over-determination of the concept with the consequent impairment of its legal meaning and scope. Obviously, this situation of illiteracy concerning the meaning of *laïcité* is closely linked to an illiteracy regarding the freedom of religion.

3 Pascal Jan, 'Il a une kippa, on veut l'interdire de voter: juridiquement, ça ne tient pas', *Le Plus* de *L'OBS*, 27 March 2015, http://leplus.nouvelobs.com/contribution/1345655-il-a-une-kippa-on-veut-l-interdire-de-voter-juridiquement-ca-ne-tient-pas.html, last accessed 12 January 2018.

4 'La RATP donne une leçon de neutralité', *L'Express*, 7 April 2015, http://blogs.lexpress.fr/pantheon-foot/2015/04/06/la-ratp-donne-une-lecon-de-neutralite/, last accessed 12 January 2018.

5 'Le "vivre-ensemble" au menu des cantines', *Le Figaro*, 18 March 2015; Le Défenseur des droits, *Rapport annuel d'activité 2013*, www.ladocumentationfrancaise.fr/var/storage/rapports-publics/144000426.pdf, last accessed 12 January 2018; Observatoire de la laïcité, 'Communiqué de presse', 10 December 2014.

Laïcité: the meaning of the principle

As the Observatoire de la laïcité recalls,

> *Laïcité* is not one opinion among others but rather the freedom to have an opinion. It is not a belief but rather the principle authorising all beliefs, provided they respect the principles of freedom of conscience and equal rights. For this reason, it is neither pro- nor anti-religious. On this basis, adherence to a faith or philosophical belief is entirely a question of freedom of conscience for every man or woman.

French *laïcité* consists in three principles: state neutrality, freedom of religion and respect of pluralism, according to the definition provided by the State Council in its *Rapport public* (2004). In 2013, the Constitutional Council supplemented this definition:

> The principle of *laïcité* is among the rights and freedoms guaranteed by the Constitution: it implies State neutrality; that the Republic does not recognise any cult; that the principle of *laïcité* especially imposes the respect of all beliefs, equality of all citizens before the law, irrespective of religion, and that the Republic protects the free exercise of cults; it implies that the Republic does not pay salaries to any cult.[6]

The principle of *laïcité* has a strong legal basis. First, the 9 December 1905 Act, which does not expressly contain the term *laïcité* but which represents its keystone, proclaiming and organising freedom of conscience, freedom of worship and the separation between churches and the state. With regards to the last point, it means that religious ministry is no longer considered a public service. The state does not recognise, subsidise or pay salaries linked to any form of worship. Consequently, the state does not interfere in the way churches operate.

The 1905 Act defines the legal regime of the relationship between the state and churches. Without any explicit reference to *laïcité*, this law provides the framework, which is grounded in two main principles: freedom of conscience and the principle of separation. The purpose of the regime established by this Act was certainly, in the first place and besides stating principles, to decide the future of recognised religions, particularly the relationship between the state and the Catholic Church. It was necessary to 'pacify minds' rather than 'think of the religious neutrality of the state in an open and pluralistic framework'. For the founding fathers of the 1905 and 1907 Acts, in the latter one concerning cults, *laïcité* is not the repression of religions or the relegation of their manifestations from the public arena to the private sphere. It is the refusal of any control on the part of religions over the state and society, and vice versa, of the state's management of religions.

Article 1 of the French Constitution of 4 October 1958 stipulates that 'France is a *République laïque*'. 'It will ensure the equality of all citizens before the law, regardless of origin, race or religion. It will respect all beliefs'. Article 10 of the *Declaration of Human and Civic Rights* of 26 August 1789 proclaims that 'No one may be disturbed on account of his opinions, even religious ones, as long as the manifestation of such opinions does not interfere with the established Law and Order'.

6 Conseil constitutionnel, *Association pour la promotion et l'expansion de la laïcité*, décision 2012-297 QPC, 21 February 2013, www.conseil-constitutionnel.fr/conseil-constitutionnel/francais/les-decisions/acces-par-date/decisions-depuis-1959/2013/2012-297-qpc/decision-n-2012-297-qpc-du-21-fevrier-2013.136084.html, last accessed 12 January 2018.

To conclude this rapid reminder of the main texts, we must add the *European Convention for the Protection of Human Rights and Fundamental Freedoms* signed in Rome on 4 November 1950 and ratified by France on 3 May 1974. The well-known Article 9 stipulates:

> 1. Everyone has the right to freedom of thought, conscience and religion; this right includes freedom to change his religion or belief and freedom, either alone or in community with others and in public or private, to manifest his religion or belief, in worship, teaching, practice and observance; 2. Freedom to manifest one's religion or beliefs shall be subject only to such limitations as are prescribed by law and are necessary in a democratic society in the interests of public safety, for the protection of public order, health or morals, or for the protection of the rights and freedoms of others.

First observation: *laïcité* is first of all a framework – that of the separation of the churches and the state.

> It is the principle which characterises a State where all political and administrative powers are exercised by the secular authorities (which means not members of the clergy), without any participation or intervention of the religious authorities and non-interference in religious affairs.
>
> (Cornu 2002)

Second observation: 'French' *laïcité* is a principle which organises the relationship between the state and the citizens. Here, the dimension of the neutrality of *laïcité* is an obligation for the state and only for the state: it does not concern the citizens as individuals, except for those who work for the state, the civil servants. Civil servants must be neutral during the exercise of their functions but not in their private life. The dimension of 'neutrality' in *laïcité* is still a very important element.

Third observation: even if the state does not recognise any religion, it must know religion and recognise the religious fact. Equality between religions is ensured by the state. It is impossible for the State to favour one religion over another. *Laïcité* does not mean for the state an ignorance of the religions but indifference. The secular state guarantees freedom of conscience, which means the personal freedom to believe or not to believe, and acknowledges the obligation to make the exercise of worship possible (for example in prisons and hospitals, where it is difficult to practise a cult). The European Court of Human Rights regularly reminds us of how important the stakes linked to the respect of freedom of thought, conscience and religion are in a society which is characterised by a plurality of opinions and confessions. According to the European Court of Human Rights,[7] 'the role of the authorities in such circumstances is not to remove the cause of tension by eliminating pluralism, but to ensure that the competing groups tolerate one other'.

According to the French Constitutional Council, 'pluralism of socio-cultural currents of expression is in itself an objective of constitutional value'. In order to ensure its respect, which is 'one of the conditions of a democracy', it should 'necessarily comply with the fundamental principles of public service and, in particular, with the principle of equality and its corollary, the principle of service neutrality'.[8]

7 'Case of *Serif* v. *Greece*' (14 December 1999), *The International Journal of Human Rights* 4:1, 2000, 106–8.

8 Conseil constitutionnel, *Loi relative à la liberté de communication*, 86-217 DC, 18 September 1986, www.conseil-constitutionnel.fr/conseil-constitutionnel/francais/les-decisions/acces-par-date/decisions-depuis-1959/1986/86-217-dc/decision-n-86-217-dc-du-18-septembre-1986.8289.html, last accessed 12 January 2018. This decision can be applied to the religious sphere.

Last observation: religious freedom is a fundamental freedom which is protected from all attacks. In such a dramatic context as the one in which we are living, it is necessary to bear in mind, as a crucial and mandatory background, that the freedom of religion is well protected and is one of people's fundamental rights. 'Preventing terrorist radicalisation and recruitment will only work if we remain fully dedicated to respecting fundamental rights, promoting integration and fighting discrimination'.[9]

There is a well-known distinction between the internal *forum* (to believe, not to believe, conversion...) and the external *forum* (manifestation of the religion). Religious freedom is not, of course, unlimited: its limitations are posed by public order, general interest and others' freedom. For example, even if acts of proselytism are permitted (except in the public services, due to their neutrality), exerting pressure on conscience and any abuse attempting to oblige a person to change his/her own religion are firmly prohibited.

Laïcité: an ambiguous use of the principle

As stated earlier, today we can observe an extension of the scope of *laïcité* whose demonstrations are numerous and related to a political or ideological view of the concept. It distorts its legal content and also has consequences in terms of the stigmatisation of certain religions because of their visibility in the public sphere. The fact is that the judicial cases we have in most cases concern the Islamic faith and its prescriptions.

As an extreme good example of these distortions, of course, there is the Baby Loup affair:[10] it was an attempt to extend the principle of *laïcité* to private companies and, consequently, stood outside its scope as management. However, according to the idea that *laïcité* must be applied to both private companies and public ones, politicians and intellectuals considered this to be obvious. Needless to say, the Court of Cassation estimated that *laïcité* does not concern private companies – even the institutions which welcome young children – if they are not public. But the idea was approved by civil society and the media in the name of *laïcité*. This position illustrates the confusions about the true meaning of the concept. In the end, the court approved the restriction of the freedom of religion because of the internal regulation of the day nursery (and in application of the Code of Labour), not in the name of *laïcité*, which would have been an aberration from a legal point of view!

However, the debate is not closed. The very recent bill concerning the modernisation of the labour law forecasts in Article 2:

> The internal regulation can include dispositions inscribing the principle of neutrality and restricting the manifestation of employees' convictions, if these restrictions are justified by the exercise of the other fundamental rights and freedoms or the necessities of the proper functioning of the company, and if they are proportionate to the aim sought.[11]

9 European Commission, DGs, Migration and Home Affairs, https://ec.europa.eu/home-affairs/what-we-do/policies/crisis-and-terrorism/radicalisation_en, last accessed 12 January 2018.

10 The French procedures and the different decisions: Conseil de prud'hommes, Mantes-la-Jolie, 13 December 2010; Cour d'appel, Versailles, 27 October 2011; Cour de cassation, Chambre sociale, 19 March 2013; Cour d'appel, Paris, 27 November 2013; Cour de cassation, Assemblée plénière, 25 June 2015.

11 Assemblée nationale, *Loi 2016-1088 du 8 août 2016 relatif au travail, à la modernisation du dialogue social et à la sécurisation des parcours professionnels*, www.legifrance.gouv.fr/eli/loi/2016/8/8/2016-1088/jo/texte, last accessed 12 January 2018.

The Observatoire de la laïcité and the Commission nationale consultative des droits de l'homme (CNCDH) immediately requested the removal of this article, reminding the government that *laïcité* is a constitutional principle which involves the neutrality of the state and public services but which ensures citizens the freedom of conscience and of the manifestation of their convictions within the limits of public order.[12]

Article 2 permits the registration of the principle of neutrality in the regulatory rules of a private company, which is in contradiction with the French Constitution, the *European Convention on Human Rights* and Community law. According to these two institutions, this article introduces the possibility of a general restriction, involves the risk of absolute prohibitions without objective justification for the employees, aiming at all their convictions concerning trade unions, politics or religion. In this way, this article is opposed to the principle of *laïcité* and opens the door to eventual discrimination and to the development of communitarian companies.

A second example of this extension is offered by the universities.[13] We must remember that in France the law prohibiting wearing an ostensible religious sign concerns only public schools, not the universities. Despite the opinion of presidents of French universities, we have had several proposals for a law whose purpose is to forbid wearing a veil at the university in the name of *laïcité*. These attempts for the moment have failed but demonstrate the crystallisation of the debate around the concept (and the Islamic veil…).

Another example concerns accompanying adults (precisely Muslim mothers wearing a veil who are not employed by the public school) and the ban to which they would be submitted.[14] There is a kind of injunction of neutrality for individuals who are not civil servants: fortunately, in France there are two institutions (and judges, of course) which make sure that *laïcité* is well applied, the Observatoire de la laïcité and the Défenseur des droits. What we must note is that 'progressively, we have moved from a requirement of the respect for public order to a requirement of symbolic neutrality' (Valentin 2015).

The breach was opened with the law of 15 March 2004 governing, by the application of the principle of *laïcité*, the wearing of symbols or clothing manifesting religious affiliation in elementary, middle and public high schools.[15] As Vincent Valentin has written, '*laïcité* requires the neutrality of appearance for individuals, without any attack on either freedom of an individual or general interest' (2015). Hence, following this logic, several parliamentary members wanted to prohibit wearing a burqa in public: it was obvious for them, and for others, that this political ban of such a religious choice must be based on *laïcité* despite the separation between the two fields (religion and politics).

12 Commission nationale consultative des droits de l'homme, 'Communiqué de presse', 19 July 2016, www.gouvernement.fr/sites/default/files/contenu/piece-jointe/2016/07/communique_de_presse_observatoire_de_la_laicite_commission_nationale_consultative_des_droits_de_lhomme_0.pdf, last accessed 12 January 2018.

13 Observatoire de la laïcité, *Avis sur la laïcité et la gestion du fait religieux dans les établissements de l'enseignement supérieur public*, 15 December 2015, www.gouvernement.fr/sites/default/files/contenu/piece-jointe/2015/12/avis_laicite_et_gestion_du_fait_religieux_dans_lenseignement_superieur_public_definitif.pdf, last accessed 12 January 2018.

14 Conseil d'État, *Application du principe de neutralité religieuse dans les services publics. Etude demandée par le Défenseur des droits le 20 décembre 2013*, www.defenseurdesdroits.fr/sites/default/files/atoms/files/ddd_avis_20130909_laicite.pdf, last accessed 12 January 2018.

15 Assemblée nationale, *Loi 2004-228 du 15 mars 2004, encadrant, en application du principe de laïcité, le port de signes ou de tenues manifestant une appartenance religieuse dans les écoles, collèges et lycées publics*, www.legifrance.gouv.fr/affichTexte.do?cidTexte=JORFTEXT000000417977&categorieLien=id, last accessed 12 January 2018.

In fact, today, we can perceive an evolution towards the relegation of religion and its manifestations to the very private sphere (the internal *forum*, in a certain measure domestic life and the place of worship *stricto sensu*). Nevertheless, this position contradicts (French and international) legal texts and mainly the freedom to exhibit one's religion.

As Jean-Louis Bianco, the president of the Observatoire de la laïcité, asserts, *laïcité* has become a portmanteau word, and it is an absolute necessity to distinguish what is public security, issues of integration and the separation of church and state. There is an illiteracy about *laïcité* and thus a great need for information, training and education, which is crucial (Leone 2014).

Since 2000, we have been able to observe this evolution from a *laïcité* of kindness to a *laïcité* of control extended to public areas. Whilst we have lived with a liberal, broad-minded conception of *laïcité*, the risk is evolving to a very intrusive design, regulating religion. The 2010 Act concerning the ban of face-covering makes the public arena an extension of the private space. Certainly, the grounds of the law are public order, but it is not a material definition of public order (security, health) but an immaterial one: references to certain minimum requirements of community life.

Conclusion

It is difficult to combat this illiteracy concerning *laïcité*, and more precisely to fight against a false use of the concept (in its legal meaning) for many reasons. First, the dramatic events France has recently witnessed (the *Charlie Hebdo* attacks, Bataclan and Nice) promote the strict vision of *laïcité*. Indeed, all these extremist episodes of violence have a link with religious behaviour. One inescapable commonality among those that have committed the recent attacks in France, Belgium and the UK is that their political radicalisation is linked to their increasing religiosity. Nonetheless, and taking into account that 'the relationship between religion and violence can never be an immediate one and always presupposes human agency' (Bielefeldt 2015), we cannot ignore the role that religious ideology, as a complete system of beliefs, values and commitments, may play in people's decisions to act, at times, violently (Francis 2015). This means that religion could be either a motivation or a justification of violent extremism. Even if the religious message is false, perverse and corrupted, even if in this perspective, religion is instrumentalised for political pursuits and violent action, religion is assumed, in the recent and dramatic events, to be either the starting point (an *a priori* motivation) or the end (an *a posteriori* justification) of these attacks. Even when these violent and terrorist acts are presented or justified in religious fundamentalist terms, many studies challenge the idea that religious fundamentalism *causes* violent radicalisation. Instead, some authors suggest religion could be the 'excuse' or the 'vehicle' to perpetrate radicalised acts, not the reason and advocate for considering a complex interaction of multiple factors (psychological, social and cultural) to understand the phenomenon. Anyway, this factor can partly explain the 'radicalisation' of *laïcité* in French society.

The second reason is perhaps the difficulties encountered in explaining the legal meaning of the concept for the experts of the law and, obviously, the difficulties of applying *laïcité*. Indeed, there are decisions from our Courts which are not clear. For example, the different judgments about the presence of Christmas cribs in the public space (Prélot 2016) can puzzle everyone! Is a Christmas crib a religious sign or a secular symbol? It depends…

And the latest decision of the French State Council (9 November 2016) on this subject does not simplify its comprehension. Indeed, considering the variety of meanings of Christmas cribs and Nativity scenes (religious ones, of course, but also elements of secular decorations put up for the Christmas season), the State Council rules that the display of Nativity scenes by a public authority in a public space is lawful, only if it has a cultural, artistic or festive purpose, but not if it expresses a public recognition or a preference for a religion. In order to examine whether a Nativity scene display fulfils a cultural, artistic or festive purpose, or, on the contrary, whether it demonstrates a public recognition or preference for a given religion, the State Council offers some suggestions: the display needs to be contextualised, taking into account the particular circumstances in which it is exhibited, the existence or the absence of local customs and the location of the display. Given the importance of the criteria of the location of the display, the State Council distinguishes two situations: first, inside public buildings, where public administrations and services are located, a Nativity scene cannot be displayed, unless specific circumstances demonstrate its cultural, artistic or festive purpose. Second, on other public properties, given the festive nature of such displays in relation to the end of the year celebrations, Nativity scenes can lawfully be displayed, unless they constitute an act of proselytism or the expression of a religious opinion.

Finally, to reply to the question 'Is illiteracy a public or a private issue?' regarding France, the answer from our point of view is complex. There is undoubtedly a gap in knowledge and pedagogy[16] on all sides. It is necessary to educate people towards *laïcité* as well as to other religions, to promote interreligious dialogue and to work with communities and families. Furthermore, legal experts have to be hearkened and understood because the legal framework is the first basis of the rules of 'living together'.

Bibliography

Baubérot, Jean 2012. *La laïcité falsifiée*, Paris, La Découverte.

Baubérot, Jean 2015. *Les 7 laïcités françaises (le modèle français de laïcité n'existe pas)*, Paris, Maison des sciences de l'homme.

Bielefeldt, Heiner 2015. *Report of the Special Rapporteur on Freedom of Religion or Belief*, United Nations, General Assembly, Human Rights Council.

Conseil d'État 2004. *Un siècle de laïcité. Rapport public*, Paris, La Documentation française.

Cornu, Gérard 2002. *Vocabulaire juridique*, 3rd edn, Paris, PUF.

Francis, Matthew 2015. 'Does Ideology Really Contribute to Radicalisation?', *Radicalisation Research*, 6 July, www.radicalisationresearch.org/debate/francis-ideology-radicalisation/, last accessed 12 January 2018.

Hermon-Belot, Rita 2016. 'Laïcité, mais pluralité', *Archives des sciences sociales des religions*, http://assr.revues.org/27197, last accessed 12 January 2018.

La Morena, Frédérique de 2016. *Les frontières de la laïcité*, Issy-les-Moulineaux, LGDJ.

Leone, Fabien 2014. 'Jean-Louis Bianco: "La laïcité n'est pas en crise en France"', *Le monde des religions*, 12 May, www.lemondedesreligions.fr/actualite/jean-louis-bianco-la-laicite-n-est-pas-en-crise-en-france-12-05-2014-3915_118.php, last accessed 12 January 2018.

Leschi, Didier and Debray, Régis 2015. *La laïcité au quotidien, guide pratique*, Paris, Gallimard.

Pena-Ruiz, Henri 1999. *Dieu et Marianne. Philosophie de la laïcité*, Paris, PUF.

Philip-Gay, Mathilde 2016. *Droit de la laïcité*, Paris, Ellipses.

Portier, Philippe 2016. *L'État et les religions en France. Une sociologie historique de la laïcité*, Rennes, PUR.

16 As an experience of explaining and talking about *laïcité* from a legal point of view to the civil society at a large: Vincente Fortier, Anne Fornerod and Françoise Curtit led, in 2014–15 and 2016–17, with the University of Strasbourg (IdEx), the project called 'Les toiles de la laïcité'.

Prélot, Pierre-Henri 2016. 'Les crèches de Noël devant le juge administratif', *Revue du droit des religions* 1, 147–53.

Rivero, Jean 1949. 'La notion juridique de laïcité', *Recueil Dalloz* 31, 137–40.

Roy, Olivier 2005. *La laïcité face à l'islam*, Paris, Stock.

Valentin, Vincent 2015. 'Le dévoiement de la laïcité', in *L'après Charlie. Quelles réponses juridiques?*, Contributions présentées dans le cadre de la journée des Rencontres du Laboratoire Forces du droit, Paris, Université de Paris 8, 20 March.

Willaime, Jean-Paul 2008. *Le retour du religieux dans la sphère publique. Vers une laïcité de reconnaissance et de dialogue*, Paris, Olivétan.

9 Secularism and religious literacy

Francesca Cadeddu

Introduction

An understanding of the political, social and cultural reality of today's Europe necessitates a variety of 'alphabets' and expertise. In this perspective, knowledge of the religious alphabet is not only an added value but an urgency. Whether we are dealing with the tragic events tied to Islamic fundamentalism, the ethical issues linked to identitarianism or the values that underpin European democracies, faith communities offer many of the historical and conceptual signposts required in the practice and study of European democratic pluralism. The lack of knowledge of these signposts – religious illiteracy – renders the above-mentioned phenomena illegible, transforming – as most of the media do – migrants into potential terrorists and 'radical' faith into an excess to be feared.

An intervention aiming to turn this trend toward illiteracy around is absolutely essential. For two decades, the academic community has pondered over just how to go about such an intervention and, albeit at a slower pace, political institutions – above all diplomacy – have also started moving in this direction.

Strategies to counter this form of illiteracy are based on the understanding of the areas appropriated by the religious and the political spheres in various geographical contexts and of the more or less inclusive ways educational systems have accommodated knowledge about religion within their curricula. There is a direct relationship between these two elements that depends, first of all, on the meaning that the category of *secular* has assumed during various historical phases. It also depends on how, on the one hand, nation-states have drawn up a doctrine from the secular (when it is not an ideology) and, on the other, how scholars have defined the resulting phenomenon of the combination of the object-secular and doctrine-secularism: secularization.

An analysis of the literature concerning this question reveals how the issue is of particular interest in Europe and North America, with specific pockets also in Australia, Russia and the Middle East (Blinkova and Vermeer 2016, Crisp 2016: 207–26).[1] One of the more recent volumes on the topic, ***Religious Literacy in Policy and Practice*** (2016), illustrates this: editors Matthew Francis and Adam Dinham, who have a background in history and sociology, position the fundamental topics of the debate (e.g., historical and theological

1 Cf. Diaa Hadid, 'Jordan Tones Down Textbooks' Islamic Content, and Tempers Rise', *The New York Times*, 14 October 2016, www.nytimes.com/2016/10/15/world/middleeast/jordan-tones-down-textbooks-islamic-content-and-tempers-rise.html, last accessed 10 June 2018; Human Rights Watch, 'Saudi Arabia: Religion Textbooks Promote Intolerance', 13 September 2017, www.hrw.org/news/2017/09/13/saudi-arabia-religion-textbooks-promote-intolerance, last accessed 10 June 2018.

contextualization, welfare, Religious Education and human rights) necessarily in the western sphere.[2] According to the authors, this is where we find the urgency to identify a multitude of strategies for religious literacy that are capable of contributing to the well-being of democratic societies marked by cultural and religious pluralism. Moreover, although these strategies are to be interpreted and translated according to the language of each national context, they stem from an inspiration and common root provided by the selfsame process of secularization (Davie 2016: IX).

However, Dinham and Francis devote little space to diachronic profundity and do not offer any reflection on the process of religious literacy within the context of western history, following a common trend found in most of the North Atlantic literature on the issue. This approach, among the other effects, ends up by offering a more limited analysis of the geographical extension of the phenomenon than the reexamination of conceptual categories, the knowledge of different languages and the involvement of Asian, African and South American scholars in the European and North American research networks could provide. Nonetheless, it is true that within the diverse scenarios of religious illiteracy[3] there are at least two elements that unite the geographical area called the 'Christianized West' that are of use in order to understand the reason for this ignorance: the definition of the *saeculum* and secularization on the one hand, and the development of educational systems on the other. The aim of this paper is to examine a selection of the most recent literature dedicated to these two contexts and to highlight the topics that mark its boundaries.

Saeculum, secularism and secularization

In 2007, Charles Taylor's milestone work, *A Secular Age*, marked the beginning of a new reflection on secularization. It posed questions concerning the conditions that made it possible to create the areas that, in the 'enchanted' world of the 1500s, gathered together readings that ran countercurrent. In four short centuries, these alternative interpretations were able to replace a society that was entirely grounded upon divine design with one based on the equally important perspective of the fullness of life that focused instead on the individual (Taylor 2007).[4] Taylor's analysis follows the developments of the separation from the immanent and transcendent in the Christianized West up to modern secularity, where – according to the author – belief in God is one of many possible forms of commitment. Set within the rich debate that began in the mid-1990s,[5] the volume places religions and the *saeculum* on a level that is neither conflictual nor alternative, disrupting the subtractive prejudice of much of twentieth-century literature,[6] assigning to modernity a creative role in

2 See Dinham and Francis (2016). 2017 also saw the release of *Teaching Religious Literacy: A Guide to Religious and Spiritual Diversity in Higher Education*, by Ariel Ennis for Routledge, which focused on the methodology and content of religious literacy rather than on an understanding of the phenomenon itself.

3 Cf. Maria Chiara Giorda's essay in this volume.

4 For an earlier debate, cf. Norris and Inglehart (2004: 3–32) and Schultz (2006).

5 The two-volume monograph *After Secularization* of *The Hedgehog Review* (8:1–2, 2006), collects the most well-known and debated dissertations of the scholars that continue to dominate the debate today. Cf. also Stark (1999), Smith (2003), Stark and Finke (2000).

6 The divergence of views between Taylor and Jürgen Habermas is well known and can be found in essays by both scholars and in a direct dialogue in *The Power of Religion in the Public Sphere*, edited by Judith Butler *et al.* (2011). In this regard, cf. the monograph issue *The Religious-Secular Divide: The U.S. Case* of *Social Research* (Mack 2009).

identifying the ever-pulsing 'bulwarks of belief' and providing solid foundations for a philosophical reflection upon which to construct a new approach to the study of secularization.

In Taylor's philosophical perspective, secularism is no longer a goal achieved through human progress, nor is it the only refuge of reason where human rights and globalization can leave aside national, cultural or religious boundaries, yet it is not the outcome of a process of invention that springs from neutral ground, either. Instead, secularism is the result of the response of the democratic state to religious diversity (Taylor 2011: 36). As a consequence, secularization, the secular and secularism – respectively the concept, the category and doctrine of the state/ideology – require new definitions that are capable of describing the relationship between the religious and the political life of the individual and of the societies in different areas of the globe. This is especially true in light of the events that have influenced the geopolitical balance since the 1970s.

The studies published by José Casanova also tend to move in this direction. Casanova agrees with Taylor in holding that medieval Christian society carried out the role of a dyad hitherto utilized exclusively to define the status of a member of the clergy – religious/secular – and that this phenomenon of appropriation proceeded along two principle guidelines: one, aimed to 'spiritualize the temporal' – in order to render life outside monasteries religiously perfect as well – and the other, intended instead to 'emancipate all secular spheres from clerical-ecclesiastical control' (Casanova 2011: 56–7). In this way, medieval Christian society is thought to have acquired an imperfect dualist architecture that, in the first case, led to societies capable of including aspects of religious life within the public area, while in the second, it developed differently along more exclusivist lines. Regardless of how any historical case is situated within the spectrum of these two extremes, there is both an institutional and a spiritual faith aspect that indivisibly typifies the concept of secularization and favors an emancipation from the merely Eurocentric perspective within which the concept of secularization has developed. According to Casanova, a step towards this emancipation can be taken from a conceptual point of view if one allows for a shift in the religious/secular binomial on a global level – thus, decontextualizing it from western history and placing it within a broader framework that can define the areas of the sacred/transcendent/religious compared to the profane/immanent/secular. The point here, however, is that this operation reveals an evident paradox,

> namely, that scholars of religion are questioning the validity of the category of 'religion' at the very same moment when the discursive reality of religion is more widespread than ever and has become for the first time global. [...] 'religion' as a discursive reality, indeed, as an abstract category and as a system of classification of reality, used by modern individuals as well as by modern societies across the world, by religious as well as by secular authorities, has become an undisputable global social fact.
>
> (Casanova 2011: 62)

'Religion' is a global social fact, but, at the same time, it can acquire different meanings within each historical, political and cultural context. We might say this is also mirrored by the 'secular', which acquires the same plurality of meanings, bringing about a multitude of forms for regulating the religious in the public sphere and for managing religious pluralism in societies: secularisms.

What meanings do secularisms assume in contemporary European society? To agree with Casanova, it is certainly possible to distinguish between a secularism-doctrine of the state and secularism-ideology: the two are fundamentally distinct in their manner of exercising authority over the boundaries of the 'religious' and the 'political':

> Political secularism falls easily into secularist ideology when the political arrogates for itself an absolute, sovereign, quasi-sacred, quasi-transcendent character or when the secular arrogates for itself the mantle of rationality and universality, while claiming that 'religion' is essentially non-rational, particularistic, and intolerant (or illiberal) and, as such, dangerous and a threat to democratic politics once it enters the public sphere.
>
> (Casanova 2011: 69)

When secularism becomes prescriptive, therefore, it inhibits the public sphere and forces faith into the private one.

However, wherever religion – especially a minoritarian religion – manifests itself with symbols, sites and rituals, it entails a necessary, continual and constant institutional adjustment. In most cases (those of France, Italy and Turkey being the most familiar), this adjustment does not find a normative equilibrium that is capable of effectively guaranteeing equal rights for all subjects involved. The solution to this impasse caused by the difficulty in drawing the boundaries between the public and the private can be found in that area where the philosophy of law shifts whenever it encounters religious rights. Taylor holds that such a solution is provided by the construction of an overlapping consensus (inspired by John Rawls) on individual policies, where each actor arrives at on the basis of moral, religious and/or political convictions, thereby guaranteeing the functioning of society without the need for each subject involved to share the initial reasons or arguments of the others. In the face of the urgency to provide answers to radical positions – for example, in cases of blasphemy or of religious fundamentalism – others, like Akeel Bilgrami, have proposed different solutions. These alternatives set political ideals (usually sanctioned by fundamental or constitutional rights) before all others (Bilgrami 2014: 87); otherwise they have advanced a cooperative approach regulated according to rules of collision that are established on different levels in each instance (Ladeur 2014: 50).

It is not until 2011 that we find a proposal for the rehabilitation of secularism. Rajeev Bhargava (2011) puts forth this idea, rooted in the historical and political experience, and the normative practices, of countries such as France, England, the USA and, above all, India. In terms of political theory, in an environment that is significantly multi-religious, the case of India has the merit of including a whole series of good practices and constitutional features that consider, among other elements: the individual and collective dimension and the rights that we should accord them; the difference between public and political; the idea of *principled distance* that

> entails a flexible approach to the question of inclusion or exclusion of religion and the engagement or disengagement of the state, which at the third level of law and policy depends on the context, nature, or current state of relevant religions. This engagement must be governed by principles undergirding a secular state, that is, principles that flow from a commitment to the values mentioned above [peace, toleration, religious liberty, and equality of citizenship in both its passive dimension and its active dimension]. This means that religion may intervene in the affairs of the state if such intervention promotes freedom, equality, or any other value integral to secularism. [...] Equally, the state may engage with religion or disengage from it, engage positively or negatively, but it does so depending entirely on whether or not these values are promoted or undermined. A state that intervenes or refrains from interference on this basis keeps a principled distance from all religions.
>
> (Bhargava 2011: 105)[7]

7 See also Bhargava (1998, 2007).

Far from imagining that these strongly contextualized characteristics could be freely applied everywhere, Bhargava posits that we can, and must, abandon the idea of the necessary opposition between the secular and the religious in favor of an institutional, social and political situation that promotes an interpretation of the world as a place inhabited by the religious and the nonreligious, that minimizes the possibility that processes of inclusion be dominated by interreligious or intra-religious dynamics or by a pre-eminence of the religious over the secular or vice-versa (111).

The development of educational systems

The ways in which the religious and the secular not only imagine themselves but also take on actual form through norms, customs, recognized rights, denied protections, narrated stories and recollected memories have the power to determine the degree to which religions may take part in public discourse and in which alphabet this discourse should occur. Denying (or offering) religions the spotlight in public life means removing them from being subjects of knowledge and of criticism (or exposing them to both).

Educational systems, the mass media and public actors play a pivotal role in the construction of knowledge and of what we call religious literacy,[8] that is, the multiple functional utilization of 'tools for the knowledge of an experience of faith, the sacred texts that underlie them, their cultural practices, their internal and external norms, and the historical dynamisms that have accompanied and modified them' (Melloni 2014: 5).

Wherever this form of literacy is lacking, it is the duty of historians to understand the vicissitudes and motivations rather than indicate the remedies. Owing to the various models that connect religions to education in Europe and to the privileges that to varying degrees are agreed upon or established for the majority of religions and the conflicts that these continue to cause, if the objective is thus to think rationally about how to create areas for religious literacy, not only should we rethink the place that religion holds in the public sphere in general, but above all, we must reexamine the historical origins of this place in the educational system.

Today, the most thorough historical analysis in terms of geographic extension, analytical outlook and type of sources utilized is *De la séparation des églises et de l'école mise en perspective historique*, by Benoît Mély, published posthumously in 2004. This work is the result of research carried out in Germany, France, Great Britain and Italy based on documents produced between 1789 and 1914 regarding the role of religion in primary and secondary education. It deconstructs the exceptionalism of French *laïcité*, setting it within a broader movement of European ideas that defined its identity between the nineteenth and twentieth century.

The uniqueness of Mély's research lies in its capacity to entwine the history of the debate on churches' monopoly of education; the history of the struggle for the complete liberation of educational systems from the clergy and from any form of religious instruction; and secularization, understood as 'la dislocation accélérée de cette conception du monde centrée sur l'importance primordiale à accorder au salut' (Mély 2004: 16). The result is a profound challenge to, and criticism of, the dichotomy between 'Catholic states' and 'Protestant states', which, according to a large amount of historiography, characterized two different models of conflict between states and churches. In Catholic states, this unrest led

8 The European Council defines functional literacy as 'the ability to read and write at a level that enables someone to develop and function in society, at home, at school and at work' concluding with multiple literacy, 'the ability to use reading and writing skills in order to produce, understand, interpret and critically evaluate written information' (Cadeddu 2014: 100).

to a violent separation within and outside schools, while in Protestant ones the separation resulted in progressive differentiation. As a consequence, hostility to church influence in schools is thought to have been a historic fact known only in 'Catholic countries' and not 'Protestant' ones. The author demonstrates, instead, how 'la nécessité de donner au peuple une solide instruction religieuse qui enseigne avant tout la docilité envers les pouvoirs établis' is part of an international process, which, in this case, was eventually interpreted and translated according to the nationalization or the laicization of modern educational systems.

As early as World War I, the monopoly of national churches over school education finds itself entirely displaced. According to Mély, if this is the case, it is because it underwent an initial revolutionary phase marked by anticlericalism and by French liberalism. This was then followed by the return of separatist expectations within the boundaries of resistance for the whole of the first half of the nineteenth century (which did not, however, lead to political consolidation) and then to its rekindling – with various manifestations depending on the nation – with the Forster Law, *Kulturkampf* and the *Risorgimento*. These gave rise to the ambiguity felt in each of these contexts in the first decade of the twentieth century. Indeed, Germany, France, Great Britain and Italy all engaged in a heated political debate on the privatization of faith (which does not necessarily correspond to a decline in any membership of a religion or doctrine on the part of the working classes); on the maturation of an idea of human and scientific progress (which in many cases derived its motivation from the Scriptures) and on the birth of a 'national religion'. By contrast, within churches there emerged situations in which questions began to be asked about the possibility of adapting doctrine to the modern world, about the relationship between science and theology and about the social message of the Scriptures. In this setting, certain balances developed concerning the position of religion in national educational systems, which from the beginning of reforms in the 1870s would undergo no significant transformations until the outbreak of World War I in 1914.[9]

A well-structured analysis that considers the plurality of voices of both minorities and the majorities in power, capable of signposting moments of common shifts in a multitude of national contexts – thus reducing their exceptional nature – and of examining the history of events and European thought (and of many of its actors) in depth and without bias, is the way in which religious literacy in Europe must be examined.

Conclusions

We have seen how the study of European secularization encompasses a broad range of visions of the totality of elements that make it possible to trace the dynamics of the common social, political and institutional development of states. However, when we wish to fully understand how these dynamics have influenced the history of education in its European totality, research no longer remains simple for two specific reasons. The first is the issue itself: the study of religion in schools is overwhelmed by the presence of different forms of Religious Education within specific instruction programs and precise time frames, and is not carried out in any systematic analysis within the overall school curricula. The second involves the establishment of disciplinary boundaries: sociologists, anthropologists, experts

9 For a broader outline of studies on the international relations between states and the Holy See cf. Melloni, Cavagnini and Grossi 2017.

in political affairs and jurists are seldom coupled with historians and theologians in the understanding of such phenomena. This in no way means that the study of Religious Education is not of the utmost importance in order to understand the current situation in Europe and to face the challenges posed by the social and political context of the times;[10] rather, it highlights the need for studies that lay out a comparative historical framework that also considers the political dynamics leading to policy choices involving the role of faith communities in the public sphere, that take into account the social equilibriums that influence the perception of the place these communities occupy and that address the educational and informative choices that introduce such communities' language – their alphabet – into the public debate.

These kinds of studies offer a multitude of benefits. Without a doubt, the first involves the benefit of critical knowledge itself, which is equally capable of questioning political and religious institutions and the illiteracies caused by the media as it is of enriching and being enriched by the interdisciplinary knowledge able to respond to societal changes.[11]

Furthermore, there is an additional reduction in social costs, upon which Paolo Naso remarked in an analysis of the case of Italy, which can easily be extended to Europe in general. It is difficult – if not impossible – to quantify the social costs of religious illiteracy in Europe, but its fallout on a social level has assumed alarming dimensions, and the fact that it has a material relevance 'on the quality of community relations and on the quality of multicultural and multi-religious cohabitation' (Naso 2014: 45) is undeniable. The reduction in this cost is the result of policies that have been able to offer long-term projects of sustainable social inclusion and which offer alternatives to the creation of ghettos through religious construction. Costs are also reduced through educational programs capable of engaging in a dialogue with students whose families or backgrounds are still anchored to cultures (including religious cultures) that are different from those of their current residence. Further policies that welcome migrants contribute to the social costs reduction through the preservation of religious identity as an essential element in an individual's life while at the same time trying to avoid the propagation of stereotypes.

On the contrary, the benefits of devoting greater attention to religious diversity can be quantified in a variety of environments, such as at work and in academia. As Brian Grim states,[12] along with political organizations such as the All-Party Parliamentary Group on Religious Education,[13] respect for diversity in religion and belief leads to advantages for both the worker (greater possibility for entrance and advancement in the labor market and professional growth) as well as for the employer – public sector included.[14] In the university

10 Among several others, see the international project called REDCo (Religion in Education. A Contribution to Dialogue or a Factor of Conflict in Transforming Societies of European Countries?). This program was financed by the European Commission within the sixth framework program and has undoubtedly established a core of scholarship that is unmatched in terms of quality, case analyses and the disciplines involved.

11 Silvio Ferrari's research on religious rights is one of the more apt and enriching examples: Ferrari (2002).

12 Brian Grim, 'Statistics on how religious literacy is important for business', 15 February 2017, https://religiousfreedomandbusiness.org/2/post/2017/02/statistics-on-how-religious-literacy-is-important-for-business.html, last accessed 10 June 2018.

13 All-Party Parliamentary Group on Religious Education, *Improving Religious Literacy. A Contribution to the Debate*, July 2016, www.reonline.org.uk/wp-content/uploads/2016/07/APPG-on-RE-Improving-Religious-Literacy-full-report.pdf, last accessed 10 June 2018.

14 In this regard, one of the most important consultancy agencies in the world, Ernst and Young, launched a religious literacy training program for organizations, see 'EY launches religious literacy training program for organizations', 6 February 2017, www.ey.com/gl/en/newsroom/news-releases/news-ey-launches-

sector, where competition is based on educational offers that correspond to precise needs for knowledge and its employment in the market, a religiously literate administrative and managerial staff is an essential resource for guaranteeing religious diversity within the university.

For some time now, the realities of European society have made a reassessment of the balance between the religious and the political spheres essential. It is that same reality that today demands a radical shift in the ability to read history and to interpret the role of religions in the public field in Europe. The duty to transform this story into an alphabet that can be understood by everyone rests with historians.

Bibliography

Bhargava, Rajeev (ed.) 1998. *Secularism and Its Critics*, New Delhi/New York, Oxford University Press.

Bhargava, Rajeev 2007. 'The Distinctiveness of Indian Secularism', in Thirukodikaval N. Srinivasan (ed.), *The Future of Secularism*, New Delhi/New York, Oxford University Press, 20–53.

Bhargava, Rajeev 2011. 'Rehabilitating Secularism', in Craig Calhoun, Mark Juergensmeyer and Jonathan VanAntwerpen (ed.), *Rethinking Secularism*, Oxford/New York, Oxford University Press, 92–113.

Bilgrami, Akeel 2014. 'Secularism. Its Content and Context', in Alfred Stepan and Charles Taylor (ed.), *Boundaries of Toleration*, New York, Columbia University Press, 79–129.

Blinkova, Alexandra and Vermeer, Paul 2016. 'Religious Education in Russia: A Comparative and Critical Analysis', *British Journal of Religious Education* 38:3, 1–13.

Butler, Judith, Habermas, Jürgen, Taylor, Charles *et al.* (ed.) 2011. *The Power of Religion in the Public Sphere*, New York, Columbia University Press.

Cadeddu, Francesca 2014. 'Definizioni e strumenti di alfabetizzazione religiosa nel panorama internazionale', in Alberto Melloni (ed.), *Rapporto sull'analfabetismo religioso in Italia*, Bologna, Il Mulino, 99–110.

Casanova, José 2011. 'The Secular, Secularizations, Secularisms', in Craig Calhoun, Mark Juergensmeyer and Jonathan VanAntwerpen (ed.), *Rethinking Secularism*, Oxford/New York, Oxford University Press, 54–74.

Crisp, Beth R. 2016. 'Religious Literacy and Social Work. The View from Australia', in Adam Dinham and Matthew Francis (ed.), *Religious Literacy in Policy and Practice*, Bristol, Policy Press, 207–26.

Davie, Grace 2016. 'Foreword', in Adam Dinham and Matthew Francis (ed.), *Religious Literacy in Policy and Practice*, Bristol, Policy Press, VII–X.

Dinham, Adam and Francis, Matthew (ed.) 2016. *Religious Literacy in Policy and Practice*, Bristol, Policy Press.

Ennis, Ariel 2017. *Teaching Religious Literacy: A Guide to Religious and Spiritual Diversity in Higher Education*, New York/Abingdon, Routledge.

Ferrari, Silvio 2002. *Lo spirito dei diritti religiosi*, Bologna, Il Mulino.

Grim, Brian 2017. 'Statistics on how religious literacy is important for business', *Religious Freedom & Business Foundation*, 15 February, https://religiousfreedomandbusiness.org/2/post/2017/02/statistics-on-how-religious-literacy-is-important-for-business.html, last accessed 10 June 2018.

Ladeur, Karl-Heinz 2014. 'The Myth of the Neutral State and the Individualization of Religion: The Relationship between State and Religion in the Face of Fundamentalism', in Susanna Mancini and

religious-literacy-training-program-for-organizations, last accessed 10 June 2018. The Center on Religion & the Professions of the University of Missouri proposes, on the other hand, a set of tools subdivided according to market sectors, http://religionandprofessions.org/religious-literacy-toolkits/, last accessed 10 June 2018.

Michel Rosenfeld (ed.), *Constitutional Secularism in an Age of Religious Revival*, Oxford/New York, Oxford University Press, 33–53.

Mack, Arien (ed.) 2009. *Social Research: An International Quarterly*, issue 'The Religious-Secular Divide: The U.S. Case' 76:4.

Melloni, Alberto 2014. 'Introduzione. L'analfabetismo religioso in Italia. *Actio finium regundorum*', in Alberto Melloni (ed.), *Rapporto sull'analfabetismo religioso in Italia*, Bologna, Il Mulino, 1–12.

Melloni, Alberto, Cavagnini, Giovanni and Grossi, Giulia (ed.) 2017. *Benedetto XV. Papa Giacomo della Chiesa nel mondo dell'«inutile strage»*, 2 vols., Bologna, Il Mulino. English translation forthcoming.

Mély, Benoît 2004. *La question de la séparation des églises et de l'école dans quelques pays européens. Allemagne, France, Grande-Bretagne, Italie. 1789–1914*, Lausanne, Editions Page Deux.

Naso, Paolo 2014. 'I costi sociali dell'analfabetismo religioso', in Alberto Melloni (ed.), *Rapporto sull'analfabetismo religioso in Italia*, Bologna, Il Mulino.

Norris, Pippa and Inglehart, Ronald (ed.) 2004. *Sacred and Secular: Religion and Politics Worldwide*, Cambridge/New York, Cambridge University Press.

Schultz, Kevin M. 2006. 'Secularization: A Bibliographic Essay', *The Hedgehog Review* 8:1–2, special issue *After Secularization?*, 170–7.

Smith, Christian 2003. *The Secular Revolution: Power, Interests, and Conflict in the Secularization of American Public Life*, Berkeley, University of California Press.

Stark, Rodney 1999. 'Secularization, R.I.P.', *Sociology of Religion* 60:3, 249–73.

Stark, Rodney and Finke, Roger 2000. *Acts of Faith: Explaining the Human Side of Religion*, Berkeley, University of California Press.

Taylor, Charles 2007. *A Secular Age*, Cambridge, MA, Harvard University Press.

Taylor, Charles 2011. 'Why We Need a Radical Redefinition of Secularism', in Judith Butler, Jürgen Habermas, Charles Taylor *et al.* (ed.), *The Power of Religion in the Public Sphere*, New York, Columbia University Press, 34–59.

10 Is 'religious' violence really religious?

John Wolffe

Introduction

The first time I visited Northern Ireland, in 1983 at the height of the Troubles, my traveling companion, frustrated by polarization between Catholics and Protestants, said with some feeling, 'I wish all the churches in this country would fall down'. A day or so later, he apologized for the remark and acknowledged that the causes of the conflict were much more complex than it had implied: religion was a factor, but by no means the only one or even the most important one.

My friend's reaction to the Northern Ireland conflict is typical of initial perceptions of wars and civil unrest – from the Crusades, through the sixteenth- and seventeenth-century 'wars of religion' to the present day 'war on terror' – for which religion is held to be responsible. Meanwhile there are many other wars – for example, the Napoleonic Wars or World War II – that are popularly perceived to have nothing to do with religion. Common sense, however, would suggest that a simple yes/no polarity – that religion either 'causes' a war or has nothing to do with it – is a crude over-simplification.

Such polarized perceptions tell us as much about the subjective assumptions of those who make them as about the historical or contemporary reality with which they are concerned. Those with secularist convictions, who believe *prima facie* that religion is a harmful delusion, are naturally inclined to exaggerate its negative impact. This perception can also be endorsed by some religious people, either because they want to highlight their own significance, or because they see war as justified by their beliefs. Other religious people, however, may be equally concerned to deny or to play down any association with violence. Hence in assessing the role of religions in causing wars and violence, it is particularly important to probe behind the perceptions of potentially partisan informants.

Such popular perceptions are more or less subtly reflected in the published literature. On the one hand, there is the new atheist polemic against religion, presenting it as a dangerous delusion that is a root cause of violence and terrorism (e.g., Harris 2004). On the other is the argument that the root inspiration of all religions is essentially peaceful, that 'religious violence' is actually attributable to the distorting impact of other political and societal factors and that in the modern era secularism has inspired far more atrocities than has religion (Armstrong 2014). Indeed William Cavanaugh writes of the 'myth of religious violence', which, he argues, was created by modern nation-states in order to justify and obscure their own violent actions (Cavanaugh 2009). There are also more nuanced middle positions such as that of the multi-authored *Oxford Handbook of Religion and Violence*, which acknowledges that 'violence in both real and symbolic forms is found in all religious traditions', while recognizing that the use of religion to justify violence does not necessarily mean that it is the primary motivation for it (Juergensmeyer, Kitts and Jerryson 2013: 11–12). Scott Appleby writes of the 'ambivalence of the sacred', by which he means that religion is an equally powerful motivator for *both* violence and peacemaking (Appleby 2000). Jonathan Sacks, formerly Chief Rabbi of the United Hebrew Congregations of the Commonwealth, similarly discerns two sides of the coin, acknowledging the sometimes violent 'sibling rivalries' among and within the three Abrahamic faiths, but also affirming the capacity of religious values to promote peace (Sacks 2015).

This short chapter similarly charts a middle course. There is insufficient space even to attempt any systematic discussion of the role of religion in individual conflicts, so the problem is best approached by outlining some general principles that can then be applied to the consideration of specific contexts.

Religion is pervasive

While religion may be a more conspicuous factor in some cases than in others, it should never be discounted, especially as conflict situations are prone to stimulate the assertion of fundamentalist beliefs that may lie dormant in peacetime. For example, the long-running Israel-Palestine conflict initially arose from essentially secular issues, particularly the territorial and refugee issues that accompanied the formation of the state of Israel in 1947. However, in recent decades it has increasingly acquired a religious dimension, with the rise of groups such as Gush Emunim, which argues on biblical grounds for Jewish colonization of the Occupied Territories, and Hamas, with its conflicting aspiration to establish an Islamic state in Palestine (Herbert 2004: 276–81). Both historically in the West and contemporaneously in most other parts of the world, religion cannot be easily separated out as a factor from other forces in culture and society. Historical analysis of the so-called 'wars of religion' in sixteenth- and seventeenth-century Europe explores the way in which apparently religious confrontations were shaped by a complex range of cultural, political, psychological and social factors alongside the religious ones (Greengrass 2013). Judgments about the role of religion in causation are not straightforward ones.

Labels often mislead

It can sometimes be a convenient shorthand to use religious labels for the two sides in a particular conflict: for example 'Catholic' v. 'Protestant' in Northern Ireland, 'Christian' v. 'Muslim' in Nigeria, 'Sunni' v. 'Shi'a' in Iraq, 'Buddhist' v. 'Hindu' in Sri Lanka. Such labels are valid to the extent that they are correctly indicative of broad alignments and of a religious dimension to the conflict in question. Their use should not, however, be taken as implying that religious difference in itself is necessarily a primary cause of the conflict in question. Many other factors may be at work, such as national and cultural tensions, and economic challenges and inequalities. Religious literacy requires one to not only give weight to the religious factor in events but also to avoid using it to explain too much.

The point can be effectively illustrated with reference to the Northern Ireland case. When asked whether he thought religion had fueled the conflict, the leading Methodist peace advocate Harold Good acknowledged that both Catholic and Protestant religious traditions had themselves contributed to confusion on that front by linking political and religious aspirations (Wolffe 2014: 246–7). However, for others awareness that in Northern Ireland 'Catholic' and 'Protestant' have become political as well as religious terms has led to religious self-identifications that are either more specific – such as 'Anglican' or 'Presbyterian' – or the more all-encompassing 'Christian' (251).

Links between texts, beliefs and actions should not be assumed

All major religions have texts and traditions that justify or even require violence under certain circumstances and conditions, but these are carefully circumscribed in practice. For example, the genocides recorded in the Old Testament – such as the slaughter of the inhabitants of Jericho after its capture (Josh 6:21) – are an embarrassment rather than an inspiration to most present-day Christians and Jews. Indeed, Jonathan Sacks argues that the underlying teaching of the Scriptures affirms the priority of peace: violence should either be understood metaphorically, as a consequence of human fallibility, or as a last resort in a specific historic crisis, rather than as an enduring divine mandate.[1]

Both Islam and Sikhism originally emerged in contexts of conflict, where believers were both exposed to violence and had to use it in self-defense. For devout Muslims, jihad is primarily the internal struggle against sin rather aggression towards nonbelievers, although violence against military objectives is justified in extreme circumstances if the faith or the Muslim community is deemed to be under attack.[2] Two young Muslim men interviewed in 2014[3] complained about the tendency of hostile critics to take Quranic texts out of context:

> [...] people can turn around and say, look, this is where extremism comes from. It comes from the Quran. But then let's evaluate the Quran. The Quran itself is a scripture that doesn't encourage injustice. So if Allah says don't be unjust... help the poor, help the orphans, and then out of context is taken, which they always do, well, go and kill them. Is that really the sentence? No, it's in the context of war, it's of defending. If they retaliate, retaliate in the same manner back. But it's better for you to forgive. You see these are the teachings and they don't mention these things. And they don't want to mention these things.[4]

Moreover, even Muslim interviewees with quite anti-western views were clear that Islamic teaching did not justify suicide attacks against innocent civilians. Similarly, although the Norwegian mass murderer Anders Behring Breivik prefaced his lengthy apologia with the Maltese Cross and claimed to be '100 per cent Christian' (Berwick 2011: 1393), the overwhelming majority of Christians would disown the ideology that he used to legitimize his killing of seventy-seven people in July 2011. If a present-day adherent resorts to violent action, it may sometimes be in spite of, rather than because of, his or her religious beliefs. And when a religious sanction for violent action is claimed, it may well arise from an eccentric interpretation of the tradition.

The specificities of particular religions and varieties of opinion within them must be understood

For example, the starting point for Christians is just war theory, which sanctions violence to defend innocent life and uphold justice and essential moral principles.[5] It was on this basis

1 Cf. Sacks (2015), especially 211–14.

2 For detailed analysis, see the forthcoming series, *Violence in Islamic Thought*, edited by Robert Gleave and István Kristó-Nagy and published by Edinburgh University Press.

3 Semi-structured interviews carried out as part of the Research Councils UK funded-project Religion, Martyrdom and Global Uncertainties, 1914–2014. Transcripts have been deposited with the UK Data Service.

4 Interview, 9 June 2014, Muslim males aged 21 and 23.

5 For a recent definitive exposition of just war theory, see Biggar (2013), and for a summary and review, see Powell (2014).

that, for example, Britain went to war with Germany in 1914 because of the latter's violation of Belgian neutrality. The then Archbishop of Canterbury, Randall Davidson, wrote of an 'assured conviction' that 'for men who desire to maintain the paramount obligation of fidelity to plighted word, and the duty of defending weaker nations against violence and wrong, no possible course was open but that which our country has taken' (Bell 1935: vol. 2, 742). Similarly, Henry Scott Holland, Regius Professor of Divinity at Oxford University, wrote in 1914 that 'War is right when it is fought on behalf of Peace – to rescue the honour of Christian Peace – without which it would be no Peace of Christ' (Paget 1921: 313–14). The Bishop of London, Arthur Winnington-Ingram, went further, asserting that the moral and spiritual case for going to war was so strong that soldiers who died in it were 'martyrs as really as St Stephen was a martyr' (Winnington-Ingram 1914: 75). Other Christians, however, took a very different stance: the soldier poet Wilfred Owen denounced war-mongering clergy and affirmed that he himself became 'more and more Christian as I walk the unchristian ways of Christendom' (Blunden 1931: 108, Stallworthy 1974: 85, 185–6).

Christian just war principles have also been used to justify violent opposition to oppressive regimes, as in the decision of the leading Lutheran theologian Dietrich Bonhoeffer to support the planned assassination of Hitler, and in the anti-apartheid struggle in South Africa. However, the most effective and inspirational Christian opponents of apartheid – notably Trevor Huddleston, Desmond Tutu and Nelson Mandela after his release from prison – adopted nonviolent methods (Appleby 2000: 34–40). Because Christians take their inspiration from Jesus, who suffered crucifixion rather than retaliate against his oppressors, there is also a strong tradition that passive resistance, which can culminate in the willing acceptance of death subsequently exemplified by Bonhoeffer, is a more appropriate response to aggression than violent defensive action.

In the past, however, Christians could sanction and perpetrate violence, notably in the era of the Crusades and the persecutions of the early modern era. Such actions were driven by a sense of a divine imperative to stamp out perceived religious error, reinforced by the prejudices of combatants on the ground, and by politically-motivated concerns to enforce religious uniformity. However, paradoxically, as Alexandra Walsham has argued, the eventual outcome of such 'charitable violence' was the advance of toleration and freedom of conscience as it proved ineffective and even counterproductive in constraining the growth of religious diversity (Walsham 2006).

Similarly, for Muslims the starting point of jihad, the struggle to maintain and promote the faith, which can be entirely peaceful, sanctions violence as a last resort, when it is believed that this is the only way that Islam can be secured. The notorious fatwa issued by Ayatollah Khomeini in 1989 calling on fellow-Muslims to execute the writer Salman Rushdie on account of his allegedly blasphemous novel *The Satanic Verses* was formally merely an opinion from an influential figure in one branch of Islam. Although there was a general consensus among Muslims that the book was offensive and should be condemned and banned, Islamic opinion was always divided on whether the extreme measure proposed by Khomeini was justified (Weller 2009: 33–48). Similarly, while it is possible for Islamist terrorist groups and individuals to justify their actions as consistent with jihad, the great majority of Islamic authorities do not sanction suicide attacks. Co-religionists, moreover, explicitly disown them: the following was a representative comment regarding the leader of the bombers who attacked London on 7 July 2005.

> Mohammad Sidique Khan is not a martyr in any shape or form as far as I am concerned. Because by the Islamic definition a martyr, you are not supposed to kill innocent people. You are not supposed to kill non-combatants. You are not supposed to kill

unarmed people. And you are not supposed to kill yourself. So, from an Islamic point of view, no he was not a martyr. Maybe just based on principles that he killed himself for the sake of his beliefs, maybe to whatever sick people agree with him that's martyrdom. But in the broader sense I don't think that he's a martyr.[6]

Religious violence should be considered alongside secular and state-sponsored violence

Historically, some of the most extreme cases of violence were perpetrated by avowedly secular regimes, notably the French revolutionaries of the Terror of 1793–4, when tens of thousands of people were either executed or murdered, and in Stalin's Soviet Union, where the death toll is estimated in the tens of millions. In other cases, violence has been unleashed in contexts where religious and secular motivations overlapped.

In particular, the alignment of religion with secular nationalisms also has great potential to unleash violence. The Archbishop of Canterbury, Robert Runcie, observed in his sermon at the Falklands Service in St Paul's Cathedral in 1982, 'War springs from the love and loyalty that should be offered to God being applied to some God substitute, one of the most dangerous being nationalism'.[7] The case of World War I, when combatants on both sides were led to believe that their cause was divinely sanctioned has already been noted. Abraham Lincoln famously reflected on the American Civil War that 'Both [sides] read the same Bible and pray to the same God, and each invokes His aid against the other. [...] The prayers of both could not be answered. That of neither has been answered fully. The Almighty has His own purposes'.[8]

Lincoln went on to speculate that 'this terrible war' should be seen as a divine judgment on the whole American people for their previous countenance of slavery. Later generations are more prone to attribute such catastrophes to human fallibility rather than divine providence and to point up the dangers of language that gives religious legitimation to a political or nationalistic cause, even a seemingly righteous one. The dangers are especially acute when the alignment of religion and nationalism is fostered by a state for its own political purposes. The militant secularism of the Spanish Second Republic (1931–9) inspired widespread persecution and murder of Catholic priests, but was met by the state-sponsored violence of General Franco's dictatorship (1936–75), which claimed to be acting in defense of the church.

The Nazi Holocaust of European Jewry is the most enduringly emotive case of state-sponsored violence. While few would argue that it was directly religiously – as opposed to racially – motivated, it still raised two uncomfortable issues for European Christians. There was both the perception that the genocidal anti-Semitism of the death camps had its roots in anti-Jewish attitudes stimulated by Christian teaching, and a sense that the churches, both within Germany and internationally, had been too passive in the face of mounting evidence of the excesses of the regime (Holtschneider 2004). These considerations highlight two wider issues: that the linkages between religious ideas and violence can often be indirect and contested, and the acute dilemmas faced by religious people in deciding when state violence and oppression has to be actively confronted rather than merely passively resisted.

6 Interview, 3 June 2014, Muslim male aged 27.

7 *The Times*, 27 July 1982, 12.

8 Second Inaugural, 4 March 1865, text in MacArthur (1996: 370).

The 'good news' stories about religion as well as the 'bad news' ones should be highlighted

Both historians and journalists tend to emphasize violence because it captures attention and demands explanation, whereas patient peace-building work of its very nature is much less visible, precisely because its success lies in preventing overt conflict. Christians, Jews and Muslims are all active in peace-building initiatives in the Middle East. Although the institutional churches in Northern Ireland struggled to transcend community divisions, individual Christian leaders, such as the Catholic Alec Reid and the Methodist Harold Good who oversaw the decommissioning of paramilitary arsenals, played crucial roles in the peace process. Contemporary Muslim leaders who advocate violence are liable to receive more exposure in the western media than moderates such as Ahmed el-Tayeb, the influential Grand Imam of al-Azhar (Cairo), who condemns ISIS and has established warm relations with Pope Francis.[9]

Conclusion

The complexities of the relationships between religion and conflict present a significant challenge for observers seeking to understand and interpret an unfamiliar situation. The previous points will, however, provide a useful checklist to assist in avoiding common pitfalls and in suggesting directions for further inquiry. Accuracy is especially important in the light of the potential for misleading assessments to inflame situations that they purport to describe. For example, analysis that appears to attribute violent actions to Islam in general, rather than to particular professing Muslims, risks not only exacerbating popular Islamophobia, but reinforcing the perception of Muslims themselves that they need to wage jihad against a hostile world. Omissions can also distort reporting and hence public perceptions. For example, the catastrophic impact of the current turmoil in Iraq and Syria on the ancient Christian churches in those countries has received little attention in mainstream secular media. Unlike Muslims, local Christians have not made themselves conspicuous by becoming active protagonists in violence, while their historic presence in the region complicates a dominant narrative that highlights its Islamic character.

I have visited Northern Ireland many times since 1983, and rejoice in the relative peace that has come to that troubled province, although deep divisions remain. That outcome has not required the churches to fall down, although it is true that there, as in most other parts of Europe, attendance has declined significantly during the last three decades. Nevertheless, committed minorities can still make a substantial difference, and through the patient work of organizations such as the Corrymeela Community and Contemporary Christianity,[10] it is clear that religion is proving to be part of the solution as well as part of the problem. We badly need more religiously literate and balanced analysis that resists stereotyping and illuminates the checkered realities of its role in this and numerous other conflict situations.

Bibliography

Appleby, R. Scott 2000. *The Ambivalence of the Sacred: Religion, Violence, and Reconciliation*, Lanham/Boulder/New York *et al.*, Rowman and Littlefield.

Appleby, R. Scott, Omer, Atalia and Little, David (ed.) 2014. *The Oxford Handbook of Religion, Conflict and Peacebuilding*, Oxford, Oxford University Press.

9 'Top Muslim cleric Ahmed al-Tayeb urges education reform to counter extremism', *The Guardian*, 23 February 2015; 'Pope Francis welcomes Sunni Muslim leader to Vatican', *Catholic Herald*, 23 May 2016.

10 See www.corrymeela.org/ and www.contemporarychristianity.net, last accessed 12 January 2018.

Armstrong, Karen 2014. *Fields of Blood: Religion and the History of Violence*, London, The Bodley Head.

Bell, George K.A. 1935. *Randall Davidson*, 2 vols., Oxford, Oxford University Press.

Bennett, Clinton 2008. *In Search of Solutions: The Problem of Religion and Conflict*, London, Equinox.

Berwick, Andrew [Breivik, Anders B.] 2011. *2083: A European Declaration of Independence*, London, self-published.

Biggar, Nigel 2013. *In Defence of War*, Oxford, Oxford University Press.

Blunden, Edmund (ed.) 1931. *The Poems of Wilfred Owen*, London, Chatto and Windus.

Brewer, John D., Higgins, Gareth I. and Teeney, Francis 2011. *Religion, Civil Society and Peace in Northern Ireland*, Oxford/New York, Oxford University Press.

Cavanaugh, William T. 2009. *The Myth of Religious Violence. Secular Ideology and the Roots of Modern Conflict*, Oxford/New York, Oxford University Press.

Ganiel, Gladys 2008. *Evangelicalism and Conflict in Northern Ireland*, Basingstoke, Palgrave Macmillan.

Greengrass, Mark 2013. 'Europe's "Wars of Religion" and their legacies', in John Wolffe (ed.), *Protestant-Catholic Conflict from the Reformation to the 21st Century. The Dynamics of Religious Difference*, Basingstoke, Palgrave Macmillan, 22–45.

Harris, Sam 2004. *The End of Faith: Religion, Terror and the Future of Reason*, New York, Norton & Co.

Herbert, David 2004. 'Religion, conflict and coexistence in Palestine/Israel', in John Wolffe (ed.), *Religion in History: Conflict, Conversion and Coexistence*, Manchester/Milton Keynes, Manchester University Press/The Open University, 249–85.

Holtschneider, K. Hannah 2004. 'Christians, Jews and the Holocaust', in John Wolffe (ed.), *Religion in History: Conflict, Conversion and Coexistence*, Manchester/Milton Keynes, Manchester University Press/The Open University, 217–48.

Juergensmeyer, Mark, Kitts, Margo and Jerryson Michael (ed.) 2013. *The Oxford Handbook of Religion and Violence*, Oxford/New York, Oxford University Press.

MacArthur, Brian (ed.) 1996. *The Penguin Book of Historic Speeches*, London, Penguin.

Omer, Atalia, Appleby, R. Scott and Little, David (ed.) 2015. *The Oxford Handbook of Religion, Conflict and Peacebuilding*, Oxford/New York, Oxford University Press.

Paget, Stephen (ed.) 1921. *Henry Scott Holland. Memoir and Letters*, New York, Dutton.

Powell, Philip 2014. 'Nigel Biggar, *In Defence of War* – A Review Essay', *Ethics in Brief* 20:2, www.klice.co.uk/uploads/Ethics%20in%20Brief/EiB_Powell_20_2_pub.pdf, last accessed 12 January 2018.

Sacks, Jonathan 2015. *Not in God's Name: Confronting Religious Violence*, London, Hodder and Stoughton.

Stallworthy, Jon 1974. *Wilfred Owen*, Oxford/New York, Oxford University Press.

Walsham, Alexandra 2006. *Charitable Hatred: Tolerance and Intolerance in England, 1500–1700*, Manchester, Manchester University Press.

Weller, Paul 2009. *A Mirror for our Times: 'The Rushdie Affair' and the Future of Multiculturalism*, London, Continuum.

Winnington-Ingram, Arthur F. 1914. *A Day of God: Being Five Addresses on the Subject of the Present War*, London, Wells Gardner.

Wolffe, John 2014. 'Conclusion: Overcoming "Religious" Conflict: History and Practice', in John Wolffe (ed.), *Irish Religious Conflict in Comparative Perspective. Catholics, Protestants and Muslims*, Basingstoke, Palgrave Macmillan, 242–60.

Wolffe, John and Moorhead, Gavin 2014. *Religion, Security and Global Uncertainties*, Milton Keynes, Open University, www.open.ac.uk/arts/research/religion-martyrdom-global-uncertainties/, last accessed 12 January 2018.

11 European law and the veil

Muslim women from victims to emblems of the enemy

Susanna Mancini

Background story

In the summer of 2016, while the controversy over the burkini was raging in southern France, I was sunbathing on a quiet Italian beach. A young woman wearing a jibab sat on the shore. Two little girls, happily playing in the water with their father, waved to her: 'Mama!' The woman waved back and remained seated on the sand, under the burning sun. The same scene occurred in the following days. After a few days, she began putting her feet in the water. She stood alone in the heat, observing her family happily splashing in the water. Then, one day, her husband took her hand and walked with her into the sea. Her jibab was floating around her as the little girls excitedly swam from one parent to the other. As the family walked out of the water, I gave them the thumbs-up sign. The spouses looked at each other and burst out laughing wholeheartedly.

As I laughed back at them, marveling at the happy ending to this little family drama, it occurred to me that had we been in one of the thirty municipalities of the French Riviera, where bans prohibiting clothes showing a religious affiliation were in effect, the police would have disrupted the idyllic moment I had witnessed and forced the young women to undress or leave. I wondered on what grounds the then French Prime Minister Manuel Valls, who supported the burkini bans, had come to the conclusion that 'The burkini is not a new range of swimwear [...]. It is the expression of a political project, a counter-society, based notably on the enslavement of women' (Valls 2016). I wondered whether Valls had ever heard the 1970s feminist slogan 'My body, my choice'. I asked myself who would have benefitted from removing the sight of this fully dressed woman playing in the water. Would our beach have become a safer place without her? As a constitutional law scholar, I could not help thinking that something in the role of the law as an instrument that holds society together had gone terribly wrong.

Muslim women and western civilization

Measures such as the burkini bans testify to a growing public discomfort concerning the increasing diversity of European societies, and, particularly, concerning the public visibility of Islam. In the last two decades, parties promoting an anti-Islam discourse have experienced increasing successes. In many countries, including EU member states, these parties are represented in parliaments and governments while fueling public anxiety toward immigration and exploiting social and economic distress by constructing Islam as an utterly irreconcilable other. By building on Orientalistic narratives and conflating ethnicity, culture and religious traditions, these parties promote notions of a 'clash of civilizations' and foster an era of 'post-truth politics', in which apocalyptic myths are built, debates appealing to emotions while disconnected from reality predominate and rational thinking and fact-based discussions virtually disappear.

Myths concerning Muslims in western societies are contradicted by all available data. Thus, one British 2016 major survey found Muslims to be 'amongst the country's most loyal, patriotic and law-abiding citizens' wanting to 'fully integrate with non-Muslims in all aspects of life', while being more opposed to terrorism than the British population as a whole (Frampton, Goodhart and Mahmood 2016). These factual findings, however, have no impact on post-truth propaganda spread by populist parties and amplified by social media, which loom as the most powerful means of mobilization on irrational and invented issues prone to incite public sentiments against Muslims. The 2015 report of the European Commission against Racism and Intolerance (ECRI) identified a dramatic increase in Islamophobia and xenophobic political discourse throughout Europe. ECRI deplored a rapid increase in hate speech disseminated principally through social media, encouraging member states to criminalize racist and xenophobic acts committed online (ECRI 2015). Many commentators, including Étienne Balibar, have pointed to the analogies between today's Islamophobic discourses and 1930s anti-Semitic propaganda (Balibar 1991: 22).

Drawing on political actors and social movements, anti-Muslim racism infiltrates decision-making processes, legislation and the judiciary in virtually all European jurisdictions, despite their deep divergences in the management of law and religion. Indeed, three key fields have a crucial impact on the equal enjoyment of rights by Muslim citizens and migrants: the display of Muslim attire, mosque construction and citizenship, and immigration law. While the latter two fields have general implications for the Muslim population in Europe, limitations on wearing traditional Muslim attire target women alone. This produces a particularly painful kind of discrimination, in which gender, religion and ethnicity intersect, affecting the equality of Muslim women and girls in education, in the workplace, in access to the public sphere and in obtaining citizenship. Muslim women in Europe encounter increasing hostility and discrimination. Their traditional clothes are constantly in the headlines. Countless politicians, legislators and judges, mostly white European males, pontificate on the significances of such clothing. Laws and bylaws have been adopted, regulating exclusively Muslim women's dresses, in the name of supposedly universal rights and principles. Simply wearing a headscarf has become a major hurdle for many women wishing nothing but to lead an ordinary life: in Belgium, as Eva Brems explains, several municipalities have prohibited the wearing of the headscarf for employees that have contact with citizens. A lawyer who wanted to practice law in Brussels was not admitted to the Bar because she was wearing a hijab. Women working in medical laboratories, in a call center and in a cleaning company have also been discriminated against because of their headscarf (Brems 2016). Despite the tiny number of women wearing full-face veils, measures criminalizing such attire are popping up across Europe. In Belgium, a law that criminalizes the mere wearing of facial veils in all public places came into effect in July 2011, targeting no more than 200 women. France adopted a similar law in 2010 to regulate less than 2,000 women. In 2009, the Danish government commissioned a study in connection with the political discussion on banning face veils. In the Netherlands, where no more than 300 women are thought to wear full-face veils, in November 2016, some MPs backed a ban on such clothing in places like schools, hospitals and public transport. Several municipalities in Italy, where fully veiled women are hardly ever seen, have enacted local bans on face-covering veils. A ban in the Spanish town of Lleida was overturned by the country's Supreme Court in February 2013. In September 2013, 65% of the electorate in the Swiss canton of Ticino voted in favor of a ban on face veils in public areas. In December 2016, chancellor Angela Merkel said the wearing of full-faced veils should be prohibited in Germany 'wherever it is legally possible'. In January 2017, the Austrian government coalition agreed to prohibit full-face veils in public spaces such as courts and schools although the number of women wearing one in Austria does not exceed 150. The government also announced that it was considering a more general ban on state employees wearing the headscarf and other religious symbols.[1]

To understand the implication of the systematic targeting of women in the proliferation of anti-Muslim measures properly, one has to bear in mind that gender difference plays a key role in defining identity and membership. Indeed, women embody cultural, as well as biological, reproduction, as the widespread use of female figures, such as Marianne or Germania to embody the nation, shows. Women represent the cultural norms and the values that define a certain group at a given historical moment and the possibility to pass on such norms and values to the next generation. This explains the great importance that all societies, and all legal systems, place on women's reproductive role: who women can marry, with whom women are permitted to have children. These rules are of key importance in defining the identity of a group and in drawing the boundaries between insiders and outsiders, which explains why women's status and women's bodies often become cultural battlefields. In the case of western/eastern relations, the battle dates back to the colonial time, when the European powers construed Muslim women to be an emblem of their backward civilization, and the veil as an obstacle to cultural surrender. In this light, the significance of the contemporary attack on Muslim women's clothes cannot be disentangled from what Robin Cohen has defined as a 'civilization panic' (Cohen 2016), that is, a profound anxiety regarding the meaning of citizenship and belonging in multicultural societies. 'Veiled' women are perceived as a challenge to the traditional representation of national identity, because they disrupt the mythical construction of the latter as uniform and homogeneous. Anti-veil measures target women in the workforce and, in the case of full-veil bans, in all public spaces, that is, women who claim a space in the European public sphere. However, the claims to wear a veil and to be part of the European public sphere are viewed as mutually incompatible, as if people of European ancestry had a monopoly in establishing what 'Europeanness' and 'European tradition' should, quite literally, look like. This understanding of 'tradition', however, relies on a stereotypical and essentialized notion of culture, as oppositional and monolithical. The first stereotype that ought to be challenged is the equation of immigration and tradition. Immigration is a modern phenomenon, and modernity not only caused a long-lasting massive immigration from former colonies but deeply affected the social structures of these societies: settling in Europe brings about changes in the relationship between parents and children and in the transmission of culture between generations (Guénif-Souilamas 2000). In the second place, one ought to bear in mind that Islam has been a key agent in the building of European identity and in the development of European 'traditions'. The latter, thus, cannot be properly understood without taking into account the influence of Europe's exposure to Islam and Islamic societies. Edward Said famously maintained that the notion of the Orient was a key in building European identity through the construction of a binary relationship between the strong, masculine and rational western self and a weak, irrational

1 'The Islamic Veil across Europe', *BBC*, 31 January 2017, www.bbc.com/news/world-europe-13038095, last accessed 27 October 2017.

and feminized Oriental other (Said 1978: 19–20). According to Bassam Tibi, the political and social evolution of Europe cannot be disentangled from the development of Islam in the Mediterranean, which constituted at the same time a source of threat and fascination for Europe (Tibi 1999: 16). Islam has been part of European history, tradition and identity as the enemy, the threatening neighbor, a colonized subject and a fascinating other. It is, thus, nonsensical to expel Islam from the notion of European identity and tradition, as Europe would not have become what it is today without its manifold encounters with Islamic societies.

By the same token, European Muslims should be viewed as contributing to the ever-changing notion of European identity. They should be entitled to claim the recognition of a complex identity that does justice to their manifold backgrounds and loyalties. In effect, as Said maintained in *Culture and Imperialism*,

> no one today is purely one thing. Labels like Indian, or woman, or Muslim, or American are no more than starting-points, which if followed into actual experience for only a moment are quickly left behind. Imperialism consolidated the mixture of cultures and identities on a global scale. But its worst and most paradoxical gift was to allow people to believe that they were only, mainly, exclusively, white, or Black, or Western, or Oriental. Yet just as human beings make their own history, they also make their cultures and ethnic identities. No one can deny the persisting continuities of long traditions, sustained habitations, national languages and cultural geographies, but there seems no reason except fear and prejudice to keep insisting on their separation and distinctiveness, as if that was all human life was about.
>
> (Said 1993: 336)

Women-protective anti-veil arguments

Measures banning or limiting the wearing of Muslim attire run counter to the fluid notion of identity upheld by Said and are rooted in the Orientalistic attitude he powerfully identified in nineteenth- and twentieth-century anthropology, history and travelogues. These measures conflate the different cultures of Eastern societies and the complex traditions of European Muslims into a homogeneous backward, misogynous and undemocratic Oriental paradigm that is pitted against European modernity. This attitude and rhetoric is by no means the monopoly of populists and right-wing Christian conservatives. On the contrary, there is a powerful liberal, supposedly gender egalitarian, Islamophobic discourse that heavily relies on the asserted subordination of women in Islam, in order to promote the notion that Muslims who adhere to their 'tradition' are culturally incompatible with the 'West' (Mancini 2010).

For many years, courts and legislators have relied on this Orientalistic notion of the subjugation of women in Islam to justify measures limiting the right to wear Muslim traditional attire. Countless bills, laws and judicial decisions have explicitly attributed to Muslim clothes an inherently anti-feminist significance, equating the wearing of headscarves and niqabs with a violation of gender equality. A paradigmatic example of this equation is provided by two cases decided by the European Court of Human Rights, which upheld, respectively, the dismissal of a teacher in Switzerland[2] and the expulsion of a student

2 *Dahlab* v. *Switzerland* [2001] EctHR 42393/98.

in Turkey,[3] for wearing a headscarf, on the grounds that the latter '[a]ppears to be imposed on women by a precept which is laid down in the Koran and which [...] is hard to square with the principle of gender equality' and that it '[a]ppears difficult to reconcile the wearing of an Islamic headscarf with the message of tolerance, respect for others and, above all, equality and non-discrimination'.[4] This line of argument also provided a justification for the two French laws that heavily limited the right of girls and women to wear traditional Muslim attire. Thus, for example, the French Stasi Commission, which set the grounds for the enactment of the 2004 law that prohibits the display of conspicuous religious symbols in state schools, asserted (without supporting this assertion with any data) that Muslim women are pressured by men from their community into wearing 'modest and asexual clothes', and are stigmatized as 'whores' if they do not conform. The committee further elaborated on the manifold subjugation of women in Muslim communities, holding that

> [y]oung women are victim of other forms of violence: sexual mutilations, polygamy, repudiation. The personal status of these women often prevents [the government] from opposing such violence because, on the grounds of bilateral agreements, the law of the country of origin might be applicable to them, including the provisions that are directly contrary to sex equality and fundamental rights.
>
> (Commission Stasi 2003: 46–7)

Similarly, the preliminary parliamentary resolution to the 2010 law criminalizing the full-face veil refers to the latter as a 'degrading garment [which] goes hand in hand with the submission of women to their spouses, to the men in their family, with the denial of their citizenship' (Assemblée nationale 2010: 14). Paradoxically, however, the French courts have established that Muslim women who are subjugated by men in the name of their religion are not entitled to French citizenship and, thus, cannot be protected from violence and gender-based discrimination. Indeed, in a case decided in 2008, the French Council of State confirmed a lower court's decision that had denied citizenship to a woman, who otherwise satisfied all the requirements and was married to a French national, on the grounds that her radical practice of Islam (manifested in her wearing the niqab and asserting an obligation to obey her husband) was incompatible with basic French values, particularly with the principle of gender equality.[5]

The imperialistic and paternalistic rationale upholding these laws and cases has been exposed by many critics (Mancini 2010), who have highlighted, *inter alia*, the lack of Muslim women's voices in the debate concerning their bodies and status. Numerous empirical researches have contradicted the assumptions behind women-protective anti-veil justifications. For example, a survey conducted in France by the Open Society Foundations indicated that the women interviewed were not coerced into wearing the facial veil; that many had decided to wear it, despite opposition from their families; that one-third did not wear it as a permanent and daily practice; and that the majority maintained active social lives. The report also revealed that the ban had contributed to discontent among these women and had reduced their autonomy and that the public discourse accompanying it had encouraged verbal abuse and physical attacks against them by members of the public.

3 *Sahin* v. *Turkey* [2007] EctHR 44774/98.

4 *Dahlab* v. *Switzerland* [2001] EctHR 42393/98, para. 13.

5 Conseil d'État, req. no. 286798, 27 Juin 2008.

From women-protective to society-protective anti-veil arguments

The notion that Muslim women have agency and might actually choose to wear headscarves and face veils has slowly made its way into the public debate. Interestingly, however, this has not prompted politicians, courts and legislators to rethink the legitimacy of veil bans. On the contrary, the suspicion that veiled women exercise a choice has turned them from victims into accomplices, and it has thus hardened measures aimed at regulating their power to choose. In other words, the rationale of anti-veil measures has shifted from women-protective to society-protective, from a justification aimed at saving Muslim women from their cultural tradition to one aimed at saving 'our' cultural tradition from Muslim women, as emblems of a threatening Islamic enemy. This shift is particularly evident in the recent case-law of the two European courts: the European Court of Human Rights (EctHR) and the European Court of Justice (ECJ).

'Living together' under the European Convention on Human Rights*:* S.A.S. *v.* France *and* Belcacemi et Oussar *v.* Belgium

Between 2010 and 2011 France and Belgium adopted laws criminalizing the wearing of facial veils in all public places.[6] These laws were upheld, respectively, by the French Constitutional Council and the Belgian Constitutional Court, on the grounds that wearing facial veils might jeopardize public safety and fails to comply with the minimum requirements of life in society. The two courts also found that women who conceal their face, voluntarily or otherwise, are objectively placed in a situation of exclusion and inferiority that is patently incompatible with the constitutional principles of liberty and equality.[7] Both the French and the Belgian laws were subsequently tested before the EctHR. The latter proceeded to evaluate the legitimacy, under the *European Convention on Human Rights*, of the three aims pursued by the French and the Belgian legislators, namely: public safety, gender equality and a certain conception of 'living together' in society. In *S.A.S.* v. *France*,[8] the court decided that a blanket ban on facial veils was not necessary for the protection of public safety, given that less restrictive alternatives, such as requesting to show the face in particular circumstances, are available. Most importantly, the court turned its back on women-protective arguments, rejecting the notion that certain attire has *per se* a discriminatory effect on women, and declared that '[a] State Party cannot invoke gender equality in order to ban a practice that is defended by women' (para. 119) and, while '[t] he clothing in question is perceived as strange by many of those who observe it [...] is the expression of a cultural identity which contributes to the pluralism that is inherent in democracy' (para. 120). Thus, it seemed as if, *prima facie*, the court had finally acknowledged that veiling practices are nothing but a manifestation of the multiplicity of cultural forms, and that veiled Muslim women may actually make a contribution to the democratic pluralistic public sphere. Unfortunately, however, in its subsequent reasoning, the court dramatically reduced the scope of pluralism, maintaining that respect for the minimum requirements of 'living together' constituted a legitimate aim for the criminalization of facial veils. 'Living together' is not listed in the *European Convention* among the legitimate grounds for limiting fundamental rights; yet the court accepted it as part of the 'protection

6 Law 2010-1192 of 11 October 2010 (France) and Law of 1st June 2011 (Belgium).

7 Decision no. 2010-613 DC of 7 October 2010 (France) and judgment of the Constitutional Court of 6 December 2012 (Belgium).

8 *S.A.S.* v. *France* [2014] EctHR 43835/11.

of the rights and freedoms of others' (para. 121), holding that 'the barrier raised against others by a veil concealing the face is perceived [...] as breaching the right of others to live in a space of socialization which makes living together easier' (para. 122). In other words, the mere sight of a fully veiled woman can objectively jeopardize 'living together' in a pluralistic society. This line of reasoning constitutes a clear shift from the victimization of veiled Muslim women to their construction as anti-system subjects. Indeed, the court accepted the use of *criminal* sanctions to suppress the visibility of facial veils, noting that the sanction is 'light' (para. 152). Clearly, however, the symbolic nature of criminal law suffices to attach a particular stigma to a religious practice, construing women who adhere to it as pernicious outcasts.

In the Belgian case *Belcacemi et Oussar* v. *Belgium*,[9] the court essentially reiterated its reasoning in *S.A.S.* v. *France*, holding that by criminalizing facial veils, Belgium had legitimately sought to respond to a practice that it considered to be incompatible with social communication and with the establishment of human relations, which were indispensable for life in a democratic society.

The conceptualization of democracy provided by the EctHR in these two cases raises worrisome questions as it indicates that legal responses to perceived 'cultural clashes' generated by the presence of Islam often deviate from the pluralistic model of democracy with which post-World War II western European countries identify themselves. Indeed, the construction of a racialized public enemy that needs to be kept out of the public sphere, or even expelled, is a central feature of the identitarian model of democracy theorized by Carl Schmitt. Schmitt argued that political communities are based on a constitutive polarity of friend and enemy (Schmitt 2007: 26). Identifying and fighting the enemy is crucial in order to preserve the principles and the values of democracy, which requires '[f]irst homogeneity and second [if the need arises] elimination or eradication' (Schmitt 1985: 9).

Discrimination in the name of neutrality: the European Court of Justice in **Achbita** *and* **Bougnaoui**

The European Union played a crucial role in the development of sex equality law in its member states. European institutions, and particularly the European Court of Justice, have made key contributions to upholding the rights of women in the workforce and to forcing national policy changes (Mulder 2017). Compared to that afforded by the *European Convention on Human Rights* (*ECHR*), protection against discrimination under EU law is stronger. Direct discrimination (i.e., treating someone less favorably because of certain attributes of who they are) can be justified under the *ECHR* if the interference with the protected right pursues a legitimate aim and is proportionate. On the contrary, under EU law, derogations are permitted only in so far as the measure in question specifically provides for them. Indirect discrimination (i.e., a practice, policy or rule which is apparently neutral but which puts certain groups of people at a disadvantage) can in some cases be excused, but only on the condition of a 'legitimate aim'. To be legitimate, an aim must be prescribed by law, respect the essence of the fundamental rights and freedoms of others and may only be pursued through measures that are appropriate, necessary and proportionate. Against this backdrop, and in the light of the disappointing EctHR 'veil jurisprudence', there were high hopes concerning the two recent decisions by the ECJ in

9 *Belcacemi et Oussar* v. *Belgium* [2017] EctHR 37798/13 (in French only).

the cases of *Achbita* and *Bougnaoui*.[10] These were referred to the court by, respectively, the Belgian and a French supreme administrative court. In both cases, a woman had been dismissed by her private employer on the grounds of her wearing a headscarf, against the company's dress policy. Unexpectedly, the court concluded that such dismissals do not violate EU law, as long as the employer adopts a general neutrality policy, that is, a ban on all religious signs. The court, thus, constructs the principle of neutrality as a legitimate aim that justifies the discrimination against minority religion employees. 'Neutrality', however, is not listed among the aims that may justify discrimination in any of the laws applicable to this case. In this respect, the use of 'neutrality' by the ECJ is analogous to that of 'living together' by the EctHR. Both are unenumerated grounds for limiting fundamental rights and vague, culturally loaded, slippery concepts. Who decides the rules according to which a society wants to live together? Who determines the standards of neutrality? Being bareheaded is no more nor less neutral that covering one's head, unless one equates neutrality with contemporary western mainstream attitudes. Like the EctHR, the ECJ did not engage in any victimization narrative. On the contrary, it departed from the assumption that wearing a headscarf is a woman's choice and it proceeded to give ammunition to the private sector against women who make this choice, in the name of a one-sided and oppressive notion of neutrality.

Concluding remarks

The recent case-law of the two European Courts dramatically reduced the protection against discrimination of a particularly vulnerable category of women. By using women's bodies to symbolically signal the existence of an unsolvable clash of civilizations, both courts failed to address the intersectional nature of the discrimination suffered by religious Muslim women. 'Intersectionality' is a term coined in the context of Black feminism to indicate the relationship between systems of oppression and marginalization and intersecting identities (Crenshaw 1989). In this light, individuals suffer discrimination on the basis of multiple and intersecting identities and belongings, such as gender, race, religion, ethnic origin, age, disability, etc. The intersection of these different identities amounts to a whole that differs from the component identities. Thus, for example, the discrimination suffered by minority women is often not 'fully described by simply adding two kinds of discrimination together' because intersectional discrimination is cumulative and 'the result is qualitatively different, or synergistic' (Fredman 2011: 140). Women who wish to wear a veil in Europe face a particularly harsh kind of discrimination that results not only from the intersection of their gender, religion and ethnicity, and from the stereotypes concerning their cultural traditions, but is also fueled by the conflation of postcolonial anxieties, demographic preoccupations and the fear of global terrorism.

'Women-protective' anti-veil measures infantilized and patronized European Muslim women under the pretense of liberating them from their misogynous religious tradition. It was the latter, not the women who complied with it, to be constructed as incompatible with western democracy. Thus, by holding that limitations to wearing the veil were meant to enable Muslim women to fully enjoy their status as citizens and rights-holders, women-protective anti-veil measures purported to uphold notions of inclusion and equality.

10 Court of Justice of the European Union, judgments in Cases C-157/15 *Achbita, Centrum voor Gelijkheid van kansen en voor racismebestrijding* v. *G4S Secure Solutions* [2017], and C-188/15 *Bougnaoui and Association de défense des droits de l'homme (ADDH)* v. *Micropole Univers* [2017].

While this hypocritical construction undoubtedly produced discrimination and oppression, it did not explicitly *outlaw* veil wearers. The escalation of the rationale of veil bans from 'women-protective' to 'society-protective' produces an even more destructive effect. It legitimizes discrimination against a vulnerable group of women, on the grounds that their mere sight jeopardizes western standards of civility. It permits the use of criminal sanctions against them, thus widening the gap between us and them, exacerbating social and ethnic division and hostility. As their bodies are increasingly constructed by the law as emblems of a culturally irreconcilable Oriental enemy, European Muslim women are losing the protection of the law and driven further toward the democratic periphery.

Bibliography

Ahmed, Leila 1992. *Women and Gender in Islam. Historical Roots of a Modern Debate*, New Haven, CT, Yale University Press.

Assemblée nationale 2010. *Rapport d'information no. 2262, Au nom de la mission d'information sur la pratique du port du voile intégral sur le territoire national*, 26 January, www.assemblee-nationale.fr/13/rap-info/i2262.asp, last accessed 29 October 2017.

Balibar, Étienne 1991. 'Is there a "Neo-Racism"?', in Étienne Balibar and Immanuel Wallerstein (ed.), *Nation, Class, Ambiguous Identities*, London/New York, Verso, 17–28.

'Berlin Court Rules in Favor of Hijab-Wearing Teacher', *Deutsche Welle*, 9 February 2017, www.dw.com/en/berlin-court-rules-in-favor-of-hijab-wearing-teacher/a-37477936, last accessed 29 October 2017.

Bowen, John R. 2008. *Why the French Don't Like Headscarves: Islam, the State, and Public Space*, Princeton, NJ, Princeton University Press.

Brems, Eva 2016. 'The Field in which Achbita will Land – A Brief Sketch of Headscarf Persecution in Belgium', *Strasbourg Observers*, 16 September, https://strasbourgobservers.com/2016/09/16/ecj-headscarf-series-5-the-field-in-which-achbita-will-land-a-brief-sketch-of-headscarf-persecution-in-belgium/, last accessed 29 October 2017.

Cohen, Robin 2016. 'The Burkini Ban as a "Civilization Panic"', University of Oxford Kellogg College's blog, 26 September, www.kellogg.ox.ac.uk/blog/the-burkini-ban-as-a-civilizational-panic/, last accessed 29 October 2017.

Commission Stasi 2003. *Commission de réflexion sur l'application du principe de laïcité dans la République: rapport au Président de la République*, 11 December, www.ladocumentationfrancaise.fr/var/storage/rapports-publics/034000725.pdf, last accessed 27 October 2017.

Crenshaw, Kimberle 1989. 'Demarginalising the Intersection of Race and Sex', *University of Chicago Legal Forum* 1, 139–67.

European Commission against Racism and Intolerance 2016. *Annual Report on Ecri's Activities*, www.coe.int/t/dghl/monitoring/ecri/activities/Annual_Reports/Annual%20report%202015.pdf, last accessed 29 October 2017.

Frampton, Martyn, Goodhart, David and Mahmood, Khalid 2016. *Unsettled Belonging: A Survey of Britain's Muslim Communities*, London, Policy Exchange.

Fredman, Sandra 2011. *Discrimination Law*, 2nd edn, Oxford, Oxford University Press.

Guénif-Souilamas, Nacira 2000. *Des 'beurettes' aux descendantes d'immigrants nord-africains*, Paris, Grasset/Le Monde.

Mancini, Susanna 2010. 'Patriarchy as the Exclusive Domain of the Other: The Veil Controversy, False Projection and Cultural Racism', *International Journal of Constitutional Law* 10:2, 411–28.

Mancini, Susanna 2014. 'The Tempting of Europe, the Political Seduction of the Cross. A Schmittian Reading of Christianity and Islam in European Constitutionalism', in Susanna Mancini and Michel Rosenfeld (ed.), *Constitutional Secularism in an Age of Religious Revival*, Oxford, Oxford University Press, 111–35.

Mulder, Jule 2017. *EU Non-Discrimination Law in the Courts: Approaches to Sex and Sexualities. Discrimination in EU Law*, Oxford, Hart Publishing.

Open Society Foundations 2011. *Unveiling the Truth: Why 32 Muslim Women Wear the Full-Face Veil in France*, www.opensocietyfoundations.org/sites/default/files/a-unveiling-the-truth-20100510_0.pdf, last accessed 29 October 2017.

Said, Edward W. 1978. *Orientalism*, New York, Pantheon Books.

Said, Edward W. 1993. *Culture and Imperialism*, New York, Knopf.

Schmitt, Carl [1923] 1985. *The Crisis of Parliamentary Democracy*, Cambridge, MA/London, The MIT Press.

Schmitt, Carl [1927] 2007. *The Concept of the Political*, Chicago, University of Chicago Press.

Tibi, Bassam 1999. *Kreuzzug und Djihad. Der Islam und die christliche Welt*, München, Bertelsmann.

Valls, Manuel 2016. 'Une vision archaïque de la place de la femme dans l'espace public', *La Provence*, 17 August, www.laprovence.com/article/politique/4078328/valls-sur-le-burkini-une-vision-archaique-de-la-place-de-la-femme-dans-lespace-public.html, last accessed 29 October 2017.

Part III

Building literacy, shaping alphabets

12 Why study religions in publicly funded schools?

Robert Jackson

Introduction

This book is concerned about the term 'religious illiteracy', the converse of the designation 'religious literacy'. To overcome religious illiteracy, it is necessary to have educational provision which aims to provide religious literacy. However, it should be noted that, in the literature about religions and education, the term 'religious literacy' is used in at least three different ways, related to: (1) learning about religions, including developing an understanding of religious uses of language in an open and impartial way (Moore 2007); (2) studying religions in order to make judgements about their truth claims, using a specific view of knowledge (Wright 1998); (3) learning religiously (Felderhof 2012).

In the present discussion, the first usage is the closest and most relevant to the study of religions in schools that are publicly funded and inclusive of young people from a variety of different religious and non-religious backgrounds. For the purposes of this contribution, 'religious illiteracy' refers to a lack of knowledge and understanding of religious diversity, together with a consequent lack of competence in engaging in the discussion of issues concerning religion and belief.

When we talk about teaching religion(s) or teaching about religion(s) in public schools, it is important to be clear about what is meant. Various terms, such as 'religious education', are used in different ways in different national contexts, and even sometimes in the same country. Some states have education systems which contribute to a form of religious upbringing or nurture for children and young people. Others have various approaches to the study of religions as an academic pursuit, with various implicit or explicit aims. The two processes are different, but there is a relationship between them. Some commentators see the academic study of religious diversity as a threat to approaches which nurture children in a particular faith or tradition. This need not be the case, and there are many who would see the two activities as complementary in principle, although not always in practice. It is arguable, for example, that anyone growing up in a religious environment should be well informed about religious and non-religious diversity, and should be able to relate their personal views to that plurality. However, some countries (such as Norway) or regions of countries (such as the province of Québec in Canada) only support some form of learning *about* religious diversity within state-funded education, leaving forms of religious nurture to private or supplementary education which parents can choose for their children. This chapter will concentrate on reasons for including studies of religious diversity as part of state-funded education. In those countries where there is some teaching about religious diversity (and sometimes religious *and* non-religious diversity), various reasons are given to justify such teaching. We shall go on to explore some of these reasons; but first we will consider why the study of religious diversity in schools has become a matter of some importance.

Religion and education in western democracies: key influences for change

The processes of secularisation, pluralisation and globalisation have influenced discussion about the place of religion in publicly funded schools, leading to some policy developments and changes in the education systems of various countries. In England, for example, where Religious Education is a separate school subject, these changes began to have an impact on practice, theory and policy in the late 1960s, eventually resulting in changes to the law in the late 1980s.

In England (Gates and Jackson 2014), to take an example, the process of secularisation was reflected in the changing attitudes of young people in schools, with research conducted in the 1960s suggesting that traditional religious instruction – essentially a Bible-based form of nondenominational Christian nurture – was considered by many upper secondary school students to be irrelevant to their personal concerns (Loukes 1965) or to include an inappropriate form of religious teaching which lacked opportunities for critical discussion (Cox 1967).

Another impetus for change, related to issues about secularisation, follows from the debate about the place of religion in the public sphere of democracies. For example, the Council of Europe, in its educational activity, promoted intercultural education and education for democratic citizenship but avoided any work on education about religious diversity. The justification for this was related to the idea that religion belonged to the private sphere, and not to the public arena. The change in Council of Europe policy in 2002, which resulted in a new project on the study of religions as a contributor to intercultural education, was galvanised by the events of 11 September 2001 in the USA, which – like so many more subsequent tragic incidents – placed religion very much in public space. We shall return to work of the Council of Europe later in this chapter.

Changes resulting from secularisation overlap with changes brought about by increasing plurality in many democratic societies. Pluralisation through migration, especially since the 1960s, has led many educators to shift the focus of religious studies in fully state-funded schools from a form of single-faith religious teaching to a 'non-confessional', inclusive, multifaith approach, including learning *about* the religions of relatively newly established minorities. In England, these minorities included Hindus, Sikhs, Muslims and Buddhists as well as Christians from the Caribbean and South Asia, joining much longer established Christian and Jewish communities. Many migrants maintained close contact with their countries of origin, bringing the dimension of globalisation to this plurality, enhanced in recent years by the development of new technologies which make international communication easy and of little or no cost.

A move towards the study of religious diversity demanded new theoretical and didactical thinking in order to facilitate appropriate teaching approaches. For example, theory and methodology from the phenomenology of religion, as developed in some university departments of Religious Studies, offered an objective approach to the study of religions which acknowledged increasing secularity and plurality. This was influential, in England, from the early 1970s. Ninian Smart was an important contributor (e.g. Smart 1968) whose work drew on continental European studies in the phenomenology of religion. While methodologies based in phenomenology have enabled an impartial stance towards the study of religions, various criticisms have been made of them, including their inability to consider material from different cultural contexts authentically in its own terms. Other methodologies include the interpretive approach (Jackson 1997, 2018), which is discussed later.

The interpretive approach is complementary to various dialogical approaches, which aim to help students to communicate with one another, in a civil way, about their various personal understandings and experiences of religions and non-religious world views (e.g. Leganger-Krogstad 2011, Ipgrave 2013).

It should be noted that any direct influence of theory and specific methodology (whether Smart's or anyone else's) on practice in schools is not always easy to assess. The relationship between theory, and its associated methodology, to policy and to general practice in schools is not straightforward to determine (Bråten 2013). Also, one should not underestimate more 'grassroots' classroom-based developments, reflecting secularisation and pluralisation as experienced by students and teachers directly in school; these have also played an important part in bringing about change (e.g. Cole 1972).

Aims

Reasons have been given for the emergence of a non-faith-based approach to teaching about religions in inclusive, publicly funded schools. However, the question of aims has not been addressed directly. Implicit in the developments described earlier are at least three aims for studying religions in inclusive educational contexts. They are not mutually exclusive, and there is no reason why they should not function together in a complementary way, despite the fact that some critics have sought to label particular approaches to the study of religious diversity as being connected with only a single aim, each linked to a specific social science discipline (e.g. Gearon 2013, replied to in Jackson 2015a, 2015b). A review of the literature shows three reasons for studying religious diversity as part of inclusive, publicly funded education. The first is its intrinsic value as a component of a liberal education covering all fundamental areas of human knowledge and experience. The second is its value as a contributor to students' individual development; this includes various ways in which students might benefit personally from reflecting on their learning. The third is its social value, through increasing knowledge and understanding of different religious perspectives within democratic societies, and through encouraging civil discussion and exchange between those having different beliefs. This aim is manifested with different emphases, related sometimes to citizenship, sometimes to social cohesion and latterly to opposition to violent extremism. The present author attempted to make this diversity of aims clear at the beginning of a large European project on dialogue and conflict in relation to studies of religions in European schools – the REDCo (Religion in Education: A contribution to Dialogue or a factor of Conflict in transforming societies of European Countries) project. In his introductory chapter in REDCo's first book the present author wrote:

> there is no intention to imply that the study of religion in schools should be solely justified through attention to social and political events and issues. I agree with the Delors Report in considering that education should include learning to know, learning to do, learning to live together and learning to be (UNESCO 1996). It is arguable that 'religious education' should be concerned with all of these, especially the fourth. The present discussion focuses on the third, but does not ignore the others. The discussion responds to recent and widespread international interest in the study of religions in schools, with particular attention to European institutions, prompted by various political events and social issues. This is why close attention is given to citizenship education.
>
> (Jackson 2007: 28)

Here, as in the present author's publications from the 1970s (e.g. Jackson 1978) to the present (e.g. Jackson 2014a), the intrinsic value of studying religions (liberal education should cover all dimensions of human experience) is set alongside its personal value, contributing to each student's individual development and its social value, for example its relevance to education for democratic citizenship.

It should be noted that there are those who would regard the 'intrinsic', liberal education argument as fundamental, leaving aside instrumental arguments as a matter of personal decision rather than as part of the remit of the inclusive school. For example, the Danish scholar Tim Jensen argues for an objective and phenomenological approach to the study of religions, regarded as worthwhile in itself. Relating the knowledge and understanding of obtained to personal and social issues is regarded as a matter of personal choice on the part of students outside the classroom (e.g. Jensen 2008). Others would regard relating new learning (whether about religion or anything else) to personal and social experience as an important component of educational activity.

Attacks on 'learning about religions'

There are many educators and parents from religious backgrounds who would support learning about religious diversity as a complement to their children's being initiated into a religious way of life. However, one critic has argued that approaches to learning about religious diversity are themselves inherently secularist, make no contribution to genuine Religious Education, and are a contributory element in the decline of religion (e.g. Gearon 2013). The same critic also claims that teaching about religious diversity has become 'politicised' and 'securitised', serving the agendas of security organisations, and with supporters who only work with a single 'social cohesion/anti-extremism' aim (Gearon 2012a, 2012b). The present author has responded in detail to these criticisms and readers are referred to the relevant publications (Jackson 2015a, 2015b).

The interpretive approach

It is difficult to separate questions of *why* we should teach about religions from issues of *how* we should do so. The questions are interrelated. Recent events involving atrocities committed by religious extremists show, for example, the importance of recognising and understanding the internal diversity of religions and of avoiding stereotypes. However, some approaches to education in this field focus on giving essentialised overviews of religions, and there are cases of young people from particular religious backgrounds who do not identify with, or even recognise, their own religion as presented by some teachers or textbooks (Ipgrave, Jackson and O'Grady 2009, Jackson, Ipgrave, Hayward *et al.* 2010, Moulin 2011). The interpretive approach includes a set of didactical principles and strategies that take account of the diversity that exists *within* religions, allowing for the interaction of religion and culture, for change over time and for different views about the nature of religions. It can begin with examples from a particular religion, or with students' questions and concerns. This does not matter, provided the three key ideas of 'representation', 'interpretation' and 'reflexivity' are covered.

The interpretive approach was developed at the University of Warwick in England (e.g. Jackson 1997, 2004, 2018), and has been used in various countries. Its methodology emerged from the experience of field studies of children and young people from different religious backgrounds in Britain, using methods developed by ethnographers in trying to understand another's religious language (e.g. Jackson and Nesbitt 1993) together with insights from scholars working in other fields, such as social psychology, hermeneutics, cultural theory, history of religions and theology. It employs particular ideas and insights from scholars working in a range of disciplines. The interpretive approach employs three key concepts in relation to the analysis of religious diversity, namely 'representation', 'interpretation' and 'reflexivity'.

Representation

Using scholarly sources, from the history of the portrayal of religion and religions in western literature, for example, the approach is critical of representing 'world religions' as entirely homogeneous belief systems (Said 1978, Smith 1978). Religions are pictured more flexibly in terms of a *relationship* between individuals who usually belong to particular groups (such as denominations or sects) and the wider religions or 'religious traditions'. The study of individuals, in the context of the various groups with which they are associated, can inform an emerging understanding of religious traditions. Similarly, key concepts from the religions can be exemplified and enlivened through the consideration of particular examples of religious faith and practice.

The approach is equally critical of simplistic representations of cultures and of the relationship between religion and culture which see religions and cultures as homogeneous. 'Cultures' are seen as dynamic, often internally contested and 'fuzzy edged', while individuals are recognised as capable of contributing to the reshaping of culture through making personal syntheses which might draw from various cultural resources, including their own ancestral traditions. The approach thus takes account of both the dimension of 'traditional' plurality – the overt diversity to be seen through the presence of different religious and ethnic groups in society – and that of 'modern' or 'postmodern' plurality (using these terms descriptively), in which individuals from any background can use cultural ideas and practices from many possible sources. The interaction of these two dimensions is reflected in the ideological and spiritual diversity to be found within religions (Jackson 2004, 2018).

With regard to the 'representation' of religions, the interpretive approach uses three 'levels'. The broadest level is the *religious tradition*, or 'religion'. Thus the Christian tradition encompasses all the different denominational and cultural manifestations of Christianity. Immediately it is evident that it would be impossible to have a full grasp of this. It is also clear that different insiders and outsiders would have different views about the tradition's scope. This does not matter. Each of us (whether teacher or student) can gradually form our own idea of the religious traditions. Every time we learn something new, our previous understanding of the religion is challenged and might be modified. Discussion and analysis of key concepts fit well into this level and can help to provide a provisional framework for understanding that can be modified as more learning takes place. It must be emphasised that this approach does *not* imply religions are not 'real'; they *are* real, but complex, and in a sense 'organic', social phenomena.

The next level is that of the *group*. This might be a denominational or sectarian group, or it might be an ethnic group whose members mainly practise a particular religion – or some combination of these. A project based on a family with both an Islamic and Pakistani background, or another about a local church would be informative about groups; and would also influence and inform our understanding of religions.

The third level is that of the *individual* religious person. Every individual is unique, but each person practising a religion usually belongs to at least one religious group, which has a relationship with the wider religious tradition. It is at the level of the individual that we can appreciate best the human face of religion and hear personal stories that break stereotypes of whole religions.

The exploration of examples which illustrate the *relationship* between these different 'levels' can bring the study of religions to life. Students do not feel that they have to know everything because every example studied illuminates the wider picture. Again it must be emphasised that the approach is *not* a postmodernist deconstruction of religions, only dealing with the beliefs and practices of individuals, but it *does* emphasise the 'organic' nature of religions; both their distinctiveness and internal diversity can be appreciated by looking at the *relationship* between individuals, groups and features of the broad religious traditions. For example, a study of biblical texts (which is worthwhile in itself), can be enhanced through looking at how particular groups use and interpret those texts, and how individuals speak of their relevance to their own lives. Using a different image, the Norwegian scholar Lars Laird Iversen uses the metaphors of liquidity, viscosity and solidity in discussing the interpretive approach (Iversen 2013).

In terms of didactics, teachers could start with an overview of key concepts from a religion or with a personal story (whether from, say, a visitor to the school or from some other source) or from the study of a group of some kind or from pupils' own previous knowledge and experience (including their own experience of religious practice or the absence of religion from their lives).

Interpretation

Rather than asking students to leave their presuppositions to one side – as in the phenomenological approach – the interpretive approach requires a comparison and contrast between the learner's concepts and those of the 'insider'. The approach moves backwards and forwards between the 'insider's' concepts in comparison with the nearest equivalent in the student's experience. Sensitivity on the part of the student is very important and a necessary condition for empathy. The other aspect of this hermeneutical approach lies in *applying* the model of representation outlined earlier – moving to and fro between individuals in the context of their groups and the wider religious tradition. These two elements overlap in practice.

This approach was not only influenced by discussions of theory and methodology, but was informed by direct experience of ethnographic fieldwork. Studies of children in Britain, from a range of different religious and cultural settings, were used as a basis for methodological reflection and as a source of material for curriculum development. Later developments of the approach used other starting points, such as key concepts or pupils' questions. The approach is flexible and can start at any point on the hermeneutical circle of learning – such as examples of religious practice, key concepts from the religion as a 'whole' or pupils' own experiences and questions.

Reflexivity

The interpretive approach does not simply set out to increase knowledge. It takes the view that, in order to increase understanding, pupils need to reflect on the impact of their new learning on their previous understanding. Thus, reflexivity covers various aspects of the relationship between the experience of students and the experience of those whose way of life they are attempting to interpret. Three elements are especially important: (1) learners reassessing their understanding of their own world view (called 'edification' in the interpretive approach); (2) learners making a distanced critique of material studied; (3) learners developing a running critique of the interpretive process through retrospective reviews of methods of study – class discussion of methods becomes a part of the subject studied.

Approaches to teaching and learning here aim to encourage reflection and constructive criticism and require methods that give a voice to pupils, allowing them to gain insight from their peers and to be able to examine different ideas of truth held within the classroom. The 'content' of lessons is thus an interactive relationship between material provided by the teacher and the knowledge and experience of the participants. The approach aims for a conversational form of learning which can accommodate diversity and difference.

Since learning is seen as a hermeneutical process, attention needs to be given to students' reflection on their own world views in the light of their studies. Reflexive activity is intimately related to the process of interpretation. Interpretation might start from the insider's language and experience, then move to that of the student, and then shift between the two. Thus the process of understanding another's way of life is inseparable in practice from that of considering the issues and questions raised by it.

The approach helps learners to engage with difference. Whatever differences there might appear to be between the student's world view and the way of life being studied, there may also be points of contact and overlap as well as common elements. What might appear to be entirely different on first acquaintance can end up linking with the learner's own experience in ways that challenge unquestioned assumptions.

Part of the reflexive process is to be able to engage critically with that which is studied. The management of such critical work is an important pedagogical issue, especially in teaching situations that are strongly pluralistic. Pupils need to learn how to be critical in a sensitive and constructive way. Another role for criticism as an element of reflexivity is pupils' involvement with reviewing study methods. This can reveal issues of representation and can also generate creative ideas for improvement, in the presentation of material studied to others. It can also help students to become more aware of bias in the techniques used in other forms of presentation. The key concepts from the interpretive approach were used as tools in classroom-based research in the European REDCo project (Jackson 2011, reprinted in Jackson 2012: 84–102).

Teachers and teacher-researchers have adapted the interpretive approach to their own situations and needs, and some have written about their particular approaches. These include action research studies carried out by teachers in different school contexts, focusing on topics such as gender issues in teaching about religions (O'Dell 2009); dialogue and conflict between teenage Religious Education students (O'Grady 2009); teaching gifted and talented students (Whittall 2009); issues concerned with assessment (Fancourt 2009). There are also various action research studies concerned with initial teacher training and in-service training of teachers in relation to the interpretive approach (Everington 2009, 2013, Miller 2009, Whitworth 2009, O'Grady 2013), and applications of the interpretive approach to particular challenges, such as religious extremism (Miller 2013). Julia Ipgrave's work, in particular, shows the complementarity of the interpretive approach and approaches fostering dialogue about religious diversity between young people (e.g. Jackson 2004: 109–25).

Having considered the main drivers of change with regard to the study of religions in publicly funded schools, aims for the study of religious diversity, and an example of how such aims relate to a particular didactical approach, we shall give an example of how an intergovernmental organisation, the Council of Europe, has changed policy with regard to teaching about religions and has addressed various issues relevant to policy and practice.

The Council of Europe now sees the study of religions, and non-religious convictions, as an important dimension of intercultural education, relating to the idea of freedom of religion or belief, as reflected in human rights codes.

The Council of Europe

Since 2002, the Council of Europe has focussed on education about religions (and also, since 2008, non-religious convictions) in public schools across its forty-seven member states. As indicated earlier, the events of 11 September in the USA triggered a reconsideration of the view that matters of religion belonged to the private sphere, and there was a policy change regarding teaching and learning about religions in publicly funded schools in Europe (Jackson 2010).

Following the publication of the *Universal Declaration of Human Rights*, the Council of Europe, based in Strasbourg, was established in 1949. The Council of Europe aims to protect human rights, pluralist democracy and the rule of law, and to seek solutions to social problems, such as xenophobia and discrimination against minorities. It also aims to promote awareness and development of Europe's cultural identity and diversity. There is an aim to develop across Europe a common commitment to the values expressed in the human rights codes – such as the value of human dignity – while also respecting and valuing Europe's cultural and religious diversity and the cultural traditions of each member state. There is a creative tension between a shared approach to human rights and a recognition of European diversity.

The Council of Europe integrates political activity with various projects undertaken via the Council's directorates. The Committee of Ministers includes all the Foreign Ministers and is empowered to make Recommendations to all member states. These are not legally binding, but are intended as tools for use in policy development at a national level.

The Council of Europe's educational work for schools concentrates on the related areas of human rights education, education for democratic citizenship and intercultural education. These fields include subjects such as language, history – and now religion and belief. Thus, the basic reasons for including religion in the Council of Europe's educational work concern social issues related to human rights, citizenship and intercultural education. However, aims concerned with the personal development of students and the value of a broadly based liberal education are also included; for example, the ingredient of moderated student-to-student dialogue is regarded as an essential component of such studies.

Towards the 2008 Council of Europe Recommendation

In 2002, the Council of Europe launched a major project on the study of religions as a contributor to intercultural education. There were several outputs from the project, including books for policy-makers and practitioners (Council of Europe 2005, Keast 2007). Most importantly, the Committee of Ministers agreed, in 2008, on a Recommendation concerning the dimension of religions and non-religious convictions within intercultural education (Council of Europe 2008) which was circulated to all member states.

The Recommendation provides guidance on education about religions and 'non-religious convictions' in the context of intercultural education. It acknowledges diversity at local, regional and international levels, and encourages connections to be made between 'local' and 'global', the exploration of issues concerning religion and identity, and the development of positive relations with parents and religious communities. The intention is to introduce young people to a variety of positions in an atmosphere of mutual tolerance, within the 'safe space' of the classroom.

There is an emphasis on competence for understanding a variety of religions and world views, including well-selected information, plus the development of skills and attitudes to facilitate dialogue. The aim is to provide knowledge but also to encourage reciprocity, sensitivity and empathy and to combat prejudice, intolerance and racism. Students are encouraged to take part in dialogues and discussions managed by teachers with specialist knowledge and facilitation skills. The Recommendation acknowledges that such provision needs to be supported by high-quality teacher training, good quality resources and on-going research and evaluation.

Whilst having clear goals, sensitivity is expressed towards the educational systems and practices already in operation in member states. The Recommendation is provided as a flexible discussion text.

The development of *Signposts*

To promote discussion and action in relation to the 2008 Recommendation, the Council of Europe and the European Wergeland Centre established a joint committee in 2009 to work on ways of helping policy-makers and practitioners in member states to discuss and apply ideas in their own national setting. The committee distributed a questionnaire to members of the Education Committee of the Council of Europe, based in each of the forty-seven member states, asking respondents to identify difficulties they felt they would have in applying the Recommendation in their own countries.

The responses identified issues common to many member states. These issues provided the framework for the main chapters of a book, which the present author was asked to write on behalf of the committee for use by policy-makers and practitioners in member states (Jackson 2014b). The ten short chapters of *Signposts: Policy and Practice for Teaching about Religions and Non-Religious World Views in Intercultural Education* (Jackson 2014b) are headed:

1. The recommendation: background, issues and challenges;
2. Introducing Signposts and its key themes;
3. Terminology associated with teaching about religions and beliefs;
4. Competence and didactics for understanding religions;
5. The classroom as a safe space;
6. The representation of religions in media;
7. Non-religious convictions and world views;
8. Human rights issues;
9. Linking schools to wider communities and organisations;
10. Promoting further discussion and action.

The chapters aim to enable policy-makers, teacher trainers and teachers to discuss the issues raised in relation to their own particular context, taking account of law and tradition in their own particular countries. The central chapters set out the key issues in relation to the particular topic being discussed and provide examples from recent research, including examples from various countries involved in the European REDCo project and current good practice in a variety of member states. The chapters draw upon illustrative examples of REDCo research with fourteen- to sixteen-year-olds in eight European countries (England, Estonia, France, Germany, the Netherlands, Norway, the Russian Federation and Spain). The selected examples deal with specific topics, but together show that studies of religious diversity are not a threat to students' own commitments, but rather can help to develop a culture of 'living together'. Most young people surveyed appreciated opportunities to learn about and from one another's religious viewpoints in the 'safe space' of the classroom, with teachers providing good quality source material, while also encouraging dialogue (Knauth, Jozsa, Bertram-Troost *et al.* 2008, Valk, Bertram-Troost, Friederici *et al.* 2009, Want, Bakker, Avest *et al.* 2009, Jackson 2012).

Central issues, such as the development of teachers' and students' competence, teaching methods and approaches, handling representations of religions in the broadcast and print media, making the classroom a safe space for civil dialogue and exchange and human rights topics, are introduced in *Signposts* in such a way as to facilitate constructive discussion by users. The general aim is to encourage politicians and educators in member states to develop policies which increase the religious literacy of their citizens.

As a result of a number of recent atrocities committed by religious extremists, the Council of Europe has taken the view that the development of higher levels religious literacy is a vital contributor to increasing understanding of religions across the population. The Committee of Ministers, the Foreign Ministers of the member states, in May 2015, issued the Declaration *United Around Our Principles Against Violent Extremism and Radicalisation Leading to Terrorism* (Council of Europe 2015a) together with an associated Action Plan (Council of Europe 2015b). The Action Plan emphasises the development of competences required for democratic culture and intercultural dialogue. There will be an emphasis on 'initiatives to combat stereotyping and discrimination, to support inclusion strategies at local level, to build trust among citizens across social and cultural differences and to support intercultural communication and skills', and it is planned that *Signposts* will be widely disseminated across member states as a tool for developing a deeper understanding of religious diversity (Council of Europe 2015b). *Signposts* has been translated into a variety of languages (Arabic, Dutch, English, French, German, Greek, Italian, Norwegian, Romanian, Russian, Spanish, Swedish and Ukrainian translations are available at the time of writing), with more to follow.[1] In the present political climate, it is important not to underplay the intrinsic value of the study of religions and its personal value, as well as its social importance. *Signposts* attempts to maintain this balance and also to encourage users in different countries and regions to have their own discussions about policy and practice, related to their own particular contexts.

Conclusion

In this chapter, various reasons for studying religions in publicly funded schools within democratic societies, with the goal of increasing religious literacy across the population, have been discussed. Issues, such as the relationship between impartial and inclusive approaches and faith-based approaches were raised and considered, and the need for complementarity between different approaches was emphasised. The intimate connection between aims for studying religions and the philosophy and design of didactical methodologies was illustrated through the example of the interpretive approach. The relationship of reasons for studying religions in publicly funded schools and policy development was discussed through the example of the Council of Europe and its on-going work in this field across the continent. Particular attention was given to the Council of Europe's Ministerial Recommendation on teaching about religions and non-religious convictions, and to its dissemination, discussion and utilisation through the book *Signposts*. It is hoped that *Signposts* will

1 Pdf copies of *Signposts* in all translations can be downloaded free of charge from www.theewc.org/Content/Library/COE-Steering-documents/Recommendations/Signposts-Policy-and-practice-for-teaching-about-religions-and-non-religious-world-views-in-intercultural-education, last accessed 15 January 2018.

be helpful for politicians and practitioners as a tool for informing discussion and debate in the development of policy and good practice. Finally, it is important to emphasise that any new policy developments which aim to increase religious literacy need to be supported by sufficient resources to fund high-quality initial training and in-service training of teachers in this field in order to be successful.

Bibliography

Bråten, Oddrun M.H. 2013. *Towards a Methodology for Comparative Studies in Religious Education: A study of England and Norway*, Münster, Waxmann.

Cole, W. Owen 1972. *Religion in the Multi-faith School*, Yorkshire, Committee for Community Relations.

Council of Europe 2005. *The Religious Dimension of Intercultural Education*, Strasbourg, Council of Europe.

Council of Europe 2008. *Recommendation CM/Rec (2008) 12 of the Committee of Ministers to Member States on the Dimension of Religions and Nonreligious Convictions within Intercultural Education*, Committee of Ministers, Brussels, 10 December, https://wcd.coe.int/ViewDoc.jsp?p=&id=1386911&Site=CM&direct=true, last accessed 15 January 2018.

Council of Europe 2015a. *Declaration of the Committee of Ministers of the Council of Europe, 'United Around Our Principles Against Violent Extremism and Radicalisation Leading to Terrorism'*, 125th Session of the Committee of Ministers, Brussels, 19 May.

Council of Europe 2015b. *The Fight against Violent Extremism and Radicalisation Leading to Terrorism. Action Plan*, 125th Session of the Committee of Ministers, Brussels, 19 May.

Cox, Edwin 1967. *Sixth Form Religion: A Study of the Beliefs and of the Attitudes to Religion, Religious Instruction, and Morals, of a Sample of Grammar School Sixth Form Pupils*, London, SCM Press.

Everington, Judith 2009. 'The Use of the Interpretive Approach in the Professional Development of Student Teachers of Religious Education', in Julia Ipgrave, Robert Jackson and Kevin O'Grady (ed.), *Religious Education Research through a Community of Practice. Action Research and the Interpretive Approach*, Münster, Waxmann, 100–13.

Everington, Judith 2013. 'The Interpretive Approach and Bridging the "Theory–Practice Gap": Action Research with Student Teachers of Religious Education in England', in Joyce Miller, Kevin O'Grady and Ursula McKenna (ed.), *Religion in Education: Innovation in International Research*, New York/London, Routledge, 149–64.

Fancourt, Nigel 2009. 'Reflexive Assessment: The Interpretive Approach and Classroom Assessment', in Julia Ipgrave, Robert Jackson and Kevin O'Grady (ed.), *Religious Education Research through a Community of Practice. Action Research and the Interpretive Approach*, Münster, Waxmann, 84–99.

Felderhof, Marius 2012. 'Secular Humanism', in L. Philip Barnes (ed.), *Debates in Religious Education*, London/New York, Routledge, 146–56.

Gates, Brian and Jackson, Robert 2014. 'Religion and Education in England', in Martin Rothgangel, Robert Jackson and Martin Jäggle (ed.), *Religious Education at Schools in Europe. Part 2: Western Europe*, Göttingen, Vienna University Press/V&R Unipress, 65–98.

Gearon, Liam 2012a. 'European Religious Education and European Civil Religion', *British Journal of Educational Studies* 60:2, 151–69.

Gearon, Liam 2012b. 'The Securitisation of Religion in Education', in Theo van der Zee and Terence J. Lovat (ed.), *New Perspectives in Religious and Spiritual Education*, Münster, Waxmann, 215–33.

Gearon, Liam 2013. *Masterclass in Religious Education: Transforming Teaching and Learning*, London, Bloomsbury.

Ipgrave, Julia 2013. 'The Language of Interfaith Encounter among Inner City Primary School Children', *Religion & Education* 40:1, 35–49 and also in Joyce Miller, Kevin O'Grady and Ursula McKenna (ed.), *Religion in Education: Innovation in International Research*, New York/London, Routledge, 90–104.

Ipgrave, Julia, Jackson, Robert and O'Grady, Kevin (ed.) 2009. *Religious Education Research through a Community of Practice. Action Research and the Interpretive Approach*, Münster, Waxmann.

Iversen, Lars L. 2013. '"Can You Be a Muslim and Not Believe in God?" How Fluid or Solid Are Religions? Introducing Viscosity to the Interpretive Approach', in Joyce Miller, Kevin O'Grady and Ursula McKenna (ed.), *Religion in Education: Innovation in International Research*, New York/London, Routledge, 167–81.

Jackson, Robert 1978. 'The World Religions Debate', in Robert Jackson (ed.), *Perspectives on World Religions*, London, University of London School of Oriental and African Studies, 3–32.

Jackson, Robert 1997. *Religious Education: An Interpretive Approach*, London, Hodder and Stoughton, available as a pdf download free of charge with a new introduction at www.theewc.org/Content/Library/Research-Development/Literature/Introducing-Religious-Education-an-Interpretive-Approach, last accessed 15 January 2018.

Jackson, Robert 2004. *Rethinking Religious Education and Plurality: Issues in Diversity and Pedagogy*, London/New York, RoutledgeFalmer.

Jackson, Robert 2007. 'European Institutions and the Contribution of Studies of Religious Diversity to Education for Democratic Citizenship', in Robert Jackson, Siebren Miedema, Wolfram Weisse *et al.* (ed.), *Religion and Education in Europe: Developments, Contexts and Debates*, Münster, Waxmann, 27–56.

Jackson, Robert 2010. 'Religious Diversity and Education for Democratic Citizenship: The Contribution of the Council of Europe', in Kath Engebretson, Marian de Souza, Gloria Durka *et al.* (ed.), *International Handbook of Inter-religious Education*, vol. 4, *Religion, Citizenship and Human Rights*, Dordrecht, Springer, 1121–51.

Jackson, Robert 2011. 'The Interpretive Approach as a Research Tool: Inside the REDCo Project', *British Journal of Religious Education* 33:2, 189–208.

Jackson, Robert 2012 (ed.). *Religion, Education, Dialogue and Conflict: Perspectives on Religious Education Research*, London, Routledge.

Jackson, Robert 2014a. 'Addressing Religious Extremism: A Positive Approach for Policy Makers and Practitioners', in Daniel Cere and Thomas Thorp (ed.), *Religion and Conflict: Responding to the Challenges*, London, Tony Blair Faith Foundation, 70–7, www.tonyblairfaithfoundationus.org/foundation/news/addressing-religious-extremism-positive-approach-policy-makers-and-practitioners, last accessed 15 January 2018.

Jackson, Robert 2014b. *Signposts: Policy and Practice for Teaching about Religions and Non-Religious World Views in Intercultural Education*, Strasbourg, Council of Europe.

Jackson, Robert 2015a. 'Misrepresenting Religious Education's Past and Present in Looking Forward: Gearon Using Kuhn's Concepts of Paradigm, Paradigm Shift and Incommensurability', *Journal of Beliefs and Values: Studies in Religion & Education* 36:1, 64–78.

Jackson, Robert 2015b. 'The Politicisation and Securitisation of Religious Education? A Rejoinder', *British Journal of Educational Studies* 63:3, 345–66.

Jackson, Robert 2018. *Religious Education for Plural Societies: The Selected Works of Robert Jackson*, London, Routledge.

Jackson, Robert and Nesbitt, Eleanor M. 1993. *Hindu Children in Britain*, Stoke-on-Trent, Trentham.

Jackson, Robert and O'Grady, Kevin 2007. 'Religions and Education in England: Social Plurality, Civil Religion and Religious Education Pedagogy', in Robert Jackson, Siebren Miedema, Wolfram Weisse *et al.* (ed.), *Religion and Education in Europe: Developments, Contexts and Debates*, Münster, Waxmann, 181–202.

Jackson, Robert, Ipgrave, Julia, Hayward, Mary *et al.* 2010. *Materials Used to Teach about World Religions in Schools in England*, Research Report DCSF-RR197, London, Department for Children, Families and Schools.

Jensen, Tim 2008. 'RS Based RE in Public Schools: A Must for the Secular State', *Numen: International Review for the History of Religions* 55:2/3, 123–50.

Keast, John (ed.) 2007. *Religious Diversity and Intercultural Education: A Reference Book for Schools*, Strasbourg, Council of Europe.

Knauth, Thorsten, Jozsa, Dan-Paul, Bertram-Troost, Gerdien *et al.* (ed.) 2008. *Encountering Religious Pluralism in School and Society. A Qualitative Study of Teenage Perspectives in Europe*, Münster, Waxmann, 207–45.

Leganger-Krogstad, Held 2011. *The Religious Dimension of Intercultural Education: Contributions to a Contextual Understanding*, Berlin, LIT.

Loukes, Harold 1965. *New Ground in Christian Education*, London, SCM Press.

Miller, Joyce 2009. 'Raising Humanities Teachers' Understanding of Their Pupils' Religious and Cultural Backgrounds', in Julia Ipgrave, Robert Jackson and Kevin O'Grady (ed.), *Religious Education Research through a Community of Practice. Action Research and the Interpretive Approach*, Münster, Waxmann, 130–47.

Miller, Joyce 2013. 'Religious Extremism, Religious Education and the Interpretive Approach', in Joyce Miller, Kevin O'Grady and Ursula McKenna (ed.), *Religion in Education: Innovation in International Research*, New York/London, Routledge, 121–33.

Moore, Diane L. 2007. *Overcoming Religious Illiteracy: A Cultural Studies Approach to the Study of Religion in Secondary Education*, New York, Palgrave Macmillan.

Moulin, Daniel 2011. 'Giving Voice to "the Silent Minority": The Experience of Religious Students in Secondary School Religious Education Lessons', *British Journal of Religious Education* 33:3, 313–26.

O'Dell, Gemma 2009. 'Action Research into Teaching about Religious Diversity: Pedagogical and Gender Issues in Applying the Interpretive Approach', in Julia Ipgrave, Robert Jackson and Kevin O'Grady (ed.), *Religious Education Research through a Community of Practice. Action Research and the Interpretive Approach*, Münster, Waxmann, 56–71.

O'Grady, Kevin 2009. '"There is a bit of Peace in England": Dialogue and Conflict between Teenage Religious Education Pupils in Sheffield', in Julia Ipgrave, Robert Jackson and Kevin O'Grady (ed.), *Religious Education Research through a Community of Practice. Action Research and the Interpretive Approach*, Münster, Waxmann, 45–55.

O'Grady, Kevin 2013. 'Action Research and the Interpretive Approach to Religious Education', in Joyce Miller, Kevin O'Grady and Ursula McKenna (ed.), *Religion in Education: Innovation in International Research*, New York/London, Routledge, 134–48.

Said, Edward W. 1978. *Orientalism*, London, Routledge & Kegan Paul.

Smart, Ninian 1968. *Secular Education and the Logic of Religion*, London, Faber and Faber.

Smith, Wilfred C. [1962] 1978. *The Meaning and End of Religion*, London, SPCK.

UNESCO 1996. *Learning: The Treasure Within. Report to UNESCO of the International Commission on Education for the Twenty-first Century*, Paris, UNESCO.

Valk, Pille, Bertram-Troost, Gerdien, Friederici, Markus *et al.* (ed.) 2009. *Teenagers' Perspectives on the Role of Religion in their Lives, Schools and Societies. A European Quantitative Study*, Münster, Waxmann.

Want, Anna van der, Bakker, Cok, Avest, Ina ter *et al.* 2009. *Teachers Responding to Religious Diversity in Europe. Researching Biography and Pedagogy*, Münster, Waxmann.

Whittall, Amy 2009. 'Developing Appropriate Principles and Strategies for the Teaching of Gifted Students of Religious Education', in Julia Ipgrave, Robert Jackson and Kevin O'Grady (ed.), *Religious Education Research through a Community of Practice. Action Research and the Interpretive Approach*, Münster, Waxmann, 72–83.

Whitworth, Linda 2009. 'Developing Primary Student Teachers Understanding and Confidence in Teaching Religious Education', in Julia Ipgrave, Robert Jackson and Kevin O'Grady (ed.), *Religious Education Research through a Community of Practice. Action Research and the Interpretive Approach*, Münster, Waxmann, 114–29.

Wright, Andrew 1998. *Spiritual Pedagogy: A Survey, Critique and Reconstruction of Contemporary Spiritual Education in England and Wales*, Abingdon, Culham College Institute.

13 Teaching faith

Mary Earl

Introduction

As soon as a new group of postgraduates come into our university setting (as they do every year), to be initiated into the mysteries of teaching about and from world religions in UK schools, I ask them one question: what do you think it means to be religiously educated? Their answers, argued in 3,000-word essays and then, more technically, worked out into practice in schools, fascinate me. These students are postgraduates, coming to us with degrees which mainly focus on either Theology, Theology and Religious Studies or Religious Studies with Philosophy. They have strong views about whether 'teaching faith' is about personally developing one's own ethical, philosophical or theological perspectives on life, about social cohesion and the needs of wider society or about achieving the foundations for a career in academe. It is common, therefore, that in any one group of postgraduate teacher trainees there will be a division, from the start, between those who see their work as being one of induction into the range of skills involved in handling theological or philosophical argumentation (a rational autonomy aim) and those who see it as part of the ethical imperative of adults in society to induct the young into debate about the right, the good, the just and the true (a citizenship aim). These twin aims seem to play out, too, in the development of school-based curricula in the UK. Having been able, through this long-term teacher training role and through an action research project funded and carried out by the Woolf Institute,[1] to find out, long term, what teachers' perception of teaching faith is, it seemed appropriate to share some of my findings here (Earl 2016).

There were five important background factors affecting our interpretation of this data. They are briefly characterised as follows:

1 From my social scientific reading it seems to me irrefutable that secularisation, migration and contested histories,[2] the malaises of modernity (Taylor 1991) and the emergence, post-1980s, of what Margaret Archer calls 'the reflexive imperative' (Archer 2012) will constantly and consistently affect the what, why, when and how of teaching faith today.
2 In the UK at least, the loss of a common understanding of what used to be seen as our linguistic heritage (Greek, Latin) means that we can no longer assume that

1 The Woolf Institute is dedicated to interfaith research, teaching and dialogue. Studying relations between Jews, Christians and Muslims throughout the ages. Their funding of this research made it possible. Its headquarters are in Cambridge, England, www.woolf.cam.ac.uk, last accessed 16 January 2018.

2 Contested histories is a term used to resituate complex academic debate about who 'owns' a particular history. It is commonly used to resituate debate about Israel, First peoples, the Crusades, etc. at university teaching level.

school students will automatically know about the languages, histories and cultures which used to lie, helpfully, in the background of school-based study of Judaism and Christianity.

3 Lack of Christian faith adhesion by many parents in the UK means that biblical narratives are to a much lesser extent 'bred into' school students' self-understanding than they were previously. Starting the project of teaching faith with an assumption that 'they know some of it anyway' from home or local faith community involvement can make teaching faith, in the case of Christianity, a project doomed to failure.
4 It is obvious from the empirical data from the following study that however teachers, whether in the UK or the USA, *want* to see their own role, their ability to carry their educational project through is constantly affected by the laws of the country they work in.
5 The prevalence of school students' sense that everything in faith is 'just your opinion' needs to be tackled seriously if anything teachers say about faith is going to be taken seriously.

The Woolf Institute/University of Cambridge Research Project (2013–15)

The twenty teachers recruited into this study all submitted case studies and questionnaires to our team of researchers as soon as they joined the project. All the schools were already committed to learning more about how to address the religious illiteracy they saw in their pluralistic school classrooms and all were already trying to do so. In both countries our team of researchers visited each school, saw a lesson where teaching was about 'the other' (e.g. in a Muslim or Jewish school, a teacher teaching about Christianity or a Jewish school teaching about Islam) – and debriefed that lesson with the teacher(s) concerned. As many teachers as could do so then met together for two days at the Faculty of Education in Cambridge, UK where, alongside academic researchers and faith community members they were presented with the six key teaching issues about teaching faith which had emerged from the preliminary data. These were: (1) the need to define aims and outcomes of teaching faith *in schools* as being different (because the schooling context is a public space within a society) from the aims of teaching faith elsewhere (e.g. in mosques, churches, etc.); (2) the need to define and understand authentically (within the tradition) all key concepts being taught; (3) the need to consider how 'insider' and 'outsider' perspectives affect teaching faith; (4) the need to define the parameters of and develop skills in the practice of using interactive teaching methods blended by exploratory talk when teaching faith; (5) the need for school students to develop other key skills for studying faith (e.g. guided research, open-minded enquiry, reasonableness); (6) the need for school teachers to constantly and consistently develop their own subject knowledge for teaching in this field – and define, for themselves, whether they are teaching Religious Studies (secular and inclusive), Dogmatic Theology or Philosophy.

During the conference, conference delegates were encouraged, in cross-country, cross-school and cross-faith groups to try to recognise any mismatch in their perceptions of what made teaching about someone else's faith challenging – and what opportunities it provided. This extremely rich data stream was later transcribed and became the backbone of both a report and a book for use in schools (Earl 2015, 2016).

Types of school and attitudes to teaching faith

The data comes from ten schools in the USA and ten in the UK. The schools, following the chief focus of work at the Woolf Institute, were largely Christian, Muslim or Jewish in foundation though, as in the UK all schools must teach about and from religions, the UK sample also included some schools with a secularised foundation. These schools, within the UK curriculum, teach six world religions and can also include the perspectives of Humanism in their teaching. Overall, our sample of twenty schools included five (one US, four UK) schools describing their schools as having no, or a secular, faith foundation; four (two US, two UK) which had a Jewish faith foundation and three (two US, one UK) which had an Islamic faith foundation. The eight schools which had a Christian faith foundation (five US, three UK) included three Catholic schools (one UK, two US), one Anglican Cathedral school, one Catholic-Anglican inter-church school (UK) and three Episcopal schools (US). All twenty teachers, together with the team who initiated the research (all working within either the Woolf Institute in Cambridge or the University of Cambridge's Faculty of Education), were concerned about how they taught (well or otherwise) about 'the other's' faiths. So questionnaires, lesson observations in the twenty schools, case studies collected and conversations held were directed towards finding 'best practice' in this area. Because of the difference in the two countries between grade ages, the study was of schooling standardised as eight to eighteen years.

Whereas the primary data (questionnaires, lesson observations and case studies) told us which issues we needed to consider when we met together, the joint conference gave us the 'thick description' of what might be involved in addressing those issues. Our data is, therefore, what Paul Ricoeur called 'testimony [which] demands to be interpreted because of the dialectic of meaning and event that traverses it' (Ricoeur 1980: 144–5). It is the testimony of twenty Religious Education teachers at two points where 'the dialectic of meaning and event' traversed their working lives (see also Ricoeur 1976: 12).

How is the 'teaching faith' curriculum being constructed?

Bernstein points out that in any construction of the curriculum, distributive, recontextualising and evaluative rules are being followed (Singh 2002). Whether you are teaching faith or teaching maths these processes operate. It is possible to see quite clearly in this data that a variety of dominant discourses govern the redistribution of knowledge from faith communities to schools in both the UK and the USA.

In some schools, as you might expect, the dominant discourse surrounding teaching faith clearly indicates that distributive rules come from within one faith only. That faith's beliefs are then being 'translated' outside that sphere, to make 'the other's' faith either 'like' or 'not like' the core ideas of the foundation faith of that school. Other schools, notably the state-maintained UK schools and some of the Episcopal schools in both the USA and the UK, choose, in the classroom, *not* to privilege any one faith's ideas but to examine the claims to truth of each faith as objectively as they can, within the rational terms of what used to be called the human sciences (Gadamer 2013). These two attitudes produce radically different ways of teaching faith. In the latter group of schools, for instance, teachers used, in the classroom, inclusive rather than exclusive language when teaching faith (for instance by stating 'Christians believe' rather than 'we believe') and did not assume or exclude diversity of faith backgrounds in their students.

Religion in the public sphere: two different cases (UK and US)

This brings us to the biggest questions about teaching faith, both of which centre on the question 'Who are we providing this education for – and in what location?' In the most recent

Agreed Syllabus[3] for Cambridge, Peterborough, Rutland and Northamptonshire (2018) religious literacy is described as both an aim and an outcome of teaching faith in local state-maintained schools. Having this in mind affects the way the curriculum is constructed – and the ways in which successful learning is 'measured'. So, here, the subject's aim is for school students, at the end of their compulsory education (age eighteen), to have 'the knowledge of, and the ability to understand, religion, beliefs, practices, spiritual insights and secular world views'. The given measure of success (Bernstein's evaluative rule) is described as students 'being able to talk with fluency and understanding about religion and belief' (Cambridge Agreed Syllabus 2018). Religious Education in the UK (but also in some US schools) forbids proselytising by law though the curriculum does emphasise (if only for heritage reasons) the teaching of Christianity over other faiths. Alongside the existence of an established (Anglican) Church and of large numbers of Anglican (especially primary) schools the distributive rules, for good or ill, favour the Anglican Church (Furbey, Dinham, Farnell *et al.* 2006). In the USA, the first amendment puts religion, automatically, into an entirely different place on (or in this case off) the curriculum of state-maintained (public) schools. None of the schools we worked with in this study were state-maintained simply because the first amendment forbids explicit teaching about faith in state-maintained (public) schools. That first amendment states that:

> Congress shall make no law respecting an establishment of religion, or prohibiting the free exercise thereof; or abridging the freedom of speech, or of the press; or the right of the people peaceably to assemble, and to petition the government for a redress of grievances.

As Charles Haynes, the senior scholar at the First Amendment Center, says, 'nowhere is it more important – or more difficult – to address our growing ideological and religious diversity than in the public schools' (Haynes and Thomas 2001: 3). In 2012 he adds 'if we can't get it right in public schools, we have little hope of getting this right in the public square of what is now the most religiously diverse nation on Earth' (Haynes 2011: 14). It was interesting, when meeting twenty teachers teaching faith against two such different legislative backgrounds, that of all the teachers the ones who agreed most about their aims were probably the Religious Education teachers in the UK and the social science teachers in the USA.

How is faith being taught?

What few if any of the teachers in this study believed they could or should do was to teach 'all about' a faith. Schools which *did* see teaching one religion in depth as their mission were mainly faith foundation schools. They worked through both the implicit *and* the explicit curriculum to address their aims, recruiting teachers who were of faith themselves and allocating a considerable amount of timetable time to teaching faith. In contrast many of the teachers who worked in state-maintained settings assumed that their students might lack even a basic understanding of what religions are. This obviously affected both their curriculum and their pedagogy (ways of teaching).

3 Agreed Syllabuses, in the UK, are revised every five years and have, since the 1988 Education Act, formed the backbone of the RE curriculum in the UK. However, with the advent of academisation and the demise of the numbers of local authority-funded schools available to implement them, these syllabi are becoming less influential in determining the RE curriculum in state-maintained schools in the UK.

Many school students, in the lessons we saw, were encouraged in every type of school to respect the 'otherness' of 'the other's' viewpoint and, in most cases, allowed time to reflect on and, sometimes, analyse critically, why one world view's perspective on a particular topic might differ from another. The most expert teachers we worked with could sustain both philosophical (including ethical) and theological lines of enquiry throughout a lesson in ways which were engaging, stimulating and challenging.

It soon became very clear to us all, as lesson observers, that the best teachers in the field ask rigorous educational questions of themselves before they plan lessons. These would include asking: 'What are the important ideas students need to understand here and what *can* students of this age understand?' Some teachers also showed a highly developed set of skills for communicating across difference and diversity in very pluralist classrooms and demonstrated very high levels of pastoral care when addressing controversial issues.[4] They saw these duties of care as part of the rigour of their professionalism. It is clearly characteristic of those teaching faith in both countries that they have deep concerns for the well-being of their students, not just for their intellectual development. It is also clear that the best practice seen did not exclude one at the expense of the other.

Teaching for religious literacy was inevitably seen by many of these teachers as a necessary part of doing their job since without this literacy little of what faiths say would, today, be understood. Most (not all) recognised that ***authentically*** knowing about and being able to understand the faith of an 'other' involves far more than a basic religious literacy. These teachers wanted to teach faith at a deeper level, one which involved an appreciation of hermeneutics (interpretation), chains of tradition in different faiths (e.g. isnad) and history (the haskalah, the Enlightenment, etc.). The selection of topic, topic aim, resources and pedagogy often involved, for instance, introducing theologically or philosophically contrasting literary, artistic, musical or other sources into the classroom or spending time making sure that a religious concept (e.g. right effort in Buddhism) was exemplified at local or regional level. One particularly good Jewish school in the UK showed that careful teaching about a concept authentically ***within*** a tradition (***tikkun olam***/repairing the world) could lead to better comparison with the same idea in secularity. Authenticity in teaching faith matters – but we repeatedly saw that difference and diversity in faith cannot be well addressed if teachers do not really understand the 'thick descriptions' behind 'the other's' use of language.[5]

Inspection agencies: conflicting aims?

The data shows multiple instances of conflicting school management and inspection agency aims, especially in faith foundation schools. This confused, for teachers, the whole issue of

4 The word 'controversial' has a very specific meaning here. Controversial issues are ones where there are reasonable arguments on two or more sides which might relevantly inform our understanding and enable us to develop arguments and eventually judgments, but where no absolute judgement has been (or sometimes can be) made about which argument is 'most true'. Some would argue, for instance, that the idea of global warming is still controversial. Others might say that the evidence is now so strong for it that it is no longer controversial. Knowing whether a topic involves controversial ideas is extremely important when teaching faith and all professional teachers think about this before they plan, resource or teach lessons.

5 You may find that asking yourself the following three questions, as you read, will also give you a sense of where you yourself stand in this debate: (1) what do you think the function of 'literacy' of any kind is in education? Why do reading, comprehending and interpreting a text matter?; (2) why do you think teachers as well as school pupils sometimes struggle to become 'literate' in relation to what others believe and practice but are perfectly comfortable when discussing their own beliefs and practices? How can teachers be helped to overcome this problem?; (3) do you think that basic 'religious literacy' is never enough – and that systematic study of a faith is the only kind of teaching of faith which is worth doing?

how, what, why and when teaching about others' beliefs and practices should take place. Teachers regularly reported feeling almost powerless to teach well (or in some cases, at all) because there were so many conflicting aims coming towards them from senior managers, governors and inspection agencies. It is noticeable in the data that state-maintained schools and those teaching about 'the other' from a social studies point of view did not encounter this problem in the same way. In the UK, for instance, the official inspection agency is Ofsted and inspection will be of the quality of the curriculum and teachers' ability to ensure that all their school students 'make progress in learning'. Here, however, is the testimony of a teacher working in a pluralist Jewish school in the UK, faced with both that agenda and the one of Pikuach:

> I have five sects of Judaism in my class of thirty. So I have to make sure that any sentence that I'm saying is not alienating. I don't want to bring Ofsted into this, but because we are a Jewish school we have an extra Ofsted called Pikuach. So if someone comes and says that I have been talking about Judaism in very general terms then that means I've failed my lesson. Forget that they made progress, forget whether they learned anything. I still taught the wrong thing because I'm not standing for Orthodox Judaism or Reform Judaism or Masorti or Liberal or atheist.
>
> (Earl 2016)

Without agreement, preferably across inspection agencies, of what best practice is, provision is unlikely to improve. These issues need to be addressed, not evaded.

For the faith communities represented here there is another journey to be faced, too. A few faith schools, despite knowing about or wanting to say that teaching about 'the other's' faith was important, were putting very little professional development into finding out, from professional sources, how to do this type of teaching well. So the actual teaching seen was of very variable standard and there were some shocking inaccuracies in the representation of 'the other's' faith. Examples include Roman Catholicism *still* being seen as a religion entirely distinct from Christianity, the use of the words Torah, Tanakh and Old Testament being horribly muddled and Christmas being described merely 'just like' Channukah. At the other end of the spectrum, however, were some highly imaginative, well-resourced and deeply sensitively aware lessons where teaching genuinely encouraged school students both to develop empathy by walking a short way in the steps of 'the other' and to comment on difference and diversity between faiths in intellectually rigorous ways which truly generated both knowledge and understanding.

Teaching and learning

The issue which arises here is whether policy-makers and governments (and, indeed, faith community leaders) are prepared to accept that what teachers do is teach, not proselytise. Teachers are trained professionally in every other subject – otherwise they are not allowed to teach in publicly funded institutions. Why should it be any different for those who teach about others' beliefs and practices? School heads, policy-makers and professional groups all seem sometimes not to understand that pupils are entitled to be given an education which sets them on an open road to understanding, not one that is prematurely sealed off by agendas not relevant to them. However some of the priests or chaplains in this cohort of teachers understood the implications of this very well. They would wear the teacher's hat first when teaching about 'the other' in a classroom – and not that of the spiritual director. As a result they did both jobs well and were respected for their work in both roles by those they taught. In the Muslim, Christian and Jewish schools, however, there were some who felt that their spiritual director role should always come first. Others turned lessons into pastoral rather than human sciences-based learning opportunities (Gadamer 2013). The result of the latter choice was usually to make the lessons ethical in focus so that the main concern was questions like: 'How should we behave towards one another?' In practice our dominant finding from the twenty-lesson observations in the two countries[6] was that for outstanding teachers the primary concern, whether or not they were both faith leaders and teachers or not, was to open up in their classrooms a dialogic space where everyone's values could be heard fairly, and where the reasonings – and faith bases – of 'the other's' beliefs and practices could be understood on their own terms. Whether we call this goal religious literacy (Furbey, Dinham, Farnell *et al.* 2006), religious understanding (Walshe and Teece 2013), critical literacy (Hella and Wright 2009) or 'recognition' of 'the other' (Jackson 2009), carrying this project through well takes enormous professional skill and judgement. It is not an amateur activity.

What brought faith and non-faith foundation schools attitudes together?

In every type of school and in both countries teachers were constantly frustrated by the fact that their subject was so poorly recognised by other teaching professionals. The range of examples of this given (Earl 2016) included the following:

1. Whether there was senior managerial support and, preferably, senior level *understanding* of why teaching about 'the other's' faith matters.
2. Whether teachers were expected to have professional training and to use collaborative and interactive teaching methods to engage the school students and enable them to make progress in learning, over time, reliably.
3. Whether the teacher (and school) encouraged open, real-world issue-influenced questioning by students. Teachers who shut down, dogmatically or otherwise, on such debate were the least effective in their teaching about 'the other'.
4. Whether high-quality professional development for teachers was available. This needed to include giving teachers an accurate sense of what professional teaching in this field looks like and then insisting that this level of teaching is reliably sustained so that students do make progress in learning. Sharing an *evidence* base for best practice always helps in this respect.
5. How far departments shared clearly defined aims for teaching about 'the other' and whether they shared the desired outcomes of their lessons transparently and collaboratively across the department.
6. How far time and space was being given, in lessons, for students to clarify their *own* values. In best practice examples this was often managed through real or virtual empathetic encounters with others' views.
7. How far examples given of 'the other's' beliefs and practices were up to date and global (e.g. in images used on PowerPoint slides and in the use of up-to-date, professionally produced, self-study booklets).

6 These observations and, indeed, the whole project, could not have taken place without the indefatigable work of Laurie Hogen from California whose vision instigated and often financially supported the project from beginning to end.

8 Whether teachers acknowledged the importance of helping students to develop discernment about the values passed on by social media. If this was acknowledged as a key concern teachers used some lessons to help students detect and handle *bias* in social media resources, too.

The need for teachers to update and recontextualise their own 'subject knowledge'

Some of the teachers in this sample were very highly theologically qualified and had many years of experience in teaching. Others were not but were just as highly motivated to learn. Yet they all shared worries, to exactly the same extent, about their personal ability to update and contextualise their subject knowledge, particularly when teaching about someone else's beliefs and practices. They also worried about how to position themselves, as teachers, in relation to that subject knowledge. Should they do so as 'insiders' or 'outsiders' to the faith? As one of the conference speakers pointed out, 'outsiders' usually present the religion as found in the 'dominant' discourse (of textbooks, of society in that time and place or of the religion itself). Insiders often privilege particular ideas and beliefs dominant in their own traditions and exclude aspects of tradition that they see as inauthentic. Therefore, neither is without its problems. This issue is exemplified again and again in our data. Many said that the main problem lay in identifying *whose* discourse about each belief and practice should be represented in the classroom and from whose perspective it needed to be represented. For instance, one professionally trained Christian teacher, teaching as objectively as he could about Paul's teaching (on Judaism in relation to Christianity) to Jewish school students in the USA began to worry that parents might see this as proselytising. His hunch was later proved true. Parents did complain. But, objectively, he knew he was simply giving information which any university-trained scholar of New Testament Theology would take for granted as being true. So where does the hermeneutic problem lie here? In another instance a Muslim teacher in the UK was teaching about the life of Jesus but without apparently noticing that the interpretation of what the texts meant was coming from Muslim sources. Christian colleagues found this difficult because one insider voice (Quranic understanding of Jesus) was dominating another insider's interpretation of their own texts (Christianity). Some found elements of the insider perspective which their students could relate to from the local community. These lessons could involve something apparently quite simple like visiting others' schools. Here the young people involved clearly learned that if 'they' are in practice, humanly 'just like us' we should not be afraid of learning from each other. More implicitly they are also at the start of learning that

> Christianity, Judaism, and Islam all have commitments to peace, justice, honesty, service, personal responsibility, forgiveness, respect, and obligation to others that can contribute to the development of trusting relationships.
>
> (Furbey, Dinham, Farnell *et al.* 2006: 10)

Because more effective teachers, whether in the UK or the USA, chose to teach from a perspective which did not set out to privilege any one viewpoint over another in the classroom (even within a faith school) they had fewer worries about whether it was 'safe' to acquire knowledge about 'the other'. Several of these teachers commented that 'because there is no assumption (for me) of any religion being "mine", effectively it means there is no "other"' (Earl 2016). Sitting in these classrooms, it was obvious that this approach worked for most teachers and for most of their students, most of the time. However it seemed odd, even in 2013, that three quarters of *all* the teachers in this study, experienced or not, felt they could not teach about or from the Quran since they did not believe it would be 'safe' to do so. When it came to teaching the Christian narrative, there was less fear of doing so but immense variety in different teachers' sense of what that narrative is. The one faith narrative all twenty agreed on was that of Judaism!

Adolescence, identity formation and teaching faith

Engaging with adolescent 'identity formation' issues and managing both pastoral and pedagogic roles in the same classroom, often at one and the same time, was creatively handled by some of the best teachers seen. The overwhelming majority of respondents said that teaching about others' beliefs and practices was important because students developed the ability to talk and reason together about others' beliefs and practices more quickly when they were engaging systematically with reflection on their own. This dialogic process was the essence of all the best practice seen in both countries (Kazepides 2013).

Everyone, said the best of these teachers, needs to be able to study 'the other's' beliefs and practices because for all of us someone or something else is other! How else will we learn at either an academic or personal, affective, level, to manage these encounters safely and productively?

Those teachers who expressed the least anxiety over teaching about 'the other' were teachers (both in maintained schools in the UK and in some independent schools in both countries) for whom inclusive teaching about 'the other' is normal. Training has taught them that since every teacher of every subject engages with some kind of 'hermeneutic' (interpretive stance) in order to take something of 'the other' into the classroom, their area of expertise must be to be able to do so consciously and with prior knowledge of what must be anticipated in terms of misconception. In this way they will help pupils reflect on the hermeneutic debates about difference and diversity which then emerge.

Teaching faith in values education mode

Many teachers are following a Rawlsian idea that we all have a right to make our own 'conception of the good' (Wenar 2017). The willingness of some teachers to explore this project of 'identity formation' with their pupils is exemplified both in school case studies and in the focus group discussions. This exploration is often conceived of, rightly, as part of the responsibility all teachers have, for 'growing' their students into the democratic communities of which they will have a participatory role in adult life. Many teachers thought hard both about pedagogy (how to teach controversial issues in the classroom) and about local social cohesion issues when they developed related schemes of work. It was somewhat disappointing, though, to find that some schools still see teaching about 'the other's' faith as somehow damaging to one's own. This was not a view shared by their students who understood very well that life in global modernity increasingly demands a capacity to work with otherness. If we waste the opportunity to do this whilst young people are in school, where else will that capacity be increased? As one US teacher in an Episcopal school said, a religiously educated person is a citizenship educated person:

> A 'religiously educated' person is one who understands that humans have, throughout history, developed a wide variety of ways of thinking about their role in the world and

how to make meaning out of an often confusing and unpredictable world. A religiously educated person then examines how the histories and cultures of various peoples have contributed to the shaping and development of religious beliefs and rituals over time.
(Earl 2016)

Faith and controversy

How, then, can this examination take place when it involves looking creatively at issues which, by definition, are likely to cause controversy? In the UK the (now archived) statutory citizenship curriculum had a very helpful description set of teaching stances which it recommended for teaching controversial issues. It did *not* recommend leaving them out of the curriculum since the understanding is that education in liberal democracies is there to help those who will hold democratic debate as adults learn how to handle it as children – not to exclude it. The shorthand for these three stances, described in the following, are *stated commitment*, *balanced* study and *procedural neutrality*:

1 A *stated commitment*-based lesson gives a clear, direct, indication of what the logical consequences are of taking a certain (political, social, theological or philosophical) stance might be.
2 *Balanced study* involves discussing a balanced set of pro and con arguments in order to help students see the value of a variety of different points of view.
3 *Procedural neutrality* is a way of teaching so that students listen first to their own internal, reflective, voice, then to those of their peers and then to the voices of adults within the room. It is a process through which young people learn, ably, to refine their own sense of judgement in both academic and personal matters.

This last way of teaching is common in schools which teach philosophy for children in the UK (P4C). In its most 'open' format philosophy for children programmes works with a Socratic principle to stimulate lively and engaging discussion about a series of questions chosen, by the students themselves, for debate. This process allows the teacher to privilege the pupils' need (and desire) to clarify their *own* values over the need of others to induct them into their own societal values. It isn't all that is necessary in values education, but it can play an important role. The process is particularly important in the later stages of both primary (9–11) and secondary (14–18) education.

For example: silence speaks volumes

A discussion can be set up that it is entirely silent for the first fifteen minutes of a lesson. The teacher simply arranges large sheets of paper on tables, with key questions on them, all relating to the same topic. A typical example at secondary level would be: 'Is it ever right to kill?' The students, silently, write down their ideas. The previously blank pages fill up. Suddenly the terms of the discussion which the question provoked become transparent. Usually this makes further learning more accessible and engaging as students get interested in each other's perspectives. Soon, the students start to move back and forwards between the sheets and add extra lines of thought to the different comments. They connect parts of the argument together with colours and lines and they start to ask 'more knowledgeable others' (peers or teachers) to explain ideas which are new to them. They are now starting to make decisions and learn about argumentation. They are also becoming aware of the value of knowledge in a classroom. Above all everybody's point of view is being heard – and valued. Allowing these silent and reflective spaces teaches school students to trust the teacher to give them time and space to explore their own commitments and concerns.

The need for greater interaction between professional development at school level and recent and relevant academic debate

The last key issue addressed here concerns the difficulty most teachers encounter, once their initial teacher education is over, of learning more about teaching faith – and about faith itself. The search for authenticity in teachers' representation of 'the other' is at the core of most of the teachers' anxiety in this study. This particular group of teachers wanted far more high-quality opportunities to interact with academic debates about the 'meta' issues which should inform the development of so-called 'best practice' in this field. These debates include issues of insider/outsider perspective taking, plural identity and the migration/contested histories debate. If teachers are expected to plan schemes of work, set tasks, assess pupils' work and make resources for classes without that 'meta' level of thinking, then the substance of what is taught about 'the other' will always tends to be reductionist – as some of our lesson observations clearly showed. In that sense, 'the act of looking at what others believe does become the act of distortion' (Angell and Demetis 2010).

Why does subject knowledge matter?

The data showed that in remarkably similar ways across the two very different countries and across many different types of school, teachers are suffering from the same basic problems. These include patchy provision, inconsistency in the amount of time available for study, an inclination, amongst some faith schools and some teachers, to preference the teaching of dogma over the professional development of a genuine religious studies curriculum and the lack of subject knowledge, when it came to teaching about 'the other's' faith, amongst the teachers.

A lack of accurate subject knowledge did, we found, 'skew' schemes of work for instance so that ideas which are not necessarily so important to insiders (e.g. the five pillars of Islam) become central to teaching about the religion. It also led to actual misrepresentation of faiths and to misrepresentation of the diversity within faiths (e.g. Catholicism being seen as a religion different from Christianity). There were some exceptional examples of how a whole school's structuring of teaching about religions *did* take into account the contested narratives involved. Best practice there had led to teachers making *understanding of contestation* the focus of the study. This Jewish school (US) had a head of Contested History and was teaching about Palestine/Israel in a deliberately balanced and critical, not automatically condemnatory, way. Many of the teachers in other schools who believed in cognitive development, not just faith development, however, were regularly in conflict with senior managers or faith-based inspection agencies which did not value this approach.

Lessons were sometimes hampered in many schools by the fact that either muddled or no explanation was being given to pupils clarify *why* they were expected to learn about others' religions. A generalised 'it's good for you to know about this' or 'you need this for your exam' approach rarely satisfied the pupils. The teachers who most used inclusive language were the ones who made the subject most accessible to all pupils in most of the lessons observed. The ability to say, in a classroom context, 'Sikhs or Muslims or Jews believe', rather than 'I believe', does make a difference to pupils' willingness to listen. Where this practice was not observed, there was more confusion about other people's faiths – and about what can be studied about them. Defining the scope and context of the study of faith was an absolute guarantor of quality teaching (Gadamer 2013).

So, what does it mean, according to these teachers, to be religiously educated?

> Religious Education in the UK has for far too long occupied an ambiguous and ambivalent ground between an academic discipline and 'learning for living'. Its compulsory nature is entirely down to the belief that it would help children to be more moral, and so RE carries that with it. As a result, RE in many schools doesn't have the status of a subject like History, which means it is often taught by non-specialists, and hence taught badly, which does not help it to seem credible. The choices of religions taught in UK state schools is based entirely on representing the UK community, not on which viewpoints are more insightful, most distinct from each other, best learned together, or least known about. Concerns about what content is most interesting do not seem to be what formed this subject into what it is.
>
> (Earl 2016)

Both rational autonomy and citizenship orientations towards teaching faith are represented in this data. Expressions of its purpose range from the simple 'Religious Education's purpose is to support the development of "good" human beings and a "just" society' (a UK independent school teacher in Earl 2016) to the more complex description to follow (US Muslim school):

> [Being religiously educated means] knowing basics of each faith, knowing sufficient to want to show interest if meet someone of same or different faith (i.e. be able to communicate with others, to want to know them as human beings as well as people of faith), to have sense of own spiritual potential. We feel this is imperative (to be religiously educated) in order to establish a pluralist and tolerant society. It is very important to be religiously educated in this day and age to prevent ignorance and to respect the other.
>
> (Earl 2016)

One very clear quality which teachers look for in successful students (and in their colleagues) is open-mindedness. But that must, they say, go alongside the ability to logically evaluate. Teaching faith is not just about developing empathy but also about developing reasonableness in relation to the claims of religions. So, here, a teacher in an independent, non-faith-based school in the UK says that

> The product of a good religious education is someone who can reflect carefully on ultimate questions and try viewpoints on for size. It takes empathy as well as analysis, and open-mindedness alongside logical evaluation.
>
> (Earl 2016)

Perhaps this teacher, in a US Episcopal foundation school puts the enterprise at its most succinct. It is, they say, about giving the next generation 'an interdisciplinary language for thinking about what it means to be human in a pluralistic world'.

Teaching faith and the impact of global modernity and reflexivity

Margaret Archer, a social scientist who is also a Catholic, has long noted that it is, in some university settings, now very difficult to find colleagues willing to talk about 'the God question' at all in the public domain (Archer, Collier and Porpora 2004). If we want young people to access and engage with critically live debates about religions publicly (i.e., in school), then we must show them how to do so safely, productively – and with support. Like Archer I would say, for instance, that just because there is debate in academia and at the popular level about whether the language religions use to express meaning will, should or already has become meaningless in global modern societies, that doesn't mean it isn't legitimate to *pose* the question 'is there G-d?' What we shouldn't be doing, though, is buying into antiquated and unscientific views of the universe in order to answer the question, and here teaching faith has, I strongly believe, to question itself. I'd sooner start a debate with school students about God as 'the ground of our being' (Tillich) than allow them for one minute to conceive of G-d as an old man up in the sky. The question of G-d is meaningful but in the light of positivism we do have to redefine the scope of teaching in the context of state-maintained schools and, more widely, think extremely carefully, as Bernstein does, about the distributive (power) rules which tend, currently, to govern teaching faith (Gadamer 2013).

School pupils want and, in the view of these teachers, have an entitlement to know, just like our academic colleagues, exactly what it is about religious discourse that we think addresses the real world problems they see, know about and live alongside day by day. They do *not* want, especially within very pluralistic school populations, to simply inherit uncritically all the most contentious, sometimes ill-informed theological and philosophical debate of centuries... and pass that on to their own children, too.

Archer talks about how, in late modernity, a reflexive anxiety exists in people's minds which I take here to include their having, frequently, an uneasy attitude towards traditional values (including religious ones). Teachers who take time to listen to this anxiety will notice that some of it concerns living in a pluralistic society where there are many competing value systems. Teachers also hear about the ways students cope with this anxiety. These can be positive, such as friendship, social media and music, or negative, such as self-harm, overuse of alcohol or drugs and political or social apathy. We cannot threaten the young people we teach into taking religions seriously. According to Charles Taylor, they are already feeling threatened enough, anyway, by what he calls 'the malaises of modernity' (Taylor 1991). Perhaps, then, we should, instead of worrying vaguely about a 'decline in values', believe more that

> Our education should provide for growth and development from the present towards a future which must be created by the efforts of individuals who are educated, rather than merely moulded by the generation before them.
>
> (Stenhouse 1967)

Young people, whether they live in New York, Newcastle or Nice, share four fundamental interests: the ability to make their own judgements about what values to adopt; acquiring the skills that will enable them to become economically self-sufficient as adults; being exposed to a range of activities and experiences that will enable them to flourish in their personal lives; and developing a sense of justice. Teaching faith should not undermine these interests and should therefore offer young people a curriculum which helps them learn to bear the difficulties of social interaction (communication) between the self and 'the other' in a pluralistic society, to act with resilience and empathy in those situations and to understand 'what a religion is and what it would mean to take a religion (or other world view) seriously' (Holm 1975). If all schools, independent, faith-based, secular, state-maintained, could collaborate more to find internationalised ways of helping young people in these tasks, then they would, for this generation, have accomplished something worthwhile.

Bibliography

Angell, Ian O. and Demetis, Dionysios S. 2010. *Science's First Mistake: Delusions in Pursuit of Theory*, London, Bloomsbury.

Archer, Margaret S. 2007. *Making Our Way through the World: Human Reflexivity and Social Mobility*, Cambridge, Cambridge University Press.

Archer, Margaret S. 2012. *The Reflexive Imperative in Late Modernity*, Cambridge, Cambridge University Press.

Archer, Margaret S., Collier, Andrew and Porpora, Douglas V. 2004. *Transcendence, Critical Realism and God*, London, Routledge.

Barnes, L. Philip 2009. 'An Alternative Reading of Modern Religious Education in England and Wales', *British Journal of Sociology of Education* 30:5, 607–19.

Barnes, L. Philip 2014. *Education, Religion and Diversity: Developing a New Model of Religious Education*, Abingdon, Routledge.

Copley, Terence [1997] 2008. *Teaching Religion: Sixty Years of Religious Education in England and Wales*, 2nd edn, Exeter, University of Exeter Press.

Earl, Mary 2015. *RE-Framing Education about Beliefs and Practices in Schools: A Lens and Tools (Concept Based) Approach*, Cambridge, University of Cambridge/Woolf Institute.

Earl, Mary 2016. *Action Research Report: UK and US Teachers' Experiences of Teaching about 'the Other'*, Cambridge, University of Cambridge/Woolf Institute.

Ferber, Michael P. 2006. 'Critical Realism and Religion: Objectivity and the Insider/Outsider Problem', *Annals of the Association of American Geographers* 96:1, 176–81.

Furbey, Robert, Dinham, Adam, Farnell, Richard *et al.* 2006. *Faith as Social Capital: Connecting or Dividing?*, Bristol, Policy Press.

Gadamer, Hans-Georg 2013. *Truth and Method*, London/New York, Bloomsbury Academic.

Gearon, Liam 2013. *Masterclass in Religious Education: Transforming Teaching and Learning*, London, Bloomsbury.

Grimmitt, Michael 1987. *Religious Education and Human Development: The Relationship between Studying Religions and Personal, Social and Moral Education*, Great Wakering, McCrimmons.

Gustafson, Andrew 2015. 'Zygmunt Bauman and Ignatius: Jesuit Values and Higher Education in an Age of Liquid Modernity', *Jesuit Higher Education: A Journal* 4:2, 57–70.

Haynes, Charles C. 2011. 'Getting Religion Right in Public Schools', *Phi Delta Kappan* 93:4, 8–14.

Haynes, Charles C. and Thomas, Oliver 2001. *Finding Common Ground: A First Amendment Guide to Religious Liberty in Public Schools*, Nashville, TN, First Amendment Center.

Hella, Elina and Wright, Andrew 2009. 'Learning "About" and "From" Religion: Phenomenography, the Variation Theory of Learning and Religious Education in Finland and the UK', *British Journal of Religious Education* 31:1, 53–64.

Holm, Jean L. 1975. *Teaching Religion in Schools: A Practical Approach*, Oxford, Oxford University Press.

Jackson, Robert 2009. 'Understanding the Religions and Worldviews of Others: The Alliance of Civilization's Goals and the Interpretive Approach', Alliance of Civilisations Forum, Istanbul, Turkey, 6–7 April, www.theewc.org/Content/Library/Conference-papers/Papers-presentations/Understanding-the-Religions-and-Worldviews-of-Others-the-Alliance-of-Civilization-s-Goals-and-the-Interpretive-Approach, last accessed 16 January 2018.

Kazepides, Tasos 2013. 'Education as Dialogue', ***Educational Philosophy and Theory*** 44:9, 913–25.

Rawls, John 1988. 'The Priority of Right and Ideas of the Good', ***Philosophy & Public Affairs*** 17:4, 251–76.

Ricoeur, Paul 1976. ***Interpretation Theory: Discourse and the Surplus of Meaning***, Fort Worth, Texas Christian University Press.

Ricoeur, Paul 1980. ***Essays on Biblical Interpretation***, Philadelphia, PA, Fortress Press.

Siegel, Harvey 2017. ***Education's Epistemology: Rationality, Diversity, and Critical Thinking***, Oxford, Oxford University Press.

Singh, Parlo 2002. 'Pedagogising Knowledge: Bernstein's Theory of The Pedagogic Device', ***British Journal of Sociology of Education*** 23:4, 571–82.

Stenhouse, Lawrence 1967. ***Culture and Education***, London, Nelson.

Taylor, Charles 1991. ***The Ethics of Authenticity***, Cambridge, MA, Harvard University Press.

Teece, Geoff 2011. 'Too Many Competing Imperatives? Does RE Need to Rediscover Its Identity?', ***Journal of Beliefs & Values: Studies in Religion & Education*** 32:2, 161–72.

Valdés, Mario J. (ed.) 1991. ***A Ricoeur Reader: Reflection and Imagination***, Toronto/Buffalo, University of Toronto Press.

Walkowitz, Daniel and Knauer, Lisa M. (ed.) 2009. ***Contested Histories in Public Space: Memory, Race, and Nation***, Durham, NC, Duke University Press.

Walshe, Karen and Teece, Geoff 2013. 'Understanding "Religious Understanding" in Religious Education', ***British Journal of Religious Education*** 35:3, 313–25.

Wenar, Leif [2008] 2017. 'John Rawls', in ***Stanford Encyclopedia of Philosophy***, https://plato.stanford.edu/entries/rawls/, last accessed 16 January 2018.

Wright, Andrew 2016. ***Religious Education and Critical Realism: Knowledge, Reality and Religious Literacy***, Abingdon, Routledge.

14 The role of the media in the development of religious illiteracy

Michael Wakelin

Introduction

The media across its many formats has not been handling religion well for quite some time. This has been evident in a number of ways. Religious specialists in written journalism are now few and far between, and usually when religion makes it into the tabloids, it is portrayed only in a negative light. Furthermore, public broadcasters have drastically cut back on religious output. In this chapter, we shall explore the perceived lack of religious consideration in news coverage and misrepresentations in dramas and more regular speech-based output. It is not a totally consistent story, but the decline in media commitment to religion is discussed here and, it will be argued, relates directly to the overall decline in religious literacy in other sectors of society.[1]

In general, programming religion is all too often presented as a problem, something that strange people do. In dramas, a religious storyline very frequently becomes spooky and weird, and there is very little representation of ordinary religious people leading decent lives contributing positively to society – which is by far and wide the norm.

The media industry (journalism, drama and entertainment, across all platforms including social media) is the one place that urgently needs proper religious literacy amongst its content creators because of the power it holds over what we watch, read and hear. Training such a diverse, busy group of people would be impossible, but there is another way – which will be explained at the end of the chapter – which may help religion find its proper place, with fair, accurate coverage in media outlets, and which may help religion achieve the goal of being an asset rather than a liability.

The fact that religion and the media are uncomfortable bedfellows has not always been the case, of course. The great British institution, the British Broadcasting Corporation (BBC), was founded by a very religious man who put religion right at the heart of the BBC's programming. As will be discussed later in this chapter, this was not necessarily a good thing for religious broadcasting or, indeed, for religious literacy in the long term; however, at that time, religion held a very different place in society and, therefore, assumed a more important position in the pecking order of broadcasters and other media priorities.

The proponents of the need for greater religious literacy bemoan the loss of religious knowledge in education, government and society in general, and the 'media' is targeted with fierce criticism for being one of the main causes of the rise of religious illiteracy.

1 For further reading: Mitchell and Gower (2012), Knott and Mitchell (2012), Knott, Poole and Taira (2013), Hoover (2016). Since 2006 Stewart Hoover, Jolyon Mitchell and David Morgan have been the editors of three collections of books about the media, religion and culture which are published by Routledge (Morgan 2008, Lynch, Mitchell and Strhan 2012, Mahan 2014).

It is easy to point one's finger and throw out general complaints but, needless to say, distinguishing the reasons for this are complex, and the situation has been negative for so long that unravelling the tangle can be a tough challenge.

Yet there is hope and, as will be demonstrated, in some areas the tide is turning, and there are important developments in progress that can address this situation and lead the way forward to a more religiously literate media and subsequently a better informed and aware audience. The latter, in turn, will be more understanding of religion and more confident in encountering religion in their daily lives.

For the present, however, we shall concentrate on the widely recognised rise of religion in the public square and a media, across all platforms, that is, by and large, ill-equipped to deal with it.

Why we are where we are

Media, of course, is itself an amorphous term; it refers to so much available content these days: from the tweet to the Hollywood blockbuster movie, via traditional journalism, memes, YouTube, blogs and Snapchats. It can refer to anything that is out there and publicly consumable. It is 'feral', as Tony Blair once said, uncontrollable and out of control but it is also owned and curated, vetted and spun. It is both a window and a mirror, a blunt instrument and a surgical blade. It is impossible to define and even harder, therefore, to analyse. However, one thing is certain, 'it' – the media at large – has a huge effect on how people see and do not perceive religion and belief.[2]

Not all is bad and negative. There is some thoughtful, insightful treatment of religion and belief across all areas of the media, but this is not the whole picture. Neither is it helpful merely to put the blame on the content creators in the media. A veteran BBC journalist with religious sympathies explains:

> I think a key problem is the failure of religious organizations to engage with the media because they believe it is hostile. So they simply don't do PR like other organizations, to offer interesting stories or comment. They have withdrawn. They have not learned how to offer stories the journalists want or how to talk to journalists to offer reasoned comment in a succinct way the journalist understands and can interpret. Because they are isolated, they don't appreciate that people outside their world don't understand theology – they speak a different language.[3]

First of all, perhaps, we should look at some of the key drivers that lie behind media coverage in general, and religion in particular, to gain a sense of the media mindset and how it has come to be so religiously illiterate.

Some key generalised drivers:

1 Editors, journalists and reporters are under constant pressure. They must distil complicated issues into short reports or articles and are subject to the changing news agenda and to the moods, prejudices and demands of editors and headline writers. Religion

2 *Living with Difference. Community, Diversity and the Common Good*, Report of The Commission on Religion and Belief in British Public Life, Cambridge, The Woolf Institute, 7 December 2015, https://corablivingwithdifference.files.wordpress.com/2015/12/living-with-difference-online.pdf, last accessed 17 January 2018.

3 Ruth Peacock, interviewed by the author on 3 April 2017.

does not fit well into this schedule. It is often complex and obscure and unless there are lots of deaths or damage, not necessarily interesting.

2 Good news is not usually news. For example, which story will make the headlines, 'Plane lands safely at Heathrow' or 'Egyptian airliner goes missing in Med'? Good news does not really sell, and most religions would claim to be about 'good news'. 'Bishop delivers sermon on three persons in the trinity' is not interesting, 'Bishop discovered with three persons in a bed romp' is.

3 The media thrives on more heat than light encounters and often pits one extreme view against another because it makes better radio/TV. Journalists would argue, of course, that they are merely interested in explaining the debate.

The clichéd sound-bite culture is also of little help. Former Archbishop of Canterbury, Rowan Williams, was sometimes a victim of this. His profound intelligence was occasionally a problem for reporters trying to grasp and condense his meaning in an erudite, subtle argument. Long, carefully phrased expositions are liable to be ignored, with perhaps only one point being seized on, taken out of a mosaic of style and context and hitting the headlines for all the wrong reasons. The controversy over his speech concerning the accommodation of Sharia law in British society is an obvious case in point. The tabloid headline 'What a Burkha' still shines out as perhaps the finest moment of complete religion and media divorce. However, the fault does not lie only with the media.[4]

Religious bodies must learn to engage with the journalists' culture better and understand their view of the world. Good PR is about finding a story that will interest a journalist and explaining it in their language. The journalist is the prism through which the wider public can understand what is going on.

The media is also disproportionately full of people poorly disposed towards religion. A BBC survey in 2011 showed that the audience was twice as likely to be religiously sympathetic than the content creators in Broadcasting House.[5] No one knows why this is the case – perhaps journalists are by nature more sceptical, but it must clearly have an impact on the selection of stories and the nature of their coverage.

Since this generally negative disposition collides with the other factors contributing to the decline in religious literacy, there has emerged a lack of expertise at the creative and commissioning levels, which has further dented the religious literacy cause. Losing so many specialist staff creates the danger of a vicious spiral – the editorial judgement that religion is of declining public interest, leading to the loss of specialist reporters and leading, in turn, to a trivialising or ignorant reporting of religious issues. If you do not understand something, you tend to treat it as a problem, which would be rather like covering football solely from the point of view of football hooliganism and never actually watching the game.

Another factor that may perhaps fail to contribute to the fairest and most helpful reporting of religion is what makes a good story. Journalists love the same ingredients – Hypocrisy,

4 Pope Benedict XVI ended up in similar hot water after giving the Regensburg lecture on 12 September 2006. He quoted a passage about Islam made at the end of the fourteenth century by Manuel II Palaiologos, the Byzantine emperor. This was then taken out of context and spread around the world. It was seen to be a grave insult to Islam and a dangerous mischaracterisation of the faith. He was called on to retract 'this objectionable statement' by the Pakistani government. The pope maintained that the comment he had quoted did not reflect his own views, and he offered an apology to Muslims. Cf. Schall (2007).

5 *Development of a BBC Diversity Strategy Summary of Responses to Public and Staff Consultations*, 31 January 2011, http://downloads.bbc.co.uk/diversity/pdf/diversity_strategy_consultation_report.pdf, last accessed 17 January 2018.

Sex, Power/Celebrity, Conflict and Deviance. Needless to say, religion can be quite a regular star character in such a concoction.

At times, a true storm may be created. A few years ago a chair of a major bank, who happened to be an ordained Christian minister, was found to have been buying drugs from a rent boy. The story ran and ran with some memorable tabloid headlines and much cynical laughter. At other times, this curious mixture of sex and religion can lead to more positive coverage as of the more recent story concerning the parentage of our current Archbishop of Canterbury, Justin Welby, who had discovered that he is the product of an affair between his mother and a government minister. Through his genuine and profound reaction, what might have been something scurrilous and disquieting became a story of healing and personal growth.

There is some logic to saying religion receives the coverage it deserves. Without listing the sickeningly regular attacks in Europe and beyond, beheadings in the desert and all the other horrors, this clearly needs to be both reported and analysed and it also sells papers and TV subscriptions. Corrupt faith leaders and the ongoing paedophile priests saga are again going to attract needed exposure to ensure justice and future prevention.

Religion also sells well when it is apparently being ridiculous in the eyes of society at large with its current pervasive ethics and morals. Not allowing a gay couple to sleep together in your hotel, or refusing to make a wedding cake for a gay wedding reception, is also going to come over badly in a secular, sometimes cynical media; or the authorities colliding with religious practice can create a media storm, for instance, the French police forcing a Muslim woman to remove her burkini on the beach. The mass availability of smartphone cameras makes all this much more accessible and available to all.

Such tasty, exciting material is being served up to the media so regularly that journalists do not need to try hard to make religion look ridiculous. One former archbishop told me that he believes it is a journalist's mission to make religious people look ridiculous: if religious are all either stupid or mad, then why should society have to take them seriously?

Certainly the issue is not the amount of religious news, which has been increasing in recent years due in no small measure to the rise in religious-based violence. It is more about the depth and quality required for proper religious coverage. Muslims, for example, are so often presented as a monochrome religion, male-dominated and on the verge of violent hostility towards the West. Little attempt is made to explore the rich variety of opinion and debate, the different denominations and community narratives – it is far easier to show the pictures we expect to see. Failure to understand the complexity of the faith and the fact that most people only ever come across Islam when it is tied to terrorism have led to a false and negative view of the faith.

Speaking from a Christian perspective, we have long since given up the idea of making a fuss when our religion is portrayed badly as it has been happening consistently for so long that we have become almost immune, although there is still much complaint in the parishes and shires. We are often and irritatingly tarred with the same brush – homophobic, down on women, Bible bashing, dinosaur-denying and so on, and it can be very offensive.

Blame for this damaging portrayal can, of course, be laid in some measure at the door of the church/synagogue/mosque, etc. The religious communities are so cautious of media coverage that the more positive messages tend to stay in the pulpit. Better 'media literacy' in the religious world is as important as better 'religious literacy' in the media.

We have concentrated thus far in particular on news coverage of religion, but the illiteracy is not limited to the news. The availability of so many, particularly, US-based dramas in box set form, or so easily downloadable, means that detrimental portrayals of religions live on and on. Many of them from a decade ago often had the Muslims as the 'bad guys', for example, which is not so surprising when you think of the proximity to 9/11, but also not fair in terms of representing the vast majority of the faithful. Once again, however, the picture is not all negative. In one episode of *The West Wing*,[6] when a group of school children visiting the White House were victims of a security shutdown, they were given an impromptu lecture in interfaith understanding by Josh Lyman, one of the senior White House staff. He presented them with a problem on a whiteboard. 'Islamic extremist is to Islamic as ______ is to Christianity'. After a suitable pause the answer 'Ku Klux Klan' was put in the space.

In an early episode of a UK-based spy drama,[7] there was much criticism over the fact that all Muslims in traditional Muslim attire were terrorists, whereas the more level-headed ones wore western clothing. But Muslims are not the only faith group singled out for poor representation.

There is very little representation of normal Christians behaving normally in UK soaps.[8] Yet, again, the picture is not consistently bad. One of the UK's most popular soaps, *Coronation Street*, has a mixed track record of its dealings with religion in storylines.

In one wedding scene in a church (which none of the characters ever attend except for rites of passage), the director decided that had to hide the cross on the altar for fear of offending viewers. In another storyline, however, they had quite an edgy plot featuring a lesbian Christian couple who were treated sympathetically by their church. However, most of the time there is no evidence of religion, even though a close community would inevitably have some practicing Christians and at least one minister or priest featuring on a regular basis in their over-colourful lives.

One religiously literate moment still makes me smile, however. While waiting for a Christening ceremony to begin, one of the more unattractive characters starts to eat an apple rather noisily. The only identifiable Christian in the whole soap opera tuts disapprovingly, and the apple eater says, 'I am sure God wouldn't mind someone eating an apple', to which the Christian lady replies, 'I'll think if you read Genesis, you'll find that he did!'

Changing attitudes in the UK

Another factor in the deteriorating relationship between the media and religion is a curious slowness of the media to adapt to, and absorb, some of the important changes in the religious make-up of society.

There have been huge social shifts in attitudes and prejudices over the past forty years. I was born in 1961 and, looking back, I can see 'the past is a foreign country – they do things differently there'.[9] It really was not so long ago that racism was rampant, for example. We were racist at school – quite openly. The best rugby player the school ever had was an Afro-Caribbean boy and we were openly racist to him (never intended unkindly – he was far too big for that) but in ways that would be totally unacceptable now, even in private. He looked down on us with quiet dignity knowing he was capable of crushing us with his fists if need be.

At senior school, we were equally racist towards the Chinese boys who showed us up in Mathematics and Science lessons and with their dedication to study, and commitment

6 *The West Wing*, 'Isaac and Ishmael', special episode 1, 2001.

7 *Spooks*, series 2, episode 2, 2003.

8 Martin Saunders, 'More TV, vicar?', *Premier Christianity*, April 2015, www.premierchristianity.com/Past-Issues/2015/April-2015/More-TV-vicar, last accessed 17 January 2018.

9 Opening sentence of Hartley 1953.

not to waste their parents' money on their education, as we were wont to do. We are only talking about the 1970s here. There was a sitcom, on the TV in the UK, *Till Death Us Do Part*[10] which thought it was funny to have a gay black man as the home help and elsewhere have black comedians mocking themselves for being black (e.g. Charlie Williams and the early Lenny Henry). I can hardly believe it but people actually threw bananas at black football players! 'The past is a foreign country and they do things differently there'.

Now we like to hope, and believe, that those days have gone and that the much sneered-at 'political correctness' has replaced such mockery with colour-blindness and respect of difference in terms of race, gender and sexuality (although of course there is still a long way to go). Strict laws are now in place, and prosecutions occur. People are banned from football stadia.

Yet attitudes to religion have not improved. In fact, as religion has slipped off government and media agendas, there has been a definite rise in hostility towards it. After sexual harassment, religious harassment, or prejudice, is now the behaviour most complained about in offices. Hate crimes against ethnic minorities, including particularly Jews and Muslims, have increased by up to 60% in the UK after the Brexit vote.[11] Perhaps a more pernicious and deeply ingrained fear has taken over from racism. Is this perhaps something that not only challenges our visual perception and abhorrence of the 'other' but also our deepest-held beliefs and suspicions?

This development has complicated, and been complicated by, the media's reactions and portrayals. Hence, not only has the religious mosaic become more fluid and unpredictable, but the assumed role of Christianity as the underlying moral principle in the UK has also been eroded. When people like myself (or those older than me) were growing up, Christianity was very much the accepted norm, and was unchallenged in the public sphere. It saw itself as the moral companion to society and the place to which everyone would naturally turn in a crisis, but people in their thirties now, or even younger, have grown up with a very different world view. Young people in general are not growing up racist; homophobia, whilst still present, is no longer as bad as it was by far. They are certainly not growing up Christian or even nominally Church of England, and now there is a tasty smorgasbord of religions and spiritualities to choose from.

However the media's attitudes have not caught up. They have, until recently, adhered to the old image of the Church of England as the main façade of UK religious life. They read 'imam' as if it were equal to an ordained priest; they show empty pews signifying the decline of Christianity but ignore the stadium-sized churches emerging from the Pentecostal movement; they focus on the radicalised youth and ignore the Mosques spilling out on to the streets for Friday prayers with thousands of the young and truly faithful.

It is hard to avoid an explanation of this sluggish media response without referring to the history of the BBC, which is to some degree, I believe, to blame for our conundrum. From its outset in 1922, the BBC was married to Religious Broadcasting and, of course, initially that was almost exclusively Christian broadcasting. Lord Reith, the son of a Scottish Presbyterian Minister, was himself a committed Christian and was convinced that his fledgling organisation could play an important role in keeping Christian values as a central part of the life of the nation.

10 It was aired on BBC1 from 1965 to 1975.

11 The data is referred particularly to Wales. Cf. 'Reported hate crimes increase by 60% since Brexit', *BBC News*, 5 September 2016, www.bbc.com/news/uk-wales-37278903, last accessed 17 January 2018. For wider analysis on the UK, see 'Race and religious hate crimes rose 41% after EU vote', *BBC News*, 13 October 2016, http://www.bbc.com/news/uk-politics-37640982, last accessed 17 January 2018.

The churches, after an initial problem with the whole notion of broadcasting the sacred to the great unwashed, soon saw that here was a great opportunity to use the BBC as a platform for continuing to propagate the traditional form of Christianity that they thought the country wanted and needed. Surely if the BBC regularly broadcast the *Book of Common Prayer*, the nation would come to its senses and flock back to the half-empty churches. They believed that the BBC was there to do its job and, at least initially, there was a tacit, if not active, agreement on the part of the Corporation with this strategy.

This was the beginning of an unhealthy relationship, which made the churches feel that in some way they had special status and would always be considered in any decisions the BBC made. This was a status quo in which the BBC management colluded for a long while – certainly until the end of World War II. The churches became complacent because their right to be on the air was unchallenged, regardless of whether it was interesting and relevant to an increasingly diverse audience, who could not only exercise their choice over the on/off switch but increasingly, over the years, move the dial to another station.

Along with this expected privilege, the churches also insisted that there should be a protection clause around any discussion of religious scriptures and the banning of anything that might alarm the delicate, innocent faith of the audience. Again, the BBC managers went along with this in the early days. However, far from protecting people, such paternalism only paved the way for great disillusionment among the audience and, I believe, resulted in a lasting attitude to religious broadcasting that it is in some ways not as 'grown up' as other programme genres.

This protectionism constituted a huge disservice beyond the walls of Broadcasting House. It undermined the credibility of the genre and, alongside the 'Honest to God' debate and, later, the Bishop of Durham's 'conjuring trick with bones' sermon, made the Christian franchise look dishonest and hopelessly fractured. This paved the way for the BBC's more secular leadership in the 80/90s to drive a coach and horses through the old agreements and, because in the early days, the genre had not been given the chance to grow up and adapt to the fast changing media scene, it left religious broadcasting very vulnerable to cuts and marginalisation. It also left the media content creators with a very jaundiced view of religion, which lasted through to 2000 and beyond.

However, it could be argued that there has been a palpable shift recently in attitudes toward religion in society, government and education, and there are signs of it in the media, too. In 2011, the Equality and Human Rights Commission, aware that religion had been ignored for too long, hired Coexist House[12] to help facilitate a programme of encounters looking at the interface between religion and society. This, in turn, led to another project with Ernst and Young (EY), who also wanted to address religion in the workplace. A major international firm such as EY offering an online Religious Literacy Training Programme for Organisations is an indication that the private sector at least has started to realise that religion needs to be taken seriously. Moreover, the programme is also being made available to the public sector, including the Civil Service and the National Health Service, to answer the government's call for greater religious literacy in society and the media. Hence, the upgrading of religious literacy in various agendas is now taking place. Some specialist religious correspondents are even returning to newspapers (e.g. *The Guardian*).

12 Coexist House is a charity devoted to establishing a London centre focussed on better religious literacy. It is supported by Cambridge University, the City of London Corporation, the Victoria and Albert Museum and the Inner Temple.

Adrian Anthony Gill wrote in *The Sunday Times* in March 2014 that 'Religion has never been more tangible in world affairs and public life. Not having more sensible and serious religious broadcasting isn't modern, it's a failure to face modernity'.[13] The problem was that broadcasting woke up to the wider world of faith rather too late. The industry was not prepared for the sudden re-emergence of religion in the public sphere. Religion was supposed to be disappearing but had now come back with a vengeance. The world of religion has burst out into a mosaic of different colours and expressions, and much of the media has not responded in kind to the opportunity to reflect this vibrant and varied culture, partly because it had been winding down its religious antennae and killing off its religious literacy; it now, like the rest of society, finds itself ill-equipped to deal with, and talk about, religion in an articulate manner.

As the world of religion has expanded and clamoured for attention, the media by and large has cut back on its expertise, budgets and time allocated to the subject. One frequently quoted example is the BBC news, which has a number of 'editors' for the leading subject areas, Finance, Politics, the Arts, World Affairs, the Middle East, etc., but for Religion it has only a 'correspondent', a more lowly ranked figure who has to fight his/her way onto the bulletins.

The current Archbishop of Canterbury, Justin Welby, recently spoke about religion and the media:

> Despite easy assumptions of secularity, true diversity also means paying proper attention to religion. After all – and this should not really need stating – it is impossible to understand the world today without understanding religion. Not religion as an exercise in private piety that needs to be covered simply to keep some strange people happy; but because religion is a prime motivator of behaviour for both individuals and communities. A religious commitment or worldview shapes the ethical choices, political priorities, economic preferences and cultural expressions of whole societies. We cannot hope to understand why people do the things they do if we don't understand what drives them – consciously or unconsciously.[14]

Compared to twenty years ago, there has been a very healthy increase in the range, quality and quantity of religious contributors to broadcasting from across the main nine faiths based in the UK. I once again find myself as an executive producer working on two major BBC religious strands but I encourage caution when thinking about where most of the audience is in relation to religious knowledge and their likely disposition towards it. I instruct all my contributors to refer solely to their own faith journeys and not assume that anyone is on the journey with them. Furthermore, I tell them to assume no knowledge at all of religious scripture or practice, that is to say, to assume religious illiteracy when referring to scripture or religious history.

It is also an encouraging sign that the way the 'God slots' are accepted within their 'host programmes' is far more positive than it used to be. The largest audience for any God slot, probably anywhere in the broadcasting world, is found for the BBC Radio 2 *Breakfast*

13 Adrian A. Gill, 'A Holy Splendid Work of Religious Comedy', *The Sunday Times*, 30 March 2014, www.thesundaytimes.co.uk/sto/culture/film_and_tv/article1392205.ece, last accessed 17 January 2018.

14 Archbishop Justin Welby's speech to the Sandford St Martin Awards, 9 June 2016, /www.archbishopofcanterbury.org/speaking-and-writing/speeches/archbishop-calls-greater-religious-literacy-media, last accessed 17 January 2018.

Show, presented by a popular DJ with no obvious religious commitment, who welcomes a live *Pause for Thought* contributor to his fast-moving, music-based show and introduces this rather strange anomaly of a religious person reading a prepared script for two unopposed minutes. Over the years, this has not been a popular item with programme presenters and producers, indeed the more serious equivalent on the more speech-based network BBC Radio 4 is very rarely welcomed by presenters or producers. However, the Radio 2 host, Chris Evans, sees the value of the slot to his audience. 'I love *Pause for Thought*', he writes in the forward to the new *Pause for Thought* book.

> I always look forward to hearing who has to say what. All of our contributors are brilliant, without exception, each bringing with them their unique mixture of character, style, wisdom and experience onto the airwaves. As the world continues to speed up at an exponential rate, it is more important now than ever before to be reminded to take a beat, take a breath and take a moment to consider why we're doing what we're doing and what we might be doing better. What's important is important. And sometimes we need a welcome reminder of what those important things might be. That's what *Pause for Thought* never fails to do. Long live those who bother to pause, think and gift us the benefit of their considered philosophies on life, love, friendship, selflessness and the myriad other virtues we humans are capable of.
>
> (Evans 2016: 4)

A proposal

Therefore, there is some evidence of a more welcoming spirit to religious thought in more popular broadcasting. In news, the evidence maybe less obvious. Serious correspondents dealing with stories from the religiously volatile and controversial Middle East are well aware and well versed in the underlying religious story and are fully aware of the importance of not misrepresenting it. Yet what is to be said of the broader picture of journalists, broadcasters, producers and commissioners? How can their religious literacy be improved?

Religious bodies often feel hard done by and complain about the way their stories are covered, and the old chummy relationship between the churches and the BBC is wistfully recalled. Some have a sense that the media has a duty to be more positive about religion. Of course, this is nonsense, but it does have a duty to cover it fairly and accurately.

I would never accuse journalists of being lazy because I do not think they are, but they have deadlines to meet, eyes to capture and will take shortcuts and go for soft targets. However, you cannot wind back the clock. We can no longer 'not do God', and what media professionals need is greater religious literacy (and, as indicated earlier, this needs to be matched with greater media literacy in the religious communities). One thing we do not need is religious broadcasting departments (except for the specialist knowledge required for worship programmes). Moreover, we certainly do not need dedicated religious channels. What we do need is a religiously literate media across all its manifestations.

Sending journalists back to college will not work; in-work training would not be taken up. Journalists are busy, not lazy; they are highly intelligent and focussed. Thus what they need is measured information offered to them in ways in which they want to receive it in order to help them tell religion stories and represent religious issues more coherently and be provided with the shortcuts to a deeper understanding, sensible and media-friendly contributors and a richer, more nuanced vocabulary so that they can tell the stories they wish to tell. In short, they need to be equipped with the tools they need to do the job.

The Science Media Centre (SMC) has transformed the way in which science is reported in the UK. Indeed, it has been so successful that it is now replicated in several other countries around the world, including Australia, New Zealand and Canada. It has no editorial line, apart from 'science matters'; it is funded with a wide cross section of stakeholders so that no single view can dominate; it does not tell journalists what to say but simply gives them the range of background they need, properly vetted contributors to represent all aspects of the debate and the resources busy and non-specialist journalists need to do their job of telling science-related stories in a responsible and nuanced way. This is the model that a new project, the Religion Media Centre, wants to replicate: it has no editorial line apart from 'religion matters'.

Unlike the SMC, it will go beyond news and journalism to offering help and advice to screen writers and drama producers so that they can avoid the inevitable stereotypes and misportrayals. The Religion Media Centre (RMC), now a registered charity, will also work with religious organisations to help them address the world outside their faith. It will be a bridge. It will not promote religion or even say that it is a good thing – both attitudes would be disastrous – but it will push for a recognition that it is important and therefore needs to be reported, discussed and examined with knowledge, fairness and respect. Moreover, to continue mocking it, misreporting it with unhelpful shorthand and careless choice of images, pretending that it is going to go away or that is only of interest to people who do not blink very much or are only intent on destruction, is simply not going to wash anymore. Things have to change, and a well-resourced and supported RMC is the way to help make this happen.

Undoubtedly, religion will continue to present challenges and it deserves the most hard-nosed journalism when it does, but for a balanced view there also needs to be an understanding of the other side of the story, and a recognition of the importance it plays in so many people's lives.

Maybe then religion and belief in all their many manifestations will be able to become something we can share and celebrate; an asset to society rather than the liability it so often appears to be.

Bibliography

Evans, Chris 2016. 'Forward', in BBC Radio 2 (ed.), *Pause for Thought*, London, Watkins.

Hartley, Leslie P. 1953. *The Go-Between*, London, Hamish Hamilton.

Hoover, Stewart M. (ed.) 2016. *Media and Religious Authority*, University Park, The Pennsylvania State University Press.

Knott, Kim and Mitchell, Jolyon 2012. 'The Changing Faces of Media and Religion', in Linda Woodhead and Rebecca Catto (ed.), *Religion and Change in Modern Britain*, London/New York, Routledge, 243–64.

Knott, Kim, Poole, Elizabeth and Taira, Teemu 2013. *Media Portrayals of Religion and the Secular Sacred: Representation and Change*, Farnham, Ashgate.

Lynch, Gordon, Mitchell, Jolyon and Strhan, Anna (ed.) 2012. *Religion, Media and Culture: A Reader*, Abingdon, Routledge.

Mahan, Jeffrey H. (ed.) 2014. *Media, Religion and Culture. An Introduction*, Abingdon, Routledge.

Mitchell, Jolyon and Gower, Owen (ed.) 2012. *Religion and the News*, Abingdon, Routledge.

Morgan, David (ed.) 2008. *Key Words in Religion, Media and Culture*, Abingdon, Routledge.

Schall, James V. 2007. *The Regensburg Lecture*, South Bend, IN, St. Augustine's Press.

Part IV

Views and experiences

15 The attitude of the media to religion

Jennifer M. Taylor

1966–2016: from description to denial: fifty years of religion in the media

On 25 October 1966, *The Guardian* published a full-page spread on the Queen's opening of the new Church Missionary Society's headquarters, in London's Waterloo area.

This you might think was not so very remarkable, unless you appreciate that *The Guardian* is now a hard-left paper, eschewing both religion and monarchy. The Queen, as both Head of State and Supreme Governor of the Church of England, has near-sacred status in the (unwritten) constitution, yet *The Guardian* is now republican banner-carrier for a campaign to abolish the monarchy. For a missionary story featuring both the monarch and the Church of England's principle agency for evangelism to receive such prominence indicates how far we have come in just fifty years. 1966 was the year of emancipation on many levels, not least by virtue of the Pill, and therefore 'emblematic of the [failed] destiny of the whole of Western Christianity' (Brown 2001: flyleaf). Yet even the permissive *Guardian* had yet to catch up.

Being not just 'neutral' towards religions, but publicly a stakeholder in the demise of Christendom, has been part of the intellectual baggage of any member of Britain's left-wing intelligentsia for a generation, with its impact on the media down to the present day. Among the left-wing press, 'Britain was cast as secular and plural, with an accompanying discourse of Christian decline and irrelevance', according to some media researchers, who recorded the opposite to be the case in the right-wing press (Knott, Poole and Taira 2013: 174). This is highly significant because as those same researchers go on to note: 'Media representations of religion [...] and their discourses on its social role and fate constitute the extent of public knowledge' (Knott, Poole and Taira 2013: 175). Therefore, before looking at the contemporary media scene, in order to see what its evasions, blind spots and occasional hilarious gaffes amount to in cultural terms, it might be helpful to look more closely at the path along which we have travelled.

The *Guardian* page was headlined 'Centre for New Missionaries' and the piece lavished praise on the new building in Waterloo Road, just a ten-minute drive from Westminster and the seat of government.[1] The piece was headed by a picture, across three columns, of the façade of the new building, 'challenging the busy street with its dramatic inscription: "Go forth into every part of the world and proclaim the good news to the whole creation"' – the words of the Great Commission at the end of St Matthew's Gospel.

The building's architect, design, purpose and vision were all examined and lauded. At the heart of the building, the writer J.R.L. Anderson exclaimed, was the Chapel of the Living Water with its huge, rough wooden cross, 'displaying only three cruelly large and

1 *The Guardian*, 24 October 1966, 12.

rusty iron nails'. He describes the font in detail with 'its flow of water across a lip of stone brought from the Abbey of Iona'. He finishes: 'The effect is intensely moving, harsh, but then life often is harsh, yet at the same time comforting, and making for a deep humility'.

Despite slightly undermining the meaning of evangelism ('Evangelism in modern terms is to bring a Christian spirit to bear on the problems of men and women in their everyday lives [...]'), this article manifests a Christian culture more or less still at ease with itself and its shared references, aware of the willingness and ability of the Established Church to modernise, while being unselfconsciously positive about the church's place in political and social life.

Yet within just under thirty years, Alastair Campbell, Prime Minister Tony Blair's Press Secretary, and a former journalist on another left-wing newspaper, the *Daily Mirror*, felt compelled to say, 'We don't do God', as he intervened to prevent Blair answering a question about his faith during an interview with *Vanity Fair* at the outbreak of the Iraq War in 2003.[2] Much later and equally as serious, in 2014, 'Don't mention the Christians' was the instruction given by a BBC producer to the senior religious correspondent before assigning her to war-torn northern Iraq, where the story was one of horrendous targeting of Christians and other minorities by the Islamic State, such that parliament two years later declared it a genocide. The correspondent expressed bemusement to me at this instruction, which she took as an example of anti-Christianity in the nation's broadcaster. What is clear anecdotally was that the Yazidis became the favourite subject of persecution stories.

The Times also buried (on page nine) comments by the King of Jordan Abdullah warning the USA at a private meeting in the spring of 2016 that 'the Third World War had begun'.[3] Despite having been trained by the Special Forces in Britain and being a reigning monarch in the very cauldron of a religious war with the West, the paper deemed it wise to relegate the piece to an inside page.

Within fifty years, key sectors of the media were denying or suppressing Christianity or Islam, following the instructions not of political leaders, for example, Tony Blair or David Cameron (who made several speeches on Britain being a Christian country), but of some within the media itself. There are, of course, other occurrences of ignorance which may or may not be symptomatic; for example, one howler in the *Caerphilly Observer* that did the rounds on Twitter was: 'We would also like to thank Mrs S.L. Evans of Oakdale who correctly pointed out that it was Noah who built Noah's Ark, and not Moses which we stated in our 12 May edition'.[4]

The question remains: Does a softly-softly approach to religion constitute a cultural or sociological generalisation? Is it more than just squeamishness about subjects deemed too complex, arcane or dangerous for volatile readerships? Is evidence of suppression merely a valiant attempt to 'hold the ring' in a time of religious plurality and heightened emotions? Is it both of these things in contexts that change with alarming rapidity? This chapter can only touch on these possibilities, based on the little research there is and on my own observations over thirty-five years as a formerly atheist journalist, the last ten of which, however, were spent as CEO of the UK's first religious literacy charity.

A more serious lack of curiosity in the media for the religious underpinnings of a seventeen-year war in northern Uganda, together with the writing of bishop and theologian

2 Colin Brown, 'Campbell interrupted Blair as he spoke of his faith: "We don't do God"', *The Telegraph*, 4 May 2003, www.telegraph.co.uk/news/uknews/1429109/Campbell-interrupted-Blair-as-he-spoke-of-his-faith-We-dont-do-God.html, last accessed 10 June 2018.

3 Dominic Kennedy, 'SAS is already in Libya fighting a world war, says King of Jordan', *The Times*, 26 March 2016, www.thetimes.co.uk/article/sas-is-already-in-libya-fighting-a-world-war-says-king-of-jordan-36v82jkbz, last accessed 10 June 2018.

4 Tweeted on 29 June 2016.

Lesslie Newbigin, gave rise to Lapido Media. Newbigin, together with sociologist Thomas Luckmann, believed that Christian truth, from which journalism itself emerged in the seventeenth-century campaign against state censorship of printing, had indeed been usurped by an alternative ideology characterised by scepticism, and this was reflected in the media (Newbigin 1991).

First, I venture a few confessional observations as a 'secular mainstream journalist' who, in 1985, became a Christian at the age of 30.

Evidence from the front line: loss of Christian objectivity in reportage produces false neutrality and blindness

Journalists are affected by genuine altruism. I was. Their stock in trade is after all human failure (sin). Indications of altruism and goodness make an impression. Despite being an atheist throughout my twenties, I hung around community projects that sought to transform the circumstances, and harness the squandered energies, of youth. I campaigned (successfully) for a new community centre for West Indians; and in 1983 became the first race relations correspondent in Westminster Press working with a range of exciting projects. But I made no connection with the church; and found the church affairs columnist deeply suspect (he did in fact go to gaol later for fraud!). Religion for me had a plausibility problem – as sociologist Peter Berger calls it in *The Sacred Canopy.* It seemed to involve a loss of intellect and autonomy, and that infected what I saw and what I reported. Religion was around, but it was largely embarrassing and kept private. Philandering clergy, loony extremists... It was easier to make religion the news than see the world with religion-aware curiosity.

But the second problem was the facile binary principle around which stories were constructed: a principle on which oppositional government depends and a hangover from modernity that renders every question a contest. Modernity gave us 'oppressor/oppressed', 'black/white', 'rich/poor'. Despite the postmodern dissolving of boundaries and greater fluidity of constructs, our western adversarial politics continues to maintain an illusion of duality and the need, apparently, for 'neutrality' in reporting it. In Britain, there are only two serious main parties, the Government and Her Majesty's Loyal Opposition, which must each be given equal airtime. And although neutrality often breaks down, as newspapers and broadcasters adopt strong political positions, so it is, it is believed, with religion. For every story about a Mother Teresa there must be a knock-down opponent to debunk her motivation – as indeed feminist and *Private Eye* journalist Germaine Greer famously did. For every Christian source, there must be a Muslim or National Secular Society one. However, religion does not work like that. Journalists generally have required little idea about differences between and within religions; and what influences, interpretation mechanisms and disciplines they subject themselves to. Why should they? There is no training in religions or how religion is done.[5] And getting it wrong can cause ridicule or disaster: the *Oldham Gazette* was firebombed, according to the paper's managing director, by Asians in 2001.[6] The solution is often to skip coverage altogether.

5 The author gave the first ever lectures on religion to the Press Association, Reuters Foundation and the National Union of Journalists in 2015 and 2016.

6 According to the BBC website: 'The attack followed earlier accusations that the paper did not give fair coverage to Asian victims of racial abuse. Philip Hirst, the paper's managing director, told BBC Radio 5 Live that allegations of bias were "complete rubbish". Mr Hirst said: "Anybody who started life working on a local paper knows we get attacked on all sides, but it's a hell of a way to make a complaint, chucking a firebomb through a window"', 28 May 2001, http://news.bbc.co.uk/1/hi/uk/1355379.stm, last accessed 10 June 2018.

As well as personal prejudice, and professional habituation, journalists are affected by their peers. In six years on news-desks of weekly and daily newspapers, I heard faith mentioned in the newsroom only once, by the women's editor profiling a Christian Justice of the Peace (magistrate). The secularisation thesis, unknown to us, was informing the zeitgeist. Although the classical secularisation thesis is largely discredited, or at least questioned, in the 1980s it still informed the newsroom. This was the view, with roots in the 1880s but particularly prevalent from the 1960s onwards when Max Weber's work began circulating the academy in translation, that traditional religious world views would become little more than 'the ghost in the machine'. Modernity with its technocracies, worker mobility and systems rationalisation had dealt a death blow to traditional patterns of belonging and believing. The evolutionary thrust of predictions, by Oxford professor Bryan Wilson and others who took up Weber's thesis, made religion's irrelevancy seem inevitable. What you did or said in the privacy of your own home was a different matter, but journalists left their faith at the door of the office when they came to work.[7]

We do, however, need here to untangle two very different things. There is the question of impartiality or fairness in reporting facts, and second, there is a much more serious 'ideology of neutralism' in regard to the religious news that maintains that there is no truth to be found. Following Descartes, all truth is relativised and we are, therefore, merely the sum of what we can think.

This attitude of ideological neutrality where religions are concerned has its reinforcement in law. 'As regards religion, the law stands neutral' was a famous legal axiom pronounced by Justice Cross, cited in Anthony Bradney's *Religions, Rights and Laws* in 1993 in the case of *Neville Estates Ltd* v. *Madden*. Bradney carried out his doctoral research on this statement and discovered that it was not actually true or possible. But an ideology, just like a religion, does not have to be true to be believed. The idea of neutrality infects the discourse. Even the otherwise superb research by Kim Knott and others on the media and religion, to which I have already referred, reveals this in its concluding remarks on two propositions about the secularity or religiosity of media professionals and the reporting of religion: 'Taken together these propositions raise questions about the identity and beliefs of those who work in the media, *their ability to be neutral*, and how they see their role in respect of their audiences and the wider society' (Knott, Poole and Taira 2013: 181).

Faith in neutrality has led to some very strange reporting. A senior commentator and journalist, Peter Oborne writes for *The Daily Telegraph* and *The Spectator*, among others. In 2010 he went to northern Nigeria to make a film for Channel 4's *Unreported World* strand, in which he blamed Christians for the massacres by Muslims in that tormented part of the world.[8] I was suspicious, having Nigerian journalist and Anglican friends, and was invited to make my own trip to Jos. Peter was good enough to give me his locations and a Muslim contact, which I followed up, driving to the villages where he filmed, and meeting the main contact in my hotel. I peered down the same wells where 'hundreds of bodies of children' were said by Peter (to the camera) to be still rotting and saw no room for four bodies, let alone corpses of hundreds. I reported the exact opposite, before it became obvious to the world, as it now is, what was going on: that, in fact, it was a combination of Fulani, Hausa and al-Qaeda influenced Boko Haram militias torching villages, shooting point blank all who refused to renounce the Christian faith and even Muslims who approved of western education. Oborne did not even mention Christians struggling not to retaliate in these

7 Comment to the author by BBC press officer.

8 *Unreported World*, 2010 episode 'Nigeria's Killing Fields'.

circumstances who therefore went uncredited.[9] When I later challenged him directly, he shrugged and said: 'Who knows where the truth lies?'

Yet the truth lies where it always has – with the best facts available: the first ever survivor of a Boko Haram massacre to testify to Congress, Habila Adamu, told his harrowing story in Washington on 14 November 2013 at the invitation of Nina Shea, director of the Religious Freedom Centre at the Hudson Institute.[10] This event contributed to the US Commission on International Religious Freedom declaring Nigeria to be 'one of the world's worst violators of religious freedom' in 2013. In April 2016, for the first time, the State Department under John Kerry included Nigeria among its Countries of Particular Concern (CPC) for religious freedom violations. These included the forced conversion of Christians, and blasphemy killings of Shia Muslims by Boko Haram. The designation warrants an array of sanctions.

An attitude of 'neutrality' prescribes the sources that will be consulted, and even counter-intuitively frames the story beforehand. Christian leaders are generally ignored as sources because they are presumed either to collude with the West or to be partisan in their 'evidence'. Oborne did not interview the Anglican Archbishop of Jos, Benjamin Kwashi, even though his wife Gloria had been attacked in their house, and even though the diocesan communications team films every atrocity in the diocese immediately after it happens. Evidence deemed good enough for use on a more stringent basis for the US channel CNN was not even consulted by Peter Oborne for Channel 4.

Again, when a crisis breaks, foreign correspondents in search of 'neutral' sources tend to consult the secular Médicins Sans Frontières personnel, not just because they speak English or French, but because, being 'secular', they are deemed to be above the fray. But these organisations were set up for emergencies, not for the long haul, and so by definition lack local knowledge. John Simpson, World Affairs editor at BBC News, when challenged by this author as to why the BBC never used church leaders as sources, although they were also always trained in English and had grassroots knowledge, said, 'You know, I never thought of it'.[11]

We journalists rightly pride ourselves in our scepticism. Rogues and fools will always speak from their own partisan perspective, and several sources are required for any story to 'stand up'. It is after all what makes four Gospels more reliable than one. But appropriate scepticism, a tool of the trade, is easily hijacked by a 'hermeneutic of suspicion' which doubts everything, including the truth, and which theologian Lesslie Newbigin attacked in his magisterial short book *Truth to Tell* and elsewhere.[12] 'A key element in contemporary western culture [is] a false concept of objectivity – of a kind of knowledge from which the human subject has been removed' (Newbigin 1991: 8). This leads to real journalistic error: the type of error Peter Oborne made which doubts that where religion is concerned there is any truth to be found. The intellectual and epistemological equivalent of doubting even the branch on which you sit leads dangerously to a loss of contact with reality. If you don't personally commit to the existence of truth because you do not believe it is there to be found, and because you believe, therefore, that all religions are a matter of partiality or

9 'Nigeria: A Case of Too Many Faultlines', *Church Times*, 29 June 2010.

10 Sam Hailes, 'Nigerian tells of 'miraculous deliverance' from execution', *Lapido Media*, 20 November 2013, www.religiousliteracyinstitute.org/nigerian-tells-miraculous-deliverance-execution, last accessed 10 June 2018.

11 Church Media Conference satellite link-up to the plenary session in 2013.

12 'From Descartes onward it has been held that reliable knowledge is to be had by the relentless exercise of the critical method [...] [but the] critical principle must ultimately destroy itself. [...] As Polanyi put it, the fuel is eventually all spent. What is left, as Nietzsche saw, is the will to power, that motif which has been at the heart of the program of enlightenment from Bacon onward. Any claim to know the truth is, [it is said] therefore, simply a concealed assertion of power' (Newbigin 1991: 29).

worse, you are likely to content yourself with less than the truth when reporting religiously impacted issues. As Einstein used to say, what you call a fact depends on the theory you bring to it. If you bring nothing but scepticism, journalism deteriorates and becomes mere 'infotainment'. Reportage becomes opinion with deleterious consequences.[13]

We are seeing the results in massively falling newspaper sales and increased use of unregulated online and social media.[14] Newbigin adds: 'We are that part of God's creation which he has equipped with the power to know the truth and to speak the praise of the whole creation in response to the truthfulness of the Creator' (Newbigin 1991: 13). The truth is out there and it can be found, but only by using the right lens. The truth is also particular, in the same way that 'the public square' in which journalists have to operate is also a *place*. Context is not neutral and never will be. It is based on historical events and behavioural habits that have been influenced, for better or worse, to become what they are.

This hermeneutic of suspicion has another manifestation which may be even more dangerous: reinterpretation, in particular the reinterpretation of religious motivation. 'When 9/11 happened, America literally did not know what had hit it', wrote commentator Paul Marshall, senior fellow at the Hudson Institute in Washington for a press release before the London launch of his book *Blind Spot: When Journalists Don't Get Religion*.[15] This was because of a habit of reinterpretation that exposed the USA and the West to unprecedented danger, despite plenty of warning that resurgent Islam had the West in its sights.[16]

In his introduction to the book, Marshall picks up a comment by CNN political analyst William Schneider, who wrote:

> On the national level, the press is one of the most secular institutions in American society. It just doesn't get religion or any idea that flows from religious conviction. The press is not necessarily contemptuous of serious religion. It's just uncomprehending.[17]

Marshall goes on to explore the catastrophic implications of this contempt and the reinterpretation of religious motivation that leads to a state of denial or false comfort. Says Marshall:

> This attitude has persisted despite the fact that on September 11, 2001, the United States was attacked by an explicitly religiously based enemy. [...] much commentary has sought to make bin Laden and his cadres theoretically domesticated by reducing their concerns to issues of poverty or globalization or US foreign policy, or even sexual frustration, or just about anything except the terrorists' repeatedly stated desire to restore a worldwide caliphate ruled by Islamic law.
>
> (Marshall 2009: 4)

13 The phenomenon of 'fake news' is a direct consequence of the loss of truth commitment and has moved centre stage since this chapter was first drafted.

14 Jasper Jackson, 'National daily newspaper sales fall by half a million in a year', *The Guardian*, 10 April 2015, www.theguardian.com/media/2015/apr/10/national-daily-newspapers-lose-more-than-half-a-million-readers-in-past-year, last accessed 10 June 2018.

15 Lapido Media launched *Blind Spot* for Oxford University Press at an event with editor Paul Marshall and historian Tom Holland.

16 'Declaration of Jihad against the Americans Occupying the Land of the Two Sacred Mosques', 23 August 1996, in Berner (2007: 40).

17 Quoted by *Los Angeles Times* media columnist Tim Rutten, 6 March 2004.

In fact, bin Laden was categorical. He declared, post-9/11:

> This war is fundamentally religious. [...] Those who try to cover this crystal clear fact, which the entire world has admitted, are deceiving the Islamic nation. This war is fundamentally religious. [...] This fact is proven in the book of God Almighty and in the teachings of our messenger, may God's peace and blessings be upon him. This war is fundamentally religious. Under no circumstances should we forget this enmity between us and the infidels. For, the enmity is based on creed.[18]

The fact that the West was ideologically oriented to view the opposite – that Islam's enmity was based on capitalism or foreign policy – exposed it to the gravest danger. Post-Christian western culture was premised upon – and journalists had internalised as 'fact' – that 'religion was dead'. Indeed, eminent historian Simon Schama told a personal story on BBC's Andrew Marr show *Start the Week*, at which Prime Ministerial hopeful, Michael Gove, was also a guest. He said:

> When I was growing up, my history teacher said, and this was the 1950s: Well boys, we are not sure about what the rest of the twentieth century has to offer, but something we know for sure, organized religion is not going to be important. So much for history teachers. Who would have thought it? [...] When I was doing [the TV series] *History of Britain*, the greatest challenge was to dive into these scream-filled caves of sectarian madness, but it had to be done, and it's unbelievably relevant to now [...] absolutely, because there was always the sense in which, of course we'd read the great seventeenth-century historians, like Christopher Hill who said religion was something that was instrumentally glued on to what was really class interest, but to live now is to understand that it actually shapes allegiance, it is not simply a reflection of it.[19]

Aaqil Ahmed, head of Religion and Ethics at the BBC, seems to have swallowed the ideological 'religion is dead' view whole. He said so at the panel to launch the new All-Party Parliamentary Group (APPG) on Religion in the Media on 4 May 2016 – although his exact words were 'Before mass immigration, Christianity in Britain was dead'.[20]

The media humbled: the late recovery of religious literacy

There are many indications in British society and in the rest of the media world that this peremptory obituary was premature. 'The media account is not unfailingly secular or driven by an ideologically secularist media', conclude the authors of *Media Portrayals of Religion and the Secular Sacred*, and this is undoubtedly the case, at least consciously. The climate has indeed been one in which Lapido Media was able to operate unhindered, helping journalists 'get' religion during a watershed decade. Senior journalists who attended the launch of Lapido in 2007, staged at a foreign correspondents' club in London in the wake of the London tube bombings, were unembarrassed to declare the unequalled size of their postbags whenever they wrote about religion. Former *Economist* and *Telegraph* editor and latterly

18 Statement issued by Osama bin Laden, 3 November 2001.

19 *Start the Week*, BBC, 30 December 2013, http://downloads.bbc.co.uk/podcasts/radio4/stw/stw_20131230-1030a.mp3, at 39'22, last accessed 10 June 2018.

20 The author was also a guest on the panel.

Independent pundit, Dominic Lawson, who hosted the event, wrote his op-ed the following day under the title: 'Could a muscular Christianity be the answer to militant Islam?' There were three pieces in the main section of *The Times* by eminent religion correspondent Ruth Gledhill. CNN's *Correspondents* slot did a full half-hour interview live from their studio that day with this author on the motivation behind Lapido. There was a huge sense of journalists waiting for the cultural moment to change so they could write more freely.

A kind of self-censorship seems to have been in operation before 7/7 bombings, long after the culture itself had changed. That gentlemanly demur against mentioning religion at dinner and in 'the club' could no longer pertain, and our event signalled change. My doctoral research into five years of government documents from 1991 to 1995 had indicated that de-secularisation had been happening for years, tested against four criteria of David Martin's secularisation theory (Martin himself examined my thesis). But what characterised de-secularisation was in part an evident end to *self*-censorship, due to the need to administer the mass immigration of religious peoples. On 21 June 1993, at the West Midlands Multi-Faith Conference on Inner Cities at the Centennial Centre, Birmingham, West Midlands Regional Director at the Department of the Environment David Ritchie told the audience:

> It is a privilege to be addressing such a distinguished gathering. I have had a longstanding interest in religion, including two years studying Theology at university. Usually I keep quiet about that, but for the first time in my career I can declare it to a sympathetic audience!
>
> (Taylor 2002: 259)

This civil servant confessed that he had absolved himself from the need to police his own religious thoughts any longer and that he was now operating within a newly religious context.

Mass immigration by religious peoples and the need to develop a discourse to administer the areas in which they settled was affecting the culture long before 9/11's cataclysmic and symbolic bombing of Manhattan's finance district. Nearly ten years earlier in 1983, as Westminster Press' first race relations correspondent, I had interviewed my teenage idol Cat Stevens just after he had become Yusuf Islam and donned the long white robe of a Muslim sheikh. It was the first interview I had ever carried out where my interviewee refused to look at me (I was not veiled) – but it was not the last,[21] and it made a profound impression on me.

The need for religious literacy in the media is now a cry going up from institutions everywhere, as the juggernaut of ideological secularism – part lazy thinking, part Marxist-inspired anti-Christian rhetoric burrowing its way, often insidiously, into the consciousness of university educators and polite civil servants – judders to a halt. The Woolf Institute's Commission on Religion and Belief in Public Life in Britain produced a report called *Living with Difference* in December 2015 which made seven recommendations in pursuit of 'serious and ongoing attempts [...] to [...] increase religion and belief literacy among all journalists and reporters on religious literacy in the media'. Proposed by Lapido, these recommendations included funding, exposure visits, placements and an award for best practice.[22]

21 My interview with a male elder at the Tablighi Jamaat headquarters in Old Delhi, India, some years ago, had to be conducted seated on the floor with my back to him to avoid eye contact.

22 *Living with Difference. Community, Diversity and the Common Good*, Report of The Commission on Religion and Belief in British Public Life, Cambridge, The Woolf Institute, 7 December 2015, 46, § 5.27, https://corablivingwithdifference.files.wordpress.com/2015/12/living-with-difference-online.pdf, last accessed 10 June 2018.

The work gave rise to the first APPG on Religion in the Media in May 2016, chaired by Muslim MP Yasmin Qureshi, intending to produce policy recommendations to government on religious literacy. This was launched the same week that another APPG, on Religious Education, heard evidence on religious literacy, at which Lapido Trustee Professor John Wolffe of the Open University gave the keynote paper. Michael Wakelin documents elsewhere in this book the combined efforts of the Church of England, Goldsmiths College and others to set up a religion media centre to feed the growing hunger among journalists for facts and accurate, accredited sources when religion stories blow up (sometimes literally), as they are now doing on a daily basis. The Research Councils' Religion and Security work, part of a £350 million study across the spectrum of post-9/11 planning, also recommended a serious review of religious literacy in the media. Quite how this is to happen is unclear, but I received three invitations in 2016 – from Reuters, the Press Association and the National Union of Journalists – for training input.

It is sobering, and I hope not premature, to note the remark by professor Raphael Liogier, director of the Observatory of Religious Affairs at Aix-en-Provence University, in answer to the cry of France following the ritual slaughter in July 2016 of Catholic priest Fr Jacques Hamel at mass: 'Why us?' He said: 'British Muslims feel that they are respected when they exercise their religion. French Muslims do not'.

The problem, I suggest, is the ideology of secularism. At the heart of French religious tensions lie secular values initially introduced to resist the influence of the Catholic Church. *Laïcité*, introduced into law in 1905, bans the acknowledgement of religion in public life. But it also means not just that religious people feel stifled and demeaned but leaves the state without discourse or mechanisms for promoting interfaith outreach or social inclusion.[23]

In Britain there has been a marked sobering up among journalists about religion. This may not yet be fully represented in what they choose to write about – but the media's silence or reticence about religion looks increasingly more like caution rather than ignorance. Andrew Brown, veteran religion correspondent for *The Guardian*, discusses the problem for journalists in reporting civilian massacres without ascribing religious motive. There is no motivational certainty that reporters can point to when news breaks. What is at stake is too salient to get wrong. In the *Church Times* 29 July 2016, Brown wrote:

> Good journalists are aware both of the emotional charge that makes 'a great story', but also of the extent to which it can disable critical thinking. That's why they can report the horror [of terrorist murders] without [Islamist] ascription for what seems a ludicrously long time.

This sense of 'waiting' for motive to clarify can be read across the reportage of globalisation's impacts as a whole. Silence no longer necessarily means ignorance.

Bibliography

Berger, Peter L. 1967. *The Sacred Canopy. Elements of a Sociological Theory of Religion*, New York, Doubleday.

Berner, Brad K. (ed.) 2007. *Jihad: Bin Laden in His Own Words. Declarations, Interviews, and Speeches*, New Delhi, Peacock Books.

Bradney, Anthony 1993. *Religions, Rights and Laws*, Leicester, Leicester University Press.

23 See Hussey (2014). Hussey is a cultural historian who lives in Paris.

Brown, Callum G. 2001. *The Death of Christian Britain. Understanding Secularisation, 1800–2000*, London/New York, Routledge.

Calhoun, Craig, Juergensmeyer, Mark and VanAntwerpen, Jonathan 2011. *Rethinking Secularism*, Oxford/New York, Oxford University Press.

Hussey, Andrew 2014. *The French Intifada: The Long War between France and Its Arabs*, London, Granta Books.

Knott, Kim, Poole, Elizabeth and Taira, Teemu 2013. *Media Portrayals of Religion and the Secular Sacred Representation and Change*, Farnham, Ashgate.

Marshall, Paul (ed.) 2009. *Blind Spot: When Journalists Don't Get Religion*, Oxford/New York, Oxford University Press.

Newbigin, Lesslie 1991. *Truth to Tell: The Gospel as Public Truth*, London, SPCK.

Taylor, Jennifer M. 2002. *After Secularism: Inner-City Governance and the New Religious Discourse*, PhD Thesis, London, School of Oriental and African Studies.

Wolffe, John and Moorhead, Gavin 2014. *Religion, Security and Global Uncertainties*, Milton Keynes, Open University, www.open.ac.uk/arts/research/religion-martyrdom-global-uncertainties/, last accessed 10 June 2018.

16 A Jewish educational approach to religious pluralism

Robin Sclafani

Introduction

Religious pluralism is a global reality, and given the effect of worldwide communications on people's lived experience, it is also a local reality regardless of the actual demographics in any one given area. How we approach the question of religion and belief literacy is inextricably linked with how we approach the opportunities and risks associated with religious pluralism.[1] Taking the definition of Diane Moore which has been adopted by the American Academy of Religion, 'Religious literacy entails the ability to discern and analyze the fundamental intersections of religion and social/political/cultural life through multiple lenses' (Moore 2006).

This definition implies that knowledge about different religions is not enough to consider oneself 'literate', although certainly such knowledge is a useful starting point. Concerns about religious illiteracy in Europe are arising now in the twenty-first century, not because of a simple curiosity about different religious traditions, but because of real concerns about a variety of issues which are appearing in the context of a Europe which is composed of a plurality of religious and nonreligious beliefs, values and practices. It is not the simple fact that religious Jews read the Torah, Muslims the Quran and Christians the New Testament which is causing such concerns. Rather, concerns arise in the way different people interpret the religious dimension when considering modern social issues such as asylum and integration policies, law enforcement practices, school lunch menus, financing of religious institutions, the wearing of religious dress and symbols, the ways in which religion is taught in public schools, civil rights for LGBTQI (lesbian, gay, bisexual, transgender, queer and intersex) people,[2] and so on.

Religious literacy is needed to discern and analyze, from different perspectives, the variety of issues which Europe currently faces in order to find practical solutions that are consistent with the core democratic principle of fundamental rights. Religion is a protected ground in a human rights framework, wherein people have the freedom to practice or not practice.[3] Europe today, in some ways, seems to be struggling with a perceived conflict between 'freedom of religion' and 'freedom from religion'. And herein lies the problem

1 Religious pluralism is understood in this chapter to imply a diversity of religions and beliefs, which can also be called convictional pluralism, including atheists, agnostics, humanists, free-thinkers as well as those who belong to organized and unorganized religions as part of the pluralistic reality which must be understood in the modern-day European context.

2 Lesbian, gay, bisexual, transgender, queer and intersex. For more information, see www.ilga-europe.org, last accessed 10 January 2018.

3 Freedom of religion or belief is enshrined in the *Universal Declaration of Human Rights* (Art. 18) and reaffirmed in the *International Covenant on Civil and Political Rights* (Art. 18) signed by over 160 states. In addition to freedom of religion, this right includes the right to adopt, change or abandon a religion or belief, or to profess no religion or belief.

with religious illiteracy: when the search for practical strategies to any given issue is reduced to a Manicheistic, polarized or dualistic paradigm, the political discourse is more likely to resort to scapegoating the 'other', the social fabric is weakened by an 'us v. them' mentality, and thus the soil is ripe for the propagation of extremisms which can more easily lead to violence.

This conflict spiral is well illustrated in the reactions and debates in Europe which have emerged over the course of the 'refugee crisis' which peaked in August 2015. The political and public discourse revolving around the fact that many of the refugees were Muslim was most certainly inflamed by the multiple terrorist attacks which had recently taken place in Europe. The burkini ban in some French coastal towns, the resistance to serving vegetarian or halal options in school lunches or the banning of religious slaughter or circumcision are all examples of how conflicts can escalate with a low capacity to understand, discern and analyze the effect of such 'us v. them' discourse on the European social fabric, which includes a very diverse population of those who identify themselves as Muslim.

In the face of emerging social issues, such as the arrival of refugees from war-torn regions, the risk of religious illiteracy is that people fall back onto limited amounts of knowledge, oversimplified generalizations or prejudices which can corrupt the process of finding practical solutions to very real and pressing issues. In contrast, religious literacy can provide an opportunity to consider possible causes and effects from multiple perspectives, thus helping to de-escalate conflicts and satisfy our higher principle of guaranteeing the fundamental rights of all people.

What can we learn from the Jewish experience?

Jewish communities came to terms with the reality of religious pluralism long before there were airplanes and the internet, long before the existence of the nation-state, long before many of today's modern religions such as Sikhism, Islam, Christianity and Buddhism even existed. The story of the Jews dates as far back as three millennia with the emergence of the ancient Hebrews as a distinct human entity. The Jewish holiday of Passover recalls the Jews' own status as 'other' in the land of Egypt and the persecution they endured. Jewish communities should understand what it means to be a minority, to be a refugee, to be blamed for illness or economic depression, to be hunted as heretics or used for racial experimentation. Jews also know what it means to be 'integrated', to rebuild one's community, to be resilient in the face of catastrophe.

'In their principled refusal to relinquish their own religio-ethnic identity, the Jews serve as a testimony to the intrinsic merit of religious pluralism' (Tirosh-Samuelson 2000: 76).

The mission of CEJI – A Jewish Contribution to an Inclusive Europe[4] is rooted in the Jewish experience of living pluralism. CEJI's vision is 'an inclusive and democratic Europe in which people enjoy their full potential with all their diversity'. This vision recognizes that Europe's diversity is not a matter of religious or ethnic origin alone, but rather each person's identity is unique in the way different social and personal dimensions interact to form a cohesive whole. Our daily experience and the ways in which we interpret the world around us are influenced simultaneously by our religious, cultural and national identifications as well as by our gender, sexual orientation, abilities and disabilities, social and economic class, education, languages spoken, family history and status, physical appearance and our personal talents, preferences, beliefs, spirituality, relationships and so on.

4 For more information on this nonprofit organization founded in 1991 in Brussels, see www.ceji.org, last accessed 10 January 2018.

While Judaism is a religion, being Jewish does not automatically imply that one is actually religious. Being Jewish is much more than belonging to a religious group; it is an identity that is shaped by numerous historical and cultural influences as well as the way one interprets a collective experience through a personal lens shaped also by nationality, religiosity, gender, socio-economic class, etc. Therefore, to understand what it means to be Jewish requires more than knowledge about the religious dimension of Judaism.

Needless to say, it is useful to have some basic religious knowledge to create an environment that is inclusive for Jews, such as to know that Rosh Hashana, Yom Kippur and Passover are important religious holidays, or that the weekly Sabbath begins at sundown on Friday and ends at sundown on Saturday, or that there are specific dietary restrictions for religious, and many nonreligious, Jews. The most basic religious literacy would need to recognize that even nonreligious Jews may well celebrate Passover with their families, just as nonreligious Christians will celebrate Christmas. If policy-makers in schools and public authorities could have even this basic religious literacy, there could already be a positive difference made in the experience of Jews in Europe. Obviously, similar parallels can be made for other religious minorities.

To create an environment that is truly inclusive, however, also requires sensitivity to the issues which are important for any collective group of people. For Jews in Europe today, two of those most highlighted issues which are often misunderstood, misused or trivialized are the Shoah[5] and Israel. Religious literacy in twenty-first-century Europe would require, for example, an understanding of the significance of the state of Israel in the history of the Jews, an ability to discern when criticism of this diverse nation falls within the realm of democratic participation or when it is used as a mask for the expression of anti-Semitism and to recognize how medieval and Nazi-era anti-Semitic conspiracy theories are propagated in so-called anti-Zionist or Holocaust denial propaganda.

There is an ethical imperative in the development of religious literacy in Europe because without it, continued ignorance, scapegoating, hatred and violence is a threat to the future stability of the region.

Learning about religious holidays, rites and rituals, sharing in multicultural meals, experiencing services of worship of other religious traditions is the easy and most pleasurable part of developing religious literacy. However, it will remain only superficial and short-lived if we do not explore honestly the ways in which stereotypes, discrimination and hatred manifest themselves towards particular religio-cultural groups.

It is for this reason that the work of CEJI to create inclusive environments requires us to help dismantle the ideas and mechanisms that perpetuate prejudice and discrimination. This work of deconstructing discrimination, on the one hand, and constructing an appreciation and ability to thrive in diversity, on the other hand, is essential to achieving our vision of a Europe in which all people can enjoy their full potential. The primary tool which CEJI uses in this deconstruction/construction process is education, such as the award-winning suite of programs called Belieforama: A Panoramic Approach to Issues of Religion and Belief.[6]

> Through working with our own stereotypes and those of others constantly, the eyes open more and more towards other groups and way of life. In training with young

5 Shoah is the Hebrew term meaning 'catastrophe' which refers to the Holocaust, when six million Jews were systematically exterminated by the Nazis and their collaborators.

6 For more information than that offered in this chapter, see www.belieforama.eu, last accessed 10 January 2018.

> people from all over Europe, I [learned] that an atheist in Poland can have similar experiences in terms of discrimination and exclusion as for example a Muslim in Germany. A discriminating majority in one place can be a discriminated minority in another. It all depends on the context and on the individual people.
>
> This helped me consider my own fixed views and stereotypes.
>
> But I also learned, in the same training, that this sharing of similar experiences of people with very different backgrounds can create new lines of solidarity. One young atheist within an activity strongly supported a religious Muslim girl's opinions, who he felt was trapped by a majority of people questioning her worldviews. He knew how it felt to be surrounded by a questioning majority and to be forced to defend oneself all alone, so he strongly started to support her. This beautiful experience of sudden and strong solidarity among people from very different backgrounds was not the only of its kind I have seen during the trainings I gave.[7]

First piloted in 2004 and still implemented today, Belieforama has been CEJI's contribution to facilitating convictional pluralism in Europe. Belieforama has brought an anti-bias diversity training approach to a field that was previously reserved for religious leaders. It aims to equip educators to facilitate learning, self-awareness, appreciation of diversity and a sense of personal responsibility on the topic of religion and belief. Over one thousand educators have participated in Belieforama train-the-trainer programs, reaching thousands of additional people across the continent. The program provides a secular space for believers and nonbelievers across the range of religio-cultural traditions to explore matters related to faith and living together from different perspectives, and find practical strategies for moving forward in our pluralistic reality.

> Through the training I can create a safe space for a group of diverse participants which helps them to understand their own baggage of religious and cultural conditioning and the impact of religious stereotypes and prejudice.
>
> I have already delivered a lot of trainings with all kinds of different groups: teachers and educators, school kids and youth, interreligious groups and employees of the administration, and I know that it works.
>
> About 8 years ago I delivered some long-term training for young representatives of different religions. The group consisted of Muslim, Jewish, Christian and atheist young adults. It was a really deep, sometimes painful but always dynamic, experience for everybody participating.
>
> Since I stayed in contact over the years with some former participants, now I can see the fruits of it, which really makes me very happy.
>
> Some of the former participants [...] developed to become important interreligious stakeholders in their communities and are now very active in the interfaith field. They do trainings with students of their own community to teach them religious openness and non-discrimination and they organise interreligious gatherings and exchange and through all this they became really very important religious ambassadors for diversity and antidiscrimination for the whole city of Berlin.
>
> Some of them directly told me that it was the training which empowered them, to do all this and they thanked me. I am very proud of them. But actually which makes me

7 Testimony of a Belieforama trainer published in *Snapshots: Stories of Change*, available at www.belieforama.eu/sites/default/files/documents/Belieforama-snapshots-web-version.pdf, last accessed 10 January 2018.

> happiest is the friendship which some of the participants developed and provides us in Berlin with a kind of informal interfaith network.[8]

Subject-specific programs, such as Overcoming Antisemitism and Overcoming Islamophobia, are within the Belieforama suite of programs as well. These programs provide educators with the tools needed to raise awareness about Jewish and Muslim communities respectively, their diversity, basic religious and cultural traditions, the stereotypes and discrimination which they face, and to facilitate a productive dialogue about the specific issues in Europe in relation to these two distinct identity groups. All the CEJI training programs take a dual approach of raising awareness and developing a sense of personal and social responsibility within a participative learning environment that promotes trust and reduces the impact of fear. These methods are all rooted in the Jewish tradition and are part of CEJI's way of making a Jewish contribution to an inclusive Europe.

Literacy presumes education

The importance of education in the Jewish tradition goes back to Rabbinic times, when 'the moral and religious training of the people from childhood up was regarded by the Jews from the very beginning of their history as one of the principle objects of life' (Hirsch, Kohler, Gottheil *et al.* 1903). The word Torah itself comes from the underlying verb *yarah*, the 'most common meaning is something like "to educate"' (Klener 2014: 46).

The Jewish historian Flavius Josephus records that the two major Jewish groupings during the later Second Temple period were the Sadducees and the Pharisees. The Pharisees advocated 'the study of both the Written and Oral Torah by all Jews, thus in some sense democratizing education and undercutting Sadducee domination. They effectively pitted the common people against the more aristocratic Sadducees'.[9]

When the Sadducees lost control of Jewish society with the destruction of the Second Temple by the Romans, the Pharisees were able to persevere and shape the becoming of Judaism today. This allowed for the flourishing of what we now understand to be a Jewish approach to education.

This illustrates not only the crucial role of education and literacy in the Jewish tradition, but it also demonstrates that in order to fully understand religious practices, one needs to consider the relevant formative cultural and political struggles over these practices. With the burning of the Second Temple, there were no longer biblical priests who had been only connected to this pivotal religious center. 'Instead their pedagogic-exegetical role was taken over by rabbinic teachers. Therefore, a rabbi's role as leader is chiefly to educate' (Klener 2014: 46).

This story from Jewish history helps to reinforce the definition offered by Diane Moore of religious literacy, in which she 'presumes that religion shapes and is shaped by the social/historical contexts out of which particular religious expressions and influences emerge' (Moore 2006). It also supports the theories of one of the most influential modern educators in the field of literacy development – the Brazilian Paolo Freire (1921–97) – whose works have been translated into numerous languages, the most well known being *Pedagogy of the Oppressed*.

8 Testimony of another Belieforama trainer, *Snapshots: Stories of Change*, www.belieforama.eu/sites/default/files/documents/Belieforama-snapshots-web-version.pdf, last accessed 10 January 2018.

9 Daron Acemoglu and James Robinson, 'Why the Jews Are so Educated?', appeared on *Why Nations Fail*'s blog on 3 September 2012, http://whynationsfail.com/blog/2012/9/3/why-the-jews-are-so-educated.html, last accessed 10 January 2018.

Through adult literacy projects aiming to deal with a variety of social and educational issues, Freire developed what is now known as 'critical pedagogy', defined by Freire's close collaborator Ira Shor[10] as

> Habits of thought, reading, writing, and speaking which go beneath surface meaning, first impressions, dominant myths, official pronouncements, traditional clichés, received wisdom, and mere opinions, to understand the deep meaning, root causes, social context, ideology, and personal consequences of any action, event, object, process, organization, experience, text, subject matter, policy, mass media, or discourse.
> (Shor 1992: 129)

Freire and Shor, like the Pharisees, understood that literacy meant more than the ability to read and write. Literacy is essential to better understand the world around us, to be able to analyze problems which we face, and to be active participants in making the world a better, more egalitarian place.

The Jewish identity would not have survived these three thousand years without a religio-cultural commitment to education, not only for the purpose of religious instruction, but to ensure the survival and success of the Jewish people in the various contexts in which they found themselves. For Jews, it is essential to assure one's literacy and therefore survival in a religiously plural world.

Jewish education as critical pedagogy

The Jewish people are, amongst themselves, an example of religious pluralism, reflecting an astonishing heterogeneity, in part due to the fact of having lived, until recently, in a global diaspora. The capacity to sustain a strong collective identity despite differences in nationality and religiosity is a further testament to an internal acceptance of diversity, albeit not without passionate debate. In fact, it is the religio-cultural tradition of argumentation that is so striking in the Talmudic method of Jewish religious instruction which helps to sustain the Jewish community in the face of internal and external changes. The culture of debate has been a unifying factor for Jews throughout history and across the world.

Called the Talmudic hypothetico-deductive method of text interpretation, those who are not accustomed to being challenged and probed may feel disconcerted by a Jewish approach to learning.

> Confronted with a statement on any subject, the Talmudic student will proceed to raise a series of questions before he satisfies himself of having understood its full meaning. If the statement is not clear enough, he will ask, 'What does the author intend to say here?' If it is too obvious, he will again ask, 'It is too plain, why then expressly say it?' If it is a statement of fact or of a concrete instance, he will then ask, 'What underlying principle does it involve?' If it is broad generalization, he will want to know exactly how much it is to include; and if it is an exception to a general rule, he will want to know how much it is to exclude. He will furthermore want to know all the circumstances under which a certain statement is true, and what qualifications are permissible.
> (Wolfson 1929: 25–6)

10 Biography on Ira Shor at http://link.springer.com/chapter/10.1007%2F978-94-6209-374-4_29#page-1, last accessed 10 January 2018.

To return to the definition of religious literacy by Diane Moore, it is crucial to recognize that the abilities to 'discern', 'explore' and 'analyze' are as important as having basic knowledge about religions. It is essential to recognize this distinction because no person can have all the knowledge about all the religions and their denominations within each political or social context in which they are living. Therefore, as society and circumstances are in a state of constant flux, it is crucial that people today have the ability and desire to be curious, to ask questions, to probe for deeper understanding, to doubt and to be willing always to consider new perspectives.

This distinction was the core challenge which CEJI sought to address in 2004 with the first Belieforama training on Religious Diversity and Anti-Discrimination. How can educators, who are not necessarily experts in any one religion and certainly not all of them, have the tools they need to facilitate learning on religion and belief diversity, and to do so in a secular context?

Jews are not 'banking'

Returning to the concept of critical pedagogy for literacy development, there are many similarities between what Paolo Freire proposes as educational methods and that which has been at the core of Jewish religious instruction since the beginning of the Common Era.

Freire referred to the traditional educational model as 'banking' through which the teacher makes knowledge deposits which the students patiently receive, memorize and repeat. 'In the banking concept of education, knowledge is a gift bestowed by those who consider themselves knowledgeable upon those whom they consider to know nothing' (Freire 1970: 58). Freire criticizes the paternalism in this approach which oppresses rather than liberates the potential of each person. Instead, the communication between teachers and students should be a dialogue wherein 'authentic education is not carried on by "A" for "B" or by "A" about "B", but rather by "A" with "B"' (Freire 1970: 70). The traditional banking model which unfortunately is still quite common today requires students to memorize facts in order to pass their tests, rather than emphasizing understanding.

Ironically, despite the stereotype of the 'Jewish banker', banking is exactly what Jewish instructional methods do *not* do. In Jewish religious instruction, students are expected to question and internalize what they are studying, and in their active participation they are simultaneously serving as learner and teacher, helping to illuminate new ways of considering the text under study.

> The Talmud's teaching method is based on a rhythm of word and reply, of arguments and rebuttals. In that sense it is based on critical questioning – in dialogue or in multilogue – about situations and texts, and from all possible points of view. This is a method that could be summarized prosaically as 'Have we asked the final question?' and which can undoubtedly broaden the fields of thought and understanding of both master and pupil.
>
> (Klener 2014: 49)

The alternative to banking education is called the 'problem-posing' approach by Freire, which involves 'listening, dialogue and action' (Wallerstein 1987: 35). Students either identify for themselves a relevant problem or they are presented with one by the teacher and they must make use of the resources available to them to find solutions. This method honors the previous experiences of the students, develops the capacity for cooperative learning and emphasizes small groups for interaction and action on the problem posed.

Over the centuries, as Jewish communities have passed through cycles of integration and persecution, they have proven to be remarkably resilient in responding to new social, political and economic models. The critical pedagogy which is inherent to the culture of transmitting the teachings of Judaism could very well have been one of the keys to their survival. The development of critical thinking skills and a high awareness of oneself in relation to others is essential to solving problems and living in a pluralistic reality. As explained by Albert Einstein:

> The association of solved problems with those unsolved may throw new light on our difficulties by suggesting new ideas. It is easy to find a superficial analogy which really expresses nothing. But to discover some essential common features, hidden beneath a surface of external differences, to form, on this basis, a new successful theory, is important creative work.
> (Einstein and Infeld 1938: 287–8)

Dialogue and relationship with the other

The Jewish tradition of questioning the religious texts and their teachers is in reality a dialogue: it affords more possibilities for people to interpret the sources and apply them appropriately in a modern-day context. Literacy in this deeper sense of the word supports the Jewish ability to adapt to new circumstances and contexts without compromising the essence of one's identity. It helps to explain oneself and one's religio-cultural traditions to others in a way that is meaningful beyond 'what scriptures say'. It facilitates Jewish relationships across differences within their identity group and also with other identity groups.

Renowned Jewish philosopher Martin Buber (1878–1965) explored profoundly the relationship between self and other in his 1923 publication *I and Thou*, which describes the qualities of the rare experience of a true encounter between entities. He distinguishes between two opposing concepts, Ich-Du (I-You) and Ich-Es (I-It), to categorize the modes of consciousness, interaction and being through which an individual engages with God, other individuals, inanimate objects and reality in general.

In the I-It relationship, two entities do not actually meet, but rather the 'it' is understood by the 'I' merely as a pre-existing idea or representation which is held in the individual's mind. This relationship is an illustration of how people encounter the 'other' only through their prejudices and projected self-interests, therefore objectifying the 'other' as an 'it'.

The I-You relationship is much more rare and precious. This is when true dialogue takes place because two beings meet each other in their authentic existence. There is no preconceived idea, judgment or objectification of one another, and the encounter is unstructured with no pre-meditated purpose. There is simply a being with, experiencing of, each other, with pure openness and no element of pursuit. If one intentionally pursued an I-You relationship, the quality of 'it-ness' would be created because the relationship would only be sought in order to fulfill one's own needs or desires.

Buber argued that many of the ills of modernity are due to the predominance of I-It relationships through which we essentially function only in monologues, sacrificing our ability to be present to each other in true mutuality and dialogue. However, as Buber and students of his have explored further, there is much hope for the I-It encounter which is in many ways part of the condition of the human mind. I-It meetings provide an opportunity for 'temporal courage', which can be harnessed in order to deconstruct prejudices and open up new possibilities for relationship (Holba 2008).

Another influential Jewish philosopher of the last century, Emmanuel Lévinas (1906–95), explored the hermeneutics of lived experience in the world. In relation to the topic of religious pluralism and literacy, his concept of 'face-to-face' relation is highly relevant, meaning that, ethically, people are responsible to each other in the face-to-face encounter. Specifically, Lévinas says that the human face calls us into 'giving and serving' the Other (Lévinas 1985: 95, 98, 119).

> For Lévinas, an 'I' lives out its embodied existence according to modalities. It consumes the fruits of the world. It enjoys and suffers from the natural elements. It constructs shelters and dwellings. It carries on the social and economic transactions of its daily life. Yet, no event is as affectively disruptive for a consciousness holding sway in its world than the encounter with another person. In this encounter (even if it later becomes competitive or instrumental), the 'I' first experiences itself as called and liable to account for itself.
>
> (Bergo 2011)

The work of Buber and Lévinas highlights the important role of the 'other' in understanding ourselves and in the educational process which must include the dimension of dialogue in the spirit of mutuality, encounter and equality.

Learning about oneself through engagement with the other

The theories of Buber and Lévinas have proven to be true in the Belieforama training courses delivered by CEJI throughout Europe with people from a variety of religio-cultural backgrounds. Through the interactive activities within the training, particularly those that explore participants' concepts of personal identity, many leave the training sessions wanting to know much more about their own religio-cultural roots. They would like to understand more clearly the influences on their way of seeing the world, to articulate better the meanings in the rites and rituals that they have always taken for granted, to experience more the richness available in their own and others' traditions.

> I very strongly believe that one of the strong points of this training programme and the philosophy of Belieforama is especially [...] that there is a space, a way of working, a very clear didactic approach, that in the group it feels okay that there is difference – we have to start at that point. We then create a space where people learn to listen to themselves about their own identity and to listen to others and to confront issues in order to be a more able citizen and to go into social action.[11]

For some, multifaith engagement can feel as a threat to their identity; a risk of dilution. In CEJI's experience, and in the philosophies offered by Buber and Lévinas, the contrary is true. Engaging with the other is an opportunity to explore one's own identity in greater depth, engendering respect for the other who has helped to serve a process of self-awareness. Engaging with the other can help to strengthen identity-affirming connections while reducing vulnerability to segregationist communitarism. Any program designed to develop religious literacy must take this aspect of learning into account. Learning about the other inherently implies a learning about oneself, but the pedagogical approach should allow for

11 Testimony of a Belieforama training participant received in the context of a survey conducted by Prof. Dr Paul Weller of the University of Derby toward production of the Belieforama policy brief *Learning from Experience, Leading to Engagement*, available in the document library of www.belieforama.eu/, last accessed 10 January 2018.

an open dialogue which reduces the impact of pre-existing filters which could prevent an authentic encounter with the other, and thus with oneself.

'In our interconnected world, we must learn to feel enlarged, not threatened, by difference' (Sacks 2002: 7).

> This training program has convinced me by the power of its learning process gradually leading to reflection, introspection, awareness, the questioning, the fight against prejudice and the transition to action. In this training, we learn not only with our head but with our emotions, not only individually but also in contact with a diverse group, not only theoretically but also by confronting reality with tough questions.
>
> On a personal level, the training has allowed me to question the subjects that I have never questioned before, for example: where do my images of God come from? What influence have my surroundings and my society had on my beliefs and convictions? The program helped me discover the concrete uniqueness of each religious identity and capture the uniqueness of each religion. I developed a greater sensitivity and empathy for people discriminated against or disadvantaged in society because of their beliefs.
>
> At the professional level, this training gave me concrete tools to create time and space for reflection and dialogue with people of diverse faiths and cultures.[12]

Bibliography

Bergo, Bettina [2006] 2011. 'Emmanuel Lévinas', in *Stanford Encyclopedia of Philosophy*, https://plato.stanford.edu/entries/levinas/#OveLev, last accessed 10 January 2018.

Einstein, Albert and Infeld, Leopold 1938. *The Evolution of Physics*, Cambridge, Cambridge University Press.

Freire, Paulo [1968] 1970. *Pedagogy of the Oppressed*, New York, The Continuum International.

Hirsch, Emil G., Kohler, Kaufmann, Gottheil, Richard *et al.* (ed.) 1903. 'Education', in *The Jewish Encyclopedia*, vol. 5, New York, Funk & Wagnalls Co., 42–8, www.jewishencyclopedia.com/articles/5438-education, last accessed 10 January 2018.

Holba, Annette 2008. 'Revisiting Martin Buber's I-It: A Rhetorical Strategy', *Human Communication* 11:4, 489–504.

Klener, Julien 2014. 'The Tanakh in the Jewish Tradition', in Maartje de Wilde (ed.), *Heilige Boeken in jodendom, christendom en islam. Sacred Books in Judaism, Christianity and Islam*, Antwerpen, BAI.

Lévinas, Emmanuel 1985. *Ethics and Infinity*, Pittsburgh, PA, Duquesne University Press.

Moore, Diane L. 2006. 'Overcoming Religious Illiteracy: A Cultural Studies Approach', *World History Connected* 4:1, http://worldhistoryconnected.press.illinois.edu/4.1/moore.html, last accessed 10 January 2018.

Sacks, Jonathan 2002. *The Dignity of Difference. How to Avoid the Clash of Civilizations*, London, Continuum.

Shor, Ira 1992. *Empowering Education. Critical Teaching for Social Change*, Chicago, IL, University of Chicago Press.

Tirosh-Samuelson, Hava 2000. 'A Jewish perspective on Religious Pluralism', *Macalester International* 8, 73–112, https://pdfs.semanticscholar.org/16c1/ddaeb960b30fe93bfef19eed35ff3050b5be.pdf, last accessed 10 January 2018.

Wallerstein, Nina 1987. 'Problem-Posing Education: Freire's Method for Transformation', in Ira Shor (ed.), *Freire for the Classroom*, Portsmouth, MA, Boynton Cook/Heinemann, 33–44.

Wolfson, Harry A. 1929. *Crescas' Critique of Aristotle*, Cambridge, MA, Harvard University Press, 25–6.

12 Testimony of a Belieforama trainer, *Snapshots: Stories of Change*, www.belieforama.eu/sites/default/files/documents/Belieforama-snapshots-web-version.pdf, last accessed 10 January 2018.

17 Positions and actions in the European Islam

Erdal Toprakyaran

Introduction

Every time a terrorist attack, motivated by Islamism, takes place, be it in Paris, in Brussels or in Istanbul, we Muslims ask ourselves the same question: how could this happen? Even the most calm-minded among us have begun raising the question of whether we are in the middle of a new global war. Pope Francis, who on 14 September 2014 spoke of the possibility that World War III might already have begun, probably became the first who brought this crisis to our attention in a significant way. This becomes even more worrying when one considers that the proclamation of the caliphate of the so-called Islamic State by Abu Bakr al-Baghdadi on 29 June 2014 coincides almost exactly with the hundred-year anniversary of the assassination of the crown prince of the Austro-Hungarian Empire Archduke Franz Ferdinand on 28 June 1914, which triggered World War I. However, the beginning of World War III can also be said to have begun on 11 September 2001, or on 20 March 2003, when an alliance under the leadership of the USA intervened in Iraq and thereby caused a continual escalation of violence.

Regardless of the discussion about whether the current crisis can be considered a world war, we must ask ourselves the question of who these Muslims are that in the name of their religious and political ideology commit mass murder? And how can we protect our societies from such terror? To some the phenomena seem utterly inexplicable, and to others the answer is always right at hand: the fault lies within Islam, and only a negation of Islam and Muslims in general can lead to the salvation of the West and of the world in general! This view often implies inhumane demands like closing the borders to refugees who, ironically, are fleeing that very same terror.

Yet another way of making sense of it all is resorting to conspiracy theories, such as those that arose after the attacks on 9/11 as a way of absolving Muslims of guilt by turning the terrorist groups responsible into mere fictions or the invention of an American and Israeli security apparatus. It is also not uncommon to encounter the argument that the so-called Islamic State is an invention of the CIA or the Mossad, as it is killing more Muslims than people of any other confession, and that the war against ISIS only serves the interests of the western weapons and energy lobbies. To some conspiracy theorists, the fact that Michel Houellebecq's novel *Submission*, which was widely viewed by Muslims as being Islamophobic, was published on the same day as the attacks on the offices of the satirical magazine *Charlie Hebdo* in France could not have been a mere coincidence. Furthermore, these critics attack the West for being racist, only standing up to its ideals of human rights when it suits its own interest. Terrorist attacks in Africa and Asia are generally ignored, or at least treated with substantially less gravity than attacks on white people from the West.

In this atmosphere of either agitation or trivialization it is a source of great comfort that so many differentiated and constructive opinions are also being heard. They emphasize that in addition to our staunch resolution to reject violence and fight terrorism, we must never lose sight of our true ideals and our solidarity with one another. Now more than ever, democrats must stand shoulder to shoulder in order to defend our free pluralistic societies. Together we must show courage and confront the enemies of freedom, democracy and humanity, without turning our societies over to regimes of control and surveillance. One step in this direction is to make sure that Muslims and refugees do not come under general suspicion. If this happens, it will be a great loss of the values we intend to defend and a victory for the enemies of freedom.

Whatever happens, we cannot avoid the need to reflect more on the global implications of our actions. It is not sufficient nowadays to speak of humanism, enlightenment and democracy; Europe must change and start to put its ideals into action both at home and abroad. 'To preach water and drink wine' will in future no longer work as we live in a globalized world in which the consequences of our actions, or inactions, almost immediately can come back to haunt us. One example is that of the failure of the European Union to take action responsibly with regard to the war in Syria or to deal with the following refugee crisis in a direct and humane manner. European countries have to reevaluate the flourishing trade and often completely uncritical dealings with authoritarian states that finance and arm Islamic militants. Europe should also not simply look away when groups of Sinti and Roma are being discriminated against or when close allies make use of systematic torture, as in the cases of Abu Ghraib and Guantanamo.

If we wish to prevent ISIS from instrumentalizing Islam, thereby making itself attractive to European youths, it is also not enough only to look for political and economic solutions to the problems. It is equally important for an Islamic theology to be established in the European states that can effectively challenge the brutal interpretations of violent militant ideologies.

I thus turn to the core issue of this chapter, namely, the dangers stemming from the religious illiteracy of European Muslims, with a particular focus on the developments in Germany.

European Islam and the problem of religious illiteracy

Islam has from the very beginning been an integral part of Europe. In a study of the historical origins of the Quran by the Arabist Angelika Neuwirth, *The Quran as a Text of Late Antiquity. A European Reading* (2010: 15–24) this becomes very clear. The Quran is a product of Mediterranean culture in late antiquity, just like the Hebrew Bible and the New Testament. The prophet Muhammad and others who participated in the discourse of revelation, such as the polytheists, the Jews and the Christians, all emerged from the culture of late antiquity, which is the reason why the Quran can also be viewed as a part of Europe's cultural inheritance.

Even if Muslims at the time of the prophet Muhammad already claimed a distinct religious identity, the dynamic discourse including Jews, Christians, Muslims and people of other faiths remained. This was especially the case in the times of the so-called rightly guided four caliphs, Abu Bakr (died 634), Umar (died 644), Uthman (died 656), Ali (died 661), but also throughout all the dynasties like that of the Umayyads (661–749), the Abbasids (749–1258), the Fatimids (909–1171), the Mamluks (1250–1517) or the Ottomans (1302–1923). With regard to a European Islam it is particularly the interreligious relations on the Iberian Peninsula, in southern Italy, in the Balkan countries, in Anatolia and in north-eastern Europe that are of special interest.

Obviously the times of peaceful coexistence were repeatedly interrupted by conflict and strife, yet Islam was never expunged from Europe in the Middle Ages or in modern times, nor was the intercultural and interreligious discourse ever silenced. The wealth and impact of Muslim culture on Europe can be seen in many areas, such as those of theology, philosophy, mathematics, astronomy, medicine, architecture, literature and music. In fact, the contributions are so numerous that it would be impossible to pursue a further description within the scope of this chapter.

Today Muslims in Europe are very present, not only in their former countries of origin, such as the Balkans and Turkey, but also in Germany, France, Great Britain, Italy and almost all the other European states. Here it is important to note that the history and identity of European Muslims varies a great deal from country to country. Ethnic background, the level of education as well as the theological and political views often differ very strongly. Thus, all case studies deal with highly complex, dynamic individuals and groups which demand a great deal of research before one can draw any definitive conclusions.

One example is the Muslim populations in the German-speaking parts of Europe, which include not only different Sunni and Shia communities but also large groups of Turkish, Arab and Kurdish Alevites. And some of the Alevite groups even no longer define themselves as belonging to the Muslim faith but instead as followers of an independent religion. The Sunnis often belong to different Turkish communities such as Diyanet, Milli Görüş, Süleymancı, Nurcu, Ülkücü, etc. Other Sunni groups belong to movements like those of Sufism, the Muslim Brotherhood or Salafism. Furthermore, one must take into account that the majority of European Muslims are not at all organized into any religious movement. None of these groups can be said to pose a threat or to promote violence in general, but as their worldviews are mainly formed in the countries of origin such as Turkey, Algeria, Egypt or Pakistan, these individuals and groups do not possess the specific theological knowledge and skills which are needed to improve religious literacy in Europe.

What, then, must really occur in order to give birth also to a truly 'European version of Islam'? That is to say, a version of Islam that is not only limited by the factors of geography, language and specific cultures, but which is able to establish a new tradition of European Islamic theology and thereby fight religious illiteracy?

The national program for the academization of Islam, which was initiated in 2010 by the German government, is proving that the realization of such an undertaking is possible. Within the framework of this program, four bounteous equipped centers of Islamic theology have been created as institutions of the universities of Tübingen, Erlangen, Frankfurt a.M. (with the junior partner of Giessen) and Münster (with the junior partner of Osnabrück). Smaller institutions of Islamic theology have also been created in Hamburg and Paderborn, which are being funded by the respective federal states. The opening of yet another theological institute is being planned in Berlin. The preliminary aspiration of this program is to educate theologians and teachers of religion. However, in the longer term, the goal is also to educate imams and other professionals to provide religious and psycho/social-services for their communities whereby they also improve the overall religious literacy of Muslims in Europe. Although it could have been taken much earlier, this brave step will in all probability create the theological foundation for the development of a 'German Islam'.

Nonetheless, the heterogeneity of opinions and interpretations will remain part of this process as the theologians who so far have been engaged by the program originate from different Islamic regions in the world and in part contradict one another in theological matters.

It will probably take several years for the difficult, time-consuming build-up phase to be concluded and a scientific routine within these new centers of theology become established. In the meantime, the predominantly young and inexperienced Muslim theologians will continue to work under a lot of pressure and constant observation on the part of the outside world. They constantly have to take into consideration the expectations of the broader public as well as the often unspoken ones of Muslim organizations, German politics, Christian churches and faculties, Orientalists, the university directorship, the students, the media and even of theologians in Islamic countries.

Consequently, theologians, PhD students and Postdocs are constantly having to react to questions and accusations with or without any connection to their true research. One example of this is the many criticisms directed against the director of the Centre for Islamic Theology in Münster, Mouhanad Khorchide, who has published a book called *Islam is Mercy* (2014). Many Muslims attack the book on the grounds that it offers a false representation of Islam. Several times he has been called upon to show regret and denounce his own writings. In the Turkish press, he was defamed for his so-called 'unislamic' position and called a 'clown' and a 'heretic'. Despite these difficulties, Islamic theology is on its way to becoming a well-established discipline in Germany, making important contributions not only to the academization of Islam, but also to the peaceful coexistence of different religions. Furthermore, it creates the foundation for the development of a 'German Islam' that truly deserves its name.

A similar development can also be found in Austria, where the universities of Vienna and Innsbruck have established new institutes of Islamic theology. The institute in Vienna, in particular, is being expanded, and more professorships will be created in the near future. In Fribourg, in Switzerland, a chair of Islamic theology already exists, and even in strictly laicistic France up to eleven positions of Islamic theology are to be created in the next few years. Institutions of Islamic theology also exist in other European countries, such as the United Kingdom and the Netherlands, but they have not been founded on a state initiative and consequently do not enjoy the same level of recognition in society at large as the previously mentioned ones.

The academization of Islam and the literarization of European Muslims could even lead to a Renaissance and a chance to reconnect to the cultural heritage of the Islamic golden ages. For such an undertaking to be successful, it is essential to develop a theology that speaks to both the hearts and the minds of Muslims. We must remind ourselves that Islam was a religion of love, peace and reason for many mystics, theologians, philosophers and poets of the Middle Ages. Once again, we must recall the giants of Muslim thought, such as Avicenna, al-Ghazali and Averroes, who all emphasized that without the constant vigilance of reason and critical thinking there can be no religion and particularly no theology, or once again turn our attention to Rabia al-Adawiyya, Ibn Arabi and Maulana Rumi, who spoke of love as the foundation and authenticity of faith and religion. The collective memory of Muslims could thereby be protected from the superficial and often puritan ideologies of Islamism.

We also have to remember that the Alhambra, the Taj Mahal, the Blue Mosque, the tales of *Arabian Nights*, contemplating Sufis or dancing Dervishes are, after all, no less representative of Islamic culture and civilization than the call to prayer or the pilgrimage to Mecca. It was not without reason that German poets and philosophers like Herder, Goethe, Lessing, Novalis, Nietzsche and Rilke were deeply fascinated by the Islamic Orient.

Furthermore, we should not forget that historically Islam has shown itself to be an ample catalyst of civilization and peace. The many wars and the many injustices, which also have been committed in the name of Islam throughout the ages, should not blind the truly intersubjective historian to the great feats of civilization for which Muslims have been responsible. Prominent examples of peaceful and productive coexistence are those of the Emirate of Cordoba and the Ottoman and the Mogul Empire. The fact that Christians and Jews were relatively well-off living in Muslim countries was the result of a very pragmatic judicial framework that was taken from interpretations of the Quran and the stories about the conduct of the prophet Muhammad. According to the Quran, (1) Abraham, Moses, Jesus and Muhammad were all Messengers of the same God (4:163–4); (2) the Torah, the Psalms and the Gospel are all inspired by God (5:44–6); (3) people of other faiths, who believe in God and the day of judgment and who act according to good morals, will not have to fear the afterlife (5:69); (4) no one must have faith forced upon them (2:256).

Because the Quran was revealed in the seventh century over a period of twenty-three years in many different contexts and situations (some in times of war, some in peace), many of which are no longer known to us today, it is of no surprise that the scripture also contains passages that will seem senseless, violent and unacceptable. However, anyone who reads the Quran without preconceived notions will also discover many beautiful, touching and contemporary-sounding verses. The text as a whole very probably contains several hundred verses that call upon people to live just, tolerant, moral, peaceful lives replete with mercy and love.

The academization of Islam can however not only be limited to uncovering the innumerable forgotten riches of Islamic culture but must also strive for renewal. Imitating Rumi, Hafiz or Averroes cannot simply bring about a renaissance of Islam. We also need to look for new, innovative answers to both old and new questions, without first asking ourselves whether a particular theological position is labeled humanistic, progressive, traditionalist, liberalist, conservative, modern or European. The prophet Muhammad himself labeled this endeavor as renewal (*tajdid*) and explained that in every century a renewer (*mujaddid*) of religion is necessary. Later, Muslims named this kind of religious restoration as 'reviving' (*ihya*), 'adjusting' (*islah*) or 'enlightening' (*tanwir/tanawwur*). Some modern thinkers also dare to use the word 'reform' which is vehemently criticized by Islamists and others who claim that this expression can't be used in the Muslim context as Islam is perfect and needs no reform. But regardless of the terminology we have to abandon the fundamentalist idea of a monolithic and never-changing Islam and start an intense discourse about the many deficiencies in Muslim societies concerning women's and children's rights, the treatment of minorities and critical intellectuals, the dealing with nature and animals, etc. We should always have in mind that severe self-criticism (*malama*) and self-observation (*muhasaba*) are not only necessary for reasons of modernity, they are also prescribed by the Islamic tradition. Contemporary scholars like Mohammed Arkoun, Nasr Hamid Abu Zayd, Salih Akdemir, Yaşar Nuri Öztürk, Fatima Mernissi, Abdou Filali-Ansary, İhsan Eliaçık, Mualla Selçuk, Abdullahi Ahmed an-Na'im, Mehmet Aydın and Süleyman Ateş can be mentioned as examples for those Muslims who continued to cultivate the (self-)critical tradition of Islam.

One of the most acute questions today is undoubtedly that of secularism and the freedom of religion as the foundation of world peace, although Muslims who at present are at home in Europe have accepted, and even appreciate, the concept of secularism (or *laïcité*) with few exceptions. Within Muslim organizations in Europe, there is almost no debate about this issue or about whether one should rather live under a theocratic regime.

This is connected to the fact that Muslims in Europe (except for the Muslim majority countries of Turkey, Bosnia and Albania) are a minority and therefore profit from the concept of secularism in the otherwise Christian majority states. The neutrality of religion is very much to their advantage. It is, however, necessary for Muslims in Muslim majority countries also to advocate the religious neutrality of the state and the freedom of religion in general. Modern Muslims should, therefore, begin to identify more with the concept of secularism and be consequent and categorical in their position. Every form of Islamism must be rejected, even when it takes on more moderate forms, because – as has been stated by Hans Küng, the initiator of the Global Ethics Foundation in Tübingen – without the peace of religions, world peace is impossible. To this, one can add that without the religious neutrality of politics, a peace between religions can never become a reality. The fact that there need not be a contradiction between Muslim theology and the secular state was already shown in the early years of the Turkish republic by famous theologians such as Mehmet Rıfat Börekçi (died 1941), Şerafettin Yaltkaya (died 1947), Kamil Miras (died 1957) and Şemsettin Günaltay (died 1961). However, Islamic theology must also emphasize this in the coming years and increasingly reject and disprove the arguments of Islamic extremists.

Conclusion

If World War III against the soldiers of extremism is to be won, one needs to think beyond the measures of theology and politics – and come together in a global alliance of love and reason. Without a common position advocating love and reason, universal human rights, the rule of law and secularity in the sense of the religious neutrality of the state, we will never be able to surmount the challenges of our time. Challenges such as terror, war, refugees, poverty, corruption, destruction of the environment, turbo-capitalism and climate change can only be met globally or not at all. This dialectical confrontation leads one to think of Samuel P. Huntington's *Clash of Civilizations*, except for the fact that the confrontation is not between monolithic cultures but between the diverse champions of love and freedom and the equally diverse and dynamic propagandists of hate and fear; between those who tear down walls and those who think barbed wire, rockets and decapitations are the way forward. The defenders of freedom must work together on a concrete utopia, in Ernst Bloch's sense, and on a universal ideal of humanity that is opposed to the ideologies of extremism. We, the European Muslims, must fight much harder than hitherto to academize our religion and thereby renew it if we also wish to make great contributions to civilization and culture in the future.

According to tradition, as a young man, the prophet Muhammad is said to have taken part in meetings of the Mecca alliance, which was called 'the alliance of the virtuous' (*khilf al-fudul*). The men of honor who gathered there – Meccan mono- and polytheists – had sworn to defend at all times the rights of the disadvantaged, whether Meccan or not, monotheists or polytheists, rich or poor. It has been narrated that Muhammad, many years later when he had long since become the prophet of Islam, rhapsodized about this alliance.

I sincerely hope, that we, the Muslims, will also be able to form such alliances in the future, in which people of different faiths and worldviews come together and strengthen one another. Once again, we should view Islam as an inspiring religious ideal, not as a petty-minded ideology. Only then will we be able to enter into a constructive competition with other religions and worldviews, something which is recommended to us not only by Lessing's *Nathan the Wise* but also by the Quran.

Bibliography

Huntington, Samuel P. 1996. *The Clash of Civilizations and the Remaking of World Order*, New York, Simon & Schuster.

Khorchide, Mouhanad 2014. *Islam is Mercy: Essential Features of a Modern Religion*, Freiburg i.Br., Herder.

Lessing, Gotthold E. 2015. *Nathan the Wise*, Mineola, NY, Dover Publications.

Neuwirth, Angelika 2010. *Der Koran als Text der Spätantike. Ein europäischer Zugang*, Berlin, Verlag der Weltreligionen.

Name Index

Index

For Product Safety Concerns and Information please contact our EU representative GPSR@taylorandfrancis.com Taylor & Francis Verlag GmbH, Kaufingerstraße 24, 80331 München, Germany

Batch number: 10726294

Printed by Printforce, the Netherlands